Fifth SIGHAN Workshop on Chinese Language Processing

Co-located with COLING/ACL 2006

Sydney, Australia
22-23 July 2006

ISBN: 978-1-62748-366-7

Printed from e-media with permission by:

Curran Associates, Inc.
57 Morehouse Lane
Red Hook, NY 12571

Some format issues inherent in the e-media version may also appear in this print version.

Printed by Curran Associates, Inc. (2013)

For permission requests, please contact the Association for Computational Linguistics at the address below.

Association for Computational Linguistics
209 N. Eighth Street
Stroudsburg, Pennsylvania 18360

Phone: 1-570-476-8006
Fax: 1-570-476-0860

acl@aclweb.org

Additional copies of this publication are available from:

Curran Associates, Inc.
57 Morehouse Lane
Red Hook, NY 12571 USA
Phone: 845-758-0400
Fax: 845-758-2634
Email: curran@proceedings.com
Web: www.proceedings.com

Table of Contents

Preface

The Fifth SIGHAN Workshop on Chinese Language Processing will be held in Sydney, Australia, on July 22 – 23, 2006, co-located with COLING/ACL 2006. The annual SIGHAN workshop is an international forum for presenting the latest research on Chinese language processing. This year, the workshop attracted 24 submissions to the main session, out of which we accepted 8 as oral paper presentations and 6 as poster paper presentations.

The Third International Chinese Language Processing Bakeoff was also organized in conjunction with this workshop. In addition to the Chinese word segmentation task of the first two bakeoffs, this year's bakeoff also included the Chinese named entity recognition task. Altogether 29 teams participated in the bakeoff, organized by Gina-Anne Levow and Olivia Oi Yee Kwong. The increase in the number of participating teams compared to the last two bakeoffs is testimony to the healthy growth of research interest in Chinese language processing.

We would like to thank all authors who submitted papers to this workshop, and all program committee members who worked hard to review the submissions. Special thanks to Gina-Anne Levow who did a fantastic job organizing a successful bakeoff. We would also like to acknowledge the help of the following people who provided the corpora used in the bakeoff: Keh-Jiann Chen and Henning Chiu (Academia Sinica), Mu Li (Microsoft Research Asia), Martha Palmer and Nianwen Xue (University of Pennsylvania/University of Colorado), Stephanie Strassel (Linguistic Data Consortium), and Benjamin K. Tsou and Olivia Oi Yee Kwong (City University of Hong Kong). We also thank Benjamin K. Tsou, Martha Palmer, and Suzanne Stevenson for their guidance and advice in our organization of this workshop.

We hope that you will have a great time attending this workshop in Sydney!

Hwee Tou Ng and Olivia Oi Yee Kwong
June 2006

Organizers

Workshop Chair:

Hwee Tou Ng, National University of Singapore

Workshop Co-Chair:

Olivia Oi Yee Kwong, City University of Hong Kong

Bakeoff Coordinators:

Gina-Anne Levow, University of Chicago
Olivia Oi Yee Kwong, City University of Hong Kong

Program Committee:

Aitao Chen, Yahoo!
Keh-Jiann Chen, Academia Sinica
David Chiang, USC Information Sciences Institute
Pascale Fung, Hong Kong University of Science and Technology
Jianfeng Gao, Microsoft Research
Julia Hockenmaier, University of Pennsylvania
Xuanjing Huang, Fudan University
Daniel Jurafsky, Stanford University
Kui-Lam Kwok, Queens College, CUNY
Gina-Anne Levow, University of Chicago
Haizhou Li, Institute for Infocomm Research
Mu Li, Microsoft Research Asia
Qun Liu, Chinese Academy of Sciences
Xiaoqiang Luo, IBM
Qing Ma, Ryukoku University
Yuji Matsumoto, Nara Institute of Science and Technology
Martha Palmer, University of Colorado
Fuchun Peng, Yahoo!
Richard Sproat, University of Illinois at Urbana-Champaign
Maosong Sun, Tsinghua University
Haifeng Wang, Toshiba (China) R&D Centre
Kam-Fai Wong, Chinese University of Hong Kong
Fei Xia, University of Washington at Seattle
Nianwen Xue, University of Pennsylvania
Jun Zhao, Chinese Academy of Sciences
Tiejun Zhao, Harbin Institute of Technology
Guodong Zhou, Institute for Infocomm Research
Ming Zhou, Microsoft Research Asia
Jingbo Zhu, Northeastern University

Workshop Program

Saturday, 22 July 2006

Saturday, 22 July 2006 (continued)

Saturday, 22 July 2006 (continued)

Session 5: Bakeoff Overview and Presentations

16:00–16:20 *The Third International Chinese Language Processing Bakeoff: Word Segmentation and Named Entity Recognition*
Gina-Anne Levow

16:20–16:35 *Chinese Named Entity Recognition with Conditional Random Fields*
Wenliang Chen, Yujie Zhang and Hitoshi Isahara

16:35–16:50 *France Telecom R&D Beijing Word Segmenter for Sighan Bakeoff 2006*
Wu Liu, Heng Li, Yuan Dong, Nan He, Haitao Luo and Haila Wang

16:50–17:05 *Voting between Dictionary-Based and Subword Tagging Models for Chinese Word Segmentation*
Dong Song and Anoop Sarkar

17:05–17:20 *BMM-Based Chinese Word Segmentor with Word Support Model for the SIGHAN Bakeoff 2006*
Jia-Lin Tsai

17:20–17:35 *On Closed Task of Chinese Word Segmentation: An Improved CRF Model Coupled with Character Clustering and Automatically Generated Template Matching*
Richard Tzong-Han Tsai, Hsieh-Chuan Hung, Cheng-Lung Sung, Hong-Jie Dai and Wen-Lian Hsu

17:35–17:50 *Chinese Word Segmentation with Maximum Entropy and N-gram Language Model*
Xinhao Wang, Xiaojun Lin, Dianhai Yu, Hao Tian and Xihong Wu

Sunday, 23 July 2006

Session 6: Bakeoff Presentations

Improving Context Vector Models by Feature Clustering for Automatic Thesaurus Construction

Jia-Ming You
Institute of Information Science
Academia Sinica
swimming@hp.iis.sinica.edu.tw

Keh-Jiann Chen
Institute of Information Science
Academia Sinica
kchen@iis.sinica.edu.tw

Abstract

Thesauruses are useful resources for NLP; however, manual construction of thesaurus is time consuming and suffers low coverage. Automatic thesaurus construction is developed to solve the problem. Conventional way to automatically construct thesaurus is by finding similar words based on context vector models and then organizing similar words into thesaurus structure. But the context vector methods suffer from the problems of vast feature dimensions and data sparseness. Latent Semantic Index (LSI) was commonly used to overcome the problems. In this paper, we propose a feature clustering method to overcome the same problems. The experimental results show that it performs better than the LSI models and do enhance contextual information for infrequent words.

1 Introduction

Thesaurus is one of the most useful linguistic resources. It provides information more than just synonyms. For example, in WordNet (Fellbaum, 1998), it also builds up relations between synonym sets, such as hyponym, hypernym. There are two Chinese thesauruses Cilin(1983) and Hownet[1]. Cilin provides synonym sets with simple hierarchical structure. Hownet uses some primitive senses to describe word meanings. The common primitive senses provide additional relations between words implicitly. However, many words occurred in contemporary news corpora are not covered by Chinese thesauruses.

Therefore, we intend to create a thesaurus based on contemporary news corpora. The common steps to automatically construct a thesaurus include a) contextual information extraction, b) finding synonym words and c) organizing synonym words into a thesaurus. The approach is based upon the fact that word meaning lays on its contextual behavior. If words act similarly in context, they may share the same meaning. However, the method can only handle frequent words rather than infrequent ones. In fact most of vocabularies occur infrequently, one has to discover extend information to overcome the data sparseness problem. We will introduce the conventional approaches for automatic thesaurus construction in section 2. Follow a discussion about the problems and solutions of context vector models in section 3. In section 4, we use two performance evaluation metrics, i.e. discrimination and nonlinear interpolated precision, to evaluate our proposed method.

2 Conventional approaches for automatic thesaurus construction

The conventional approaches for automatic thesaurus construction include three steps: (1) Acquire contextual behaviors of words from corpora. (2) Calculate the similarity between words. (3) Finding similar words and then organizing into a thesaurus structure.

2.1 Acquire word sense knowledge

One can model word meanings by their co-occurrence context. The common ways to extract co-occurrence contextual words include simple window based and syntactic dependent based (You, 2004). Obviously, syntactic dependent relations carry more accurate information than window based. Also, it can bring additional information, such as POS (part of speech) and semantic roles etc. To extract the syntactic de-

[1] *http://www.HowNet.com(Dong Zhendong, Dong Qiang:HowNet)*

pended relation, a raw text has to be segmented, POS tagged, and parsed. Then the relation extractor identifies the head-modifier relations and/or head-argument relations. Each relation could be defined as a triple (w, r, c), where w is the thesaurus term, c is the co-occurred context word and r is the relation between w and c.

Then context vector of a word is represented differently by different models, such as: tf, weight-tf, Latent Semantic Indexing (LSI) (Deerwester, S.,et al., 1990) and Probabilistic LSI (Hofmann, 1999). The context vectors of word x can be express by:

a) tf model: word $x = \{tf_1^x, tf_2^x, ..., tf_n^x\}$,where tf_i^x is the term frequency of the *ith* context word when given word x.

b) weight-tf model: assume there are n contextual words and m target words. word x=

$$\{tf_1^x \times \text{weight}1, tf_2^x \times \text{weight}2 ... tf_n^x \times \text{weight}n\}$$

,where weight$_i$, we used here, is defined as [log$m$-entropy(word$i$)]/log$m$

$$\text{entropy}(\text{word}i) = \sum_{k=1}^{m} - p(word_k^i) \log p(word_k^i);$$

$p(\text{word}_k^i)$ is the co-occurrence probability of word$k$ when given word$i$.

c) LSI or PLSI models: using tf or weighted-tf co-occurrence matrix and by adopting LSI or PLSI to reduce the dimension of the matrix.

2.2 Similarity between words

The common similarity functions include

a) Adopting simple frequency feature, such as cosine, which computes the angle between two context vectors;

$$\cos(x, y) = \frac{x \bullet y}{\|x\| \times \|y\|}$$

b) Represent words by the probabilistic distribution among contexts, such as Kull-Leiber divergence (Cover and Thomas, 1991).

The first step is to convert the co-occurrence matrix into a probabilistic matrix by simple formula.

$$\text{word}x = p = \{p_1^x, p_2^x, ... p_n^x\}, p_i^x = tf_i^x \Big/ \textstyle\sum_{k=1}^{n} tf_k^x$$

$$\text{word}y = q = \{q_1^x, q_2^x, ... q_n^x\}, q_i^x = tf_i^y \Big/ \textstyle\sum_{k=1}^{n} tf_k^y$$

Then calculate the distance between probabilistic vectors by sums up the all probabilistic difference among each context word so called cross entropy.

$$\text{KL Distance : KL}(p, q) = \sum_{i=1}^{n} p(i) \bullet \log_2 p_i / q_i$$

Due to the original KL distance is asymmetric and is not defined when zero frequency occurs. Some enhanced KL models were developed to prevent these problems such as Jensen-Shannon (Jianhua, 1991), which introducing a probabilistic variable m, or α -Skew Divergence (Lee, 1999), by adopting adjustable variable α. Research shows that Skew Divergence achieves better performance than other measures. (Lee, 2001)

$$\text{D(SkewDivergence)} = S_x^y \alpha = KL(x \parallel \alpha x + (1-\alpha) y)$$

$$\text{D(Jensen - Shannon)} = \text{JS}(x, y) = \{KL(x \parallel m) + KL(y \parallel m)\} / 2,$$

$$m = (x + y) / 2$$

To convert distance to similarity value, we adopt the formula inspired by Mochihashi, and Matsumoto 2002.

$$\text{similarity(word}x, \text{word}y) = \exp\{-\lambda \cdot \text{distance}(x, y)\}$$

2.3 Organize similar words into thesaurus

There are several clustering methods can be used to cluster similar words. For example, by selecting N target words as the entries of a thesaurus, then extract top-n similar words for each entry; adopting HAC(Hierarchical agglomerative clustering, E.M. Voorhees,1986) method to cluster the most similar word pairs in each clustering loop. Eventually, these similar words will be formed into synonyms sets.

3 Difficulties and Solutions

There are two difficulties of using context vector models. One is the enormous dimensions of contextual words, and the other is data sparseness problem. Conventionally LSI or PLSI methods are used to reduce feature dimensions by mapping literal words into latent semantic classes. The researches show that it's a promising method (April Kontostathis, 2003). However the latent semantic classes also smooth the information content of feature vectors. Here we proposed a different approach to cope with the feature reduction and data sparseness problems.

3.1 Feature Clustering

Reduced feature dimensions and data sparseness cause the problem of inaccurate contextual information. In general, one has to reduce the feature dimensions for computational feasibility and also to extend the contextual word information to overcome the problem of insufficient context information.

In our experiments, we took the clustered-feature approaches instead of LSI to cope with these two problems and showed better performances. The idea of clustered-feature approaches is by adopting the classes of clustering result of the frequent words as the new set of features which has less feature dimensions and context words are naturally extend to their class members. We followed the steps described in section 2 to develop the synonyms sets. First, the syntactic dependent relations were extracted to create the context vectors for each word. We adopted the skew divergence as the similarity function, which is reported to be the suitable similarity function (Masato, 2005), to measure the distance between words.

We used HAC algorithm to develop the synonyms classes, which is a greedy method, simply to cluster the most similar word pairs at each clustering iteration.

The HAC clustering process:

While the similarity of the most similar word pair (wordx, wordy) is greater than a threshold ε

then cluster wordx, wordy together and replace it with the centroid between wordx and wordy

Recalculate the similarity between other words and the centroid

3.2 Clustered-Feature Vectors

We obtain the synonyms sets S from above HAC method. Let the extracted synonyms sets S = { S^1, S^2,…S^R} which contains R synonym classes; S^i_j stands for the *jth* element of the *ith* synonym class; the *i*th synonym class S^i contains Q_i elements.

$$S = \begin{bmatrix} S_1^1 & S_2^1 & \dots & S_{Q1}^1 \\ S_1^2 & S_2^2 & \dots & S_{Q2}^2 \\ \dots & \dots & \dots & \dots \\ S_1^R & S_2^R & \dots & S_{QR}^R \end{bmatrix}$$

The feature extension processing transforms the coordination from literal words to synonyms sets. Assume there are *N* contextual words {C_1,C_2,…C_N}, and the first step is to transform the context vector of of C_i to the distribution vector among S. Then the new feature vector is the summation of the distribution vectors among S of its all contextual words.

The new feature vector of word_j =

$$\sum_{i=1}^{N} tf_i^j \times \text{Distribution\_Vector\_among\_S}(C_i)$$

,where tf_i^j is the term frequency of the context word C_i occurs with word_j.

$\text{Distribution\_Vector\_among\_S}(C_i) = \{P_i^{S_1}, P_i^{S_2}, \dots P_i^{S_R}\}$,

, where $P_i^{S_j} = \dfrac{\sum_{q=1}^{Qj} freq(S_q^j, Ci)}{freq(Ci)}$, means the distribution of context words of *Ci* at the *jth* synonyms S^j.

Due to the transformed coordination no longer stands for either frequency or probability, we use simple cosine function to measure the similarity between these transformed clustered-feature vectors.

4 Evaluation

To evaluate the performance of the feature clustering method, we had prepared two sets of testing data with high and low frequency words respectively. We want to see the effects of feature reduction and feature extension for both frequent and infrequent words.

4.1 Discrimination Rates

The discrimination rate is used to examine the capability of distinguishing the correlation between words. Given a word pair (*wordi,wordj*), one has to decide whether the word pair is similar or not. Therefore, we will arrange two different word pair sets, related and unrelated, to estimate the discrimination. By given the formula below

$$\text{Discrimination rate} = \frac{1}{2}\left(\frac{na}{Na} + \frac{nb}{Nb}\right)$$

,where Na and Nb are respectively the numbers of synonym word pairs and unrelated word pairs. As well as, na and nb are the numbers of correct labeled pairs in synonyms and unrelated words.

4.2 Nonlinear interpolated precision

The Nap evaluation is used to measure the performance of restoring words to taxonomy, a similar task of restoring words in WordNet (Dominic Widdows, 2003).

The way we adopted Nap evaluation is to reconstruct a partial Chinese synonym set, and measure the structure resemblance between original synonyms and the reconstructed one. By doing so, one has to prepare certain number of synonyms sets from Chinese taxonomy, and try to reclassify these words.

Assume there are *n* testing words distributed in *R* synonyms sets. Let R^i_1 stands for the represented word of the *ith* synonyms set. Then we will compute the similarity ranking between each represented word and the rest *n-1* testing words. By given formula

$$\text{NAP} = \frac{1}{R}\sum_{i=1}^{R}\sum_{j=1}^{n-1}\frac{Z^i_j}{j}\left(1+\sum_{k=1}^{j-1}Z^i_k\right)$$

S^i_j represents the *jth* similar word of R^i_1 among the rest *n-1* words

$$Z^i_j = \begin{cases} 1, \text{if } S^i_j \text{ and } R^i_1 \text{ are synonym} \\ 0 \end{cases}$$

The NAP value means how many percent synonyms can be identified. The maximum value of NAP is 1, means the extracted similar words are exactly match to the synonyms.

5 Experiments

The context vectors were derived from a 10 year news corpus from The Central News Agency. It contains nearly 33 million sentences, 234 million word tokens, and we extracted 186 million syntactic relations from this corpus. Due to the low reliability of infrequent data, only the relation triples (w, r, c), which occurs more than 3 times and POS of w and c must be noun or verb, are used. It results that nearly 30,000 high frequent nouns and verbs are used as the contextual features. And with feature clustering[2], the contextual dimensions were reduced from 30,988 literal words to 12,032 semantic classes.

In selecting testing data, we consider the words that occur more than 200 times as high frequent words and the frequencies range from 40 to 200 as low frequent words.

Discrimination

For the discrimination experiments, we randomly extract high frequent word pairs which include 500 synonym pairs and 500 unrelated word pairs from Cilin (Mei et. al, 1983). At the mean time, we also prepare equivalent low frequency data.

We use a mathematical technique Singular Value Decomposition (SVD) to derive principal components and to implement LSI models with respect to different feature dimensions from 100 to 1000. We compare the performances of different models. The results are shown in the following figures.

discrimination	related recall	unrelated words	discrimination rate
TF	81.20%	84.00%	82.60%
Weight_TF	77%	88.40%	82.70%
Feature Clustering	81.80%	82%	81.90%
SVD 100	60.80%	89.80%	75.30%
SVD200	65.60%	85.80%	75.70%
SVD300	64.20%	90.20%	77.20%
SVD400	69.40%	86.20%	77.80%
SVD500	74%	84.60%	79.30%
SVD600	74.80%	85.40%	80.10%
SVD700	75.20%	84.80%	80%
SVD800	72.40%	89.40%	80.90%
SVD900	70.80%	91%	80.90%
SVD1000	78.60%	83.60%	81.10%

Figure1. Discrimination for high frequent words

The result shows that for the high frequent data, although the feature clustering method did not achieve the best performance, it performances better at related data and a balanced performance at unrelated data. The tradeoffs be-

[2] *Some feature clustering results are listed in the Appendix*

tween related recalls and unrelated recalls are clearly shown. Another observation is that no matter of using LSI or literal word features (tf or weight_tf), the performances are comparable. Therefore, we could simply use any method to handle the high frequent words.

discrimination	related recall	unrelated recall	discrimination rate
TF	53.13%	97.19%	75.16%
Weight_TF	53.13%	97.62%	75.38%
Feature Clustering	**59.18%**	**94.17%**	**76.67%**
SVD 100	64.58%	78.19%	71.38%
SVD200	53.56%	94.17%	73.87%
SVD300	54.43%	94.60%	74.51%
SVD400	53.56%	96.11%	74.84%
SVD500	60.04%	88.98%	74.51%
SVD600	51.40%	95.68%	73.54%
SVD700	54.21%	95.03%	74.62%
SVD800	50.54%	96.98%	73.76%
SVD900	53.56%	96.54%	75.05%

Figure2 Discrimination for low frequent word

For the infrequent words experiments, neither LSI nor weighted-tf performs well due to insufficient contextual information. But by introducing feature clustering method, one can gain more 6% accuracy for the related data. It shows feature clustering method could help gather more information for the infrequent words.

Nonlinear interpolated precision

For the Nap evaluation, we prepared two testing data from Cilin and Hownet. In the high frequent words experiments, we extract 1311 words within 352 synonyms sets from Cilin and 2981 words within 570 synonyms sets from Hownet.

Nap Performance	Cilin	Hownet
TF	38.34%	28.56%
Weight_TF	40.38%	29.00%
Feature Clustering	37.71%	27.61%
SVD100	20.13%	13.12%
SVD200	22.46%	15.73%
SVD300	23.26%	16.21%
SVD400	26.04%	17.28%
SVD500	26.95%	17.37%
SVD600	27.31%	17.93%
SVD700	28.80%	18.58%
SVD800	29.10%	19.14%
SVD900	29.07%	19.48%
SVD1000	29.15%	19.67%

Figure 3. Nap performance for high frequent words

In high frequent experiments, the results show that the models retaining literal form perform better than dimension reduction methods. It means in the task of measuring similarity of high frequent words using literal contextual feature vectors is more precise than using dimension reduction feature vectors.

In the infrequent words experiments, we can only extract 202 words distributed in 62 synonyms sets from Cilin and 1089 words within 222 synonyms sets. Due to fewer testing words, LSI was not applied in this experiment.

Nap Performance	Cilin	Hownet
TF	22.30%	15.60%
Weighted TF	23.60%	17.23%
Feature Clustering	22.56%	16.43%

Figure 4. Nap performance for low frequent words

It shows with insufficient contextual information, the feature clustering method could not help in recalling synonyms because of dimensional reduction.

6. Error Analysis and Conclusion

Using context vector models to construct thesaurus suffers from the problems of large feature dimensions and data sparseness. We propose a feature clustering method to overcome the problems. The experimental results show that it performs better than the LSI models in distinguishing related/unrelated pairs for the infrequent data, and also achieve relevant scores on other evaluations.

Feature clustering method could raise the ability of discrimination, but not robust enough to improve the performance in extracting synonyms. It also reveals the truth that it's easy to distinguish whether a pair is related or unrelated once the word pair shares the same sense in their senses. However, it's not the case when seeking synonyms. One has to discriminate each sense for each word first and then compute the similarity between these senses to achieve synonyms. Because feature clustering method lacks the ability of senses discrimination of a word, the method can handle the task of distinguishing correlation pairs rather than synonyms identification.

Also, after analyzing discrimination errors made by context vector models, we found that some errors are not due to insufficient contextual information. Certain synonyms have dissimilar contextual contents for different reasons. We observed some phenomenon of these cases:

a) Some senses of synonyms in testing data are not their dominant senses.

Take *guang1hua2* (光華) for example, it has a sense of "splendid" which is similar to the sense of *guang1mang2* (光芒). *Guang1hua2* and *guang1mang2* are certainly mutually changeable in a certain degree, *guang1hua2jin4shi4 (*光華盡失) and *guang1mang2jin4shi4* (光芒盡失), or *xi2ri4guang1hua2* (昔日光華) and *xi2ri4guang1mang2* (昔日光芒). However, the dominated contextual sense of *guang1hua2* is more likely to be a place name, like *guang1hua2shi4chang3(* 光華市場) or *hua1lian2guang1hua2* (花蓮光華) etc[3].

b) Some synonyms are different in usages for pragmatic reasons.

Synonyms with different contextual vectors could be result from different perspective views. For example, we may view *wai4jie4* (外界) as a container image with viewer inside, but on the other hand, *yi3wai4* (以外) is an omnipotence perspective. This similar meaning but different perspective makes distinct grammatical usage and different collocations.

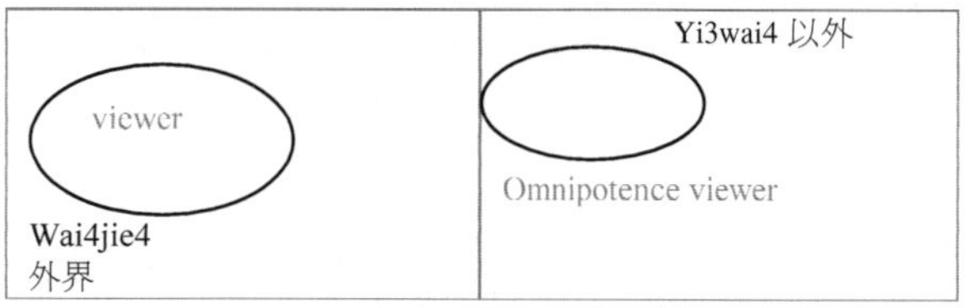

Similarly, *zhong1shen1* (終身) and *sheng1ping2* (生平) both refer to "life-long time". *zhong1shen1* explicates things after a time point, which differs from *sheng1ping2*, showing matters before a time point.

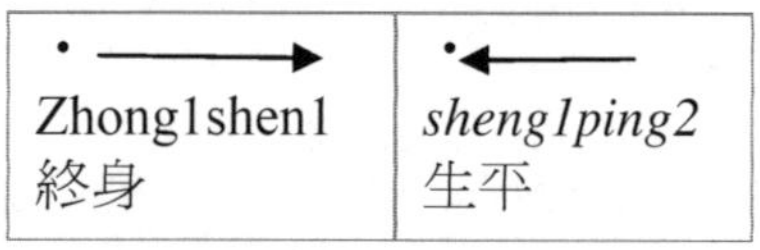

c) **Domain specific usages**.

For example, in medical domain news ,*wa1wa1* (娃娃) occurs frequently with *bo1li2* (玻璃) refer to kind of illness. Then the corpus reinterpret *wa1wa1* (娃娃) as a sick people, due to it occurs with medical term. But the synonym of *wa1wa1* (娃娃), xiao3peng2you3(小朋友) stands for money in some finance news. Therefore, the meanings of words change from time to time. It's hard to decide whether meaning is the right answer when finding synonyms.

With above observations, our future researches will be how to distinguish different word senses from its context features. Once we could distinguish the corresponding features for different senses, it will help us to extract more accurate synonyms for both frequent and infrequent words.

References

April Kontostathis, William M. Pottenger 2003. , *A Framework for Understanding LSI Performance*, *In the* Proceedings of the ACM SIGIR Workshop on Mathematical/Formal Methods in Information Retrieval, *Annual International SIGIR Conference, 2003.*

Christiance Fellbaum, editor 1998,*WordNet*: An alectronic lwxical database. MIT press, Cambrige MA.

Deerwester, S.,et al. 1990 *Indexing by Latent Semantic Analysis.* Jorunal of the American Society for Information Science, 41(6):391-407

Dominic Widdows. 2003. *Unsupervised methods for developing taxonomies by combining syntactic and statistical information*. In *Proceeding of HLT-NAACL 2003 Main papers,* pp, 197-204.

E.M. Voorhees, "*Implement agglomerative hierarchical clustering algorithm for use in document retrieval"*, Information Processing & Management. , no. 22 pp.46-476,1986

Hofmann, T.1999. *Probabilistic Latent Semantic Indexing*. Proc.of the 22nd International conference on Research and Development in Information Retrieval (SIGIR'99),50-57

James R.Curran and Marc Moens. 2002. I*mprovements in Automatic Thesaurus Extraction. Proceedings of the Workshop of the ACL Special Interest Group on the Lexicon (SIGLEX)*, pp. 59-66

Jia-Ming You and Keh-Jiann Chen, 2004 *Automatic Semantic Role Assignment for a Tree Structure,* Pro-

[3] This may due to different genres. In newspapers the proper noun usage of *guang1hua2* is more common than in a literature text.

ceedings of 3rd ACL SIGHAN Workshop

Jiahua Lin. 1991. *Divergence measures based on the Shannon Entropy*. IEEE transactions on Information Theory, 37(1): 145-151

Lillian Lee. 2001. *On the effectiveness of the skew divergence for statistical language analysis*. In Artificial Intelligence and Statistics 2001, page 65-72.

Lillian Lee. 1999. *Measure of distributional similarity*. In Proceeding of the 37th Annual Meeting of the Association for Computational Linguistics (ACL-1999), page 23-32.

Masato Hagiwara, Yasuhiro Ogawa, and Katsuhiko Toyama. 2005. *PLSI Utilization for Automatic Thesaurus Construction. IJCNLP 2005, LNAI 651,* pp. 334-345.

Mei,Jiaju,Yiming Lan, Yunqi Gao, Yongxian Ying (1983) *同義詞詞林 [A Dictionary of Synonyms]*,Shanghai Cishu Chubanshe.

Mochihashi, D., Matsumoto, Y.2002. *Probabilistic Representation of Meanings*. IPSJ SIG Notes Natural Language, 2002-NL-147:77-84.

T.Cover and J.Thomas, 1991. *Element of Information Theory*. Wiley & sons, New York

Appendix:

Some feature clustering results

一下 一陣子

一千多 四百多 一百多 二百多

一切 災難性

一月份 二月份 類型

一生 畢生 一輩子 生平

一年級 國一 大學部

一成 三成 兩成 二成

一百多萬 三百多萬 一千多萬

一段 大半 較多 多一點 空檔 美東 間隔 尖峰 睡眠 美西 需要

一家人 家人 親人

一席之地 優勢

一氧化碳 沼氣 食物 河豚 粉塵

一級 黨務 行庫 原由 二級

一般性 計畫型

一號機 二號機

一銀 二銀 五金

一審 原審 陪審團 審法院

一樓 大會堂 中庭

一舉一動 動向 事項 言行 舉止

一體 中西文

乙級 技術士 廚師 中餐

丁等 甲等 乙等 丙等 中醫師 優等

七人 九人 六人 九人決策

七夕 西洋

七月號 月刊 八月號 雜誌 消息報 週報 二月號

七成 六成 八成 五成 四成 九成

七股 鰲鼓

七美 東引

九孔 草蝦 鰻魚 石斑魚 虱目魚 文蛤 吳郭魚 牡蠣 甲魚 箱網 蝦子 魚蝦 蚵仔 黑鯛 魚群 蝸牛

九份 草嶺 國姓鄉 瑞芳鎮 竹北市

二仁溪 大漢溪 淡水河 漢江 新店溪 游泳池 泳池 鴨綠江 朴子溪 後龍溪 農漁局

二月 十二月 九月 十一月 十月 七月 元月

二年制 四年制

二年級 五年級 大二

二次大戰 第二次世界大戰 大戰 韓戰

二兵 上士 准將 新聞官

二者 兩者 三者

二金 三金 一金

二段 三段

二胡 琵琶 古箏 吉他

二重 疏洪道

二氧化碳 廢氣 污染物 廢水 二氧化硫 氣體 柴油車 氧化物 臭氣 污染源

二專 四技二專 學校院 校院

二組 三組 五組 八組 標準組 組別 梯隊

二號 三號 四號 五號 一號 太原 風雲 型號

二路 三路

二線 三線 四線

二壘 三壘 隊友

二讀會 三讀會 讀會 提案

人人 舉世 舉國 兩性

人力 物力 頻寬

人口 人數 人口數 救濟金 大軍 週數 戶數 家數 次數 隊數 保險金 頻率 斷面

人才 人材 師資 運動選手 增長點 搖籃 英才 專才

人文 美學 藝能 科展

人文組 數理組

人犯 罪犯 煙毒犯

人生 寶島 山城

人生觀 價值觀 觀念

人次 車次

人行道 騎樓

人身 信仰 言論 性行為

人事費 醫療費用 利息 保費 保險費

人協 黨代表 會員 懇親 股東 社員 締約國

人命 性命 生命

人物 學府 旅遊點 傑作 寶庫 勁旅

Regional Variation of Domain-Specific Lexical Items: Toward a Pan-Chinese Lexical Resource

Oi Yee Kwong and Benjamin K. Tsou
Language Information Sciences Research Centre
City University of Hong Kong
Tat Chee Avenue, Kowloon, Hong Kong
{rlolivia,rlbtsou}@cityu.edu.hk

Abstract

This paper reports on an initial and necessary step toward the construction of a Pan-Chinese lexical resource. We investigated the regional variation of lexical items in two specific domains, finance and sports; and explored how much of such variation is covered in existing Chinese synonym dictionaries, in particular the Tongyici Cilin. The domain-specific lexical items were obtained from subsections of a synchronous Chinese corpus, LIVAC. Results showed that 20-40% of the words from various subcorpora are unique to the individual communities, and as much as 70% of such unique items are not yet covered in the Tongyici Cilin. The results suggested great potential for building a Pan-Chinese lexical resource for Chinese language processing. Our next step would be to explore automatic means for extracting related lexical items from the corpus, and to incorporate them into existing semantic classifications.

1 Introduction

Many cities have underground railway systems. Somehow one takes the *tube* in London but the *subway* in New York. In a more recent edition of the Roget's Thesaurus (Kirkpatrick, 1987), *subway*, *tube*, *underground railway* and *metro* are found in the same semicolon-separated group under head *624 Way*. Similarly if one looks up WordNet (http://wordnet.princeton.edu; Miller et al., 1990), the synset to which *subway* belongs also contains the words *metro*, *tube*, *underground*, and *subway system*; and it is further indicated that "in Paris the subway system is called the 'metro' and in London it is called the 'tube' or the 'underground'". Such regional lexical variation is also found in Chinese. For instance, the subway system in Hong Kong, known as the Mass Transit Railway or MTR, is called 地鐵 in Chinese. The subway systems in Beijing and Shanghai, as well as the one in Singapore, are also known as 地鐵, but that in Taipei is known as 捷運. Their counterpart in Japan is written as 地下鉄 in Kanji. Such regional variation, as part of lexical knowledge, is important and useful for many natural language applications, including natural language understanding, information retrieval, and machine translation. Unfortunately, existing Chinese lexical resources often lack such comprehensiveness.

To fill this gap, Tsou and Kwong (2006) proposed a comprehensive Pan-Chinese lexical resource, based on a large and unique synchronous Chinese corpus as an authentic basis for lexical acquisition and analysis across various Chinese speech communities. For a significant world language like Chinese, a useful lexical resource should have maximum *versatility* and *portability*. It is not sufficient to target at one particular community speaking the language and thus cover only language usage observed from that particular community. Instead, such a lexical resource should document the core and universal substances of the language on the one hand, and also the more subtle variations found in different communities on the other. As is evident from the above example on the variation of *subway*, regional variation should be captured for the lexical resource to be useful in a wide range of applications.

In this study, we investigate and compare the regional variation of lexical items from two specific domains, finance and sports, as an initial and necessary step toward the more important undertaking of building a Pan-Chinese lexical resource. In addition, we make use of an existing Chinese synonym dictionary, the *Tongyici Cilin* (Mei et al., 1984) as leverage, and explore its coverage of such variation and thus the potential for enriching it. The lexical items under study were obtained from a synchronous Chinese corpus, LIVAC, which will be further introduced in Section 4. Corpus data from four Chinese speech communities were compared with respect to their commonality and uniqueness, and also against Cilin for their coverage. Results showed that 20-40% of the words extracted from the corpus are unique to the individual communities, and as much as 70% of such unique items are not yet covered in Cilin. It therefore suggests that the synchronous corpus is a rich source for mining region-specific lexical items, and there is great potential for building a Pan-Chinese lexical resource for Chinese language processing.

In Section 2, we will briefly review existing resources and related work. Then in Section 3, we will briefly outline the design and architecture of the Pan-Chinese lexical resource proposed by Tsou and Kwong (2006). In Section 4, we will further describe the Chinese synonym dictionary and the synchronous Chinese corpus used in this study. The comparison of their lexical items will be discussed in Section 5. Future directions will be presented in Section 6, followed by a conclusion.

2 Existing Resources and Related Work

The construction and development of large lexical resources is relying more and more on corpus-based approaches, not only as a result of the increased availability of large corpora, but also for the authoritativeness and authenticity allowed by the approach. The Collins COBUILD English Dictionary (Sinclair, 1987) is amongst the most well-known lexicographic fruit based on large corpora.

For natural language applications, much of the information in conventional dictionaries targeted at human readers must be made explicit. Lexical resources for computer use thus need considerable manipulation, customisation, and supplementation (e.g. Calzolari, 1982). WordNet (Miller et al., 1990), grouping words into synsets and linking them up with relational pointers, is probably the first broad coverage general computational lexical database. In view of the intensive time and effort required in resource building, some researchers have taken an alternative route by extracting information from existing machine-readable dictionaries and corpora semi-automatically (e.g. Vossen et al., 1989; Riloff and Shepherd, 1999; Lin et al, 2003).

Compared to the development of thesauri and lexical databases, and research into semantic networks for major languages such as English, similar work for the Chinese language is less mature. This gap was partly due to the lack of authoritative Chinese corpora as a basis for analysis, but has been gradually reduced with the recent availability of large Chinese corpora including the LIVAC synchronous corpus (Tsou and Lai, 2003) used in this work and further described below, the Sinica Corpus (Chen et al., 1996), the Chinese Penn Treebank (Xia et al., 2000), and the like.

An important issue which is seldom addressed in the construction of Chinese lexical databases is the problem of versatility and portability. For a language such as Chinese which is spoken in many different communities, different linguistic norms have emerged as a result of the individualistic evolution and development of the language within a particular community and culture. Such variations are seldom adequately reflected in existing lexical resources, which often only draw reference from one particular source. For instance, Tongyici Cilin (同義詞詞林) (Mei et al., 1984) is a thesaurus containing some 70,000 Chinese lexical items in the tradition of the Roget's Thesaurus for English, that is, in a hierarchy of broad conceptual categories. First published in the 1980s, it was based exclusively on Chinese as used in post-1949 Mainland China. Thus for the subway example above, the closest word group found is 火車, 列車 (train) only, let alone the subway itself and its regional variations.

With the recent availability of large corpora, especially synchronous ones, to construct an authoritative and timely lexical resource for Chinese is less distant than it was in the past. A large synchronous corpus provides authentic examples of the language as used in a variety of locations. It thus enables us to attempt a comprehensive and in-depth analysis of the core common language in constructing a lexical resource; and to incorporate useful information relating to location-sensitive linguistic variations.

3 Proposal of a Pan-Chinese Thesaurus

The Pan-Chinese lexicon proposed by Tsou and Kwong (2006) is expected to capture not only the core senses of lexical items but also senses and uses specific to individual Chinese speech communities.

The lexical database will be organised into a core database and a supplementary one. The core database will contain the core lexical information for word senses and usages which are common to most Chinese speech communities, whereas the supplementary database will contain the language uses specific to individual communities, including "marginal" and "sublanguage" uses.

A network structure will be adopted for the lexical items. The nodes could be sets of near-synonyms or single lexical items (in which case synonymy will be one type of links). The links will not only represent the paradigmatic semantic relations but also syntagmatic ones (such as selectional restrictions).

We thus begin by investigating in depth the regional variation of lexical items, especially domain-specific words, among several Chinese speech communities. In addition, we explore the potential of enriching existing resources as a start. In the following section, we will discuss the Tongyici Cilin and the synchronous Chinese corpus used in this study in greater details.

4 Materials and Method

4.1 The Tongyici Cilin

The Tongyici Cilin (同義詞詞林) (Mei et al., 1984) is a Chinese synonym dictionary, or more often known as a Chinese thesaurus in the tradition of the Roget's Thesaurus for English. The Roget's Thesaurus has about 1,000 numbered semantic heads, more generally grouped under higher level semantic classes and subclasses, and more specifically differentiated into paragraphs and semicolon-separated word groups. Similarly, some 70,000 Chinese lexical items are organized into a hierarchy of broad conceptual categories in the Tongyici Cilin. Its classification consists of 12 top-level semantic classes, 94 sub-classes, 1,248 semantic heads and 3,925 paragraphs.

4.2 The LIVAC Synchronous Corpus

LIVAC (http://www.livac.org) stands for Linguistic Variation in Chinese Speech Communities. It is a synchronous corpus developed by the Language Information Sciences Research Centre of the City University of Hong Kong since 1995 (Tsou and Lai, 2003). The corpus consists of newspaper articles collected regularly and synchronously from six Chinese speech communities, namely Hong Kong, Beijing, Taipei, Singapore, Shanghai, and Macau. Texts collected cover a variety of domains, including front page news stories, local news, international news, editorials, sports news, entertainment news, and financial news. Up to December 2005, the corpus has already accumulated about 180 million character tokens which, upon automatic word segmentation and manual verification, amount to over 900K word types.

For the present study, we make use of the subcorpora collected over the 9-year period 1995-2004 from Hong Kong (HK), Beijing (BJ), Taipei (TW), and Singapore (SG). In particular, we focus on the *financial news* and *sports news* to investigate the commonality and uniqueness of the lexical items used in these specific domains in the various communities. We also evaluate the adequacy of the Tongyici Cilin in terms of its coverage of such domain-specific terms especially from the Pan-Chinese perspective, and thus assess the room for its enrichment with the synchronous corpus. Table 1 shows the sizes of the subcorpora used for this study.

Subcorpus	Overall (rounded to nearest 0.01M)		Financial News (rounded to nearest 1K)		Sports News (rounded to nearest 1K)	
	Word Token	Word Type	Word Token	Word Type	Word Token	Word Type
HK	14.39M	0.22M	970K	38K	1041K	39K
BJ	11.70M	0.19M	232K	20K	443K	28K
TW	12.32M	0.20M	254K	22K	657K	33K
SG	13.22M	0.21M	621K	28K	998K	34K

Table 1 Sizes of individual subcorpora

4.3 Procedures

Word-frequency lists were generated from the financial and sports subcorpora from each individual community. For each resulting list, the steps below were followed to remove irrelevant items and retain only the potentially useful content words:

(a) Remove all numbers and non-Chinese words.

(b) Remove all proper names, including those annotated as personal names, geographical names, and organisation names. Proper names have been annotated in the corpora during the process of word segmentation.

(c) Remove function words.

(d) Remove lexical items with frequency 5 or below.

The numbers of remaining items in each subcorpus after the above steps are listed in Tables 2 and 3 for the two domains respectively. The lexical items retained, which are expected to contain a substantial amount of content words, are potentially useful for the current study. The lists in each domain (from the various subcorpora) were compared in terms of the items they share and those unique to individual communities. Their unique items were also compared against the Tongyici Cilin to investigate its adequacy and explore how it might be enriched with the synchronous corpus.

Subcorpus	All	After (a)	After (b)	After (c)	After(d)
HK	37,525	27,937	20,422	17,162	5,238
BJ	20,025	17,361	14,460	12,134	2,791
TW	22,142	19,428	16,316	13,496	3,088
SG	28,193	22,829	16,863	13,822	3,836

Table 2 Number of word types remaining after various data cleaning steps for the financial domain

Subcorpus	All	After (a)	After (b)	After (c)	After(d)
HK	39,190	35,720	25,289	21,502	6,316
BJ	27,971	26,049	19,799	16,598	3,878
TW	32,706	30,231	20,361	17,248	4,601
SG	34,040	31,974	19,995	16,780	5,120

Table 3 Number of word types remaining after various data cleaning steps for the sports domain

5 Results and Discussion

5.1 Lexical Items from LIVAC

The four subcorpora of the financial domain differ considerably in their sizes, and slightly less so for the sports domain. Despite this, we observed for both domains from Tables 2 and 3 that in general about 40-50% of all word types are numbers, non-Chinese words, proper names, and function words. Of the remaining items, about 20-30% have frequency greater than 5. These several thousand word types from each subcorpus are expected to be amongst the more interesting items and form the "candidate sets" for further investigation.

5.2 Commonality among Various Regions

Comparing the candidate sets from various subcorpora, which reflect the use of Chinese in various Chinese speech communities, Tables 4 and 5 show the sizes of the intersection sets among different places for the two domains respectively.

The intersection set for all four places contains slightly more than 1,000 lexical items in the financial domain. A quick skim through these common lexical items suggests that they contain, on the one hand, the many general concepts in the financial domain (e.g. 公司 company, 市場 market, 銀行 bank, 投資 invest / investment, 業務 business, 發展 develop / development, 集團 corporation, 股份 stock shares, 股東 shareholder, 資金 capital, etc.); and on the other hand, many reportage and cognitive verbs often used in news articles (e.g. 表示 express, 認為 reckon, 出現 appear, 反映 reflect, etc.).

In the sports domain, more than 1,700 lexical items were found in all of the four subcorpora. Like its financial counterpart, we found many general concepts at the top of the list (e.g. 球員 player, 球隊 team, 賽事 match, 比賽 competition, 聯賽 league, 教練 coach, 對手 opponent, 冠軍 champion, etc.).

The numbers of overlaps in Tables 4 suggest that lexical items used in Mainland China (as evident from BJ data) seem to have the least in common with the rest. For instance, compared to the overlap amongst all four regions (i.e. 1,039), the overlap has increased most when BJ was not included in the comparison; and when we compare any two regions, the overlap between BJ and TW is smallest. Nevertheless, such uniqueness of BJ data is less apparent in the sports domain. In particular, the difference between HK/BJ and BJ/TW is even slightly less than that in the financial domain.

If we look at the individual regions, HK apparently shares most (about 50%) with SG, and vice versa (about 68%), in the financial domain. At the same time, BJ also shares more with HK than with the other two regions, and so does TW. But surprisingly, BJ has over 60% overlap with SG and about 55% with TW in the sports domain. The overlaps of TW with HK and with BJ differ by more than 20% in the finance domain, but only by about 10% in the sports domain. All these patterns might suggest lexical items in the financial domain are more versatile and have more varied focus in different communities, whereas those in the sports domain reflect the more common interests of different places.

Regions	Overlap	Proportion to individual lists (%)			
		HK	BJ	TW	SG
HK / BJ / TW / SG	1039	19.84	37.23	33.65	27.09
HK / BJ / TW	1126	21.50	40.34	36.46	
HK / BJ / SG	1327	25.33	47.55		34.59
HK / TW / SG	1581	30.18		51.20	41.21
BJ / TW / SG	1092		39.13	35.36	28.47
HK / BJ	1609	30.72	57.65		
HK / TW	1912	36.50		61.92	
HK / SG	2607	49.77			67.96
BJ / TW	1250		44.79	40.48	
BJ / SG	1505		53.92		39.23
TW / SG	1795			58.13	46.79

Table 4 Commonality amongst various regions for the financial domain

Regions	Overlap	Proportion to individual lists (%)			
		HK	BJ	TW	SG
HK / BJ / TW / SG	1668	26.41	43.01	36.25	32.58
HK / BJ / TW	1782	28.21	45.95	38.73	
HK / BJ / SG	2047	32.41	52.78		39.98
HK / TW / SG	2249	35.61		48.88	43.93
BJ / TW / SG	1864		48.07	40.51	36.41
HK / BJ	2318	36.70	59.77		
HK / TW	2693	42.64		58.53	
HK / SG	3305	52.33			64.55
BJ / TW	2124		54.77	46.16	
BJ / SG	2554		65.86		49.88
TW / SG	2709			58.88	52.91

Table 5 Commonality amongst various regions for the sports domain

5.3 Uniqueness of Various Regions

Next we compared the lists with respect to what they have unique to themselves. Table 6 shows the numbers of unique items found in each list, together with examples from the most frequent 20 unique items in each case.

Again, taking the size difference among the candidate sets into account, about 40% of the lexical items found in HK data are unique to the region, which re-echoes the versatility and wide coverage of interests of HK data. This is especially evident when compared to only about 20% of the candidate sets for SG are unique to Singapore.[1]

Looking at the unique lexical items found in individual regions, it is not difficult to see the region-specific lexicalisation of certain concepts. For instance, in terms of housing, 居屋 (housing under the Home Ownership Scheme) is a specific kind of housing in Hong Kong, 組屋 is a specific term in Singapore (as seen in SG data), whereas housing is generally expressed as 住房 in Mainland China (as seen in BJ data). Similarly, 操練 (HK) and 冬訓 (BJ) both refer to training, but may relate to different practice in the two communities. Such regional variation lends strong support to the importance of a Pan-Chinese lexical resource.

The lists of unique items also suggest the various focus and orientation in different Chinese speech communities. For example, while Hong Kong pays much attention to the real estate market and stock market, Mainland China may be focusing more on the basic needs like water, farming, poverty alleviation, etc., and Singapore is relatively more concerned with local affairs like port management. The passion for baseball, among other more popular sports like soccer, is most obvious from the unique lexical items found in TW data.

5.4 Comparison with Tongyici Cilin

As mentioned earlier, the Tongyici Cilin contains some 70,000 lexical items under 12 broad semantic classes, 94 subclasses, and 1,428 heads. It was first published in the 1980s and was based on lexical usages mostly of post-1949 Mainland China. In this section, we discuss the results obtained from comparing the unique lexical items found from individual subcorpora with Cilin, which are shown in Table 7.

On the one hand, Cilin's collection of words may be considerably dated and obviously will not include new concepts and neologisms arising in the last two decades. On the other hand, the data in LIVAC come from newspaper materials in the 1990s. So overall speaking, for each of the unique word lists, much less than 50% are covered in Cilin.

Nevertheless, there is still an apparent gap between Cilin's coverage of the unique items from various places. About 40% of the unique items found in BJ for both domains are covered; but for other places, the coverage is more often less than 30% in either or both domains. Again, this could be considered a result of Cilin's bias toward lexical usages in Mainland China.

In addition, while almost 40% of the unique items in BJ data are found in Cilin, many of these unique items covered are amongst the most frequent items. On the contrary, even though about 560 unique items in HK data are also found in Cilin, only 3 out of the 20 most frequent items are amongst them. In addition, the apparent coverage does not necessarily suggest the correct match of word senses. For instance, 居屋 is found under head *Bn1* together with other items like 住房, 住宅, etc., all of which only refer to the general concept of housing, instead of the housing specifically under the Home Ownership Scheme as known in Hong Kong. Also, coverage of words like 晨曦, 帝王 and 水手 in the sports domain does not match their actual usages which refer to team names. A more interesting example might be 火鍋, which is used in the basketball context in TW data, and in no way refers to the literal "hot pot" sense.

Results from the above comparisons thus support that (1) different Chinese speech communities have their distinct usage of Chinese lexical items, in terms of both form and sense; (2) such variation is found in different domains, such as the financial and sports domain; (3) existing lexical resources, the Tongyici Cilin in particular as in our current study, should be enriched and enhanced by capturing lexical usages from a variety of Chinese speech communities, to represent the lexical items from a Pan-Chinese perspective; and (4) lexical items obtained from the synchronous Chinese corpus can supplement the existing content of the Tongyici Cilin, with more contemporarily lexicalised concepts, as well as variant expressions of similar and related concepts from various Chinese speech communities.

Hence it remains for us to further investigate how the related lexical items obtained from the synchronous corpus should be grouped and incorporated into the semantic classification of existing lexical resources; and to further explore how they might be extracted in a large scale by automatic means. These will definitely be amongst the most important future directions as discussed in the next section.

[1] Upon further analysis, on average about 60% of these "unique" items were actually found in one or more of the other regions, but with frequency 5 or below. Since the difference in frequency is quite large for most items, we can reasonably treat them as unique to a particular community.

6 Future Work

In the current study, we have investigated the regional variation of lexical items from the financial and sports domain, and the coverage of the Tongyici Cilin for such variation. The results suggested great potential for building a Pan-Chinese lexical resource for Chinese language processing. Our next step would thus be to further investigate more automatic means for extracting the near-synonymous or closely related items from the various subcorpora. To this end, we would explore algorithms like those used in Lin et al. (2003). Of similar importance is the mechanism for grouping the related lexical items and incorporating them into the semantic classifications of existing lexical resources. In this regard we will proceed with further in-depth analysis of the classificatory structures of individual resources and fit in our Pan-Chinese architecture.

Apart from the Tongyici Cilin, there are other existing Chinese lexical resources such as HowNet (Dong and Dong, 2000), SUMO and Chinese WordNet (Huang et al., 2004), as well as other synonym dictionaries from which we might draw reference to build up our Pan-Chinese lexical resource.

7 Conclusion

In this paper, we have investigated the regional variation of lexical items in two specific domains from a synchronous Chinese corpus, and explored their coverage in a Chinese synonym dictionary. Results are encouraging in the sense that 20-40% of the candidate words from various subcorpora are unique to the individual communities, and as much as 70% of such unique items are not yet covered in the Tongyici Cilin. It therefore suggests great importance and potential for a Pan-Chinese lexical resource which we aim to construct. The synchronous corpus is a valuable resource for mining the region-specific expressions while existing synonym dictionaries might provide a ready-made semantic classificatory structure. Our next step would be to explore automatic means for extracting related lexical items from the corpus, and to incorporate them into existing semantic classifications.

Acknowledgements

This work is supported by Competitive Earmarked Research Grant (CERG) of the Research Grants Council of Hong Kong under grant No. CityU1317/03H. The authors would like to thank the anonymous reviewers for comments.

References

Calzolari, N. (1982) Towards the organization of lexical definitions on a database structure. In E. Hajicova (Ed.), *COLING '82 Abstracts*, Charles University, Prague, pp.61-64.

Caraballo, S.A. (1999) Automatic construction of a hypernym-labeled noun hierarchy. In *Proceedings of the 37th Annual Meeting of the Association for Computational Linguistics (ACL'99)*, College Park, Maryland, pp.120-126.

Chen, K-J., Huang, C-R., Chang, L-P. and Hsu, H-L. (1996) Sinica Corpus: Design Methodology for Balanced Corpora. In *Proceedings of the 11th Pacific Asia Conference on Language, Information, and Computation (PACLIC 11)*, Seoul, Korea, pp.167-176.

Dong, Z. and Dong, Q. (2000) *HowNet*. http://www.keenage.com.

Huang, C-R., Chang, R-Y. and Lee, S-B. (2004) *Sinica BOW (Bilingual Ontological Wordnet): Integration of Bilingual WordNet and SUMO*. In *Proceedings of the 4th International Conference on Language Resources and Evaluation (LREC2004)*, Lisbon, Portugal.

Kirkpatrick, B. (1987) *Roget's Thesaurus of English Words and Phrases*. Penguin Books.

Lin, D., Zhao, S., Qin, L. and Zhou, M. (2003) Identifying Synonyms among Distributionally Similar Words. In *Proceedings of the 18th Joint International Conference on Artificial Intelligence (IJCAI-03)*, Acapulco, pp.1492-1493 .

Mei et al. 梅家駒、竺一鳴、高蘊琦、殷鴻翔 (1984) 《同義詞詞林》 (*Tongyici Cilin*). 商務印書館 (Commerical Press) / 上海辭書出版社.

Miller, G.A., Beckwith, R., Fellbaum, C., Gross, D. and Miller, K.J. (1990) Introduction to WordNet: An online lexical database. *International Journal of Lexicography, 3(4)*:235-244.

Riloff, E. and Shepherd, J. (1999) A corpus-based bootstrapping algorithm for semi-automated semantic lexicon construction. *Natural Language Engineering, 5(2)*:147-156.

Sinclair, J. (1987) *Collins COBUILD English Language Dictionary*. London, UK: HarperCollins.

Tsou, B.K. and Kwong, O.Y. (2006) Toward a Pan-Chinese Thesaurus. In *Proceedings of the Fifth International Conference on Language Resources and Evaluation (LREC 2006)*, Genoa, Italy.

Tsou, B.K. and Lai, T.B.Y. 鄒嘉彥、黎邦洋 (2003) 漢語共時語料庫與信息開發. In B. Xu, M. Sun and G. Jin 徐波、孫茂松、靳光瑾 (Eds.),《中文信息處理若干重要問題》 (*Issues in Chinese Language Processing*). 北京：科學出版社, pp.147-165.

Vossen, P., Meijs, W. and den Broeder, M. (1989) Meaning and structure in dictionary definitions. In B. Boguraev and T. Briscoe (Eds.), *Computational Lexicography for Natural Language Processing*. Essex, UK: Longman Group.

Xia, F., Palmer, M., Xue, N., Okwrowski, M.E., Kovarik, J., Huang, S., Kroch, T. and Marcus, M. (2000) Developing Guidelines and Ensuring Consistency for Chinese Text Annotation. In *Proceedings of the 2nd International Conference on Language Resources and Evaluation (LREC-2000)*, Athens, Greece.

Region	Unique Items and Examples (Financial)	Unique Items and Examples (Sports)
HK	**2105 (40.19%)** 按揭 證劵界 銷情 招股 錄得 開售 地產股 加推 樓盤 收報 寬頻 純利 大市 入市 減價 居屋 息率 新盤 貨尾 低位	**2410 (38.16%)** 今季 球證 轉投 客軍 球手 種籽 操練 披甲 現時 超聯 友賽 歐國盃 港隊 反勝 12 碼 力壓 決賽周 早前 周一 爭標
BJ	**933 (33.43%)** 農村 住房 黨 質檢 退耕還林 下崗 節水 品種 查處 群眾 走私 城鄉 非典 優化 專項 扶貧 抽查 運行 水資源 林業	**907 (23.39%)** 自行車 攀岩 奧神隊 江蘇隊 登山 特級 自行車賽 自治區 遼寧隊 宏遠隊 前衞 體質 名人戰 中學生 棋院 彩票 山東隊 軍區 散打王 冬訓
TW	**891 (28.85%)** 金控 投信 經理人 降息 計劃 釋股 董監事 執行長 投資人 成長率 團隊 立委 網路 升息 坪 個股 營收 買超 契約 專案	**1302 (28.30%)** 安打 金剛 牛隊 獅隊 中華隊 雷公 三振 主投 投手 保送 球團 戰神 職棒 國中 打點 二壘 全壘打 撞球 鯨隊 大陸隊
SG	**890 (23.20%)** 新元 脫售 馬股 私宅 獻議 港務 財政年 海事 閉市 戶頭 文告 財年 公寓 董事部 組屋 辦公樓 平方英尺 共管 地契 輪船	**1044 (20.39%)** 新加坡隊 阿申納隊 芽蘢隊 丹戎巴葛隊 正賽 效勞 大決賽 76 人隊 新元 利物浦隊 切爾西隊 利茲隊 射腳 受訪 瓶分 星期六 軍團隊 新麒隊 賽項 網隊

Table 6 Uniqueness of individual subcorpora

Region	Financial		Sports	
	Found in Cilin	Not in Cilin	Found in Cilin	Not in Cilin
HK	**560 (26.60%)** 減價 純利 居屋 戶口 拆息 憧憬 容許 倒退 通告 結餘	**1545 (73.40%)**	**884 (36.68%)** 現時 操練 披甲 晨曦 攻堅 大勇 帝王 蛋 答 爭勝	**1526 (62.32%)**
BJ	**369 (39.55%)** 農村 抽查 住房 運行 黨 走私 品種 林業 鄉鎮 森林	**564 (60.45%)**	**355 (39.14%)** 自行車 特級 中學生 前衞 自治區 彩票 農民 解放軍 棋壇 幹部	**552 (60.86%)**
TW	**265 (29.74%)** 契約 專案 不動產 改選 股利 通路 關卡 週 終場 席次	**626 (70.26%)**	**354 (27.19%)** 投手 金剛 雷公 保送 打點 地主 水手 報導 總和 晚間	**948 (72.81%)**
SG	**333 (37.42%)** 公寓 平方英尺 港務 戶頭 共管 文告 地契 海事 輪船 開銷	**557 (62.58%)**	**281 (26.91%)** 效勞 星期六 星期三 城門 補足 星期四 星期五 星期天 腳踏車 星期二	**763 (73.08%)**

Table 7 Coverage of the *Tongyici Cilin* for the unique lexical items in individual subcorpora

Mining Atomic Chinese Abbreviation Pairs: A Probabilistic Model for Single Character Word Recovery

Jing-Shin Chang
Department of Computer Science & Information Engineering
National Chi-Nan University
Puli, Nantou, Taiwan, ROC.
jshin@csie.ncnu.edu.tw

Wei-Lun Teng
Department of Computer Science & Information Engineering
National Chi-Nan University
Puli, Nantou, Taiwan, ROC.
S3321512@ncnu.edu.tw

Abstract

An HMM-based Single Character Recovery (SCR) Model is proposed in this paper to extract a large set of "atomic abbreviation pairs" from a large text corpus. By an "atomic abbreviation pair," it refers to an abbreviated word and its root word (i.e., unabbreviated form) in which the abbreviation is a single Chinese character.

This task is interesting since the abbreviation process for Chinese compound words seems to be "compositional"; in other words, one can often decode an abbreviated word, such as "台大" (Taiwan University), character-by-character back to its root form. With a large atomic abbreviation dictionary, one may be able to recover multiple-character abbreviations more easily.

With only a few training iterations, the acquisition accuracy of the proposed SCR model achieves 62% and 50 % precision for training set and test set, respectively, from the ASWSC-2001 corpus.

1 Introduction

Chinese abbreviations are widely used in the modern Chinese texts. They are a special form of *unknown words*, which cannot be exhaustively enumerated in an ordinary dictionary. Many of them originated from important lexical units such as *named entities*. However, the sources for Chinese abbreviations are not solely from the noun class, but from most major categories, including verbs, adjectives adverbs and others. No matter what lexical or syntactic structure a string of characters could be, one can almost always find a way to abbreviate it into a shorter form. Therefore, it may be necessary to handle them beyond a class-based model. Furthermore, abbreviated words are semantically ambiguous. For example, "清大" can be the abbreviation for "清華大學" or "清潔大隊"; on the opposite direction, multiple choices for abbreviating a word are also possible. For instance, "台北大學" may be abbreviated as "台大", "北大" or "台北大". This results in difficulty for correct Chinese processing and applications, including word segmentation, information retrieval, query expansion, lexical translation and much more. An abbreviation model or a large abbreviation lexicon is therefore highly desirable for Chinese language processing.

Since the smallest possible Chinese lexical unit into which other words can be abbreviated is a single character, identifying the set of multi-character words which can be abbreviated into a single character is especially interesting. Actually, the abbreviation of a compound word can often be acquired by the principle of *composition*. In other words, one can decompose a compound word into its constituents and then concatenate their single character equivalents to form its abbreviated form. The reverse process to predict the unabbreviated form from an abbreviation shares the same compositional property.

The Chinese abbreviation problem can be regarded as an *error recovery* problem in which the suspect root words are the "errors" to be recovered from a set of candidates. Such a problem can be mapped to an HMM-based generation model for both abbreviation identification and root word recovery; it can also be integrated as part of a unified word segmentation model when the input extends to a complete sentence. As such, we can find the most likely root words, by finding those candidates that maximizes the likelihood of the whole text. An abbreviation lexicon, which consists of the root-abbreviation pairs, can thus be constructed automatically.

In a preliminary study (Chang and Lai, 2004), some probabilistic models had been developed to handle this problem by applying the models to a parallel corpus of compound words and their abbreviations, without knowing the context of the abbreviation pairs. In this work, the same framework is extended and a method is proposed to automatically acquire a large abbreviation lexicon for indivisual characters from web texts or large corpora, instead of building abbreviation models based on aligned abbreviation pairs of short compound words. Unlike the previous task, which trains the abbreviation model parameters from a list of known abbreviation pairs, the current work aims at extracting abbreviation pairs from a corpus of free text, in which the locations of prospective abbreviations and full forms are unknown and the correspondence between them is not known either.

In particular, a Single Character Recovery (SCR) Model is exploited in the current work to extract "atomic abbreviation pairs" from a large text corpus. With only a few training iterations, the acquisition accuracy achieves 62% and 50 % precision for training set and test set from the ASWSC-2001 corpus.

1.1 Chinese Abbreviation Problems

The modern Chinese language is a highly abbreviated one due to the mixed uses of ancient single character words as well as modern multi-character words and compound words. The abbreviated form and root form are used interchangeably everywhere in the current Chinese articles. Some news articles may contain as high as 20% of sentences that have suspect abbreviated words in them (Lai, 2003). Since abbreviations cannot be enumerated in a dictionary, it forms a special class of *unknown words*, many of which originate from *named entities*. Many other open class words are also abbreviatable. This particular class thus introduces complication for Chinese language processing, including the fundamental *word segmentation* process (Chiang *et al.*, 1992; Lin *et al.*, 1993; Chang and Su, 1997) and many word-based applications. For instance, a keyword-based information retrieval system may requires the two forms, such as "中研院" and "中央研究院" ("Academia Sinica"), in order not to miss any relevant documents. The Chinese word segmentation process is also significantly degraded by the existence of unknown words (Chiang *et al.*, 1992), including unknown abbreviations.

There are some heuristics for Chinese abbreviations. Such heuristics, however, can easily break (Sproat, 2002). Unlike English abbreviations, the abbreviation process of the Chinese language is a very special word formation process. Almost all characters in all positions of a word can be omitted when used for forming an abbreviation of a compound word. For instance, it seems that, by common heuristics, "most" Chinese abbreviations could be derived by keeping the first characters of the constituent words of a compound word, such as transforming '台灣大學' into '台大', '清華大學' into '清大' and '以色列(及)巴勒斯坦' into '以巴'. Unfortunately, it is not always the case. For example, we can transform '台灣香港' into '台港', '中國石油' into '中油', and, for very long compounds like '雲林嘉義台南' into '雲嘉南' (Sproat, 2002). Therefore, it is very difficult to predict the possible surface forms of Chinese abbreviations and to guess their base (non-abbreviated) forms heuristically.

<table>
<tr><th>P(bit|n)</th><th>Score</th><th>Examples</th></tr>
<tr><td>P(10|2)</td><td>0.87</td><td>(德|德國),(美|美國)</td></tr>
<tr><td>P(101|3)</td><td>0.44</td><td>(宜縣|宜蘭縣),
(限級|限制級)</td></tr>
<tr><td>P(1010|4)</td><td>0.56</td><td>(公投|公民投票),
(清大|清華大學)</td></tr>
<tr><td>P(10101|5)</td><td>0.66</td><td>(環保署|環境保護署),
(航警局|航空警察局)</td></tr>
<tr><td>P(101001|6)</td><td>0.51</td><td>(化工系|化學工程學系),
(工工系|工業工程學系)</td></tr>
<tr><td>P(1010001|7)</td><td>0.55</td><td>(國科會|國家科學委員會),
(中科院|中山科學研究院)</td></tr>
<tr><td>P(10101010|8)</td><td>0.21</td><td>(一中一台|一個中國一個台灣),
(一大一小|一個大人一個小孩)</td></tr>
</table>

Table 1. High Frequency Abbreviation Patterns [by P(bit|n)] (Chang and Lai, 2004)

The high frequency abbreviation patterns revealed in (Chang and Lai, 2004) further break the heuristics quantitatively. Table 1 lists the distribution of the most frequent abbreviation patterns for word of length 2~8 characters.

The table indicates which characters will be deleted from the root of a particular length (n) with a bit '0'; on the other hand, a bit '1' means that the respective character will be retained. This table does support some general heuristics for native Chinese speaker quantitatively. For instance, there are strong supports that the first character in a two-character word will be retained in most cases, and the first and the third characters in a 4-character word will be retained in 56% of the cases. However, the table also shows that around 50% of the cases cannot be uniquely determined by character position simply by consulting the word length of the un-abbreviated form. This does suggest the necessity of either an abbreviation model or a large abbreviation lexicon for resolving this kind of unknown words and named entities.

There are also a large percentage (312/1547) of "*tough*" abbreviation patterns (Chang and Lai, 2004), which are considered "*tough*" in the sense that they violate some simple assumptions, and thus cannot be modeled in a simple way. For instance, some tough words will actually be *recursively* abbreviated into shorter and shorter lexical forms; and others may change the word order (as in abbreviating "第一核能發電廠" as "核一廠" instead of "一核廠".). As a result, the abbreviation process is much more complicated than a native Chinese speaker might think.

1.2 Atomic Abbreviation Pairs

Since the abbreviated words are created continuously through the abbreviation of new (mostly compound) words, it is nearly impossible to construct a complete abbreviation lexicon. In spite of the difficulty, it is interesting to note that the abbreviation process for Chinese compound words seems to be "compositional". In other words, one can often decode an abbreviated word, such as "台大" ("Taiwan University"), character-by-character back to its root form "台灣大學" by observing that "台" can be an abbreviation of "台灣" and "大" can be an abbreviation of "大學" and "台灣大學" is a frequently observed character sequence.

Since character is the smallest lexical unit for Chinese, no further abbreviation into smaller units is possible. We therefore use "atomic abbreviation pair" to refer to an abbreviated word and its root word (i.e., unabbreviated form) in which the abbreviation is a single Chinese character.

On the other hand, abbreviations of multi-character compound words may be synthesized from single characters in the "atomic abbreviation pairs". If we are able to identify all such "atomic abbreviation pairs", where the abbreviation is a single character, and construct such an atomic abbreviation lexicon, then resolving multiple character abbreviation problems, either by heuristics or by other abbreviation models, might become easier.

Furthermore, many ancient Chinese articles are composed mostly of single-character words. Depending on the percentage of such single-character words in a modern Chinese article, the article will resemble to an ancient Chinese article in proportional to such a percentage. As another application, an effective single character recovery model may therefore be transferred into an auxiliary translation system from ancient Chinese articles into their modern versions. This is, of course, an overly bold claim since lexical translation is not the only factor for such an application. However, it may be consider as a possible direction for lexical translation when constructing an ancient-to-modern article translation system. Also, when a model for recovering atomic translation pair is applied to the "single character regions" of a word segmented corpus, it is likely to recover unknown abbreviated words that are previously word-segmented incorrectly into individual characters.

An HMM-based Single Character Recovery (SCR) Model is therefore proposed in this paper to extract a large set of "atomic abbreviation pairs" from a large text corpus.

1.3 Previous Works

Currently, only a few quantitative approaches (Huang *et al.*, 1994a; Huang *et al.*, 1994b) are available in predicting the presence of an abbreviation. There are essentially no prior arts for automatically extracting atomic abbreviation pairs. Since such formulations regard the word segmentation process and abbreviation identification as two independent processes, they probably cannot optimize the identification process jointly with the *word segmentation* process, and thus may lose some useful contextual information. Some class-based segmentation models (Sun *et al.*, 2002; Gao *et al.*, 2003) well integrate the identification of some regular non-lexicalized units (such as named entities). However, the abbreviation process can be applied to almost all word forms (or classes of words). Therefore, this particular word formation process may have to be handled as a separate layer in the segmentation process.

To resolve the Chinese abbreviation problems and integrate its identification into the word segmentation process, (Chang and Lai, 2004) proposes to regard the abbreviation problem in the word segmentation process as an "error recovery" problem in which the suspect root words are the "errors" to be recovered from a set of candidates according to some generation probability criteria. This idea implies that an HMM-based model for identifying Chinese abbreviations could be effective in either identifying the existence of an abbreviation or the recovery of the root words from an abbreviation.

Since the parameters of an HMM-like model can usually be trained in an unsupervised manner, and the "output probabilities" known to the HMM framework will indicate the likelihood for an abbreviation to be generated from a root candidate, such a formulation can easily be adapted to collect highly probable root-abbreviation pairs. As a side effect of using HMM-based formulation, we expect that a large abbreviation dictionary could be derived automatically from a large corpus or from web documents through the training process of the unified word segmentation model.

In this work, we therefore explore the possibility of using the theories in (Chang and Lai, 2004) as a framework for constructing a large abbreviation lexicon consisting of all Chinese characters and their potential roots. In the following section, the HMM models as outlined in (Chang and Lai, 2004) is reviewed first. We then described how to use this framework to construct an abbreviation lexicon automatically. In particular, a Single Character Recovery (SCR) Model is exploited for extracting possible root (un-abbreviated) forms for all Chinese characters.

2 Chinese Abbreviation Models

2.1 Unified Word Segmentation Model for Abbreviation Recovery

To resolve the abbreviation recovery problem, one can identify some root candidates for suspect abbreviations (probably from a large abbreviation dictionary if available or from an ordinary dictionary with some educated guesses), and then confirm the most probable root by consulting local context. This process is identical to the operation of many error correction models, which generate the candidate corrections according to a *reversed* word formation process, then justify the best candidate.

Such an analogy indicates that we may use an HMM model (Rabiner and Juang, 1993), which is good at finding the best *unseen* state sequence, for root word recovery. There will be a direct map between the two paradigms if we regard the observed input character sequence as our "observation sequence", and regard the unseen word candidates as the underlying "state sequence".

To integrate the abbreviation process into the word segmentation model, firstly we can regard the segmentation model as finding the best underlying words $w_1^m \equiv w_1, \cdots, w_m$ (which include only base/root forms), given the surface string of characters $c_1^n \equiv c_1, \cdots, c_n$ (which may contain abbreviated forms of compound words.) The segmentation process is then equivalent to finding the best (un-abbreviated) word sequence $\vec{w}*$ such that:

$$
\begin{aligned}
\vec{w}* &= \mathop{\arg\max}_{w_1^m : w_1^m \Rightarrow c_1^n} P\left(w_1^m \mid c_1^n\right) \\
&= \mathop{\arg\max}_{w_1^m : w_1^m \Rightarrow c_1^n} P\left(c_1^n \mid w_1^m\right) \times P\left(w_1^m\right) \\
&= \mathop{\arg\max}_{w_1^m : w_1^m \Rightarrow c_1^n} \prod_{\substack{i=1,m \\ w_i \Rightarrow \vec{c}_i}} P\left(\vec{c}_i \mid w_i\right) \times P\left(w_i \mid w_{i-1}\right)
\end{aligned}
$$

Equation 1. Unified Word Segmentation Model for Abbreviation Recovery where $\vec{c}_i$ refers to the surface form of w_i, which could be in an abbreviated or non-abbreviated root form of w_i. The last equality assumes that the generation of an abbreviation is independent of context, and the language model is a word-based bigram model.

If no abbreviated words appears in real text, such that all surface forms are identical to their "root" forms, we will have $P(\vec{c}_i \mid w_i) = 1$, $\forall i = 1, m$, and **Equation 1** is simply a word bigram model for word segmentation (Chiang *et al.*, 1992). In the presence of abbreviations, however, the generation probability $P(\vec{c}_i \mid w_i)$ can no longer be ignored, since the probability $P(\vec{c}_i \mid w_i)$ is not always 1 or 0.

As an example, if two consecutive $\vec{c}_i$ are '台' and '大' then their roots, w_i, could be '台灣' plus '大學' (Taiwan University) or '台灣' plus '大聯盟' (Taiwan Major League). In this case, the parameters in P(大學|台灣) x P(台|台灣) x P(大|大學) and P(大聯盟|台灣) x P(台|台灣) x P(大|大聯盟) will indicate how likely '台大' is an abbreviation, and which of the above two compounds is the root form.

Notice that, this equation is equivalent to an HMM (Hidden Markov Model) (Rabiner and Juang, 1993) normally used to find the best "state" sequence given the observation symbols. The parameters $P(w_i \mid w_{i-1})$ and $P(\vec{c}_i \mid w_i)$ represent the transition probability and the (word-wise) output probability of an HMM, respectively; and, the formulations for $P(w_1^m)$ and $P(c_1^n \mid w_1^m)$ are the respective "language model" of the Chinese language and the "generation model" for the abbreviated words (i.e., the "abbreviation model" in the current context). The "state" sequence in this case is characterized by the hidden root forms $w_1^m \equiv w_1, \cdots, w_m$; and, the "observation symbols" are characterized by $c_1^n \equiv c_1, \cdots, c_n \equiv \vec{c}_1, \cdots, \vec{c}_m$, where the surface form $\vec{c}_i \equiv c_{b(i)}^{e(i)}$ is a chunk of characters beginning at the b(i)-th character and ending at the e(i)-th character.

The word-wise transition probability $P(w_i \mid w_{i-1})$ in the language model is used to provide contextual constraints among root words so that the underlying word sequence forms a legal sentence with high probability.

Notice that, after applying the word segmentation model **Equation 1** to the word lattice, some of the above candidates may be preferred and others be discarded, by consulting the neighboring words and their transition probabilities. This makes the abbreviation model *jointly* optimized in the word segmentation process, instead of being optimized independent of context.

2.2 Simplified Abbreviation Models

Sometimes, it is not desirable to use a generation probability that is based on the root-abbreviation pairs, since the number of parameters will be huge and estimation error due to data sparseness might be high. Therefore, it is desirable to simplify the abbreviation probability by using some simpler features in the model. For instance, many 4-character compound words are abbreviated as 2-character abbreviations (such as in the case for the <台灣大學, 台大> pair.) It was also known that many such 4-character words are abbreviated by preserving the first and the third characters, which can be represented by a '1010' bit pattern, where the '1' or '0' means to preserve or delete the respective character. Therefore, a reasonable simplification for the abbreviation model is to introduce the *length* and the positional *bit pattern* as additional features, resulting in the following augmented model for the abbreviation probability.

$$
\begin{aligned}
P(\vec{c} \mid w) &= P(c_1^m, bit, m \mid r_1^n, n) \\
&\equiv P(c_1^m \mid r_1^n) \times P(bit \mid n) \times P(m \mid n)
\end{aligned}
$$

$$
\text{where} \begin{cases} c_1^m : \text{surface characters.} \\ r_1^n : \text{root word characters.} \\ m\text{: length of surface characters.} \\ n\text{: length of root word characters.} \\ \text{bit: bit pattern of abbreviation} \end{cases}
$$

Equation 2. Abbreviation Probability using Abbreviation Pattern and Length Features.

All these three terms can be combined freely to produce as many as 7 sub-models for the abbreviation model. Note, the first term $\Pr(c_1^m \mid r_1^n)$ plays the same role as the older notation of $\Pr(\vec{c} \mid w)$. To use the simple length and position features, this term can be unused in the above augmented abbreviation model.

3 The Single Character Recovery (SCR) Model

As mentioned earlier, many multiple character words are frequently abbreviated into a single Chinese character. Compound words consisting of a couple of such multiple character words are then abbreviated by concatenating all the single character abbreviations. This means that those N-to-1 abbreviation patterns may form the basis for the underlying Chinese abbreviation process. The other M-to-N abbreviation patterns might simply be a composition of such basic N-to-1 abbreviations. The N-to-1 abbreviation patterns can thus be regarded as the atomic abbreviation pairs.

Therefore, it is interesting to apply the abbreviation recovery model to acquire all basic N-to-1 abbreviation patterns, in the first place, so that abbreviations of multi-character words can be detected and predicted more easily.

Such a task can be highly simplified if each character in a text corpus is regarded as an abbreviated word whose root form is to be recovered. In other words, the surface form $\vec{c}_i$ in Equation 1 is reduced to a single character. The abbreviation recovery model based on this assumption will be referred to as the SCR Model.

The root candidates for each single character will form a word lattice, and each path of the lattice will represent a non-abbreviated word sequence. The underlying word sequence that is most likely to produce the input character sequence will then be identified as the best word sequence. Once the best word sequence is identified, the model parameters can be re-estimated. And the best word sequence is identified again. Such process is repeated until the best sequence no more changes. In addition, the corresponding <root, abbreviation> pairs will be extracted as atomic abbreviation pairs, where all the abbreviations are one character in size.

While it is overly simplified to use this SCR model for conducting a general abbreviation enhanced word segmentation process (since not all single characters are abbreviated words), the single character assumption might still be useful for extracting roots of real single-character abbreviations. The reason is that one only care to use the contextual constraints around a true single character abbreviation for matching its root form against the local context in order to confirm that the suspect root did conform to its neighbors (with a high language model score). An alternative to use a two-stage recovery strategy, where the first stage applies a baseline word segmentation model to identify most normal words and a second stage to identify and recover incorrectly segmented single characters, is currently under investigation with other modes of operations. For the present, the SCR model is tested first as a baseline.

The HMM-based recovery models enables us to estimate the model parameters using an unsupervised training method that is directly ported from the Baum-Welch re-estimation formula (Rabiner and Juang, 1993) or a generic EM algorithm (Dempster *et al.*, 1977). Upon convergence, we should be able to acquire a large corpus of atomic abbreviation pairs from the text corpus.

If a word-segmented corpus is available, we can also use such re-estimation methods for HMM parameter training in an unsupervised manner, but with initial word transition probabilities estimated in a supervised manner from the seed.

The initial candidate <root, abbreviation> pairs are generated by assuming that all word-segmented words in the training corpus are potential roots for each of its single-character constituents. For example, if we have "台灣" and "大學" as two word-segmented tokens, then the abbreviation pairs <台, 台灣>, <灣, 台灣>, <大, 大學> and <學, 大學> will be generated. Furthermore, each single character by default is its own abbreviation.

To estimate the abbreviation probabilities, each abbreviation pair is associated with a frequency count of the root in the word segmentation corpus. This means that each single-character abbreviation candidate is equally weighted. The equal weighting strategy may not be absolutely true (Chang and Lai, 2004). In fact, the character position and word length features may be helpful as mentioned in **Equation 2**. The initial probabilities are therefore weighted differently according to the position of the character and the length of the root. The weighting factors are directly acquired from a previous work in (Chang and Lai, 2004). Before the initial probabilities are estimated, Good-Turning smoothing (Katz, 1987) is applied to the raw frequency counts of the abbreviation pairs.

4 Experiments

To evaluate the SCR Model, the Academia Sinica Word Segmentation Corpus (dated July, 2001), ASWSC-2001 (CKIP, 2001), is adopted for parameter estimation and performance evaluation. Among the 94 files in this balanced corpus, 83 of them (13,086KB) are randomly selected as the training set and 11 of them (162KB) are used as the test set.

Table 3 shows some examples of atomic abbreviation pairs acquired from the training corpus. The examples here partially justify the possibility to use the SCR model for acquiring atomic abbreviation pairs from a large corpus.

Abbr : Root	Example	Abbr : Root	Example
籃:籃球	籃賽	宣:宣傳	文宣
檢:檢查	安檢	農:農業	農牧
媒:媒體	政媒	艙:座艙	艙壓
宿:宿舍	男舍	攜:攜帶	攜械
臺:臺灣	臺幣	汽:汽車	汽機車
漫:漫畫	動漫	咖:咖啡店	網咖
港:香港	港人	職:職業	現職
網:網路	網咖	設:設計	工設系
股:股票	股市	湖:澎湖	臺澎
韓:韓國	韓流	海:海洋	海生館
祕:祕書	主秘	文:文化	文建會
植:植物	植被	生:學生	新生
儒:儒家	新儒學	新:新加坡	新國
盜:強盜	盜匪	花:花蓮	花東
房:房間	機房	資:資訊	資工

Table 3. Examples of atomic abbreviation pairs.

The iterative training process converges quickly after 3~4 iterations. The numbers of unique abbreviation patterns for the training and test sets are 20,250 and 3,513, respectively. Since the numbers of patterns are large, a rough estimate on the acquisition accuracy rates is conducted by randomly sampling 100 samples of the <root, abbreviation> pairs. The pattern is then manually examined to see if the root is correctly recovered. The precision is estimated as 50% accuracy for the test set, and 62% for the training set on convergence. Although a larger sample may be necessary to get a better estimate, the preliminary result is encouraging. Figures 1~4 demonstrate the curve of convergence for the iterative training process in terms of pattern number and accuracy.

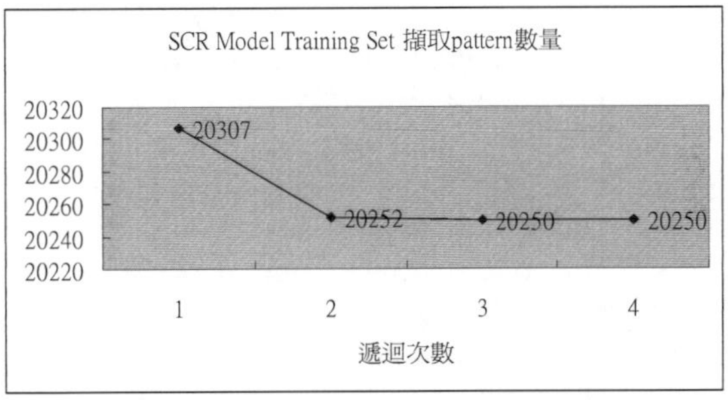

Figure 1. Numbers of abbreviation patterns in each iteration. (Training Set)

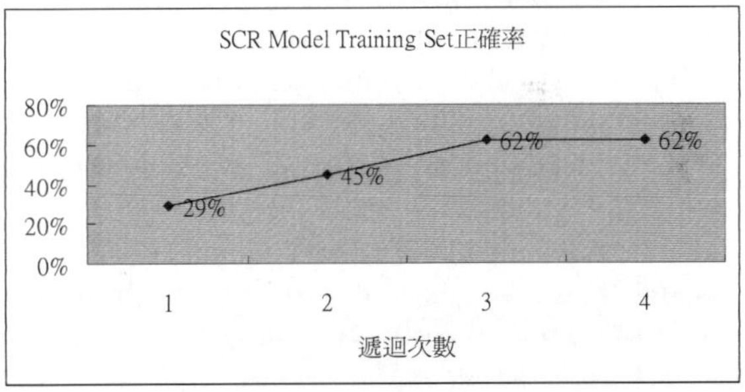

Figure 2. Acquisition accuracy for each iteration. (Training Set)

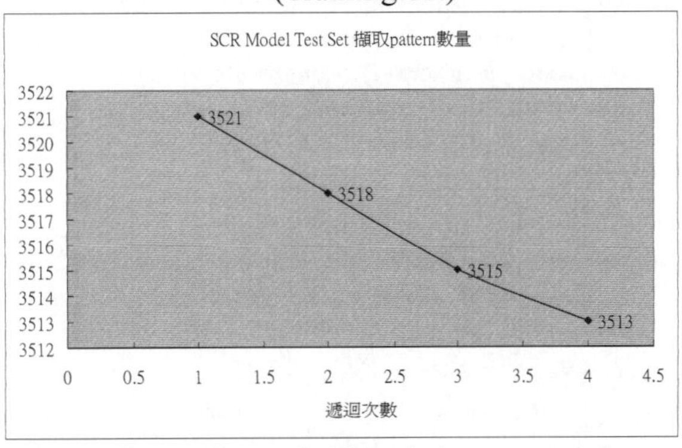

Figure 3. Numbers of abbreviation patterns in each iteration. (Test Set)

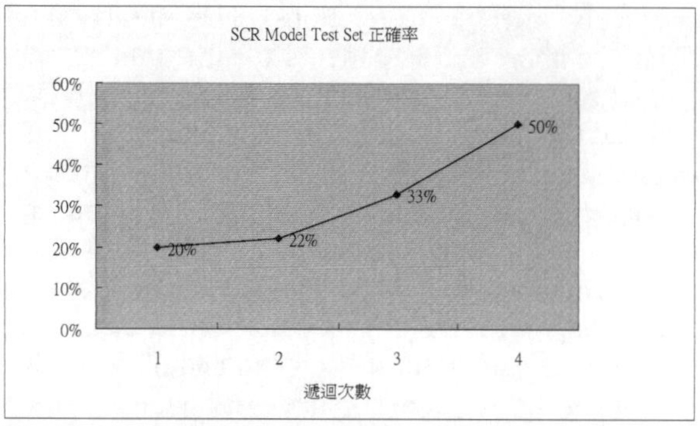

Figure 4. Acquisition accuracy for each iteration. (Test Set)

5 Concluding Remarks

Chinese abbreviations, which form a special kind of unknown words, are widely seen in the modern Chinese texts. This results in difficulty for correct Chinese processing. In this work, we had applied a unified word segmentation model developed in a previous works (Chang and Lai, 2004), which was able to handle the kind of "errors" introduced by the abbreviation process. An iterative training process is developed to automatically acquire an abbreviation dictionary for single-character abbreviations from large corpora. In particular, a Single Character Recovery (SCR) Model is exploited. With only a few training iterations, the acquisition accuracy achieves 62% and 50 % precision for training set and test set from the ASWSC-2001 corpus. For systems that choose to lexicalize such lexicon entities, the automatically constructed abbreviation dictionary will be an invaluable resource to the systems. And, the proposed recovery model looks encouraging.

References

Chang, Jing-Shin and Keh-Yih Su, 1997. "An Unsupervised Iterative Method for Chinese New Lexicon Extraction", *International Journal of Computational Linguistics and Chinese Language Processing (CLCLP)*, 2(2): 97-148.

Chang, Jing-Shin and Yu-Tso Lai, 2004. "A Preliminary Study on Probabilistic Models for Chinese Abbreviations." *Proceedings of the Third SIGHAN Workshop on Chinese Language Learning,* pages 9-16, ACL-2004, Barcelona, Spain.

Chiang, Tung-Hui, Jing-Shin Chang, Ming-Yu Lin and Keh-Yih Su, 1992. "Statistical Models for Word Segmentation and Unknown Word Resolution," *Proceedings of ROCLING-V*, pages 123-146, Taipei, Taiwan, ROC.

CKIP 2001, *Academia Sinica Word Segmentation Corpus, ASWSC-2001, (中研院中文分詞語料庫)*, Chinese Knowledge Information Processing Group, Acdemia Sinica, Tiapei, Taiwan, ROC.

Dempster, A. P., N. M. Laird, and D. B. Rubin, 1977. "Maximum Likelihood from Incomplete Data via the EM Algorithm", *Journal of the Royal Statistical Society*, 39 (b): 1-38.

Gao, Jianfeng, Mu Li, Chang-Ning Huang, 2003. "Improved Source-Channel Models for Chinese Word Segmentation," *Proc. ACL 2003*, pages 272-279.

Huang, Chu-Ren, Kathleen Ahrens, and Keh-Jiann Chen, 1994a. "A data-driven approach to psychological reality of the mental lexicon: Two studies on Chinese corpus linguistics." In *Language and its Psychobiological Bases*, Taipei.

Huang, Chu-Ren, Wei-Mei Hong, and Keh-Jiann Chen, 1994b. "Suoxie: An information based lexical rule of abbreviation." In *Proceedings of the Second Pacific Asia Conference on Formal and Computational Linguistics II*, pages 49–52, Japan.

Katz, Slava M., 1987. "Estimation of Probabilities from Sparse Data for the Language Model Component of a Speech Recognizer," *IEEE Trans. ASSP-35 (3)*.

Lai, Yu-Tso, 2003. *A Probabilistic Model for Chinese Abbreviations,* Master Thesis, National Chi-Nan University, ROC.

Lin, Ming-Yu, Tung-Hui Chiang and Keh-Yih Su, 1993. "A Preliminary Study on Unknown Word Problem in Chinese Word Segmentation," *Proceedings of ROCLING VI*, pages 119-142.

Rabiner, L., and B.-H., Juang, 1993. *Fundamentals of Speech Recognition*, Prentice-Hall.

Sun, Jian, Jianfeng Gao, Lei Zhang, Ming Zhou and Chang-Ning Huang, 2002. "Chinese named entity identification using class-based language model," *Proc. of COLING 2002*, Taipei, ROC.

Sproat, Richard, 2002. "Corpus-Based Methods in Chinese Morphology", *Pre-conference Tutorials*, COLING-2002, Taipei, Taiwan, ROC.

Features, Bagging, and System Combination for the Chinese POS Tagging Task

Fei Xia
University of Washington
Seattle, WA 98195-4340, USA
fxia@u.washington.edu

Lap Cheung
University of Washington
Seattle, WA 98195-4340, USA
lapcheung@gmail.com

Abstract

In recent years more and more NLP packages become available to the public, and many of them are implementations of general machine learning methods. A natural question is how one can quickly build a good system using those packages. To address this issue, we built three part-of-speech taggers (i.e., trigram, TBL, and MaxEnt taggers) for Chinese using existing packages. Our experiments showed that adapting and extending a package is relative easy if the package is well-written and source code is available. We studied the contribution of each type of feature templates to the tagging accuracy and showed that adding some templates could help one tagger but hurt another one. Furthermore, we demonstrated that bagging (Breiman, 1996) provides a moderate gain for the TBL tagger, and combining TBL and MaxEnt taggers work better than using all three taggers.

1 Introduction

In recent years, there has been much progress in the NLP field, and more and more NLP packages become available to the public. Many of those packages are implementations of general machine learning methods, and their usefulness has been demonstrated by some particular tasks for certain languages. Given those resources, how can we quickly build a good system for a new language? For instance, how do packages differ and what kind of packages should we choose for a particular task? If a package requires additional input such as feature templates besides the training data, what kinds of templates help and what do not? Will the same templates have the same effect on different methods? Is it easy to extend a package to accept new types of templates? If multiple packages are available, will system combination provide an additional boost?

In order to answer those questions, we did a case study: the goal was to quickly develop a Chinese Part-of-speech (POS) tagger that performs well. Our approach has three steps. First, we built three baseline POS taggers using existing packages. Two of the taggers require feature templates as input, in addition to training data. In the second step, we created several types of templates for Chinese and studied the contribution of each type to the tagging accuracy. In the third step, we applied the bagging technique (Breiman, 1996) and showed that bagging provide a moderate gain for one of the taggers, and combining two taggers work better than combining all three. In the next three sections, we shall describe each step in detail.

2 Baseline taggers

POS tagging is an important task for many NLP applications. Some common approaches are Hidden Marcov Models (HMM), transformation-based learning (TBL) (Brill, 1995; Florian and Ngai, 2001), maximum entropy models (MaxEnt) (Ratnaparkhi, 1996), boosting (Abney et al., 1999), decision tree (Màrquez, 1999), just to name a few.

For our case study, we trained three taggers:

a trigram tagger using Carmel (Knight and Al-Onaizan, 1999) as a decoder, a TBL tagger using the fnTBL package (Ngai and Florian, 2001), and a MaxEnt tagger built by Le Zhang.[1] We chose these packages mainly because they all provide source codes and are well-packaged with detailed tutorials.

Both MaxEnt and TBL taggers take feature templates as input. There are a series of interesting questions with respect to feature templates. For instance, are there some types of templates that are allowed by one tagger, but not by the other? If so, are those templates useful? When we use the same templates, do they have similar effects on both taggers? If we want to add a new type of templates, is it easier for one tagger than the other? Before answering those questions, let us take a closer look at the two taggers.

2.1 POS tagging as a classification problem

In a standard classification problem, there are a finite set of input attributes and a target (a.k.a. label or class). For supervised learning, a training corpus T is a set of classified examples; that is, T is a set of (x_i, y_i) pairs, where x_i is an example, and y_i is the correct label for x_i. At the training stage, a learner induces a classifier from T, and at the test stage the classifier labels new examples.

The POS tagging task is different from the standard classification problem in that its goal is to find the best tag sequence, not the best tag for each word. The MaxEnt tagger and the TBL tagger resolve this issue in different ways, as we shall discuss in the remaining of the section.

2.2 The MaxEnt tagger

The flowchart for the training stage of the MaxEnt tagger is shown in Figure 1. The tagger requires two inputs: an original training corpus (OT), which is a set of tagged sentences, and a set of feature templates (FT). They are fed to the C&FI module, which converts OT into the attribute-value representation and instantiate features based on FT. The converted corpus (CT) and the instantiated features (F) are sent to the MaxEnt learner, which iteratively adjusts feature weights.

Table 1: Attribute-value representation for the sentence *time flies like an arrow* in MaxEnt

x_i			y_i
w_0	t_{-1}	t_{-2}, t_{-1}	Target
time	-	-,-	N
flies	N	-,N	V
like	V	N,V	P
an	P	V,P	DT
arrow	DT	P,DT	N

The conversion from OT to CT is straightforward. For instance, let us assume that the FT contains only three templates: (1) the current word w_0, (2) the tag t_{-1} of the previous word, and (3) the tags "t_{-2}, t_{-1}" of the two previous words. If the OT contains only one sentence as in (#1), the corresponding CT is shown in Table 1: each word in the sentence corresponds to a row in the table; each column except the last one corresponds to a feature template, and the last column lists the tag for the word.

```
(#1) Time/N flies/V like/P an/DT arrow/N
```

At the test stage, in order to find the best tag sequence, the MaxEnt tagger uses beam search and labels words from left to right, as described in (Ratnaparkhi, 1996). Because the decoding is done from left to right, a feature template cannot contain the tag of the current word or tags in the right context such as t_1.[2]

2.3 The TBL tagger

Like MaxEnt, the TBL tagger takes two inputs: the original training corpus (OT) and feature templates (FT), as shown in Figure 2. TBL differs from MaxEnt and many other machine learning methods in that for each (x_i, y_i) in the training data, TBL also maintains a y_i', which is the current label of x_i. Therefore, the converted corpus (CT) is a list of (x_i, y_i', y_i) tuples.

The training stage has three steps: (1) Each x_i is labeled y_i' by an initial tagger (e.g., a unigram tagger), and the converted corpus (CT) is formed; (2) The current label y_i' is compared with the gold standard y_i, and the TBL learner

[1] The MaxEnt package can be downloaded from http://homepages.inf.ed.ac.uk/s0450736.

[2] In this paper w_i means the i-th word from the current word, not the i-th word in the sentence. t_i is defined similarly.

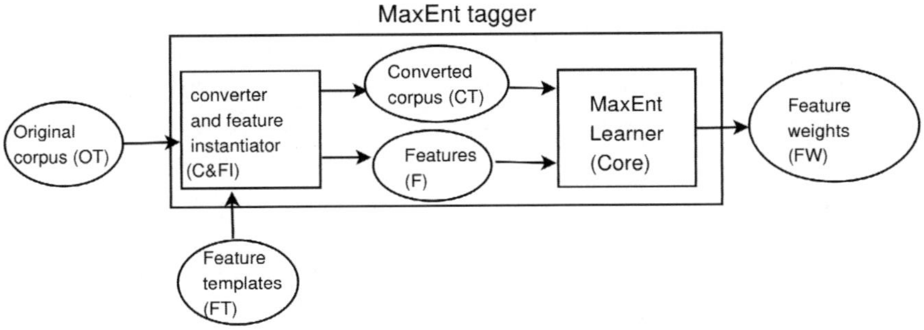

Figure 1: The training stage of the MaxEnt tagger

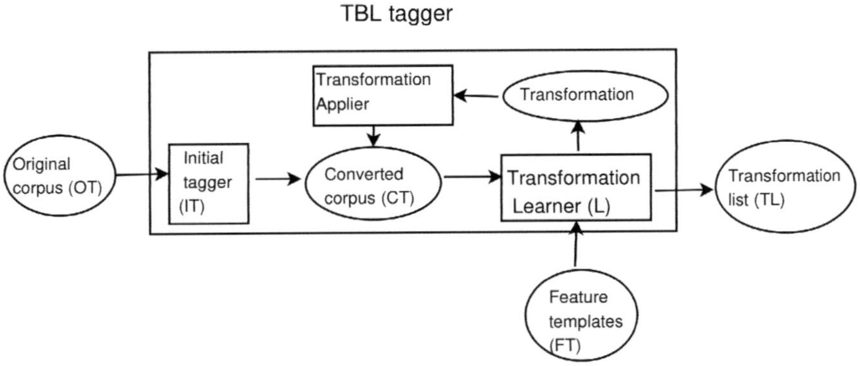

Figure 2: The training stage of the TBL tagger

selects a transformation that reduces the errors the most; (3) The CT is updated as the newly learned transformation is applied to it. Steps (2)-(3) are repeated until no more good transformations can be learned.

At the test stage, the test data are first labeled by the initial tagger, then the transformations learned at the training stage are applied to the test data one by one in the same order as they were learned.

We illustrate the main steps of TBL with an example. Suppose the TBL tagger uses the same set of feature templates and training data as in the MaxEnt tagger, and let (#2) be the result produced by the initial tagger. Table 2 shows the CT after the initial tagging. This table has one more column than Table 1, and the column, CurTag, stores the tag for the current word.[3] Also, if a feature template contains a t_i, the value of t_i comes from the CurTag column, not from the Target column.

[3]In this paper, CurTag is the same as t_0. We use CurTag in the running text, tables, and on the right-hand side of a transformation, and use t_0 when it appears in a feature template or on the left-hand side of a transformation.

Table 2: The training corpus after initial tagging in TBL

x_i			y_i'	y_i
w_0	t_{-1}	t_{-2}, t_{-1}	CurTag	Target
time	-	-,-	N	N
flies	N	-,N	**N**	V
like	**N**	N,**N**	**V**	P
an	**V**	**N,V**	DT	DT
arrow	DT	**V**,DT	N	N

Therefore, the errors in CurTag column are passed to the second and third columns, as marked in boldface.

```
(#2) Time/N flies/N like/V an/DT arrow/N
```

In the second step of the training, y_i and y_i' in the CT are compared and the best transformation is selected at each iteration. Let us assume the transformation selected at this iteration is t_{-1}=*N* ⇒ *CurTag*=*V*, which means that if the tag of the previous word is N and the CurTag for the current word is not V, then set CurTag to be V.

In the third step of training, the selected transformation is applied to the whole corpus, and the updated corpus is shown in Table 3. Notice that the CurTag for word *flies* is

Table 3: The training corpus after applying the transformation "t_{-1}=N ⇒ *CurTag*=V" (The updated parts are underlined).

x_i			y'_i	y_i
w_0	t_{-1}	t_{-2}, t_{-1}	CurTag	Target
time	-	-,-	N	N
flies	N	-,N	$\underline{\text{V}}$	V
like	$\underline{\text{V}}$	N,$\underline{\text{V}}$	**V**	P
an	**V**	$\underline{\text{V}}$,**V**	DT	DT
arrow	DT	**V**,DT	N	N

changed, and its corresponding values in the second and third columns are updated too.[4]

2.4 Differences between MaxEnt and TBL taggers

TBL and MaxEnt are very different learning methods: TBL is rule-based, whereas MaxEnt is statistical. Because MaxEnt is statistical, MaxEnt taggers can treat the tagging of each word as a classification problem, produce the top-N best tags for each word, and then use beam search to find the best tag sequence. Such an option is not available to the TBL method, because TBL does not provide scores or probabilities for its decisions.

In addition, the two methods have several major differences that are relevant to our present work:

- The CT in MaxEnt is a list of (x_i, y_i) pairs and is unchanged once created, whereas the CT in TBL is a list of (x_i, y'_i, y_i) tuples and is updated at each iteration.

- The feature set F in MaxEnt is unchanged once created; whereas the TBL learner may generate new features at each iteration because the CT keeps changing.

- It is easy to extend the MaxEnt tagger to accept new *types* of feature templates: we only need to change the C&FI module. Doing the same for TBL is harder as we need to change the transformation learner, which is more complicated.[5]

- The MaxEnt tagger labels a sentence from left to right, which implies that features used in MaxEnt cannot refer to tags in the right context. In contrast, TBL does not label words from left to right, and the CurTags for the words in the right context are always available. Therefore, features in TBL can refer to tags of any words in the sentence.

- Feature templates are used differently in the two taggers, as we shall explain in Section 3.

To summarize, adding new feature template types to the MaxEnt tagger is easier than adding them to the TBL tagger because both CT and instantiated features are unchanged during the iteration in the MaxEnt tagger. However, the MaxEnt tagger cannot use features that refer to the tag of the current word and the tags in the right context, while the TBL tagger can. But are those features useful? We shall answer that question in Section 5.

3 Feature templates

Feature templates can be divided into two types: contextual templates that look at the context (e.g., neighboring words), and lexical templates that look at word spelling and the like.

MaxEnt and TBL taggers use feature templates in different ways. For instance, given a template "t_{-1}" and the training corpus in Table 1, the MaxEnt tagger will create the following feature for the word *flies*:

$$f_j(h,t) = \begin{cases} 1 & \text{if } t_{-1} = N \text{ and } t = V \\ 0 & \text{otherwise} \end{cases} \tag{1}$$

Each feature f_j has a weight λ_j, and is used to calculate the probability of a history h and the tag t as defined below:

$$p(h,t) = \frac{e^{\sum_{j=1}^{k} \lambda_j f_j(h,t)}}{Z} \tag{2}$$

In contrast, for the same feature template t_{-1} and for the corpus in Table 2, the TBL tagger will create a transformation for the word *flies*:

$$t_{-1} = N \Rightarrow CurTag = V \tag{3}$$

[4]The fnTBL package stores the training corpus in a slightly different representation, but our statement about TBL still holds.

[5]In the fnTBL package, a template is a conjunction of so-called *atomic* templates, and each atomic template is defined as a C++ class. If a new template includes new types of atomic templates, we have to define additional C++ classes for the new atomic templates.

This transformation is applicable if the CurTag is **not** V and the previous tag is N; when the transformation applies, it will set the CurTag to be V.

If we treat a transformation as a rule, CurTag can appear in both sides of the rule. For instance for the template "$t_0\ t_{-1}$" and the word *flies* in Table 2, the TBL tagger will create a transformation

$$t_0 = N \text{ and } t_{-1} = N \Rightarrow CurTag = V \quad (4)$$

Notice that the transformations in (3) and (4) are different, as (4) will not fire unless the CurTag is N. In Section 5, we shall show that whether or not CurTag is included in the templates could affect tagging accuracy significantly.

3.1 Contextual templates

To study the contribution of each type of templates, we define three types of contextual templates:[6]

C1: seven templates that are used in both the TBL tagger and the original MaxEnt tagger

C2: seventeen less commonly used templates

C3: thirteen templates that include tags from the right context

To test the effect of including CurTag, we also define a set C_i' for each C_i: templates in C_i' are the same as the ones in C_i except that they include CurTag. For instance, "t_{-1}" in C_1 becomes "t_0, t_{-1}" in C_1'.

3.2 Lexical templates

In addition to contextual templates, both taggers use lexical templates to handle unknown words. In our experiments, we use three types of lexical templates that are defined in the fnTBL package:

L1: Affix: An Affix template checks whether a word starts (or ends) with a character n-gram.

[6]We started with the templates used in the fnTBL package and then made some modifications. The complete contextual template list is given in the Appendix.

L2: WordInVoc: A WordInVoc template checks whether removing or adding a character n-gram will result in a word that has appeared in the training data.

L3: SubString: A SubString template checks whether a word contains a particular substring.

The original MaxEnt package uses features in C1 and L1. We modified the code so that it accepts features in C2, L2, and L3 as well.

4 Bagging

Bagging (Bootstrap Aggregating) is a method for generating multiple versions of a predictor and using them to get an aggregated predictor (Breiman, 1996).[7] The bagging algorithm is very simple: during the training stage, multiple bootstrap replicates[8] are generated from the training data and each replicate induces a predictor. During the decoding stage, each test example is processed by all the predictors and the final result is created in a voting approach.

Breiman (1996) shows that bagging achieves impressive results when applied to unstable learning algorithms (e.g., decision tree), but it could degrade the performance of stable algorithms (e.g., kNN). Henderson and Brill (2000) used bagging and boosting to improve a Treebank parser. For the POS tagging task, Màrquez et al. (1999) shows that bagging decision-tree taggers improves tagging accuracy on English text, and similar improvement is observed for Hungarian text when bagging TBL taggers (Kuba et al., 2005).

In our present work, we test the effect of bagging on our three baseline taggers for Chinese text.

5 Experiments

We ran our experiment on the Chinese Penn Treebank (CTB) version 5.0, which contains 500 thousand words of newspaper and magazine articles from three sources: Xinhua News Agency from Mainland China, HKSAR from

[7]A predictor can be any function that maps input to output, and in this case, a predictor is simply a POS tagger.

[8]Given a training set of n examples, a bootstrap replicate is created by randomly drawing with replacement n times.

Hong Kong, and Sinorama Magazine from Taiwan. Three previous work (Xue et al., 2002; Florian and Ngai, 2001; Ng and Low, 2004) were trained on various earlier versions of the treebank, which contain 100K, 160K, and 250K words respectively. (Tseng et al., 2005) is the only previous work that was trained on version 5.0; therefore we used the same data split as they did.[9] Table 4 shows the sources and sizes of the data sets. The average sentence length is 27 words, and the OOV rate (the percentage of unknown tokens) is 6.42% on the DevSet and 5.86% on the TestSet. The unigram tagging accuracy on the DevSet is 86.31%.

Table 4: Training, development, and test data

Data Set	Sections	words
Training		461406
Xinhua	026-270, 301-325, 400-454, 600-931	213910
HKSAR	none	0
Sinorama	1003-1039, 1043-1151	247496
DevSet		23839
Xinhua	001-025	7844
HKSAR	500-527	8202
Sinorama	590-593, 1001-1002	7793
TestSet		23522
Xinhua	271-300	8008
HKSAR	528-554	7153
Sinorama	594-596, 1040-1042	8361

5.1 TBL results

To test the effects of contextual templates on TBL, we first use an empty lexical template set, which means all the unknown words are assigned a default tag at both the training and the test stages. The results are in Table 5, where the three columns list the tagging accuracy for all words, known words, and unknown words, respectively. As shown in the first two rows, C1' works much better than C1, indicating that it is useful to include CurTag in the feature templates for this template set.

Then we add either $C2$ or $C2'$ to $C1'$. In both cases, the tagging accuracy improves, and $C2$ works slightly better than $C2'$. Next, we add C3 or C3', and the results are further improved.

To test the effect of lexical templates, we start with the best result from Table 5, which uses C1'+C2+C3'. The results are in Table 6. The lexical templates greatly improve the accuracy of unknown words, and the overall accuracy increases from 92.13% to 92.83%.

[9]Our training data plus the DevSet is the same as the Training III defined in their paper.

Table 5: Effects of contextual templates for TBL (on the DevSet)

Features	Overall	Known	Unk
C1	88.82	91.24	53.52
C1'	91.35	93.46	60.76
C1'+C2	91.70	93.83	60.69
C1'+C2'	91.60	93.80	59.71
C1'+C2+C3	92.05	94.22	60.52
C1'+C2+C3'	**92.13**	94.26	61.15

Table 6: Effects of lexical templates for TBL (on the DevSet)

Features	Overall	Known	Unk
C1'+C2+C3'	92.13	94.26	61.15
C1'+C2+C3'+L1	92.74	94.17	71.90
C1'+C2+C3'+L1+L2	92.46	93.89	71.66
C1'+C2+C3'+L1+L2+L3	**92.83**	94.29	71.56

5.2 MaxEnt results

The MaxEnt tagger cannot use C1', C2', C3' (which refer to the tag of the current word) and C3 (which refers to tags of words to the right). We ran the tagger with other template sets, and the results are in Table 7. When we compare this with TBL results, we observe that some templates can have opposite effects on the two taggers. For instance, while adding C2 helps the TBL tagger, it hurts the MaxEnt tagger.

Table 7: Tagging accuracy of the MaxEnt tagger (on the DevSet)

Features	Overall	Known	Unk
C1	92.75	94.46	67.99
C1+C2	92.56	94.28	67.54
C1+L1	**93.65**	94.83	76.53
C1+L1+L2	93.62	94.79	76.60
C1+L1+L2+L3	93.42	94.76	74.05

5.3 Bagging results

Table 8 shows the bagging results. The first row is the baseline result without bagging. The rest are the results when the number of bags ranges from 1 to 100.

A few observations are in order: First, among three taggers, bagging helps TBL the most (from 92.83% to 93.25%) with a relative error reduction of 5.85%, but the gain is very

Table 8: Bagging with different numbers of bags (on the DevSet)

	Trigram	TBL	MaxEnt	Trigram+TBL+MaxEnt	TBL+MaxEnt
no bagging	90.41	92.83	**93.65**	93.25	N/A
1 bag	89.71	91.71	92.73	92.87	N/A
3 bags	90.06	92.70	93.15	93.32	93.55
10 bags	90.30	93.08	93.45	93.46	93.85
25 bags	90.43	93.13	93.58	93.47	93.91
50 bags	90.50	93.20	93.60	93.48	93.93
75 bags	90.48	93.23	93.61	93.49	93.93
100 bags	90.51	93.25	93.60	93.50	**93.95**

moderate.[10] Second, the last two columns indicate that leaving out the trigram tagger from voting yields better results. Overall, bagging and system combination together improves the tagging accuracy from 93.65% (the best single system) to 93.95% (TBL+MaxEnt with 100 bags), achieving a relative error rate deduction of 4.72%.

5.4 Results on the test data

Table 9 shows the results on the test data. It follows the same pattern as Table 8, and the overall improvement is from 93.14% to 93.58%.

Table 9: Tagging accuracy on the TestSet

	Trigram	TBL	MaxEnt	TBL + MaxEnt
no bagging	90.32	92.41	**93.14**	N/A
1 bags	89.63	91.19	92.31	N/A
3 bags	89.95	92.13	92.73	93.17
10 bags	90.16	92.49	93.00	93.42
25 bags	90.32	92.65	93.08	93.52
100 bags	90.33	92.69	93.10	**93.58**

For comparison, among all the previous work on the Chinese POS tagging, (Tseng et al., 2005) was the only one that was trained and tested on the Chinese Penn Treebank version 5.0. However, in their experiments, the whole corpus was cleaned up before training, which yielded a 0.46% absolute performance gain when their tagger was trained on a subset of the whole training data. Because of the clean-up step and the fact that they used a different MaxEnt package, their MaxEnt baseline result on the test set was 93.51% whereas ours was 93.14%. By adding seven new types of templates, their tagging accuracy improves from 93.51% to 93.74%, whereas our tagging accuracy improves from 93.14% to 93.58% when MaxEnt and TBL output were combined. The two sets of experiments show that both adding features and system combination could improve tagging accuracy.

[10] In comparison, Kuba et al. (2005) reports a relative error reduction of 18% (tagging accuracy changes from 98.26% to approximately 98.58%) on Hungarian text. Because the two experiments used texts from different languages and the baseline results (92.83% vs. 98.26%) are quite different, comparing the error reduction rates is not very meaningful. Nevertheless, we plan to look into this difference in the future.

6 Conclusion

In this paper, we investigated the possibility of quickly adapting existing tools for a new language. We learned a few important lessons.

First, one should choose good NLP packages as the starting point. For our experiments, it is crucial that the packages include source code, which allows us to modify or extend the packages. For instance, we modified the MaxEnt tool so that it can accept feature templates in (C2), (L2), and (L3).

Second, both MaxEnt and TBL taggers use feature templates, but the same templates (e.g., C2, L2, and L3) could have opposite effects on the two taggers. In addition, TBL taggers can use feature templates that refer to the tags of the current word and the words to the right. Including CurTag in C1 greatly improves the tagging accuracy (from 88.82% to 91.35%), but adding it in C2 hurts the accuracy slightly (from 91.70% to 91.60%). Adding templates that refer to tags of the words to the right helps a little bit (from 91.70% to 92.13%).

Third, among the three taggers bagging helps TBL the most, and it has little effect on the trigram and the MaxEnt taggers. Combining TBL and MaxEnt provides a moderate gain, and it is better to leave out the Trigram tagger from the system combination.

For future work, we plan to experiment with other learning algorithms such as SVM, and other methods of system combination.

A Contextual templates used in the TBL and MaxEnt taggers

We follow the template format used in the fnTBL package. All the numbers in the templates are relative positions with respect to the current word. For instance, pos_-1 is the tag of the previous word, and word_1 is the next word. [i,j] is a range of the context. For instance, word:[-3,-1] means one of the previous three words. Notice that C3 is used only in TBL.

```
C1: seven basic templates that do not use
    tags in the right context.

word_0
word_-1
word_1
word_-2
word_2
pos_-1
pos_-2 pos_-1

C2: seventeen more templates that do not
    use tags in the right context.

word_0 word_1 word_2
word_-1 word_0 word_1
word_0 word_-1
word_0 word_1
word_0 word_2
word_0 word_-2
word:[1,2]
word:[-2,-1]
word:[1,3]
word:[-3,-1]
word_0 pos_-2
word_0 pos_-1
pos_-2
pos:[-3,-1]
pos:[-2,-1]
pos_-1 word_-1 word_0
pos_-1 word_0 word_1

C3: thirteen templates that use the tags in
    the right context.

word_0 pos_1
word_0 pos_2
pos_-1 pos_1
pos_1 pos_2
pos_1
pos_2
pos_1 word_0 word_1
pos_1 word_0 word_-1
pos:[1,3]
pos:[1,2]
pos_1 pos_2 word_1
pos_1 word_0 word_1
pos_1 word_0 word_-1
```

References

Steven Abney, Robert E. Schapire, and Yoram Singer. 1999. Boosting Applied to Tagging and PP Attachment. In *Proceedings of the 1999 Joint SIGDAT Conference on Empirical Methods in Natural Language Processing and Very Large Corpora (EMNLP-1999)*, pages 38–45.

Leo Breiman. 1996. Bagging predictors. *Machine Learning*, 24(2):123–140.

Eric Brill. 1995. Transformation-based error-driven learning and natural language processing: A case study in part-of-speech tagging. *Computational Linguistics*, 21(4):543–565.

Radu Florian and Grace Ngai. 2001. Multidimensional transformation-based learning. In *Proceedings of the 5th Conference on Computational Natural Language Learning (CoNLL-2001)*.

John Henderson and Eric Brill. 2000. Bagging and boosting a treebank parser. In *Proceedings of the 6th Applied Natural Language Processing Conference (ANLP-2000)*.

Kevin Knight and Yaser Al-Onaizan. 1999. A primer on finite-state software for natural language processing. downloadable from http://www.isi.edu/licensed-sw/carmel/carmel-tutorial2.pdf.

András Kuba, László Felföldi, and András Kocsor. 2005. Pos tagger combinations on hungarian text. In *2nd International Joint Conference on Natural Language Processing (IJCNLP-2005)*.

Lluís Màrquez, Horacio Rodríguez, Josep Carmona, and Josep Montolio. 1999. Improving pos tagging using machine-learning techniques. In *Proceedings of the 1999 Joint SIGDAT Conference on Empirical Methods in Natural Language Processing and Very Large Corpora (EMNLP-1999)*, pages 53–62.

Lluís Màrquez. 1999. *Part-of-speech Tagging: A Machine Learning Approach based on Decision Trees.* Ph.D. thesis, Universitat Politècnica de Catalunya.

Hweee Tou Ng and Jin Kiat Low. 2004. Chinese Part-of-speech Tagging: One-at-a-Time or All-at-Once? Word-based or Character-based? In *Proc. of the 9th Conf. on Empirical Methods in Natural Language Processing (EMNLP-2004)*.

Grace Ngai and Radu Florian. 2001. Transformation-based learning in the fast lane. In *Proceedings of North American ACL (NAACL-2001)*, pages 40–47, June.

Adwait Ratnaparkhi. 1996. A Maximum Entropy Model for Part-of-speech Tagging. In *Proc. of Joint SIGDAT Conference on Empirical Methods in Natural Language Processing and Very Large Corpora (EMNLP-1996)*.

Huihsin Tseng, Daniel Jurafsky, and Christopher Manning. 2005. Morphological features help pos tagging of unknown words across language varieties. In *Proc. of the 4th Workshop on Chinese Language Processing (SIGHAN-2005)*.

Nianwen Xue, Fu dong Chiou, and Martha Palmer. 2002. Building a Large-scale Annotated Chinese Corpus. In *Proc. of the 19th International Conference on Computational Linguistics (COLING-2002)*.

Semantic Analysis of Chinese Garden-Path Sentences

Yaohong Jin
Institute of Acoustics, Chinese Academy of Sciences, Beijing 100080, China
jinyaohong@hotmail.com

Abstract

This paper presents a semantic model for Chinese garden-path sentences. Based on the Sentence Degeneration model of HNC theory, a garden-path can arise from two types of ambiguities: SD type ambiguity and NP allocated ambiguity. This paper provides an approach to process garden-paths, in which ambiguity detection and analysis take the place of revision. The performance of the approach is evaluated on a small manually annotated test set. The results show that our algorithm can analyze Chinese garden-path sentences effectively.

1 Introduction

A characteristic of garden-path sentences is that they contain a temporarily ambiguous verb structure, in which a participle is confused with the main verb of the sentence. For example, consider the sentence *While Anna dressed the baby spit up on the bed*. Initially *the baby* is assumed to be the object of *dressed*, but when *spit up* is encountered, some sort of error arises. This initial process, then, must be somehow revised. This paper models the phenomenon of garden-path sentences in Chinese and addresses the mechanisms of semantic analysis. Let v1 be the first verb in the sentence and v2 the second verb. Modeling the garden-path that arising from two verbs like v1 and v2 will the focus of this paper.

Models of reanalysis, which concern the syntactic relationships between the error signal and the head of the phrase that has been misanalyzed (Frazier, 1998), attempt to explain how the revisions take place. However, for Chinese garden-path sentence analysis, the syntactic relationship is not enough because the same syntactic relationship can have different semantic interpretations. For example, *咬死猎人的狗* which is temporarily ambiguous in Chinese has different interpretations in the following two sentences. In the first sentence *狗(dog)* is the subject of *咬死(killed)*, and in the second it is the object of *咬死(killed)*.

(1) 咬死猎人的狗逃跑了 (The dog, which killed the hunter, had run away).

(2) 咬死猎人的狗是熊逃跑的唯一出路 (It is the only way for the bear to run away that killed the hunter's dog).

So, semantic analysis is important for Chinese garden-path sentences. In this paper, garden-path sentences will be modeled using the Sentence Degeneration model (SD) of the Hierarchical Network of Concepts theory (HNC) (Huang, 1998; 2004). Furthermore, our analysis algorithm, in which ambiguity analysis takes the place of a revision process, is introduced. We evaluated the model and the algorithm using a small sentence set with grammatical structures like *NP1+V1+NP2+v2+NP3*. The experiment results show that our algorithm can efficiently process Chinese garden-path sentences.

In the rest of this paper: Section 2 discusses previous work. Section 3 gives a detailed definition of the Sentence Degeneration model. Section 4 describes in detail the Semantic Model of Chinese garden-path sentences. Section 5 describes the algorithm and section 6 gives evaluation results. Section 7 presents our conclusions and future work.

2 Previous Work

The phenomenon of garden-path sentences has attracted a lot of attention in the research communities of psycholinguistics and computational linguistics. The goal of this research is to discover how people understand garden-path sentences and how to analyze them automatically.

In English, garden-path sentences always involve a subordinate clause and a main clause together with an NP that attaches initially to the former but ultimately to the latter (Karl and Fernanda, 2003). This NP is the point of misunderstanding and the verb after the NP is always the error signal. Models of reanalysis are aimed at describing and motivating the mechanisms used by the sentence comprehension system to detect errors, deduce useful information about the nature of the necessary repair of those errors, and ultimately create a successful analysis (Ferreira and Christianson, 2001). Fodor and Inoue(1998) proposed the principles of Attach Anyway and Adjust to explain how reanalysis processes operate. Ferreira and Christianson(2001) stated that Reflexive Absolute Transitive (RAT) verbs, such as *wash*, *bathe*, *shave*, *scratch*, *groom,* and so on, are likely to give rise to garden-paths. Michael J. Pazzani(1984) demonstrated how to reanalyze one type of garden-path sentence that arises from a passive participle and a main verb conflicting. However Ferreira and Henderson(2001) demonstrated that reanalysis is more difficult when the head of the misanalyzed phrase (*baby* in *the baby that was small and cute*) is distant from the error signal.

In Chinese, there has been little research that directly addresses the problem of garden-paths. Zhiwei Feng(2003) interpreted the temporarily ambiguous verb structure in a garden-path in two ways; one is as a subordinate clause (MV), the other is a Reduced Relative (RR). He defined Garden Path Degree (GPD) as MV/RR. He studied some types of temporarily ambiguous verb structures such as *NP1+VP+NP2+de+NP3, VP+NP1+de+NP2, V+Adj+de+N and V+V+de+N*, and stated that when GPD is larger than 3, the temporarily ambiguous verb structure may give rise to a garden-path. Moreover he used the Earley algorithm to process garden-path sentences.

3 Sentence Degeneration model (SD)

The Sentence Degeneration model, which is one model of the Hierarchical Network of Concepts theory (HNC), focuses on representing the subordinate clause in a sentence. The theory of the Hierarchical Network of Concepts (HNC theory), founded by Prof. Zengyang Huang of the Institute of Acoustics, Chinese Academy of Sciences, is a theoretical approach to Natural Language Processing (NLP). The objective of HNC is to establish natural language representation patterns based on the association veins of concepts, which can simulate the language perception process of the human brain and can be applied to computational Natural Language Understanding.

Sentence Degeneration (SD) represents the semantic patterns of the subordinate clause in a sentence. There are three types of SD: prototype SD, key-element SD, and packed SD.

In Prototype SD a subordinate clause wholly acts as one role of the other sentence without any alteration. For example, *中国加入世界贸易组织(China joined the WTO)* is a complete sentence. However in sentence (3) this sentence acts as the subject of *促进(accelerate)*. Unlike English, in Chinese there is no relative pronoun, such as *that* or *which*, to indicate that this is a subordinate clause. This phenomenon is named Prototype SD.

(3) 中国加入世界贸易组织会促进全球经济的发展 (That China joined the WTO will accelerate the development of global economics.).

Key-element SD involves an NP which semantically is an attributive clause. For example, although in sentence (4) *加入世界贸易组织的中国* is an NP, it can be transformed from the sentence *中国加入世界贸易组织* by moving the subject *中国* to the tail and adding the Chinese word *的(of or 's)* in front of it. We look at this NP as a specific attributive clause[1] in Chinese, and look at *中国* as the core concept of this clause. Because the core concept of this clause is the subject, which is the key element, this phenomenon is called key-element SD. Besides the subject, the object and the verb of the sentence can be the core of key-element SD. For example, in sentence (5) *中国对世界经济的影响* is one key-element SD transformed from the sentence *中国影响世界经济*, and the verb *影响* is its core.

(4) 加入世界贸易组织的中国将严格遵守贸易规则 (China, which joined WTO, will strictly confirm the world trade rule.)

(5) 这一切体现了中国对世界经济的影响 (Everything of all reflected the influence that China economics impacts on the world).

Packed SD is also an NP in which the attrib-

[1] This NP has to be translated as an attributive clause using *which* in English.

uter is a prototype SD or key-element SD. For example, in sentence (6) and (7) both noun phrases *中国加入世界贸易组织的消息* and *中国对世界经济的影响程度* are Packed SD's. Moreover, the attributer of *消息* is *中国加入世界贸易组织* which is a prototype SD, and the attributer of *程度* is *中国对世界经济的影响* which is a key-element SD. The words *消息* and *程度* are called packed words.

(6) 中国加入世界贸易组织的消息令人激动 (The news that China joined WTO is exciting.)

(7) 中国对世界经济的影响程度将越来越大 (The degree of influence that Chinese economics impacts on the world is deeper and deeper.)

Let *ElJ* be the semantic structure of the subordinate clause, *GBKi* be the subject/object, and *El* be the verb of the clause. The semantic pattern of the clause can be given as *ElJ=GBK1+El+GBK2+GBK3*, where *GBK2* and *GBK3* can be absent and the position of *GBKi* can be changed. Suppose *ElJ-GBKi* stands for the action of subtracting the *GBKi* from *ElJ*, *ElJ-El* stands for subtracting the *El*. The semantic patterns of SD can be given as follows:

1. *ElJ*. It means that *ElJ* is a prototype SD.
2. *(ElJ-GBKi)+ 的+GBKi*. It means that this key-element SD can be transformed from the clause *ElJ* by moving *GBKi* to the tail and adding the Chinese word *的* in front of GBKi.
3. *(ElJ-El)+ 的 +El*. It means that this key-element SD can be transformed from the clause *ElJ* by moving *El* to the tail and adding the Chinese word *的* in front of *El*. Although this *El* looks like a noun because there is Chinese word *的* in front of it, it is regarded as a verb when restored back to the *ElJ*.
4. *a prototype SD or key-element SD+{ 的 }+noun*. It means the three patterns above can serve as the attributer of the packed SD.

Although the key-element SD and packed SD look like NP's in Chinese, they need to be transformed back into clauses during semantic analysis. It means that in patterns 2 and 3 the *GBKi* and *El* have to be restored into *ElJ*. This is why we named these phenomena Sentence Degeneration. Moreover, in patterns 2 and 3, the Chinese word *的* is necessary to indicate the transformation, and we call it a sign of SD.

Therefore, if an NP or other structure includes a verb and the Chinese word *的*, it has to be analyzed as one type of SD. These semantic patterns of SD are useful for describing the interpretation of temporarily ambiguous verb structures, such as those in garden-path sentences.

4 Semantic Model of Chinese Garden-Path Sentence

Based on the Sentence Degeneration model, there are two types of Chinese Garden-Path Sentences: SD type ambiguity garden-paths and NP allocated ambiguity garden-paths.

A temporarily ambiguous verb structure in a sentence always has more than one semantic interpretation that can be represented as a type of SD. This phenomenon we call SD type ambiguity. If an SD type ambiguity includes a prototype SD, a garden-path arises. For example, an ambiguous structure like *咬死猎人的狗* has two different interpretations as A and B in sentence (1) and (2):

A. It is a key-element SD in sentence (1), where *狗(dog)* is the subject of *咬死(kill)*, and *猎人(hunter)* is the object of *咬死(kill)*.

B. It is a prototype SD in sentence (2), where *狗(dog)* is the object of *咬死(kill)*, and *猎人(hunter)* is the attributer of *狗(dog)*.

Obviously, *咬死猎人的狗* has SD type ambiguity, and one type of SD is prototype SD. Therefore, sentence (1) and sentence (2) are garden-path sentences.

An NP allocated ambiguity garden-path is a sentence in which one *NP* can be both the object of *v1* and the subject of *v2*. Given the structure *NP1+v1+NP2+v2+NP3*, if *NP1+v1+NP2* is a clause, *NP2+v2+NP3* is a clause, too; there is an ambiguity about whether *NP2* serves as either the object of the first clause or the subject of the second clause. Unlike the garden-path that arises from an SD type ambiguity, NP allocated ambiguity garden-paths confuse the main verb of the sentence. For example, Sentence (8) has two different interpretations as A and B. The difference in the two interpretations is the role of *the solution*. So, sentence (8) is a garden-path sentence with an NP allocated ambiguity.

(8)这个学生忘记答案在书的背后 (The student forgot the solution was in the back of the book.)

A. *the solution* is the subject of *was*, the main verb is *forgot*; *the solution was in the back of the book,* which is a prototype SD, is the object of *forgot*.

B. *the solution* is the object of *forgot*, the main verb is *was*, *the student forgot the solution,* which is a prototype SD, is the subject of *was*.

We can see that it is necessary for both types of garden-path that *NP1+v1+NP2* be a clause. If there is an NP allocated ambiguity garden-path, *NP1+v1+NP2* is a clause together with *NP2+v2+NP3* as a clause. If there is an SD type ambiguity garden-path, *NP1+v1+NP2* has to be a prototype SD together with one of other two types of SD (Key-element SD or packed SD). Thus, this clause, *NP1+v1+NP2*, is called a garden-path detecting signal.

Therefore, in our model the garden-path is represented as one of two types of ambiguity: the SD type ambiguity and NP allocated ambiguity. Garden-path processing involves detecting and analyzing these two types of ambiguities.

5 Algorithm for processing Chinese Garden-Path Sentences

A Chinese Garden-Path Sentence is processed in four steps:

(1) Initially, *v1* is analyzed as the main verb.
(2) When *v2* is encountered, if there is a clause before *v2*, this is a garden-path detecting signal. It is necessary to detect and analyze the garden-path in this sentence.
(3) Detect if v1 and v2 can give rise to a garden-path (see section 5.1).
(4) Determine the main verb of the sentence and the semantic interpretation of the garden-path sentence (see section 5.2).

5.1 Garden-path detection

Given an input string *S*, suppose its grammatical structure is *NP1+v1+NP2+v2+NP3*, where *NP1* and *NP3* can be absent. Therefore, a garden-path detecting signal means that *NP1+v1+NP2* is a clause.

The garden-path can be detected in two steps as follows:

Step 1: test if there is SD type ambiguity in *NP1+v1+NP2*.

We can look at the clause *NP1+v1+NP2* as a prototype SD without any change. If this prototype SD can be analyzed as another type of SD, such as key-element or packed SD, an SD type ambiguity is found, and the input *S* is a garden-path sentence. Otherwise, if there is no SD type ambiguity, the input *S* is a non garden-path sentence.

As mentioned above, sentence (1) has an ambiguity between a prototype and a key-element SD, and it is a garden-path sentence. Consider another sentence (9), with grammatical structure *NP1+v1+NP2+v2*. Because the Chinese word 的(of) in *NP2* is a sign of SD, the structure can be rewritten as *NP1+v1+NP21+的+NP22+v2*.

(9) 小王研究鲁迅的文章发表了 (The paper which Mr. wang research on Luxun is published.)

The structure *NP1+v1+NP21+的+NP22* can be analyzed in two different ways as follows. Obviously there is an ambiguity between prototype SD and packed SD, and sentence (9) is a garden-path sentence.

A. It is a prototype SD, where *文章(paper)* is the object of *研究(research)*, and *文章(paper)* was written by *鲁迅(Luxun)*.

B. It is a packed SD, where *鲁迅(Luxun)* is the object of *研究(research)*, and *文章(paper)* was written by *小王(Mr. wang)*.

Although the structure *v1+NP2+v2* in sentence (1) and the structure *NP1+v1+NP2+v2* in sentence (9) can give rise to garden-paths, not all the instances of these two structures are like this. For example, in sentence group (10) *年轻人(younger)* and *刀(knife)* disfavor being objects of *热爱(love)* and *削(peel)*, so *热爱祖国的年轻人* is only analyzed as a key-element SD, and *小王削苹果的刀* is only analyzed as a packed SD. There is no garden-path detecting signal, so these sentences are non garden-path sentences.

(10) 热爱祖国的年轻人回国了 (The younger who love his country go back.)

小王削苹果的刀不见了 (The knife with which Mr. wang peeled the apple is lost.)

Furthermore, in sentence group (11), *v1+NP2* is a clause, so there is a garden-path detecting signal. However, *皮(fruit skin)* disfavors being the subject of *削(peel)*, and *门(door)* is not a packed word, so *削苹果的皮* and *小王推开房间的门* are only analyzed as prototype SD. There is no SD type ambiguity, so these sentences are non garden-path sentences.

(11) 削苹果的皮要小心 (Peeling the apple need to be careful.)

小王推开房间的门走了 (Mr. wang opened the door and went away.)

Step 2: test if *NP2+v2+NP3* is a clause.

If *NP2+v2+NP3* is not a clause, definitely there is no NP allocated ambiguity, and the sentence is not a garden-path sentence. For example, in sentence (12) *伊拉克起因于能源危机(Iraq is due to the crisis of energy)* is not a clause, so sentence (12) is a non garden-path sentence.

(12) 美国打击伊拉克起因于能源危机 (That USA attacked Iraq is due to the crisis of energy)

If *NP2+v2+NP3* is a clause, there are two interpretations for *v1* and *v2*.

First, *v1* and *v2* are serial verbs, and the sentence can be divided into two separate sentences; one is *NP1+v1+NP2*, the other is *NP2+v2+NP3* and the subject of v2 is *NP2*. For example, sentence (13) can be divided into sentences (14) and (15). This phenomenon can be interpreted as sentence (15) sharing *大会(conference)* with sentence (14), which is not NP allocated ambiguity, so the sentence (13) is a non garden-path sentence.

(13) 文件将提交给大会讨论 (The file will be given to the conference to discuss.)

(14) 文件将提交给大会 (The file will be given to the conference.)

(15) 大会讨论这个文件 (The conference will discuss the file.)

Second, one of *v1* and *v2* is the main verb of the sentence, and *NP2* has to be in *NP1+v1+NP2* or *NP2+v2+NP3*, and cannot be shared. For example, in sentence (8), the *solution* cannot be shared by *forgot* and *was*. Absolutely this is an NP allocated ambiguity, and the sentence is a garden-path sentence.

The difference between a serial verb interpretation and an NP allocated ambiguity interpretation is the semantic information of the two verbs. Suppose *VS(pro)* is the set of all verbs whose subject can be a prototype SD, *VO(pro)* is the set of all verbs whose object can be a prototype SD. Verbs about mental acts, emotions or other human feelings, such as *forget, worry, cry*, belong to the *VS(pro)*. Verbs about propositions, causes and results, such as *be, result in, be due to*, belong to both *VO(pro)* and *VS(pro)*.

If *NP2+v2+NP3* is a clause, and if *v1* is not one of *VO(pro)* and *v2* is not one of *VS(pro)*, the sentence is a non garden-path sentence and these two verbs are serial verbs. Otherwise, the sentence is a garden-path sentence.

5.2 Garden-path analysis

A garden-path is always affected by the selection of the main verb of a sentence. In the garden-path caused by SD ambiguity, *v1* is regarded as the main verb initially, however, in the end, *v2* is the real main verb. In the garden-path caused by NP allocated ambiguity, both *v1* and *v2* can be the main verb. So, the garden-path analysis includes two steps: the first step is determining the main verb of the sentence; the second step is disambiguating the SD type or the NP allocated ambiguity, and determining the semantic structure of the sentence.

Given a garden-path sentence with grammatical structure *NP1+v1+NP2+v2+NP3*, the analysis process is as follows:

First, if an SD type ambiguity is detected, it means *NP1+v1+NP2* can be a prototype SD and key-element or packed SD, and *v2* always is the main verb of the sentence. The ambiguity can be processed as in Figure 1. For example, In sentences (1) and (2), *是(is)* is one of VS(pro) and *逃跑(run away)* is not, so *咬死猎人的狗* is processed as a key-element SD in sentence (1) and a prototype SD in sentence (2).

Second, if an NP allocated ambiguity is detected, it means that both *NP1+v1+NP2* and *NP2+v2+NP3* can be clauses. The main verb can be determined in Figure 2. The NP allocated ambiguity can be processed as in Figure 3.

(16) 张先生看见李小姐正在跳舞 (Mr. Zhang saw Miss. Li dancing.)

The result of garden-path analysis is a semantic structure for the sentence. In Figures 1 and 3, a flag of prototype SD, key-element SD and packed SD, which indicates the semantic interpretation, is added to the grammatical structure of the sentence. Therefore, the main verb, which is always outside the flag, and the semantic structure of the sentence are both represented.

v2 is	*NP1+v1+NP2* is	Sentence semantic structure	Example
one of VS(pro)	a prototype SD	(NP1+v1+NP2)+v2+NP3	Sentence (2)
not one of VS(pro)	a key-element SD	<NP1+v1+NP2>+v2+NP3	Sentence (1)
not one of VS(pro)	a packed SD	{NP1+v1+NP2}+v2+NP3	Sentence (9)

Figure 1: The process of SD type ambiguity in garden-path sentences. Where ( ) is the flag

indicating that the content in it is prototype SD, < > is the flag of key-element SD, and { } is the flag of packed SD.

V1 is	v2 is	the main verb is	Example
one of VO(pro)	not one of VS(pro)	v1	Sentence (16)
one of VO(pro)	one of VS(pro)	prior to be v1	Sentence (8)
not one of VO(pro)	one of VS(pro)	v2	Sentence (12)

Figure 2: The main verb determining in garden-path sentences. Here *prior to* means that if v1 is one of VO(pro) and v2 is one of VS(pro), the main verb is v1 in most cases. In some cases it depends on the meaning of v1 and v2, whether v1 is the main verb. These cases are out of the scope of consideration of this paper.

Main verb is	NP2 is	Sentence semantic structure	Example	Comment
v1	The subject of v2	NP1+v1+(NP2+v2 +NP3)	Sentence (8),(16)	NP2+v2+NP3 is a prototype SD, this SD is the object of v1.
v2	The object of v1	(NP1+v1+NP2)+v2 +NP3	Sentence (12)	NP1+v1+NP2 is a prototype SD, this SD is the subject of v2.

Figure 3: The process of NP allocated ambiguity in garden-path sentence. Where ( ) is the flag indicating that the content in it is prototype SD.

6. Evaluation and Discussion

To conduct a reliable evaluation, a test sentence set and a simple knowledge base were developed. The test set includes 100 manually annotated Chinese garden-path sentences and 100 non garden-path sentences with grammatical structure *NP1+v1+NP2+v2+NP3*. The knowledge base includes two aspects: one is if the verb is one of VS(pro) or VO(pro), the other is the concepts which the subject/object of the verb favor. And there are about 800 verbs in our knowledge base.

Next, two experiments have been conducted. The first one is designed to test if our model can detect garden-paths effectively. The second one is designed to evaluate if garden-path sentences can be correctly analyzed. The results of the experiments are shown in Tables 1 and 2.

Total Num	Detected	Correct	P(%)	R(%)	F(%)
100	85	79	92.9	79	85.4

Table 1: Performance of detection algorithm.

Total of Detected	SD type ambiguity Analysis Correct	NP allocated ambiguity Analysis Correct	Total of Correct	P(%)
85	53	24	77	90.6

Table 2: Performance of analysis algorithm.

Where, P is precision ratio, R is recall ratio, and F is F-measure (F β =1, which is defined as 2PR/(P+R)).

We can see that on this small test set, our algorithm achieves good performance in detection and analysis of Chinese garden-path sentences. We also conducted an error analysis, showing that two main factors lead to detection errors.

The first is that attributer processing of NP2's is not considered. For example, in *管理朋友的*

公司(manage the friend's company), *朋友的公司(the friend's company)* is an NP which cannot be divided to *NP21(朋友 friend)+的+NP22(公司 company)* and cannot be detected if there is an SD type ambiguity.

The second is coordination ambiguity interacting with NP allocated ambiguity, as in *Sandra bumped into the busboy and the waiter told her to be careful*, which has not been considered.

Furthermore, there are two sentences correctly detected as Chinese garden-path sentences, but there are neither SD type ambiguities nor NP allocated ambiguities in them. This is why there are 79 correct detections in Table 1, but only 77 correct analyses in Table 2. One of these sentences is sentence (17), in which *我是县长(I am the mayor)* looks like a prototype SD, however "是…的" is used to emphasized 县长(the mayor) in Chinese.

(17) 我是县长派来的（It is the mayor that instructed me to come here）

7. Conclusions and Future Work

The contributions of this paper are three-fold.

First, the Sentence Degeneration model is introduced which can represent the differences in interpretation of the same grammatical structure.

Second, we represent garden-paths as SD type ambiguity and NP allocated ambiguity. These two ambiguities come from semantics but not grammar.

Third, we present a unified approach to processing garden-paths, in which ambiguity detection and analysis take the place of revision. The result of our approach is the semantic structure of a garden-path sentence.

The results of two experiments we conducted show that our model and algorithm can analyze Chinese garden-path sentences effectively. In our future work, we will build a complex knowledge base for verbs to support our semantic analysis. We will also develop attributer processing and coordination disambiguation to improve the performance of our algorithm.

Moreover, we will extend our algorithm to detect and analyze garden-paths caused by sentences which have no verbs. This phenomenon is a typical ambiguity in Chinese sentences, such as. Sentence (18):

(18) 她穿裙子很漂亮(She is beautiful dressing skirt).

Acknowledgments

I thank Prof. Zengyang Huang and Dr. Chuanjiang Miao for their valuable comments on an early draft of this paper. I also thank Zheng Wu for his wonderful work in algorithm development.

References

Frazier, L., & Clifton, C., Jr. 1998. Sentence reanalysis and visibility. In J. D. Fodor & F.Ferreira (Eds.), *Reanalysis in sentence processing*. Dordrecht, Kluwer.

Fernanda Ferreira,etc. 2001. Misinterpretations of Garden-Path Sentences: Implications for Models of Sentence Processing and Reanalysis. *Journal of Psycholinguistic Research*, 30(1).

Michael J. Pazzani. 1984. Conceptual Analysis of Garden-Path Sentences. *Proceedings of the 10th international conference on Computational linguistics*.

Karl G.D. Bailey, etc. 2003. Disfluencies affect the parsing of garden-path sentences. *Journal of Memory and Language*, 49:183–200.

Zengyang Huang. 1998. *The theory of Hierarchical Network of Concepts* (in Chinese). Tsinghua University Press, Beijing, China.

Zengyang Huang. 2004. *The Basic Concepts and expression of the Concepts space* (in Chinese). Ocean Press, Beijing, China.

Zhiwei Feng. 2003. The automatic parsing algorithm for garden-path sentence (in Chinese). *Contemporary Linguistics*, 5(4)

A Clustering Approach for Unsupervised Chinese Coreference Resolution

Chi-shing Wang **Grace NGAI**

Department of Computing

Hong Kong Polytechnic University

Kowloon, HONG KONG

{cscswang, csgngai}@comp.polyu.edu.hk

Abstract

Coreference resolution is the process of identifying expressions that refer to the same entity. This paper presents a clustering algorithm for unsupervised Chinese coreference resolution. We investigate why Chinese coreference is hard and demonstrate that techniques used in coreference resolution for English can be extended to Chinese. The proposed system exploits clustering as it has advantages over traditional classification methods, such as the fact that no training data is required and it is easily extended to accommodate additional features. We conduct a set of experiments to investigate how noun phrase identification and feature selection can contribute to coreference resolution performance. Our system is evaluated on an annotated version of the TDT3 corpus using the MUC-7 scorer, and obtains comparable performance. We believe that this is the first attempt at an unsupervised approach to Chinese noun phrase coreference resolution.

1 INTRODUCTION

Noun phrase coreference resolution is the process of detecting noun phrases (NPs) in a document and determining whether the NPs refer to the same *entity*, where an entity is defined as "a construct that represents an abstract identity". The NPs that refer to the entity are known as *mentions*. Mentions can be antecedents or anaphors. An anaphor is an expression that refers back to a previous expression in a discourse. In Figure 1, 克林頓總統 (President Clinton) refers to 克林頓 (Clinton) and is described as an anaphoric reference to克林頓 (Clinton). 克林頓總統 (President Clinton) is described as the antecedent of 他 (he). 克林頓 (Clinton), 克林頓總統 (President Clinton) and the second 他 (he) are all mentions of the same entity that refers to former U.S. president Bill Clinton.

[克林頓$_1$]説，華盛頓將逐步落實對[韓國$_2$]的經濟援助。[金大中$_3$]對[克林頓$_1$]的講話報以掌聲。[他$_3$]説：「[克林頓總統$_1$]在會談中重申，[他$_1$]堅定地支持[韓國$_2$]擺脱經濟危機。」

[Clinton$_1$] said that Washington would progressively follow through on economic aid to [Korea$_2$]. [Kim Dae-Jung$_3$] applauded [Clinton$_1$]'s speech. [He$_1$] said, "[President Clinton$_1$] reiterated in the talks that [he$_1$] would provide solid support for [Korea$_2$] to shake off the economic crisis.

Figure 1: An excerpt from the text, with coreferring noun phrases annotated. *English translation in italics.*

NP coreference resolution is an important subtask in natural language processing (NLP) applications such as text summarization, information extraction, data mining and question answering. This task has attracted much attention in recent years (Cardie and Wagstaff, 1999; Harabagiu et al., 2001; Soon et al., 2001; Ng and Cardie, 2002; Yang et al., 2004; Florian et al., 2004; Zhou et al., 2005), and has been included as a subtask in the MUC (Message Understanding Conferences) and ACE (Automatic Content Extraction) competitions.

Coreference resolution is a difficult task for various reasons. Firstly, a list of features can play a role to support coreference resolution such as gender agreement, number agreement, head noun matches, semantic class, positional information, contextual information, appositive, abbreviation etc. Ng and Cardie (2002) found 53 features which are useful for this problem. However, no single feature is completely reliable since there are always exceptions: e.g. the number agreement test returns false when 這個部隊 (*this army*, singular) is matched against 眾隊員 (*army members*, plural), despite the two phrases being coreferential. Secondly, identifying features automatically and accurately is hard. Features such as semantic class come from named entity recognition (NER) systems and ontologies and gazetteers, but they are not always accurate, especially where new terms are concerned. Thirdly, coreference resolution subsumes the pronoun resolution problem, which is already difficult since pronouns carry limited lexical and semantic information.

In addition to the aforementioned, Chinese coreference resolution is also made more difficult due to the lack of morphological and orthographic clues. Chinese words contain less exterior information than words in many Indoeuropean languages. For example, in English, number agreement can be detected through word inflections and part-of-speech (POS) tags, but there are no simple rules in Chinese to distinguish whether a word is singular or plural. Proper name and abbreviations are identified by capitalization in English, but Chinese does not use capitalization. Moreover, written Chinese does not have word boundaries, so word segmentation is a crucial problem, as we cannot get the true meaning of the sentence based on characters alone. A simple sentence can be segmented in several different ways to get different meanings. This characteristic affects the performance of all parts and leads to irrecoverable errors. In addition, there are very few Chinese coreference data sets available for research purposes (none of them freely available) and as a result, no easily obtainable benchmarking dataset for training and measuring performance. Building a reasonably large coreference corpus is a labor-consuming task.

To our knowledge, there have only been two Chinese coreference systems in previously published work: Florian et al. (2004), which presents a statistical framework and reports experiment results on Chinese texts; and Zhou et al. (2005), which proposed a unified transformation based learning framework for Chinese entity detection and tracking. It consists of two models: the detection model locates possibly coreferring NPs and the tracking model links the coreference relations.

This paper presents research performed on Chinese noun phrase coreference resolution. Since there are no freely available Chinese coreference resources, we used an unsupervised method that partially borrows from Cardie and Wagstaff's (1999) clustering-based technique, with features that are specially designed for Chinese. In addition, we perform and present the results of experiments designed to investigate the contribution of each feature.

2 Experiment Setup

Identifying coreferent NPs in an unannotated document actually involves two tasks: mention detection, which identifies the anaphors and antecedents in a document, followed by noun phrase coreference resolution. In order to reduce the complexity of the final system, we follow the usual approach in handling these two phases separately.

2.1 Corpus

Even though we are using an unsupervised approach, a gold standard corpus is still needed for experiment evaluation. Since we did not have access to the ACE multilingual entity tracking corpus, we created our own corpus by selecting 30 documents from the TDT3 Chinese corpus. This resulted in a corpus of approximately 36K Chinese characters, about the same size as the MUC dryrun test sets. We then had our corpus annotated by a native Chinese speaker following the MUC-7 (Hirschman and Chinchor, 1997) and ACE Chinese entity guidelines (LDC, 2004) by picking out noun phrase mentions corresponding to one of the following nine types of entities: Person, Organization, Location, Geo-Political Entity (GPE), Facility, Vehicle, Weapon, Date and Money, and for each pair of mentions, deciding whether they refer to the same entity following MUC-7 definitions. According to the guidelines, each mention participates in exactly one entity, and all mentions in the same entity are coreferent. The NPs that are marked include proper nouns, nominal nouns and pronouns and the entity types are a superset of those used in the MUC and ACE competitions. The resulting corpus includes 1640 mentions, referring to 410 entities.

Once our corpus had been determined, the first step was to determine the possible mentions in a plain text. We first used a dictionary-based word segmentation system (Lancashire, 2005) to segment the Chinese characters into words. The segmented words are then labeled with POS tags by a statistical POS tagging system (Fung et al., 2004).

3 Mention Detection

After the corpus has been preprocessed, mention detection involves the identification of NPs in the corpus that refer to some entity. Most of these NPs correspond to non-recursive NPs, which makes this task simpler as most syntactic parsers identify NPs as part of the parsing process. This approach, however, suffers from two problems: firstly, the parser itself is unlikely to be 100% accurate; and secondly, the boundaries of the NPs identified by the parser may not correspond exactly with those of the entities identified by the human annotator.

Another approach is simply to use heuristics based on the POS tag sequence to identify potential NPs of interest. The advantage of this method is that the NPs thus extracted should be closer to the human-annotated entities since the heuristics will be constructed specifically for this task.

To investigate the effect of different approaches on the result of the coreference resolution, we applied both methods separately to our corpus. The corpus was parsed with a state-of-the-art multilingual statistical parser (Bikel 2004), which is trained on the Chinese Penn Treebank. After parsing, we extracted all non-recursive NP chunks tagged by the parser as possible mentions.

For the heuristic-based approach, we applied a few simple heuristics, which had been previously developed during unrelated work for English named-entity resolution (i.e. they were not written with foreknowledge of the gold standard entities) and which are based on the part-of-speech tags of the words. Some examples of our heuristics were to look for pronouns, or to extract all noun sequences, or sequences of determiners followed by adjectives and nouns.

Table 1 shows the performance of the parsing-based approach versus the heuristic-based approach. The parser-based approach suffers mainly because the NPs that it extracts tend to be on the long side, resulting in recall errors when the boundaries of the parser-identified NPs mismatch with the human-annotated entities. In addition, the parser also tends to extract more NPs than needed, which results in a hit to precision.

4 Coreference Resolution

The final step after the mention detection phase is to determine which of the extracted phrases refer to the same entity, or are coreferent.

The small size of our corpus made it quite obvious that we would not be able to perform supervised learning, as there would not be enough data for generalization purposes. Therefore we chose to use an unsupervised clustering approach for this step. Clustering is a natural choice as it partitions the data into groups; used on coreference resolution, we expect to gather coreferrent NPs into the same cluster. Furthermore, most clustering methods can easily incorporate both context-dependent and independent constraints into their features.

4.1 Features

Our features use both lexical and syntactic information designed to capture both the content of the phrase and its role within the sentence. With the exception of the last three features, which are defined with respect to a noun phrase pair, all our features describe various aspects of a single noun phrase:

Lexical String – This is just simply the string of words in the phrase.

Head Noun – The head noun in a phrase is the noun that is not a modifier for another noun.

Sentence Position – This measures the position of the phrase within the document.

Gender – For each phrase, we use a gazetteer to assign it a gender. The possible values are male (e.g. **先生**, *mister*), female (e.g. **小姐**, *miss*), either (e.g. **團長**, *leader*) and neither (e.g. **工廠**, *factory*).

Number – A phrase can be either singular (e.g. **一隻貓**, *one cat*), plural (e.g. **兩隻狗**, *two dogs*), either (e.g. **產品**, *product*) or neither (e.g. **安全**, *safety*).

	Recall	Precision	F-Measure
Heuristics	83	59.3	69.2
Parser-Based	62.7	28.7	39.4

Table 1: Mention Detection Results

Semantic Class – To give the system more information on each phrase, we generated our own gazetteer from a combination of gazetteers compiled from web sources and heuristics. Our gazetteer consists of 4700 entries, each of which is labeled with one of the following semantic classes: person, organization, location, facility, GPE, date, money, vehicle and weapon. Phrases in the corpus that are found in the gazetteer are given the same semantic class label; phrases not in the gazetteer are marked as UNKNOWN.

Proper Name – The part-of-speech tag "NR" and a list of common proper names were used to label each noun phrase as to whether it is a proper name (values: true/false).

Pronoun – Determined by the part-of-speech "PN". Values: true/false.

Demonstrative Noun Phrase – A demonstrative noun phrase is a phrase that consists of a noun phrases preceded by one of the characters [這那該] (*this/that/some*).

Appositive – Two noun phrases are in apposition when the first phrase is headed by a common noun while the second one is a proper name with no space or punctuation between them. e.g. [美國總統][克林頓]上星期到朝鮮訪問。(*[US president] [Clinton] visited Pyongyang last week.*) This differs from English where two nouns are considered to be in apposition when one of them is an anaphor and separated by a comma from the other phrase, which is the most immediate proper name. (e.g. "Bill Gates, the chairman of Microsoft Corp")

Abbreviation – A noun phrase is an abbreviation when it is formed by using part of another noun phrase, e.g. 朝鮮中央通訊社 (*Pyongyang Central Communications Office*) is commonly abbreviated as 朝中社. Since name abbreviations in Chinese are often given in an ad-hoc manner, it would be infeasible to generate a list of nam and abbreviations in advance. We therefore use the following heuristic: given two phrases, we test if one is an abbreviation of another by extracting each successive character from the shorter phrase and testing to see if it is included in the corresponding word from the longer phrase. Intuitively, we know that this is a common way of abbreviating terms; empirically, it usually gives us a correct result.

Edit Distance – Abbreviations and nicknames

Feature *f*	**Function**
Noun Phrase Match	-1 if the string of NP_i matches the string of NP_j; else 0
Head Noun Match	-1 if head noun of NP_i matches the head noun of NP_j; else 0
Sentence Distance	0 if NP_i and NP_j are in the same sentence; For non-pronouns: 1/10 if they are one sentence apart; and so on with maximum value 1; For pronouns: if more than two sentences apart, then 1
Gender Agreement	1 if they do not match in gender; else 0
Number Agreement	1 if they do not match in number; else 0
Semantic Agreement	1 if they do not match in semantic class or unknown; else 0
Proper Name Agreement	1 if both are proper names, but mismatch on every word; else 0
Pronoun Agreement	1 if either NP_i or NP_j is pronoun and mismatch in gender or number; else 0
Demonstrative Noun Phrase	-1 if NP_i is demonstrative and NP_i contains NP_j; else 0
Appositive	-1 if NP_i and NP_j are in an appositive relationship; else 0
Abbreviation	-1 if NP_i and NP_j are in an abbreviative relationship; else 0
Edit Distance	0 if NP_i and NP_j are the same, 1/(length of longer string) if one edit is needed to transform one to another, and so on.

Table 2: Features and functions used in clustering algorithm

are very commonly used in Chinese and even though the previous feature will work on most of them, there are some common exceptions. To make sure that we catch those as well, we introduced a Chinese-specific feature as a further test. Since abbreviations and nicknames are not usually substrings of the original strings, but will still share some common characters, we measure the Levenshtein distance, defined as the number of character insertions, deletions and substitutions, between every potential antecedent-anaphor pair.

4.2 Distance Metric

In order for the clustering algorithm to be able to group instances together by similarity, we need to determine a distance metric between two instances – in our case, two noun phrases. For our system, we borrowed a simple distance metric from Cardie and Wagstaff (1999) that sums up the results of a series of functions over the two phrases:

$$dist(NP_i, NP_j) = \sum_{f \in F} function_f(NP_i, NP_j)$$

Table 2 presents the features and the corresponding functions that were used in our system. Each function calculates a distance between the two phrases that is an indicator of the degree of incompatibility between the two phrases with respect to a particular feature. The NOUN PHRASE, HEAD NOUN, DEMONSTRATIVE, APPOSITIVE and ABBREVIATIVE functions test for compatibility and return a negative value when the two phrases are compatible for that term's feature. The reason for the negative value returned is that if the two phrases match on this particular feature, then it is a strong indicator of coreference. Therefore, we reduce the distance between two phrases, making it more likely that they will be clustered together into the same entity. When there is a mismatch, however, it does not necessarily indicate that the two NPs are non-coreferential, so we leave the distance between the NPs unchanged.

Conversely, there are some features where a mismatch would indicate that the two NPs are absolutely non-compatible and will definitely not refer to the same entity. The DISTANCE, GENDER, NUMBER, SEMANTIC, PROPER NAME, PRONOUN and EDIT_DISTANCE functions return a positive value when the two phrases mismatch on that particular feature. A positive value results in a greater distance between two phrases, which makes it less likely for them to be clustered together.

4.3 Clustering Algorithm

Most of the previous work in clustering-based noun phrase coreference resolution has centered around the use of bottom-up clustering methods, where each noun phrase is initially assigned to a singleton cluster by itself, and clusters which are "close enough" to each other are merged (Cardie & Wagstaff, 1999; Angheluta et al., 2004).

In our system, we use a method called modified k-means clustering (Wilpon & Rabiner 1985), which takes the opposite approach and uses a top-down approach to split clusters, interleaved with a k-means iterative phase. Modified k-means clustering has been successfully applied to speech recognition and it has the advantage of always being able to come to the optimal clustering (i.e. it is not dependent upon the starting state or merging order).

Modified k-means starts off with all the instances in one big cluster. The system then iteratively performs the following steps:

1. For each cluster, find its centroid, defined as the instance which is the closest to all other instances in the same cluster.
2. For each instance:
    a. Calculate its distance to all the centroids.
    b. Find the centroid with the minimum distance, and join its cluster.
3. Iterate 1-2 until instances stop moving between clusters.
4. Find the cluster with the largest intra-cluster distance. (Call this $Cluster_{max}$ and its centroid, $Centroid_{max}$.) If this distance is smaller than some threshold r, stop.
5. From the instances inside $Cluster_{max}$, find the pair that are the furthest apart from each other.
    a. Add the pair of instances to the list of centroids and remove $Centroid_{max}$ from the list.
    b. Repeat from Step 2.

The algorithm thus alternates traditional k-means clustering with a step that adds new clusters to the pool of existing ones. Used for coreference resolution, it splits up the instances into clusters in which the instances are more similar to each other than to instances in other clusters.

The only thing left to do is to determine a suitable threshold. As functions that check for compatibility return negative values while positive distances indicate incompatibility, a threshold of 0 would separate compatible and incompatible

	Recall	Precision	F-Measure
Gold Standard Entities	78	88.5	82.9
Baseline (Heuristic-based Entities)	80.9	44.1	57.1
Baseline (Noun Phrase Match Only)	50.9	77.2	61.3
Heuristic-Based Entity Recognition	62.9	77.1	69.3
Parsing-Based Entity Recognition	42.5	62.9	50.7

Table 3: Coreference Resolution Performance

elements. However, since the feature extraction will not be totally accurate, (especially for the GENDER and NUMBER features which test for incompatibility) we chose to be more lenient with deciding whether two phrases should be clustered together, and used a threshold of $r = 1$ to allow for possible errors.

5 Evaluation

Evaluation of coreference resolution systems has traditionally been performed with precision and recall. The MUC competition defines recall as follows (Vilain et al., 1995):

$$R = \frac{\sum(|C_i| - |p(C_i)|)}{\sum(|C_i| - 1)}$$

Each C_i is a gold standard cluster (i.e. a set of phrases which we know refer to the same entity), and $p(C_i)$ is the partitioning of C_i by the automatically-generated clusters. For precision, the role of the automatic and gold standard clusters are reversed. Our results were evaluated using the MUC scoring program which reports recall, precision and F-measure, where the F-measure is defined as the harmonic mean of precision and recall:

$$F = \frac{2PR}{P + R}$$

Table 3 presents the results of our coreference resolution system on the outputs of both the parsing-based and heuristic-based entity detection systems, as measured by the MUC-7 scoring program. For the purposes of comparison, we also present results of our clustering algorithm on the gold standard entities. This gives us a sense of the upper bound that we could potentially achieve if we got 100% accuracy on our mention detection phase. An additional baseline is generated by implementing a system that assumes that all phrases refer to the same entity – i.e. it takes all the heuristically-generated phrases and puts them into one big cluster. This gives us an upper bound on the recall of the system. Yet another baseline, to see how easy the task is, is to merge mentions together if the "Noun Phrase Match" function tests true.

From the results, it can be seen that our system achieves a performance gain of over 10 F-Measure points over the simplest baseline, and over 8 F-Measure points over the more sophisticated baseline. Unfortunately, due to corpus differences, we cannot conduct a comparison with results found in previous work.

An interesting observation is the fact that the heuristic-based entity recognizer achieves better performance than the one based on statistical parsing. The parser is trained on the Chinese Penn Treebank, which tends to have relatively longer noun phrases, and as result, the phrases generated by the parser also tend to be on the long side. This causes errors at the entity recognition phase, which results in a performance hit for the overall system.

6 Analysis

One interesting question to ask about the results is the contribution of any given individual feature to the result of the overall system. We have already investigated the effect of entity recognition, and in this section, we take a look at the features for the clustering algorithm. **Error! Reference source not found.** presents the results of a series of experiments in which one feature at a time was removed from the clustering algorithm. The last entry in the table shows the results of the full system; the drop in performance when a feature is removed is indicative of its contribution. Judging from the results, the 3 features that contribute the most to performance are the NOUN PHRASE MATCH, SEMANTIC AGREEMENT and EDIT DISTANCE features. Two out of the three, NOUN PHRASE and EDIT DISTANCE, operate on lexical information. The importance of string matching to coreference resolution is consistent with findings in previous work (Yang et al. 2004), which arrived at the same conclusion for English.

In addition, we note that the two Chinese-specific features that were introduced, ABBREVIATION and EDIT DISTANCE, both contribute significantly (as measured by a student's t-test) to the performance of the final system.

Removed feature	Recall	Precision	F-measure
Noun Phrase Match	**59.8**	**75.9**	**66.9**
Head Noun Match	60.4	76.2	67.4
Sentence Distance	63.2	73.3	67.8
Gender Agreement	62.9	76.3	68.9
Number Agreement	63.2	75.9	69
Semantic Agreement	**60.5**	**73**	**66.2**
Proper Name Agreement	63	76.2	69
Pronoun Agreement	61.3	76.9	68.2
Demonstrative Noun Phrase	62.2	77.9	69.2
Appositive	60.1	76.9	67.5
Abbreviation	61.6	77	68.4
Edit Distance	**62.4**	**72.8**	**67.2**
None (All Features)	62.9	77.1	69.3

Table 4: Contribution of individual features to overall performance.

Of our features, those that contribute the least to the overall performance are the GENDER, NUMBER and DEMONSTRATIVE NOUN PHRASE features. For DEMONSTRATIVE NOUN PHRASE, the reason is because of data sparsity – there are just simply not enough examples that it would make any significant impact. For the GENDER and NUMBER features, we find that the problem is mostly with errors in feature generation.

To our knowledge, this is the first published result on unsupervised Chinese coreference resolution. Due to differences in data, it is not possible to conduct a comparison of our work with previous results.

7 Related Work

Coreference resolution has attracted much attention in recent years, especially as a result of the MUC and ACE competitions. The approaches taken have exhibited a shift from knowledge-based approaches to learning-based approaches. Many of the learning-based approaches recast coreference resolution as a binary classification task, which, given a pair of NPs, uses a trained classifier to determine whether they are coreferent. Soon et al. (2001) used this approach with a 12-feature decision tree-based classifier and Ng and Cardie (2002) extended this approach with extra machine learning frameworks and a larger set of features. Yang et al. (2004) extended this approach into an NP-cluster based approach, which considers the relationships between phrases and coreferential clusters.

In addition, several unsupervised approaches have been proposed. Cardie and Wagstaff (1999) re-cast the problem as a clustering task which applied a set of incompatibility functions and weights in the distance metric. Bean and Riloff (2004) used information extraction patterns to identify contextual clues that would determine the compatibility between NPs.

All of the previously mentioned work has been for English. There has been relatively little work in Chinese: Florian et al. (2004) provides results using a language-independent framework on the Entity Detection and Tracking task (EDT). They formulate the detection subtask as a classification problem using a Robust Risk Minimization classifier combined with a Maximum Entropy classifier. Their system performs significantly well on English, Chinese and Arabic, however, the system suffers from small amount of training data (90K characters for Chinese, in contrast with 340K words for English). Their system obtained an ACE value of 58.8 on the ACE evaluation data on Chinese. Finally, Zhou et al. (2005) proposed a unified Transformation-Based Learning framework on Chinese EDT. The TBL tracking model looks at pairs of NPs at a time and classifies them as being coreferent or not based on the values of six features. They report an ACE score of 63.3 on their dataset.

8 Conclusions and Future Work

In this paper, we have presented an unsupervised approach to Chinese coreference resolution. Our approach performs resolution by clustering, with the advantage that no annotated training data is needed. We evaluated our approach using a corpus which we developed using standard annotation schemes, and find that our system achieves an error reduction rate of almost 30% over the baseline. We also analyze the performance of our system by investigating the contribution of individual features to our system. The analysis illustrates the contribution of the new language-specific features.

While the results produced by our system are impressive, it should be noted that all our features consider only the mention phrase itself. We consider this to be a rather simplistic and incomplete. In future work, we plan to investigate the use of more sophisticated features, including contextual features, to improve the performance of our system.

References

ANGHELUTA R., JEUNIAUX P., RUDRADEB M., MOENS M.F. 2004. Clustering Algorithms for Noun Phrase Coreference Resolution. *Proceedings of the 7th International Conference on the Statistical Analysis of Textual Data.*

BEAN, D. and RILOFF, E. 2004. Unsupervised learning of contextual role knowledge for coreference resolution. In *Proc. of HLT/NAACL*, pages 297–304.

BIKEL, D. M. 2004. A Distributional Analysis of a Lexicalized Statistical Parsing Model. In *Proceedings of EMNLP*, Barcelona

CARDIE, C. and WAGSTAFF, K. 1999. Noun phrase coreference as clustering. In *Proceedings of the 1999 Joint SIGDAT Conference on Empirical Methods in Natural Language Processing and Very Large Corpora*, pages 82-89.

FLORIAN, R., HASSAN, H., ITTYCHERIAH, A., JING, H., KAMBHATLA, N., LUO, X., NICOLOV, N., and ROUKOS, S. 2004. Statistical Model for Multilingual Entity Detection and Tracking. In *Proceedings of 2004 annual meeting of the North American Chapter of the Association for Computational Linguistics (HLT-NAACL 2004).*

FUNG, P., NGAI, G., YANG, Y. S., and CHEN, B.F. 2004. A maximum-entropy Chinese parser augmented by Transformation-Based Learning. *ACM Transactions on Asian Language Information Processing (TALIP)*, 3(2), pp 159-168.

GAO J.F., LI M. and HUANG C.N. 2003. Improved souce-channel model for Chinese wordsegmentation. In *Proc. of ACL2003.*

HARABAGIU, S., BUNESCU, R.,and MAIORANO, S. 2001. Text and Knowledge Mining for Coreference Resolution, in *Proceedings of the 2nd Meeting of the North American Chapter of the Association of Computational Linguistics (NAACL-2001).*

HIRSCHMAN, L. and CHINCHOR, N. 1997. MUC7 Coreference Task Definition, http://www.itl.nist.gov/iaui/894.02/related_projects/muc/proceedings/co_task.html.

LANCASHIRE, D. 2005. Adsotrans Chinese-English annotation. http://www.adsotrans.com/.

LDC. 2004. Chinese Annotation Guidelines for Entity Detection and Tracking. http://www.ldc.upenn.edu/Projects/ACE/Data.

MUC-7. 1998. *Proceedings of the Seventh Message Understanding Conference (MUC-7).* Morgan Kaufmann, San Francisco, CA.

NG V. 2005. Machine learning for coreference resolution: From local classification to global ranking. *In Proceedings of the 43rd Annual Meeting of the Association for Computational Linguistics (ACL), 2005.*

NG, V. and CARDIE, C. 2002. Improving machine learning approaches to coreference resolution. In *Proceedings of the 40rd Annual Meeting of the Association for Computational Linguistics,* Pages 104-111.

NG V. and CARDIE C. 2003. Bootstrapping Coreference Classifiers with Multiple Machine Learning Algorithms. *Proceedings of the 2003 Conference on Empirical Methods in Natural Language Processing (EMNLP-2003), Association for Computational Linguistics, 2003.*

SOON, W., NG, H., and LIM, D. 2001. A machine learning approach to coreference resolution of noun phrases. *Computational Linguistics*, 27(4):521-544.

VILAIN, M., BURGER, J., ABERDEEN, J., CONNOLLY, D., and HIRSCHMAN, L. 1995. A model-theoretic coreference scoring scheme. In *Proceedings of the Sixth Message Understanding Conference (MUC-6)*, pages 45–52, San Francisco, CA. Morgan Kaufmann.

WILPON, J., AND RABINER, L. 1985. A modified K-means clustering algorithm for use in isolated word recognition. In *IEEE Transactions on Acoustics, Speech, Signal Processing*. ASSP-33(3), 587-594.

YANG, X., ZHOU, G., SU, J., and TAN, C. L. 2004. An NP-Cluster Based Approach to Coreference Resolution. *Proceedings of the 20th International Conference on Computational Linguistics (COLING2004).*

ZHOU Y., HUANG C., GAO J., WU L. 2005. Transformation Based Chinese Entity Detection and Tracking. *Proceedings of the Second International Joint Conference on Natural Language Processing.*

Latent Features in Automatic Tense Translation between Chinese and English

Yang Ye[†], **Victoria Li Fossum**[§], **Steven Abney** [† §]
[†] Department of Linguistics
[§] Department of Electrical Engineering and Computer Science
University of Michigan

Abstract

On the task of determining the tense to use when translating a Chinese verb into English, current systems do not perform as well as human translators. The main focus of the present paper is to identify features that human translators use, but which are not currently automatically extractable. The goal is twofold: to test a particular hypothesis about what additional information human translators might be using, and as a pilot to determine where to focus effort on developing automatic extraction methods for features that are somewhat beyond the reach of current feature extraction. The paper shows that incorporating several latent features into the tense classifier boosts the tense classifier's performance, and a tense classifier using only the latent features outperforms one using only the surface features. Our findings confirm the utility of the latent features in automatic tense classification, explaining the gap between automatic classification systems and the human brain.

1 Introduction

Language speakers make two types of distinctions about temporal relations: the first type of relation is based on precedence between events and can be expanded into a finer grained taxonomy as proposed by (Allen, 1981). The second type of relation is based on the relative positioning between the following three time parameters proposed by (Reichenbach, 1947): speech time (S), event time (E) and reference time (R). In the past couple of decades, the NLP community has seen an emergent interest in the first type of temporal relation. In the cross-lingual context, while the first type of relationship can be easily projected across a language pair, the second type of relationship is often hard to be projected across a language pair. In contrast to this challenge, cross-lingual temporal reference distinction has been poorly explored.

Languages vary in the granularity of their tense and aspect representations; some have finer-grained tenses or aspects than others. Tense generation and tense understanding in natural language texts are highly dynamic and context-dependent processes, since any previously established time point or interval, whether explicitly mentioned in the context or not, could potentially serve as the reference time for the event in question. (Bruce, 1972) captures this nature of temporal reference organization in discourse through a multiple temporal reference model. He defines a set (S_1, S_2, ..., S_n) that is an element of tense. S_1 corresponds to the speech time, S_n is the event time, and (S_i, i=2, ..., n-1) stand for a sequence of time references from which the reference time of a particular event could come. Given the elusive nature of reference time shift, it is extremely hard to model the reference time point directly in temporal information processing. The above reasons motivate classifying temporal reference distinction automatically, using machine learning algorithms such as Conditional Random Fields (CRFs).

Many researchers in Natural Language Processing seem to believe that an automatic system does not have to follow the mechanism of human brain in order to optimize its performance, for example, the feature space for an automatic classification system does not have to replicate the knowledge sources that human beings utilize. There has been very little research that pursues to testify this faith.

The current work attempts to identify which features are most important for tense generation in Chinese to English translation scenario, which can point to direction of future research effort for automatic tense translation between Chinese and English.

The remaining part of the paper is organized as follows: Section 2 summarizes the significant related works in temporal information annotation and points out how this study relates to yet differs from them. Section 3 formally defines the problem, tense taxonomy and introduces the data. Section 4 discusses the feature space and proposes the latent features for the tense classification task. Section 5 presents the classification experiments in Conditional Random Fields as well as Classification Tree and reports the evaluation results. Section 6 concludes the paper and section 7 points out directions for future research.

2 Related Work

There is an extensive literature on temporal information processing. (Mani, et al., 2005) provides a survey of works in this area. Here, we highlight several works that are closely related to Chinese temporal information processing. (Li, 2001) describes a model of mining and organizing temporal relations embedded in Chinese sentences, in which a set of heuristic rules are developed to map linguistic patterns to temporal relations based on Allen's thirteen relations. Their work shows promising results via combining machine learning techniques and linguistic features for successful temporal relation classification, but their work is concerned with another type of temporal relationship, namely, the precedence-based temporal relation between a pair of events explicitly mentioned in text.

A significant work worth mentioning is (Olsen et. al. 2001)'s paper, where the authors examine the determination of tense for English verbs in Chinese-to-English translation. In addition to the surface features such as the presence of aspect markers and certain adverbials, their work makes use of the telicity information encoded in the lexicons through the use of Lexical Conceptual Structures (LCS). Based on the dichotomy of grammatical aspect and lexical aspect, they propose that past tense corresponds to the telic (either inherently or derived) LCS. They propose a heuristic algorithm in which grammatical aspect markings supersede the LCS, and in the absence of grammatical aspect marking, verbs that have telic LCS are translated into past tense and present tense otherwise. They report a significant performance improvement in tense resolution from adding a verb telicity feature. They also achieve better performance than the baseline system using the telicity feature alone. This work, while alerting researchers to the importance of lexical aspectual feature in determination of tense for English verbs in Chinese-to-English machine translation, is subject to the risk of adopting a one-to-one mapping between grammatical aspect markings and tenses hence oversimplifies the temporal reference problem in Chinese text. Additionally, their binary tense taxonomy is too coarse for the rich temporal reference system in Chinese.

(Ye, et al. 2005) reported a tense tagging case study of training Conditional Random Fields on a set of shallow surface features. The low inter-annotator agreement rate reported in the paper illustrates the difficulty of tense tagging. Nevertheless, the corpora size utilized is too small with only 52 news articles and none of the latent features was explored, so the evaluation result reported in the paper leaves room for improvement.

3 Problem Definition

3.1 Problem Formulation

The problem we are interested in can be formalized as a standard classification or labeling problem, in which we try to learn a classifier

$$C : V \to T \tag{1}$$

where V is a set of verbs (each described by a feature vector), and T is the set of possible tense tags.

Tense and aspect are morphologically merged in English and coarsely defined, there can be twelve combinations of the simple tripartite tenses (present, past and future) with the progressive and perfect grammatical aspects. For our classification experiments, in order to combat sparseness, we ignore the aspects and only deal with the three simple tenses: present, past and future.

3.2 Data

We use 152 pairs of parallel Chinese-English articles from LDC release. The Chinese articles come from two news sources: Xinhua News Service and Zaobao News Service, consisting of 59882 Chinese characters in total with roughly 350 characters per article. The English parallel articles are from Multiple-Translation Chinese (MTC) Corpus from LDC with catalog number LDC2002T01. We chose to use the best human translation out of 9 translation teams as our gold-standard parallel English data. The verb tenses are obtained through manual alignment between the Chinese source articles and the English translations. In order to avoid the noise brought by errors and be focused on the central question we try to answer in the paper, we did not use automatic tools such as GIZA++ to obtain the verb alignments, which typically comes with significant amount of errors. We ignore Chinese verbs that are not translated into English as verbs because of "nominalization" (by which verbal expressions in Chinese are translated into nominal phrases in English). This exclusion is based on the rationale that another choice of syntactic structure might retain the verbal status in the target English sentence, but the tense of those potential English verbs would be left to the joint decision of a set of disparate features. Those tenses are unknown in our training data. This preprocessing yields us a total of 2500 verb tokens in our data set.

4 Feature Space

4.1 Surface Features

There are many heterogeneous features that contribute to the process of tense generation for Chinese verbs in the cross-lingual situation. Tenses in English, while manifesting a distinction in temporal reference, do not always reflect this distinction at the semantic level, as is shown in the sentence "I will leave when he comes." (Hornstein, 1990) accounts for this phenomenon by proposing the Constraints on Derived Tense Structures. Therefore, the feature space we use includes the features that contribute to the semantic level temporal reference construction as well as those contributing to tense generation from that semantic level. The following is a list of the surface features that are directly extractable from the training data:

1. Feature 1: Whether the verb is in quoted speech or not.
2. Feature 2: The syntactic structure in which the current verb is embedded. Possible structures include sentential complements, relative clauses, adverbial clauses, appositive clauses, and null embedding structure.
3. Feature 3: Which of the following signal adverbs occur between the current verb and the previous verb: yi3jing1(already), ceng2jing1(once), jiang1(future tense marker), zheng4zai4(progressive aspect marker), yi4zhi2(have always been).
4. Feature 4: Which of the following aspect markers occur between the current verb and the subsequent verb: le0, zhe0, guo4.
5. Feature 5: The distance in characters between the current verb and the previously tagged verb (We descretize the continuous distance into three ranges: $0 < distance < 5$, $5 \leq distance < 10$, or $10 \leq distance < \infty$).
6. Feature 6: Whether the current verb is in the same clause as the previous verb.

Feature 1 and feature 2 are used to capture the discrepancy between semantic tense and syntactic tense. Feature 3 and feature 4 are clues or triggers of certain aspectual properties of the verbs. Feature 5 and feature 6 try to capture the dependency between tenses of adjacent verbs.

4.2 Latent Features

The bottleneck in Artificial Intelligence is the unbalanced knowledge sources shared by human beings and a computer system. Only a subset of the knowledge sources used by human beings can be formalized, extracted and fed into a computer system. The rest are less accessible and are very hard to be shared with a computer system. Despite their importance in human language processing, latent features have received little attention in feature space exploration in most NLP tasks because they are impractical to extract. Although there have not yet been rigorous psycholinguistic studies demonstrating the extent to which the above knowledge types are used in human temporal relation processing, we hypothesize that they are very significant in assisting human's temporal relation decision. Nevertheless, a quantitative assessment of the utility of the latent features in NLP tasks has yet to be explored. (Olsen, et al., 2001) illustrates the value of latent features by showing how the telicity feature alone can help with tense resolution in Chinese to English machine translation. Given the prevalence of latent features in human language processing, in order to emulate human beings performance of the disambiguation, it is crucial to experiment with the latent features in automatic tense classification.

(Pustejovsky, 2004) discusses the four basic problems in event-temporal identification:

他***说***，河南省不仅***具有***外商投资所需的硬件，而且还根据国家政策、结合本省实际***制定***了优惠政策。

He ***said*** that Henan Province not only ***possesses*** the hardwares necessary for foreign investment, but also has, on the basis of the State policies and Henan's specific conditions, ***formulated*** its own preferential policies.

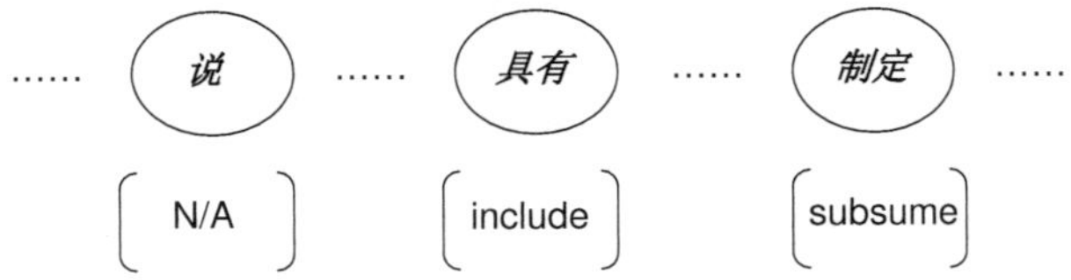

Figure 1: Temporal Relations between Adjacent Events

1. Time-stamping of events (identifying an event and anchoring it in time)

2. Ordering events with respect to one another

3. Reasoning with contextually under-specified temporal expressions

4. Reasoning about the persistence of events (how long does an event or the outcome of an event last?)

While time-stamping of the events and reasoning with contextually under-specified temporal expressions might be too informative to be features in tense classification, information concerning orderings between events and persistence of events are relatively easier to be encoded as features in a tense classification task. Therefore, we experiment with these two latent knowledge sources, both of which are heavily utilized by human beings in tense resolution.

4.3 Telicity and Punctuality Features

Following (Vendler, 1947), temporal information encoded in verbs is largely captured by some innate properties of verbs, of which telicity and punctuality are two very important ones. Telicity specifies a verb's ability to be bound in a certain time span, while punctuality specifies whether or not a verb is associated with a point event in time. Telicity and punctuality prepare verbs to be assigned different tenses when they enter the context in the discourse. While it is true that isolated verbs are typically associated with certain telicity and punctuality features, such features are contextually volatile. In reaction to the volatility exhibited in verb telicity and punctuality features, we propose that verb telicity and punctuality features should be evaluated only at the clausal or sentential level for the tense classification task. We manually obtained these two features for both the English and the Chinese verbs. All verbs in our data set were manually tagged as "telic" or "atelic", and "punctual" or "apunctual", according to context.

4.4 Temporal Ordering Feature

(Allen, 1981) defines thirteen relations that could possibly hold between any pair of situations. We experiment with six temporal relations which we think represent the most typical temporal relationships between two events. We did not adopt all of the thirteen temporal relationships proposed by Allen for the reason that some of them would require excessive deliberation from the annotators and hard to implement. The six relationships we explore are as follows:

1. event A precedes event B

2. event A succeeds event B

3. event A includes event B

4. event A subsumes event B

5. event A overlaps with event B

6. no temporal relations between event A and event B

For each Chinese verb in the source Chinese texts, we annotate the temporal relation between the verb and the previously tagged verb as belonging to one of the above classes. The annotation of the temporal relation classes mimics a deeper semantic analysis of the Chinese source text. Figure 1 illustrates a sentence in which each verb is tagged by the temporal relation class that holds between it and the previous verb.

5 Experiments and Evaluation

5.1 CRF learning algorithms

Conditional Random Fields (CRFs) are a formalism well-suited for learning and prediction on sequential data in many NLP tasks. It is a probabilistic framework proposed by (Lafferty et al., 2001) for labeling and segmenting structured data, such as sequences, trees and lattices. The conditional nature of CRFs relaxes the independence assumptions required by traditional Hidden Markov Models (HMMs). This is because the conditional model makes it unnecessary to explicitly represent and model the dependencies among the input variables, thus making it feasible to use interacting and global features from the input. CRFs also avoid the label bias problem exhibited by maximum entropy Markov models (MEMMs) and other conditional Markov models based on directed graphical models. CRFs have been shown to perform well on a number of NLP problems such as shallow parsing (Sha and Pereira, 2003), table extraction (Pinto et al., 2003), and named entity recognition (McCallum and Li, 2003). For our experiments, we use the MALLET implementation of CRF's (McCallum, 2002).

5.2 Experiments

5.2.1 Human Inter-Annotator Agreement

All supervised learning algorithms require a certain amount of training data, and the reliability of the computational solutions is intricately tied to the accuracy of the annotated data. Human annotations typically suffer from errors, subjectivity, and the expertise effect. Therefore, researchers use consistency checking to validate human annotation experiments. The Kappa Statistic (Cohen, 1960) is a standard measurement of inter-annotator agreement for categorical data annotation. The Kappa score is defined by the following formula, where P(A) is the observed agreement rate from multiple annotators and P(E) is the expected rate of agreement due to pure chance:

$$k = \frac{P(A) - P(E)}{1 - P(E)} \quad (2)$$

Since tense annotation requires disambiguating grammatical meaning, which is more abstract than lexical meaning, one would expect the challenge posed by human annotators in a tense annotation experiment to be even greater than for word sense disambiguation. Nevertheless, the tense annotation experiment carried as a precursor to our tense classification task showed a kappa Statistic of 0.723 on the full taxonomy, with an observed agreement of 0.798. In those experiments, we asked three bilingual English native speakers who are fluent in Chinese to annotate the English verb tenses for the first 25 Chinese and English parallel news articles from our training data.

We could also obtain a measurement of reliability by taking one annotator as the gold standard at one time, then averaging over the precisions of the different annotators across different gold standards. While it is true that numerically, precision would be higher than Kappa score and seems to be inflating Kappa score, we argue that the difference between Kappa score and precision is not limited to one measure being more aggressive than the other. Rather, the policies of these two measurements are different. The Kappa score cares purely about agreement without any consideration of trueness or falseness, while the procedure we described above gives equal weight to each annotator being the gold standard, and therefore considers both agreement and truthness of the annotation. The advantage of the precision-based agreement measurement is that it makes comparison of the system performance accuracy to the human performance accuracy more direct. The precision under such a scheme for the three annotators is 80% on the full tense taxonomy.

5.2.2 CRF Learning Experiments

We train a tense classifier on our data set in two stages: first on the surface features, and then on the combined space of both surface features (discussed in 4.1) and latent features (discussed in 4.2-4.4). It is conceivable that the granularity of sequences may matter in learning from data with sequential relationship, and in the context of verb tense tagging, it naturally maps to the granularity of discourse. (Ye, et al., 2005) shows that there is no significant difference between sentence-level sequences and paragraph-level sequences. Therefore, we experiment with only sentence-level sequences.

5.2.3 Classification Tree Learning Experiments

To verify the stability of the utility of the latent features, we also experiment with classification tree learning on the same features space as

Tense	Precision	Recall	F
Present tense	0.662	0.661	0.627
Past tense	0.882	0.915	0.896
Future tense	0.758	0.487	0.572

Table 1: Evaluation Results for CRFs Classifier in Precision, Recall and F Using All Features

	Surface Features	Latent Features	Surface and Latent Features
Accuracy for Training Data	79.3%	82.9%	85.9%

Table 2: Apparent Accuracy for the Training Data of the Classification Tree Classifiers

discussed above. Classification Trees are used to predict membership of cases or objects in the classes of a categorical dependent variable from their measurements on one or more predictor variables. The main idea of Classification Tree is to do a recursive partitioning of the variable space to achieve good separation of the classes in the training dataset. We use the Recursive Partitioning and Regression Trees(Rpart) package provided by R statistical computing software for the implementation of classification trees. In order to avoid over-fitting, we prune the tree by setting the minimum number of objects in a node to attempt a split and the minimum number of objects in any terminal node to be 10 and 3 respectively. In the constructed classification tree when we use all features including both surface and latent features, the top split at the root node in the tree is based on telicity feature of the English verb, indicating the importance of telicity feature for English verb among all of the features.

5.3 Evaluation Results

All results are obtained by 5-fold cross validation. The classifier's performance is evaluated against the tenses from the best-ranked human-generated English translation. To evaluate the performance of the CRFs tense classifier, we compute the precision, recall, general accuracy and F, which are defined as follow.

$$Accuracy = \frac{n_{prediction}}{N_{prediction}} \tag{3}$$

$$Recall = \frac{n_{hit}}{S} \tag{4}$$

$$Precision = \frac{n_{hit}}{N_{hit}} \tag{5}$$

$$F = \frac{2 \times Precision \times Recall}{Precision + Recall} \tag{6}$$

where

1. $N_{prediction}$: Total number of predictions;
2. $n_{prediction}$: Number of correct predictions;
3. N_{hit}: Total number of hits;
4. n_{hit}: Number of correct hits;
5. S: Size of perfect hitlist;

From Table 1, we see that past tense, which occurs most frequently in the training data, has the highest precision, recall and F. Future tense, which occurs least frequently, has the lowest F. Precision and recall do not show clear pattern across different tense classes.

Table 2 presents the apparent classification accuracies for the training data, we see that latent features still outperform the surface features. Table 3 summarizes the general accuracies of the tense classification systems for CRFs and Classification Trees. The CRFs classifier and the Classification Tree classifier demonstrate similar scales of improvement from surface features, latent features to both surface and latent features.

Methodology	Surface Features	Latent Features	Surface and Latent Features
CRFs	75.8%	80%	83.4%
Classification Tree	74.1%	81%	84.5%

Table 3: Evaluations in General Accuracy

5.4 Baseline Systems

To better evaluate our tense classifiers, we provide two baseline systems here. The first baseline system is the tense resolution from the best ranked machine translation system's translation results in the MTC corpus mentioned above. When evaluated against the reference tense tags from the best ranked human translation team, the best MT system yields a accuracy of 47%. The second baseline system is a naive system that assigns the most frequent tense in the training data set, which in our case is past tense, to all verbs in the test data set. Given the fact that we are deadling with newswire data, this baseline system yields a high baseline system with an accuracy of 69.5%.

6 Discussion and Conclusions

To the best of our knowledge, the current paper is the first work investigating the utility of latent features in the task of machine-learning based automatic tense classification. We significantly outperform the two baseline systems as well as the automatic tense classifier performance reported by (Ye, et al., 2005) by 15% in general accuracy. A crucial finding of our experiments is that utility of only three latent features, i.e. verb telicity, verb punctuality and temporal ordering between adjacent events, outperforms that of all the surface linguistic features we discussed earlier in the paper. While one might think that the lack of existing techonology of latent feature extraction would discount research effort on latent features' utilities, we believe that such efforts guide the research community to determine where to focus effort on developing automatic extraction methods for features that are beyond the reach of current technologies. Such research effort will also help to shed light on the enigmatic research question of whether automatic NLP systems should take effort to make use of the features employed by human beings to optimize the system performance and shorten the gap between the system and human brain. The results of the current paper point to the fact that bottleneck of cross-linguistic tense classification is acquisition and modeling of the more latent linguistic knowledge. To our surprise, CRF tense classifier performance is consistently tied with classification tree tense classifier performance in all of our experiments. One might expect that CRFs would accurately capture sequential dependencies among verbs. Reflecting upon the similar evaluation results of the CRFs classifier and the Classification Tree classifier, it is unlikely for this to be due to the over-fitting of the Classification Tree because of the pruning we did to the Classification Trees. Therefore, we speculate that the dependencies between the tense tags of verbs in the texts may not be strong enough for CRFs to outperform Classification Tree. This might also be contributable to the built-in variable selection procedures of Classification Trees, which makes it more robust to interacting and interdependent features. A confirmative explanation towards the equal performances between the CRFs and the Classification Tree classifiers requires more experiments with other machine learning algorithms.

In conclusion, this paper makes the following contributions:

1. It demonstrates that an accurate tense classifier can be constructed automatically by combining off-the-shelf machine learning techniques and inexpensive linguistic features.

2. It shows that latent features (such as verb telicity, verb punctuality and temporal ordering between adjacent events) have higher utility in tense classification than the surface linguistic features.

3. It reveals that the sequential dependency between tenses of adjacent verbs in the discourse may be rather weak.

7 Future Work

Temporal reference is a complicated semantic domain with rich connections among the disparate features. We investigate three latent features: telicity, punctuality, and temporal ordering between adjacent verbs. We summarize several interesting questions for future research in this section. First, besides the latent features we examined in the current paper, there are other interesting latent features to be investigated under the same theme, e.g. classes of temporal expression associated with the verbs and causal relationships among disparate events. Second, currently, the latent features are obtained through manual annotation by a single annotator. In an ideal situation, multiple annotators are desired to provide the reliability of the annotations as well as reduce the noise in annotations. Thirdly, it would be interesting to examine the utility of the same latent features for classification in the opposite direction, namely, aspect marker classification for Chinese verbs in the English-to-Chinese translation scenario. Finally, following our discussion of the degree of dependencies among verb tenses in the texts, it is desirable to study rigorously the dependencies among tenses and aspect markers for verbs in extensions of the current research.

References

James Allen. 1981. Towards a General Theory of Action and Time. Artificial Intelligence, 23(2): 123-160.

Hans Reichenbach. 1947. Elements of Symbolic Logic. Macmillan, New York, N.Y.

B. Bruce. 1972. A Model for Temporal Reference and its Application in a Question Answering System, Artificial Intelligence. Vol. 3, No. 1, 1-25.

Inderjeet Mani, James Pustejovsky and Robert Gaizauskas. 2005. The Language of Time, Oxford Press.

Wenjie Li, Kam-Fai Wong, Caogui Hong, Chunfa Yuan. 2004. Applying Machine Learning to Chinese Temporal Relation Resolution. Proceedings of the 42nd Annual Meeting of the Association for Computational Linguistics, 582-588.

Mari Olson, David Traum, Carol Van-ess Dykema, and Amy Weinberg. 2001. Implicit Cues for Explicit Generation: Using Telicity as a Cue for Tense Structure in a Chinese to English MT System. Proceedings Machine Translation Summit VIII, Santiago de Compostela, Spain.

Yang Ye, Zhu Zhang. 2005. Tense Tagging for Verbs in Cross-Lingual Context: a Case Study. Proceedings of IJCNLP 2005, 885-895

Norbert Hornstein. 1990. As Time Goes By: Tense and Universal Grammar. The MIT Press.

James Pustejovsky, Robert Ingria, Roser Sauri, Jose Castano, Jessica Littman, Rob Gaizauskas, Andrea Setzer, Graham Katz, and Inderjeet Mani. 2004. The Specification Language TimeML. The Language of Time: A Reader. Oxford, 185-96.

Zeno Vendler. 1967. Verbs and Times. Linguistics in Philosophy, 97-121.

Lafferty, J., McCallum, A. and Pereira, F. 2001. Conditional random fields: Probabilistic models for segmenting and labeling sequence data. In Proceedings of ICML-01, 282-289.

Sha, F. and Pereira, F. 2003. Shallow Parsing with Conditional Random Fields. Proceedings of the 2003 Human Language Technology Conference and North American Chapter of the Association for Computational Linguistics (HLT/NAACL-03)

Pinto, D., McCallum, A., Lee, X. and Croft, W. B. 2003. Table Extraction Using Conditional Random Fields. Proceedings of the 26th Annual International ACM SIGIR Conference on Research and Development in Information Retrieval (SIGIR 2003)

McCallum, A. and Li, W. 2003. Early Results for Named Entity Recognition with Conditional Random Fields, Feature Induction and Web-Enhanced Lexicons. Proceedings of the Seventh Conference on Natural Language Learning (CoNLL)

McCallum, A. K. 2002. MALLET: A Machine Learning for Language Toolkit, http://mallet.cs.umass.edu.

Jacob Cohen, 1960. A Coefficient of Agreement for Nominal Scales, Educational and Psychological Measurement, 20, 37-46.

Ross Ihaka and Robert Gentleman. 1996. R: A Language for Data Analysis and Graphics, Journal of Computational and Graphical Statistics, Vol. 5. 299?14.

Cluster-based Language Model for Sentence Retrieval in Chinese Question Answering

Youzheng Wu **Jun Zhao** **Bo Xu**
National Laboratory of Pattern Recognition
Institute of Automation Chinese Academy of Sciences
No.95 Zhongguancun East Road, 100080, Beijing, China
(yzwu, jzhao,boxu)@nlpr.ia.ac.cn

Abstract

Sentence retrieval plays a very important role in question answering system. In this paper, we present a novel cluster-based language model for sentence retrieval in Chinese question answering which is motivated in part by sentence clustering and language model. Sentence clustering is used to group sentences into clusters. Language model is used to properly represent sentences, which is combined with sentences model, cluster/topic model and collection model. For sentence clustering, we propose two approaches that are One-Sentence-Multi-Topics and One-Sentence-One-Topic respectively. From the experimental results on 807 Chinese testing questions, we can conclude that the proposed cluster-based language model outperforms over the standard language model for sentence retrieval in Chinese question answering.

1 Introduction

To facilitate the answer extraction of question answering, the task of retrieval module is to find the most relevant passages or sentences to the question. So, the retrieval module plays a very important role in question answering system, which influences both the performance and the speed of question answering. In this paper, we mainly focus on the research of improving the performance of sentence retrieval in Chinese question answering.

Many retrieval approaches have been proposed for sentence retrieval in English question answering. For example, Ittycheriach [Ittycheriah, et al. 2002] and H. Yang [Hui Yang, et al. 2002] proposed vector space model. Andres [Andres, et al. 2004] and Vanessa [Vanessa, et al. 2004] proposed language model and translation model respectively. Compared to vector space model, language model is theoretically attractive and a potentially very effective probabilistic framework for researching information retrieval problems [Jian-Yun Nie. 2005].

However, language model for sentence retrieval is not mature yet, which has a lot of difficult problems that cannot be solved at present. For example, how to incorporate the structural information, how to resolve data sparseness problem. In this paper, we mainly focus on the research of the smoothing approach of language model because sparseness problem is more serious for sentence retrieval than for document retrieval.

At present, the most popular smoothing approaches for language model are Jelinek-Mercer method, Bayesian smoothing using Dirichlet priors, absolute discounting and so on [C. Zhai, et al. 2001]. The main disadvantages of all these smoothing approaches are that each document model (which is estimated from each document) is interpolated with the same collection model (which is estimated from the whole collection) through a unified parameter. Therefore, it does not make any one particular document more probable than any other, on the condition that neither the documents originally contains the query term. In other word, if a document is relevant, but does not contain the query term, it is still no more probable, even though it may be topically related.

As we know, most smoothing approaches of sentence retrieval in question answering are learned from document retrieval without many adaptations. In fact, question answering has some characteristics that are different from traditional document retrieval, which could be used to improve the performance of sentence retrieval. These characteristics lie in:

1. The input of question answering is natural language question which is more unambiguous than query in traditional document retrieval.

For traditional document retrieval, it's difficult to identify which kind of information the users want to know. For example, if the user submit the query {发明/invent, 电话/telephone}, search engine does not know what information is needed, who invented telephone, when telephone was invented, or other information. On the other hand, for question answering system, if the user submit the question {谁发明了电话? /who invented the telephone?}, it's easy to know that the user want to know the person who invented the telephone, but not other information.

2. Candidate answers extracted according to the semantic category of the question's answer could be used for sentence clustering of question answering.

Although the first retrieved sentences are related to the question, they usually deal with one or more topics. That is, relevant sentences for a question may be distributed over several topics. Therefore, treating the question's words in retrieved sentences with different topics equally is unreasonable. One of the solutions is to organize the related sentences into several clusters, where a sentence can belong to about one or more clusters, each cluster is regarded as a topic. This is sentence clustering. Obviously, cluster and topic have the same meaning and can be replaced each other. ***In the other word, a particular entity type was expected for each question, and every special entity of that type found in a retrieved sentence was regarded as a cluster/topic.***

In this paper, we propose two novel approaches for sentence clustering. The main idea of the approaches is to conduct sentence clustering according to the candidate answers which are also considered as the names of the clusters.

For example, given the question {谁发明了电话? /who invented telephone?}, the top ten retrieved sentences and the corresponding candidate answers are shown as Table 1. Thus, we can conduct sentence clustering according to the candidate answers, that are, {贝尔/Bell, 西门子/Siemens, 爱迪生/Edison,库珀/Cooper, 斯蒂芬/Stephen}.

ID	Top 10 Sentences	Candidate Answer
S1	1876年3月10日贝尔发明电话/Bell invented telephone on Oct. 3th, 1876.	贝尔/Bell
S2	西门子发明了电机，贝尔发明电话，爱迪生发明电灯。/ Bell, Siemens and Edison invented telephone, electromotor and electric light respectively.	西门子/ Siemens 贝尔/Bell 爱迪生/ Edison
S3	最近，“移动电话之父”库珀再次成为公众焦点。/Recently, the public paid a great deal of attention to Cooper who is Father of Mobile Phone.	库珀/Cooper
S4	1876年，发明家贝尔发明了电话。/In 1876, Bell invented telephone.	贝尔/Bell
S5	接着，1876年，美国科学家贝尔发明了电话；1879年美国科学家爱迪生发明了电灯。/Subsequently, American scientist Bell invented the phone in 1876; Edison invented the electric light in 1879.	贝尔/Bell 爱迪生/Edison
S6	1876年3月7日，贝尔成为电话发明的专利人。/On March 7th, 1876, Bell became the patentee of telephone.	贝尔/Bell
S7	贝尔不仅发明了电话，还成功地建立了自己的公司推广电话。/Bell not only invented telephone, but also established his own company for spreading his invention.	贝尔/Bell
S8	在首只移动电话投入使用30年以后，其发明人库珀仍梦想着未来电话技术实现之日到来。/Thirty years after the invention of first mobile phone, Cooper still anticipated the date of the realization of future phone's technology.	库珀/Cooper

S9	库珀表示，消费者采纳移动电话的速度之快令他意外，但移动电话的普及率还没有达到无所不在，这让他有些失望。/Cooper said, he was surprised at the speed that the consumers switched to mobile phones; but the popularization of mobile phone isn't omnipresent, which made him a little bit disappointed.	库珀/Cooper
S10	英国发明家斯蒂芬将移动电话的所有电子元件设计在一张纸一样厚薄的芯片上。/England inventor Stephen designed the paper-clicked CMOS chip which included all electronic components.	斯蒂芬/Stephen

Table 1 The Top 10 Retrieved Sentences and its Candidate Answers

Based on the above analysis, this paper presents cluster-based language model for sentence retrieval of Chinese question answering. It differs from most of the previous approaches mainly as follows. 1. Sentence Clustering is conducted according to the candidate answers extracted from the top 1000 sentences. 2. The information of the cluster of the sentence, which is also called as topic, is incorporated into language model through aspect model. For sentence clustering, we propose two novel approaches that are One-Sentence-Multi-Topics and One-Sentence-One-Topic respectively. The experimental results show that the performances of cluster-based language model for sentence retrieval are improved significantly.

The framework of cluster-based language model for sentence retrieval is shown as Figure 1.

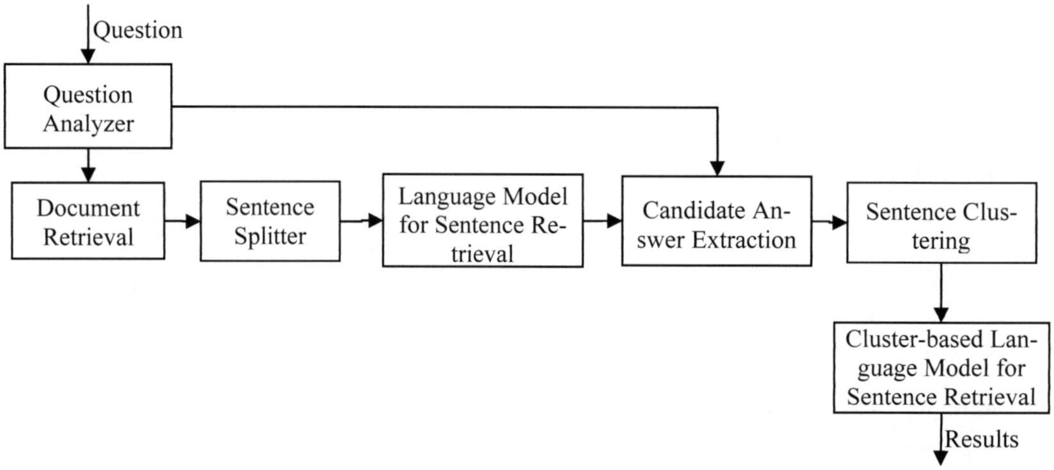

Figure 1 The Framework of Cluster-based Language Model for Sentence Retrieval

2 Language Model for Information Retrieval

Language model for information retrieval is presented by Ponte & Croft in 1998[J. Ponte, et al. 1998] which has more advantages than vector space model. After that, many improved models are proposed like J.F. Gao [J.F Gao, et al. 2004], C. Zhai [C. Zhai, et al. 2001], and so on. In 1999, Berger & Lafferty [A. Berger, et al. 1999] presented statistical translation model for information retrieval.

The basic approach of language model for information retrieval is to model the process of generating query Q. The approach has two steps. 1. Constructing document model for each document in the collection; 2. Ranking the documents according to the probabilities $p(Q|D)$. A classical unigram language model for IR could be expressed in equation (1).

$$p(Q \mid D) = \prod_{w_i \in Q} p(w_i \mid D) \quad (1)$$

where, w_i is a query term, $p(w_i|D)$ is document model which represents terms distribution over document. Obviously, estimating the probability $p(w_i|D)$ is the key of document model. To solve the sparseness problem, Jelinek-Mercer is commonly used which could be expressed by equation (2).

$$p(w \mid D) = a \times p_{ML}(w \mid D) + (1-a) \times p_{ML}(w \mid C) \quad (2)$$

where, $p_{ML}(w|D)$ and $p_{ML}(w|C)$ are document model and collection model respectively estimated via maximum likelihood.

As described above, the disadvantages of standard language model is that it does not make any one particular document any more probable than any other, on the condition that neither the documents originally contain the query term. In the other word, if a document is relevant, but does not contain the query term, it is still no more probable, even though it may be topically related. Thus, the smoothing approaches based on standard language model are improper. In this paper, we propose a novel cluster-based language model to overcome it.

3 Cluster-based Language Model for Sentence Retrieval

Note that document model *p(w|D)* in document retrieval is replace by *p(w|S)* called sentence model in sentence retrieval.

The assumption of cluster-based language model for retrieval is that topic-related sentences tend to be relevant to the same query. So, incorporating the topic of sentences into language model can improve the performance of sentence retrieval based on standard language model.

The proposed cluster-based language model is a mixture model of three components, that are sentence model $p_{ML}(w|S)$, cluster/topic model $p\_topic_{ML}(w|T)$ and collection model $p_{ML}(w|C)$. We can formulate our model as equation (3).

$$p(w\mid S) = a \times p_{ML}(w\mid S) + (1-a)\times \left(\beta \times p\_topic_{ML}(w\mid T) + (1-\beta)\times p_{ML}(w\mid C)\right) \tag{3}$$

In fact, the cluster-based language model can also be viewed as a two-stage smoothing approach. The cluster model is first smoothed using the collection model, and the sentence model is then smoothed with the smoothed cluster model.

In this paper, the cluster model is in the form of term distribution over cluster/topic, associated with the distribution of clusters/topics over sentence, which can be expressed by equation (4).

$$p\_topic(w\mid T) = \sum_{t\in T} p(w\mid t)p(t\mid S) \tag{4}$$

where, *T* is the set of clusters/topics. *p_topic(w|T)* is cluster model. *p(t|S)* is topic sentence distribution which means the distribution of topic over sentence. And *p(w|t)* is term topic distribution which means the term distribution over topics.

Before estimating the sentence model *p(w|S)*, topic-related sentences should be organized into clusters/topics to estimate *p(t|S)* and *p(w|t)* probabilities. For sentence clustering, this paper presents two novel approaches that are One-Sentence-Multi-Topics and One-Sentence-One-Topic respectively.

3.1 One-Sentence-Multi-Topics

The main idea of One-Sentence-Multi-Topics can be summarized as follows.

1. If a sentence includes M different candidate answers, then the sentence consists of M different topics.

For example, the sentence S5 in Table 1 includes two topics which are "贝尔发明电话/Bell invented telephone" and "爱迪生发明电灯/Edison invented electric light" respectively.

2. Different sentences have the same topic if two candidate answers are same.

For example, the sentence S4 and S5 in Table 1 have the same topic "贝尔发明电话/Bell invented telephone" because both of sentences have the same candidate answer "贝尔/Bell".

Based on the above ideas, the result of sentence clustering based on One-Sentence-Multi-Topics is shown in Table 2.

Name of Clusters	Sentences
贝尔/Bell	S1 S2 S4 S5 S6 S7 S8
西门子/Siemens	S2
爱迪生/Edison	S2 S5
库珀/Cooper	S3 S8 S9
斯蒂芬/Stephen	S10

Table 2 The Result of One-Sentence-Multi-Topics Sentence Clustering

So, we could estimate term topic distribution using equation (5).

$$p(w\mid t) = \frac{n(w,t)}{\sum_{w'} n(w',t)} \tag{5}$$

Topic sentence distribution can be estimated using equation (6) and (7).

$$p(t\mid S) = \frac{1/kl_{st}}{\sum_{t} 1/kl_{st}} \tag{6}$$

$$kl_{st} = KL(s\,\|\,t) = \sum_{w} p_{ML}(w\mid s)\times \log\frac{p_{ML}(w\mid s)}{p_{ML}(w\mid t)} \tag{7}$$

where, kl_{st} means the Kullback-Leibler divergence between the sentence with the cluster/topic. k denotes the number of cluster/topic. The main idea of equation (6) is that the closer the Kullback-Leibler divergence, the larger the topic sentence probability *p(t|S)*.

3.2 One-Sentence-One-Topic

The main idea of One-Sentence-One-Topic also could be summarized as follows.

1. A sentence only has one kernel candidate answer which represents the kernel topic no matter how many candidate answers is included.

For example, the kernel topic of sentence S5 in Table 1 is "贝尔发明电话/Bell invented telephone" though it includes three different candidate answers.

2. Different sentences have the same topic if two kernel candidate answers are same.

For example, the sentence S4 and S5 in Table 1 have the same topic "贝尔发明电话/Bell invented telephone".

3. The kernel candidate answer has shortest average distance to all query terms.

Based on the above ideas, the result of sentence clustering based on One-Sentence-One-Topic is shown in Table 3.

Name of Clusters	Sentences
贝尔/Bell	S1 S2 S4 S5 S6 S7
库珀/Cooper	S3 S8 S9
斯蒂芬/Stephen	S10

Table 3 The Result of One-Sentence-One-Topic Sentence Clustering

Equation (8) and (9) can be used to estimate the kernel candidate answer and the distances of candidate answers respectively. Term topic distribution in One-Sentence-One-Topic can be estimated via equation (5). And topic sentence distribution is equal to 1 because a sentence only belongs to one cluster/topic.

$$a_i^* = \underset{a_i}{argmin}\{SemDis_{a_i}\} \quad (8)$$

$$SemDis_{a_i} = \frac{\sum_j SemDis(a_i, q_j)}{N} \quad (9)$$

$$SemDis(a_i, q_j) = \left|Position_{a_i} - Position_{q_j}\right| \quad (10)$$

where, a_i* is the kernel candidate answer. a_i is the i-th candidate answer, $SemDis_{a_i}$ is the average distance of i-th candidate answer. q_j is the j-th query term, N is the number of all query terms. $Position_{q_j}$ and $Position_{a_i}$ mean the position of query term q_j and candidate answer a_i.

4 Experiments and Analysis

Research on Chinese question answering, is still at its early stage. And there is no public evaluation platform for Chinese question answering. So in this paper, we use the evaluation environment presented by [Youzheng Wu, et al. 2004] which is similar to TREC question answering track [Ellen. M. Voorhees. 2004]. The documents collection is downloaded from Internet which size is 1.8GB. The testing questions are collected via four different approaches which has 7050 Chinese questions currently.

In this section, we randomly select 807 testing questions which are fact-based short-answer questions. Moreover, the answers of all testing questions are named entities identified by [Youzheng Wu, et al. 2005]. Figure 2 gives the details. Note that, LOC, ORG, PER, NUM and TIM denote the questions which answer types are location, organization, person, number and time respectively, SUM means all question types.

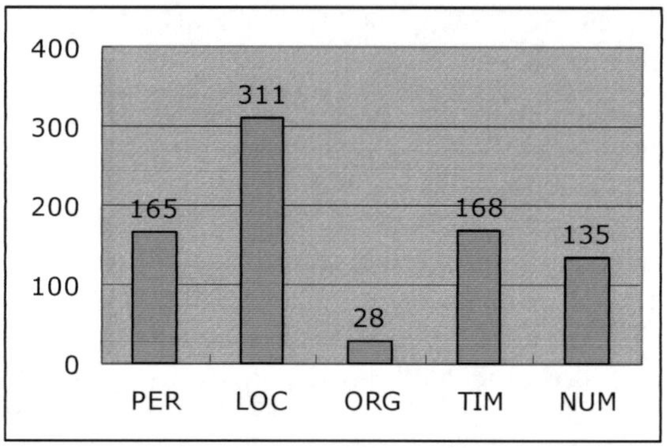

Figure 2 The Distribution of Various Question Types over Testing Questions

Chinese question answering system is to return a ranked list of five answer sentences per question and will be strictly evaluated (unsupported answers counted as wrong) using mean reciprocal rank (MRR).

4.1 Baseline: Standard Language Model for Sentence Retrieval

Based on the standard language model for information retrieval, we can get the baseline performance, as is shown in Table 4, where α is the weight of document model.

α	0.6	0.7	0.8	0.9
LOC	49.95	51.50	52.63	54.54
ORG	53.69	51.01	50.12	51.01
PER	63.10	64.42	65.94	65.69
NUM	48.43	49.86	51.78	53.26
TIM	56.97	58.38	58.77	61.49
SUM	53.98	55.28	56.40	57.93

Table 4 The Baseline MRR5 Performance

In the following chapter, we conduct experiments to answer two questions.

1. Whether cluster-based language model for sentence retrieval could improve the performance of standard language model for sentence retrieval?

2. What are the performances of sentence clustering for various question types?

4.2 Cluster-based Language Model for Sentence Retrieval

In this part, we will conduct experiments to validate the performances of cluster-based language models which are based on One-Sentence-Multi-Topics and One-Sentence-One-Topic sentence clustering respectively. In the following experiments, $\beta = 0.9$.

4.2.1 Cluster-based Language Model Based on One-Sentence-Multi-Topics

The experimental results of cluster-based language model based on One-Sentence-Multi-Topics sentence clustering are shown in Table 5. The relative improvements are listed in the bracket.

α	0.6	0.7	0.8	0.9
LOC	55.57 (+11.2)	55.61 (+7.98)	56.59 (+7.52)	57.70 (+5.79)
ORG	59.05 (+9.98)	59.46 (+16.6)	59.46 (+18.6)	59.76 (+17.2)
PER	67.73 (+7.34)	68.03 (+5.60)	67.71 (+2.68)	67.45 (+2.68)
NUM	52.79 (+9.00)	53.90 (+8.10)	54.45 (+5.16)	55.51 (+4.22)
TIM	60.17 (+5.62)	60.63 (+3.85)	62.33 (+6.06)	61.68 (+0.31)
SUM	58.14 (+7.71)	58.63 (+6.06)	59.30 (+5.14)	59.54 (+2.78)

Table 5 MRR5 Performance of Cluster-based Language Model Based on One-Sentence-Multi-Topics

From the experimental results, we can find that by integrating the clusters/topics of the sentence into language model, we can achieve much improvement at each stage of α. For example, the largest and smallest improvements for all types of questions are about 7.7% and 2.8% respectively. This experiment shows that the proposed cluster-based language model based on One-Sentence-Multi-Topics is effective for sentence retrieval in Chinese question answering.

4.2.2 Cluster-based Language Model Based on One-Sentence-One-Topic

The performance of cluster-based language model based on One-Sentence-One-Topic sentence clustering is shown in Table 6. The relative improvements are listed in the bracket.

α	0.6	0.7	0.8	0.9
LOC	53.02 (+6.15)	54.27 (+5.38)	56.14 (+6.67)	56.28 (+3.19)
ORG	58.75 (+9.42)	58.75 (+17.2)	59.46 (+18.6)	59.46 (+16.6)
PER	66.57 (+5.50)	67.07 (+4.11)	67.44 (+2.27)	67.29 (+2.44)
NUM	49.95 (+3.14)	50.87 (+2.02)	52.15 (+0.71)	53.51 (+0.47)
TIM	59.75 (+4.88)	60.65 (+3.89)	62.71 (+6.70)	62.20 (+1.15)
SUM	56.48 (+4.63)	57.65 (+4.29)	58.82 (+4.29)	59.22 (+2.23)

Table 6 MRR5 Performance of Cluster-based Language Model Based on One-Sentence-One-Topic

In Comparison with Table 5, we can find that the improvement of cluster-based language model based on One-Sentence-One-Topic is slightly lower than that of cluster-based language model based on One-Sentence-Multi-Topics. The reasons lie in that Clusters based on One-Sentence-One-Topic approach are very coarse and much information is lost. But the improvements over baseline system are obvious.

Table 7 shows that MRR1 and MRR20 scores of cluster-based language models for all question types. The relative improvements over the baseline are listed in the bracket. This experiment is to validate whether the conclusion based on different measurements is consistent or not.

	One-Sentence-Multi-Topics		One-Sentence-One-Topic	
α	MRR1	MRR20	MRR1	MRR20
0.6	50.00 (+14.97)	59.60 (+7.66)	48.33 (+10.37)	57.70 (+4.23)
0.7	50.99 (+13.36)	60.03 (+6.12)	49.44 (+9.92)	58.62 (+3.62)
0.8	51.05 (+8.99)	60.68 (+5.06)	51.05 (+8.99)	60.01 (+3.90)
0.9	51.92 (+5.81)	61.05 (+2.97)	51.30 (+4.54)	60.25 (+1.62)

Table 7 MRR1 and MRR20 Performances of Two Cluster-based Language Models

Table 7 also shows that the performances of two cluster-based language models are higher than that of the baseline system under different measurements. For MRR1 scores, the largest improvements of cluster-based language models based on One-Sentence-Multi-Topics and One-Sentence-One-Topic are about 15% and 10% respectively. For MRR20, the largest improvements are about 7% and 4% respectively.

Conclusion 1: The experiments show that the proposed cluster-based language model can improve the performance of sentence retrieval in Chinese question answering under the various measurements. Moreover, the performance of clustering-based language model based on One-Sentence-Multi-Topics is better than that based on One-Sentence-One-Topic.

4.3 The Analysis of Sentence Clustering for Various Question Types

The parameter β in equation (3) denotes the balancing factor of the cluster model and the collection model. The larger β, the larger contribution of the cluster model. The small β, the larger contribution of the collection model. If the performance of sentence retrieval decreased with the increasing of β, it means that there are many noises in sentence clustering. Otherwise, sentence clustering is satisfactory for cluster-based language model. So the task of this experiment is to find the performances of sentence clustering for various question types, which is helpful to select the most proper β to obtain the best performance of sentence retrieval.

With the change of β and the fixed α ($\alpha = 0.9$), the performances of cluster-based language model based on One-Sentence-Multi-Topics are shown in Figure 3.

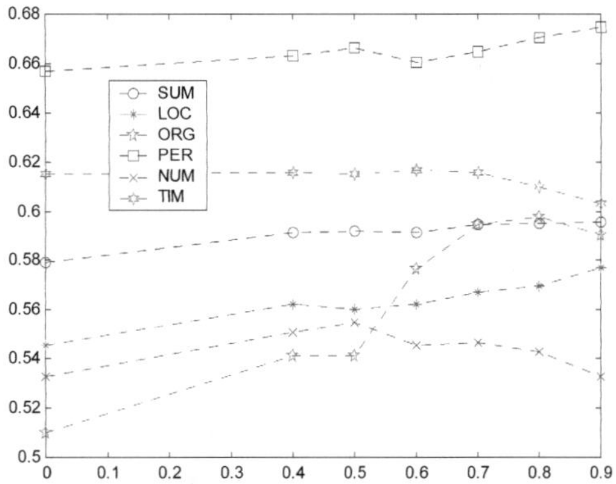

Figure 3 MRR5 Performances of Cluster-based Language Model Based on One-Sentence-Multi-Topics with the Change of β

In Figure 3, the performances of TIM and NUM type questions decreased with the increasing of the parameter β (from 0.6 to 0.9), while the performances of LOC, PER and ORG type questions increased. This phenomenon showed that the performance of sentence clustering based on One-Sentence-Multi-Topics for TIM and NUM type questions is not as good as that for LOC, PER and ORG type questions. This is in fact reasonable. The number and time words frequently appeared in the sentence, which does not represent a cluster/topic when they appear. While PER, LOC and ORG entities can represent a topic when they appeared in the sentence.

Similarly, with the change of β and the fixed α ($\alpha=0.9$), the performances of cluster-based language model based on One-Sentence-One-Topic are shown in Figure 4.

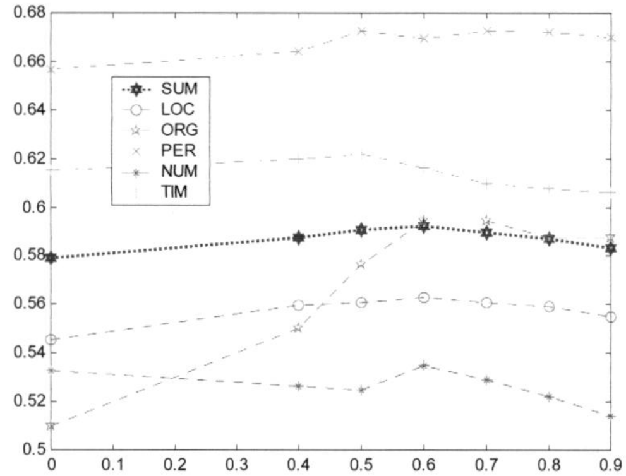

Figure 4 MRR5 Performance of Cluster-based Language Model Based on One-Sentence-One-Topic with the Change of β

In Figure 4, the performances of TIM, NUM, LOC and SUM type questions decreased with the increasing of β (from 0.6 to 0.9). This phenomenon shows that the performances of sentence clustering based on One-Sentence-One-Topic are not satisfactory for most of question types. But, compared to the baseline system, the cluster-based language model based on this kind of sentence clustering can still improve the performances of sentence retrieval in Chinese question answering.

Conclusion 2: The performance of the proposed sentence clustering based on One-Sentence-Multi-Topics for PER, LOC and ORG type questions is higher than that for TIM and NUM type questions. Thus, for PER, LOC and ORG questions, we should choose the larger β value (about 0.9) in cluster-based language model based on One-Sentence-Multi-Topics. While for TIM and NUM type questions, the *value of β should be smaller (about 0.5). But, the performance of sentence clustering based on One-Sentence-One-Topic for all questions is not ideal, so the value for cluster-based language model based on One-Sentence-One-Topic should be smaller (about 0.5) for all questions.*

5 Conclusion and Future Work

The input of a question answering system is natural language question which contains richer information than the query in traditional document retrieval. Such richer information can be used in each module of question answering system. In this paper, we presented a novel cluster-based language model for sentence retrieval in Chinese question answering which combines the sentence model, the cluster/topic model and the collection model.

For sentence clustering, we presented two approaches that are One-Sentence-Multi-Topics and One-Sentence-One-Topic respectively. The experimental results showed that the proposed cluster-based language model could improve the performances of sentence retrieval in Chinese question answering significantly.

However, we only conduct sentence clustering for questions, which have the property that their answers are named entities in this paper. In the future work, we will focus on all other type questions and improve the performance of the sentence retrieval by introducing the structural, syntactic and semantic information into language model.

Reference

J. Ponte, W. Bruce Croft. A Language Modeling Approach to Information Retrieval. In the Proceedings of ACM SIGIR 1998, pp 275-281, 1998.

C. Zhai, J. Lafferty. A Study of Smoothing Techniques for Language Modeling Applied to ad hoc Information Retrieval. In the Proceedings of the ACM SIGIR Conference on Research and Development in Information Retrieval, 2001.

Ittycheriah, S. Roukos. IBM's Statistical Question Answering System-TREC 11. In the Eleventh Text Retrieval Conference (TREC 2002), Gaithersburg, Maryland, November 2002.

Hui Yang, Tat-Seng Chua. The Integration of Lexical Knowledge and External Resources for Question Answering. In the Proceedings of the Eleventh Text REtrieval Conference (TREC'2002), Maryland, USA, 2002, page 155-161.

Andres Corrada-Emmanuel, W.Bruce Croft, Vanessa Murdock. Answer Passage Retrieval for Question Answering. In the Proceedings of the 27th Annual International Conference on Research and Development in Information Retrieval, pp. 516 – 517, 2004.

Ellen M. Voorhees. Overview of the TREC 2004 Question Answering Track. In Proceedings of the Twelfth Text REtrieval Conference (TREC 2004), 2004.

Vanessa Murdock, W. Bruce Croft. Simple Translation Models for Sentence Retrieval in Factoid Question Answering. In the Proceedings of the SIGIR 2004 Workshop on Information Retrieval for Question Answering, pp.31-35, 2004.

Thomas Hofmann. Probabilistic Latent Semantic Indexing. In the Proceedings of the Twenty-Second Annual International SIGIR Conference on Research and Development in Information Retrieval, 1999.

A. Berger and J. Lafferty. Information Retrieval as Statistical Translation. In the Proceedings of ACM SIGIR-1999, pp. 222—229, Berkeley, CA, August 1999.

A. Echihabi and D.Marcu. A noisy-channel approach to question answering. In the Proceeding of the 41st Annual Meeting of the Association for Computational Linguistics, Sappora, Japan, 2003.

Leif Azzopardi, Mark Girolami and Keith van Rijsbergen. Topic Based Language Models for ad hoc Information Retrieval. In the Proceeding of IJCNN 2004 & FUZZ-IEEE 2004, July 25-29, 2004, Budapest, Hungary.

Jian-Yun Nie. Integrating Term Relationships into Language Models for Information Retrieval. Report at ICT-CAS.

Jianfeng Gao, Jian-Yun Nie, Guangyuan Wu and Guihong Cao. 2004b. Dependence language model for information retrieval. In SIGIR-2004. Sheffield, UK, July 25-29.

Youzheng Wu, Jun Zhao, Bo Xu. Chinese Named Entity Recognition Model Based on Multiple Features. In the Proceeding of HLT/EMNLP 2005, Vancouver, B.C., Canada, pp.427-434, 2005.

Youzheng Wu, Jun Zhao, Xiangyu Duan and Bo Xu. Building an Evaluation Platform for Chinese Question Answering Systems. In Proceeding of the First National Conference on Information Retrieval and Content Security. Shanghai, China, December, 2004.(In Chinese)

The Role of Lexical Resources in CJK Natural Language Processing

Jack Halpern（春遍雀來）
The CJK Dictionary Institute (CJKI) (日中韓辭典研究所)
34-14, 2-chome, Tohoku, Niiza-shi, Saitama 352-0001, Japan
jack@cjk.org

Abstract

The role of lexical resources is often understated in NLP research. The complexity of Chinese, Japanese and Korean (CJK) poses special challenges to developers of NLP tools, especially in the area of word segmentation (WS), information retrieval (IR), named entity extraction (NER), and machine translation (MT). These difficulties are exacerbated by the lack of comprehensive lexical resources, especially for proper nouns, and the lack of a standardized orthography, especially in Japanese. This paper summarizes some of the major linguistic issues in the development NLP applications that are dependent on lexical resources, and discusses the central role such resources should play in enhancing the accuracy of NLP tools.

1 Introduction

Developers of CJK NLP tools face various challenges, some of the major ones being:

1. Identifying and processing the large number of orthographic variants in Japanese, and alternate character forms in CJK languages.
2. The lack of easily available comprehensive lexical resources, especially lexical databases, comparable to the major European languages.
3. The accurate conversion between Simplified and Traditional Chinese (Halpern and Kerman 1999).
4. The morphological complexity of Japanese and Korean.
5. Accurate word segmentation (Emerson 2000 and Yu et al. 2000) and disambiguating ambiguous segmentations strings (ASS) (Zhou and Yu 1994).
6. The difficulty of lexeme-based retrieval and CJK CLIR (Goto et al. 2001).
7. Chinese and Japanese proper nouns, which are very numerous, are difficult to detect without a lexicon.
8. Automatic recognition of terms and their variants (Jacquemin 2001).

The various attempts to tackle these tasks by statistical and algorithmic methods (Kwok 1997) have had only limited success. An important motivation for such methodology has been the poor availability and high cost of acquiring and maintaining large-scale lexical databases.

This paper discusses how a lexicon-driven approach exploiting large-scale lexical databases can offer reliable solutions to some of the principal issues, based on over a decade of experience in building such databases for NLP applications.

2 Named Entity Extraction

Named Entity Recognition (NER) is useful in NLP applications such as question answering, machine translation and information extraction. A major difficulty in NER, and a strong motivation for using tools based on probabilistic methods, is that the compilation and maintenance of large entity databases is time consuming and expensive. The number of personal names and their variants (e.g. over a hundred ways to spell *Mohammed*) is probably in the billions. The number of place names is also large, though they are relatively stable compared with the names of organizations and products, which change frequently.

A small number of organizations, including The CJK Dictionary Institute (CJKI), maintain databases of millions of proper nouns, but even such comprehensive databases cannot be kept fully up-to-date as countless new names are created daily. Various techniques have been used to automatically detect entities, one being the use of keywords or syntactic structures that co-occur with proper nouns, which we refer to as *named entity contextual clues* (NECC).

Table 1. Named Entity Contextual Clues

Headword	Reading	Example
センター	せんたー	国民生活**センター**
ホテル	ほてる	**ホテル**シオノ
駅	えき	朝霞**駅**
協会	きょうかい	日本ユニセフ**協会**

Table 1 shows NECCs for Japanese proper nouns, which when used in conjunction with entity lexicons like the one shown in Table 2 below achieve high precision in entity recognition. Of course for NER there is no need for such lexicons to be multilingual, though it is obviously essential for MT.

Table 2. Multilingual Database of Place Names

English	Japanese	Simplified Chinese	LO	Traditional Chinese	Korean
Azerbaijan	アゼルバイジャン	阿塞拜疆	L	亞塞拜然	아제르바이잔
Caracas	カラカス	加拉加斯	L	卡拉卡斯	카라카스
Cairo	カイロ	开罗	O	開羅	카이로
Chad	チャド	乍得	L	查德	차드
New Zealand	ニュージーランド	新西兰	L	紐西蘭	뉴질랜드
Seoul	ソウル	首尔	O	首爾	서울
Seoul	ソウル	汉城	O	漢城	서울
Yemen	イエメン	也门	L	葉門	예멘

Note how the lexemic pairs ("L" in the **LO** column) in Table 2 above are not merely simplified and traditional *orthographic* ("O") versions of each other, but independent lexemes equivalent to American *truck* and British *lorry*.

NER, especially of personal names and place names, is an area in which lexicon-driven methods have a clear advantage over probabilistic methods and in which the role of lexical resources should be a central one.

3 Linguistic Issues in Chinese

3.1 Processing Multiword Units

A major issue for Chinese segmentors is how to treat compound words and multiword lexical units (MWU), which are often decomposed into their components rather than treated as single units. For example, 录像带 *lùxiàngdài* 'video cassette' and 机器翻译 *jīqifānyì* 'machine translation' are not tagged as segments in Chinese Gigaword, the largest tagged Chinese corpus in existence, processed by the CKIP morphological analyzer (Ma 2003). Possible reasons for this include:

1. The lexicons used by Chinese segmentors are small-scale or incomplete. Our testing of various Chinese segmentors has shown that coverage of MWUs is often limited.
2. Chinese linguists disagree on the concept of wordhood in Chinese. Various theories such as the Lexical Integrity Hypothesis (Huang 1984) have been proposed. Packard's outstanding book (Packard 98) on the subject clears up much of the confusion.
3. The "correct" segmentation can depend on the application, and there are various segmentation standards. For example, a search engine user looking for 录像带 is not normally interested in 录像 'to videotape' and 带 'belt' per se, unless they are part of 录像带.

This last point is important enough to merit elaboration. A user searching for 中国人 *zhōngguórén* 'Chinese (person)' is *not* interested in 中国 'China', and vice-versa. A search for 中国 should *not* retrieve 中国人 as an instance of 中国. Exactly the same logic should apply to 机器翻译, so that a search for that keyword should only retrieve documents containing that string in its entirety. Yet performing a Google search on 机器翻译 in normal mode gave some 2.3 million hits, hundreds of thousands of which had zero occurrences of 机器翻译 but numerous occurrences of unrelated words like 机器人 'robot', which the user is not interested in.

This is equivalent to saying that *headwaiter* should not be considered an instance of *waiter*, which is indeed how Google behaves. More to the point, English space-delimited lexemes like *high school* are not instances of the adjective *high*. As shown in Halpern (2000b), "the degree of solidity often has nothing to do with the status of a string as a lexeme. *School bus* is just as legitimate a lexeme as is *headwaiter* or *word-processor*. The presence or absence of spaces or hyphens, that is, the orthography, does not determine the lexemic status of a string."

In a similar manner, it is perfectly legitimate to consider Chinese MWUs like those shown below as indivisible units for most applications, especially information retrieval and machine translation.

丝绸之路 *sīchóuzhīlù* silk road
机器翻译 *jīqìfānyì* machine translation
爱国主义 *àiguózhǔyì* patriotism
录像带 *lùxiàngdài* video cassette
新西兰 *Xīnxīlán* New Zealand
临阵磨枪 *línzhènmóqiāng*
start to prepare at the last moment

One could argue that 机器翻译 is compositional and therefore should be considered "two words." Whether we count it as one or two "words" is not really relevant – what matters is that it is *one lexeme* (smallest distinctive units associating meaning with form). On the other extreme, it is clear that idiomatic expressions like 临阵磨枪, literally "sharpen one's spear before going to battle," meaning 'start to prepare at the last moment,' are indivisible units.

Predicting compositionality is not trivial and often impossible. For many purposes, the only practical solution is to consider all lexemes as indivisible. Nonetheless, currently even the most advanced segmentors fail to identify such lexemes and missegment them into their constituents, no doubt because they are not registered in the lexicon. This is an area in which expanded lexical resources can significantly improve segmentation accuracy.

In conclusion, lexical items like 机器翻译 'machine translation' represent stand-alone, well-defined concepts and should be treated as single units. The fact that in English *machineless* is spelled solid and *machine translation* is not is an historical accident of orthography unrelated to the fundamental fact that both are full-fledged lexemes each of which represents an indivisible, independent concept. The same logic applies to 机器翻译, which is a full-fledged lexeme that should not be decomposed.

3.2 Multilevel Segmentation

Chinese MWUs can consist of nested components that can be segmented in different ways for different levels to satisfy the requirements of different segmentation standards. The example below shows how 北京日本人学校 *Běijīng Rìběnrén Xuéxiào* 'Beijing School for Japanese (nationals)' can be segmented on five different levels.

1. 北京日本人学校 multiword lexemic
2. 北京+日本人+学校 lexemic
3. 北京+日本+人+学校 sublexemic
4. 北京 + [日本 + 人] [学+校] morphemic
5. [北+京] [日+本+人] [学+校] submorphemic

For some applications, such as MT and NER, the multiword lexemic level is most appropriate (the level most commonly used in CJKI's dictionaries). For others, such as embedded speech technology where dictionary size matters, the lexemic level is best. A more advanced and expensive solution is to store presegmented MWUs in the lexicon, or even to store nesting delimiters as shown above, making it possible to select the desired segmentation level.

The problem of incorrect segmentation is especially obvious in the case of neologisms. Of course no lexical database can expect to keep up with the latest neologisms, and even the first edition of Chinese Gigaword does not yet have 博客 *bókè* 'blog'. Here are some examples of MWU neologisms, some of which are not (at least bilingually), compositional but fully qualify as lexemes.

电脑迷 *diànnǎomí* cyberphile
电子商务 *diànzǐshāngwù* e-commerce
追车族 *zhuīchēzú* auto fan

3.3 Chinese-to-Chinese Conversion (C2C)

Numerous Chinese characters underwent drastic simplifications in the postwar period. Chinese written in these simplified forms is called Simplified Chinese (SC). Taiwan, Hong Kong, and most overseas Chinese continue to use the old, complex forms, referred to as Traditional Chinese (TC). Contrary to popular perception, the process of accurately converting SC to/from TC is full of complexities and pitfalls. The linguistic issues are discussed in Halpern and Kerman (1999), while technical issues are described in Lunde (1999). The conversion can be implemented on three levels in increasing order of sophistication:

1. Code Conversion. The easiest, but most unreliable, way to perform C2C is to transcode by using a one-to-one mapping table. Because of the numerous one-to-many ambiguities, as shown below, the rate of conversion failure is unacceptably high.

Table 3. Code Conversion

SC	TC1	TC2	TC3	TC4	Remarks
门	們				one-to-one
汤	湯				one-to-one
发	發	髮			one-to-many
暗	暗	闇			one-to-many
干	幹	乾	干	榦	one-to-many

2. Orthographic Conversion. The next level of sophistication is to convert orthographic units, rather than codepoints. That is, meaningful linguistic units, equivalent to lexemes, with the important difference that the TC is the traditional version of the SC on a character form level. While code conversion is ambiguous, orthographic conversion gives much better results because the orthographic mapping tables enable conversion on the lexeme level, as shown below.

Table 4. Orthographic Conversion

English	SC	TC1	TC2	Incorrect
Telephone	电话	電話		
Dry	干燥	乾燥		干燥 幹燥 榦燥
	阴干	陰乾	陰干	

As can be seen, the ambiguities inherent in code conversion are resolved by using orthographic mapping tables, which avoids false conversions such as shown in the **Incorrect** column. Because of segmentation ambiguities, such conversion must be done with a segmentor that can break the text stream into meaningful units (Emerson 2000).

An extra complication, among various others, is that some lexemes have one-to-many orthographic mappings, *all* of which are correct. For example, SC 阴干 correctly maps to both TC 陰乾 'dry in the shade' and TC 陰干 'the five even numbers'. Well designed orthographic mapping tables must take such anomalies into account.

3. Lexemic Conversion. The most sophisticated form of C2C conversion is called *lexemic conversion,* which maps SC and TC lexemes that are semantically, not orthographically, equivalent. For example, SC 信息 *xìnxī* 'information' is converted into the semantically equivalent TC 資訊 *zīxùn*. This is similar to the difference between British *pavement* and American *sidewalk.* Tsou (2000) has demonstrated that there are numerous lexemic differences between SC and TC, especially in technical terms and proper nouns, e.g. there are more than 10 variants for *Osama bin Laden.*

Table 5. Lexemic Conversion

English	SC	Taiwan TC	HK TC	Incorrect TC
Software	软件	軟體	軟件	軟件
Taxi	出租汽车	計程車	的士	出租汽車
Osama Bin Laden	奥萨马本拉登	奧薩瑪賓拉登	奧薩瑪賓拉丹	奧薩馬本拉登
Oahu	瓦胡岛	歐胡島		瓦胡島

3.4 Traditional Chinese Variants

Traditional Chinese has numerous variant character forms, leading to much confusion. Disambiguating these variants can be done by using mapping tables such as the one shown below. If such a table is carefully constructed by limiting it to cases of 100% semantic interchangeability for polysemes, it is easy to normalize a TC text by trivially replacing variants by their standardized forms. For this to work, all relevant components, such as MT dictionaries, search engine indexes and the related documents should be normalized. An extra complication is that Taiwanese and Hong Kong variants are sometimes different (Tsou 2000).

Table 6. TC Variants

Var. 1	Var. 2	English	Comment
裏	裡	Inside	100% interchangeable
著	着	Particle	variant 2 not in Big5
沉	沈	sink; surname	partially interchangeable

4 Orthographic Variation in Japanese

4.1 Highly Irregular Orthography

The Japanese orthography is highly irregular, significantly more so than any other major language, including Chinese. A major factor is the complex interaction of the four scripts used to write Japanese, e.g. kanji, hiragana, katakana, and the Latin alphabet, resulting in countless words that can be written in a variety of often unpredictable ways, and the lack of a standardized orthography. For example, *toriatsukai* 'handling' can be written in six ways: 取り扱い, 取扱い, 取扱, とり扱い, 取りあつかい, とりあつかい.

An example of how difficult Japanese IR can be is the proverbial 'A hen that lays golden eggs.' The "standard" orthography would be 金の卵を産む鶏 *Kin no tamago o umu niwatori*. In reality, *tamago* 'egg' has four variants (卵, 玉子, たまご, タマゴ), *niwatori* 'chicken' three (鶏, にわとり, ニワトリ) and *umu* 'to lay' two (産む, 生む), which expands to 24 permutations like 金の卵を生むニワトリ, 金の玉子を産む鶏 etc. As can be easily verified by searching the web, these variants occur frequently.

Linguistic tools that perform segmentation, MT, entity extraction and the like must identify and/or normalize such variants to perform dictionary lookup. Below is a brief discussion of what kind of variation occurs and how such normalization can be achieved.

4.2 Okurigana Variants

One of the most common types of orthographic variation in Japanese occurs in kana endings, called *okurigana*, that are attached to a kanji stem. For example, *okonau* 'perform' can be written 行う or 行なう, whereas *toriatsukai* can be written in the six ways shown above. Okurigana variants are numerous and unpredictable. Identifying them must play a major role in Japanese orthographic normalization. Although it is possible to create a dictionary of okurigana variants algorithmically, the resulting lexicon would be huge and may create numerous false positives not semantically interchangeable. The most effective solution is to use a lexicon of okurigana variants, such as the one shown below:

Table 7. Okurigana Variants

HEADWORD	READING	NORMALIZED
書き著す	かきあらわす	書き著す
書き著わす	かきあらわす	書き著す
書著す	かきあらわす	書き著す
書著わす	かきあらわす	書き著す

Since Japanese is highly agglutinative and verbs can have numerous inflected forms, a lexicon such as the above must be used in conjunction with a morphological analyzer that can do accurate stemming, i.e. be capable of recognizing that 書き著しませんでした is the polite form of the canonical form 書き著す.

4.3 Cross-Script Orthographic Variation

Variation across the four scripts in Japanese is common and unpredictable, so that the same word can be written in any of several scripts, or even as a hybrid of multiple scripts, as shown below:

Table 8. Cross-Script Variation

Kanji	Hiragana	katakana	Latin	Hybrid	Gloss
人参	にんじん	ニンジン			carrot
		オープン	OPEN		open
硫黄		イオウ			sulfur
		ワイシャツ		Y シャツ	shirt
皮膚		ヒフ		皮フ	skin

Cross-script variation can have major consequences for recall, as can be seen from the table below.

Table 9: Hit Distribution for 人参 'carrot' *ninjin*

ID	Keyword	Normalized	Google Hits
A	人参	人参	67,500
B	にんじん	人参	66,200
C	ニンジン	人参	58,000

Using the ID above to represent the number of Google hits, this gives a total of $A+B+C+\alpha_{123} = 191{,}700$. α is a coincidental occurrence factor, such as in '100 人参加, in which '人参' is unrelated to the 'carrot' sense. The formulae for calculating the above are as follows.

Unnormalized recall:

$$\frac{C}{A+B+C+\alpha_{123}} = \frac{58,000}{191,700} \ (\approx 30\%)$$

Normalized recall:

$$\frac{A+B+C}{A+B+C+\alpha_{123}} = \frac{191,700}{191,700} \ (\approx 100\%)$$

Unnormalized precision:

$$\frac{C}{C+\alpha_{3}} = \frac{58,000}{58,000} \ (\approx 100\%)$$

Normalized precision:

$$\frac{C}{A+B+C+\alpha_{123}} = \frac{191,700}{191,700} \ (\approx 100\%)$$

人参 'carrot' illustrates how serious a problem cross-orthographic variants can be. If orthographic normalization is not implemented to ensure that all variants are indexed on a standardized form like 人参, recall is only 30%; if it is, there is a dramatic improvement and recall goes up to nearly 100%, without any loss in precision, which hovers at 100%.

4.4 Kana Variants

A sharp increase in the use of katakana in recent years is a major annoyance to NLP applications because katakana orthography is often irregular; it is quite common for the same word to be written in multiple, unpredictable ways. Although hiragana orthography is generally regular, a small number of irregularities persist. Some of the major types of kana variation are shown in the table below.

Table 10. Kana Variants

Type	English	Standard	Variants
Macron	computer	コンピュータ	コンピューター
Long vowels	maid	メード	メイド
Multiple kana	team	チーム	ティーム
Traditional	big	おおきい	おうきい
づ vs. ず	continue	つづく	つずく

The above is only a brief introduction to the most important types of kana variation. Though attempts at algorithmic solutions have been made by some NLP research laboratories (Brill 2001), the most practical solution is to use a katakana normalization table, such as the one shown below, as is being done by Yahoo! Japan and other major portals.

Table 11. Kana Variants

HEADWORD	NORMALIZED	English
アーキテクチャ	アーキテクチャー	Architecture
アーキテクチャー	アーキテクチャー	Architecture
アーキテクチュア	アーキテクチャー	Architecture

4.5 Miscellaneous Variants

There are various other types of orthographic variants in Japanese, described in Halpern (2000a). To mention some, kanji even in contemporary Japanese sometimes have variants, such as 才 for 歳 and 巾 for 幅, and traditional forms such as 發 for 発. In addition, many *kun* homophones and their variable orthography are often close or even identical in meaning, i.e., *noboru* means 'go up' when written 上る but 'climb' when written 登る, so that great care must be taken in the normalization process so as to assure semantic interchangeability for all senses of polysemes; that is, to ensure that such forms are *excluded* from the normalization table.

4.6 Lexicon-driven Normalization

Leaving statistical methods aside, lexicon-driven normalization of Japanese orthographic variants can be achieved by using an orthographic mapping table such as the one shown below, using various techniques such as:

1. Convert variants to a standardized form for indexing.
2. Normalize queries for dictionary lookup.
3. Normalize all source documents.
4. Identify forms as members of a variant group.

Table 12. Orthographic Normalization Table

HEADWORD	READING	NORMALIZED
空き缶	あきかん	空き缶
空缶	あきかん	空き缶
明き罐	あきかん	空き缶
あき缶	あきかん	空き缶
あき罐	あきかん	空き缶
空きかん	あきかん	空き缶
空きカン	あきかん	空き缶
空き罐	あきかん	空き缶
空罐	あきかん	空き缶
空き鑵	あきかん	空き缶
空鑵	あきかん	空き缶

Other possibilities for normalization include advanced applications such as domain-specific synonym expansion, requiring Japanese thesauri based on domain ontologies, as is done by a select number of companies like Wand and Convera who build sophisticated Japanese IR systems.

5 Orthographic Variation in Korean

Modern Korean has is a significant amount of orthographic variation, though far less than in Japanese. Combined with the morphological complexity of the language, this poses various challenges to developers of NLP tools. The issues are similar to Japanese in principle but differ in detail.

Briefly, Korean has variant hangul spellings in the writing of loanwords, such as 케이크 *keikeu* and 케익 *keik* for 'cake', and in the writing of non-Korean personal names, such as 클린턴 *keulrinteon* and 클린톤 *keulrinton* for 'Clinton'. In addition, similar to Japanese but on a smaller scale, Korean is written in a mixture of hangul, Chinese characters and the Latin alphabet. For example, 'shirt' can be written 와이셔츠 *wai-syeacheu* or Y 셔츠 *wai-syeacheu*, whereas 'one o'clock' *hanzi* can written as 한시, 1 시 or 一時. Another issue is the differences between South and North Korea spellings, such as N.K. 오사까 *osakka* vs. S.K. 오사카 *osaka* for 'Osaka', and the old (pre-1988) orthography versus the new, i.e. modern 일군 'worker' (*ilgun*) used to be written 일꾼 (*ilkkun*).

Lexical databases, such as normalization tables similar to the ones shown above for Japanese, are the only practical solution to identifying such variants, as they are in principle unpredictable.

6 The Role of Lexical Databases

Because of the irregular orthography of CJK languages, procedures such as orthographic normalization cannot be based on statistical and probabilistic methods (e.g. bigramming) alone, not to speak of pure algorithmic methods. Many attempts have been made along these lines, as for example Brill (2001) and Goto et al. (2001), with some claiming performance equivalent to lexicon-driven methods, while Kwok (1997) reports good results with only a small lexicon and simple segmentor.

Emerson (2000) and others have reported that a robust morphological analyzer capable of processing lexemes, rather than bigrams or n-grams, must be supported by a large-scale computational lexicon. This experience is shared by many of the world's major portals and MT developers, who make extensive use of lexical databases.

Unlike in the past, disk storage is no longer a major issue. Many researchers and developers, such as Prof. Franz Guenthner of the University of Munich, have come to realize that "language is in the data," and "the data is in the dictionary," even to the point of compiling full-form dictionaries with millions of entries rather than rely on statistical methods, such as Meaningful Machines who use a full form dictionary containing millions of entries in developing a human quality Spanish-to-English MT system.

CJKI, which specializes in CJK and Arabic computational lexicography, is engaged in an ongoing research and development effort to compile CJK and Arabic lexical databases (currently about seven million entries), with special emphasis on proper nouns, orthographic normalization, and C2C. These resources are being subjected to heavy industrial use under real-world conditions, and the feedback thereof is being used to further expand these databases and to enhance the effectiveness of the NLP tools based on them.

7 Conclusions

Performing such tasks as orthographic normalization and named entity extraction accurately is beyond the ability of statistical methods alone, not to speak of C2C conversion and morphological analysis. However, the small-scale lexical resources currently used by many NLP tools are inadequate to these tasks. Because of the irregular orthography of the CJK writing systems, lexical databases fine-tuned to the needs of NLP applications are required. The building of large-scale lexicons based on corpora consisting of even billions of words has come of age. Since lexicon-driven techniques have proven their effectiveness, there is no need to overly rely on probabilistic methods. Comprehensive, up-to-date lexical resources are the key to achieving major enhancements in NLP technology.

References

Brill, E. and Kacmarick, G. and Brocket, C. (2001) *Automatically Harvesting Katakana-English Term Pairs from Search Engine Query Logs*. Microsoft Research, Proc. of the Sixth Natural Language Processing Pacific Rim Symposium, Tokyo, Japan.

Packard, L. Jerome (1998) "New Approaches to Chinese Word Formation", Mouton Degruyter, Berlin and New York.

Emerson, T. (2000) *Segmenting Chinese in Unicode. Proc. of the 16th International Unicode Conference*, Amsterdam

Goto, I., Uratani, N. and Ehara T. (2001) *Cross-Language Information Retrieval of Proper Nouns using Context Information*. NHK Science and Technical Research Laboratories. Proc. of the Sixth Natural Language Processing Pacific Rim Symposium, Tokyo, Japan

Huang, James C. (1984) *Phrase Structure, Lexical Integrity, and Chinese Compounds,* Journal of the Chinese Teachers Language Association, 19.2: 53-78

Jacquemin, C. (2001) *Spotting and Discovering Terms through Natural Language Processing*. The MIT Press, Cambridge, MA

Halpern, J. and Kerman J. (1999) *The Pitfalls and Complexities of Chinese to Chinese Conversion*. Proc. of the Fourteenth International Unicode Conference in Cambridge, MA.

Halpern, J. (2000a) *The Challenges of Intelligent Japanese Searching*. Working paper (www.cjk.org/cjk/joa/joapaper.htm), The CJK Dictionary Institute, Saitama, Japan.

Halpern, J. (2000b) *Is English Segmentation Trivial?*. Working paper, (www.cjk.org/cjk/reference/engmorph.htm) The CJK Dictionary Institute, Saitama, Japan.

Kwok, K.L. (1997) *Lexicon Effects on Chinese Information Retrieval*. Proc. of 2nd Conf. on Empirical Methods in NLP. ACL. pp.141-8.

Lunde, Ken (1999) *CJKV Information Processing*. O'Reilly & Associates, Sebastopol, CA.

Yu, Shiwen, Zhu, Xue-feng and Wang, Hui (2000) *New Progress of the Grammatical Knowledge-base of Contemporary Chinese*. Journal of Chinese Information Processing, Institute of Computational Linguistics, Peking University, Vol.15 No.1.

Ma, Wei-yun and Chen, Keh-Jiann (2003) *Introduction to CKIP Chinese Word Segmentation System for the First International Chinese Word Segmentation Bakeoff,* Proceedings of the Second SIGHAN Workshop on Chinese Language Processingpp. 168-171 Sapporo, Japan

Yu, Shiwen, Zhu, Xue-feng and Wang, Hui (2000) *New Progress of the Grammatical Knowledge-base of Contemporary Chinese*. Journal of Chinese Information Processing, Institute of Computational Linguistics, Peking University, Vol.15 No.1.

Tsou, B.K., Tsoi, W.F., Lai, T.B.Y. Hu, J., and Chan S.W.K. (2000) *LIVAC, a Chinese synchronous corpus, and some applications*. In "2000 International Conference on Chinese Language ComputingICCLC2000", Chicago.

Zhou, Qiang. and Yu, Shiwen (1994) *Blending Segmentation with Tagging in Chinese Language Corpus Processing,* 15th International Conference on Computational Linguistics (COLING 1994)

Hybrid Models

for Chinese Named Entity Recognition

Lishuang Li, Tingting Mao, Degen Huang, Yuansheng Yang
Department of Computer Science and Engineering
Dalian University of Technology
116023 Dalian, China
{computer, huangdg, yangys}@dlut.edu.cn
maotingting1007@sohu.com

Abstract

This paper describes a hybrid model and the corresponding algorithm combining support vector machines (SVMs) with statistical methods to improve the performance of SVMs for the task of Chinese Named Entity Recognition (NER). In this algorithm, a threshold of the distance from the test sample to the hyperplane of SVMs in feature space is used to separate SVMs region and statistical method region. If the distance is greater than the given threshold, the test sample is classified using SVMs; otherwise, the statistical model is used. By integrating the advantages of two methods, the hybrid model achieves 93.18% F-measure for Chinese person names and 91.49% F-measure for Chinese location names.

1 Introduction

Named entity (NE) recognition is a fundamental step to many language processing tasks such as information extraction (IE), question answering (QA) and machine translation (MT). On its own, NE recognition can also provide users who are looking for person or location names with quick information. Palma and Day (1997) reported that person (PER), location (LOC) and organization (ORG) names are the most difficult sub-tasks as compared to other entities as defined in Message Understanding Conference (MUC). So we focus on the recognition of PER, LOC and ORG entities.

Recently, machine learning approaches are widely used in NER, including the hidden Markov model (Zhou and Su, 2000; Miller and Crystal, 1998), maximum entropy model (Borthwick, 1999), decision tree (Qin and Yuan, 2004), transformation-based learning (Black and Vasilakopoulos, 2002), boosting (Collins, 2002; Carreras et al., 2002), support vector machine (Takeuchi and Collier, 2002; Yu et al., 2004; Goh et al., 2003), memory-based learning (Sang, 2002). SVM has given high performance in various classification tasks (Joachims, 1998; Kudo and Matsumoto, 2001). Goh et al. (2003) presented a SVM-based chunker to extract Chinese unknown words. It obtained higher F-measure for person names and organization names.

Like other classifiers, the misclassified testing samples by SVM are mostly near the decision plane (i.e., the hyperplane of SVM in feature space). In order to increase the accuracy of SVM, we propose a hybrid model combining SVM with a statistical approach for Chinese NER, that is, in the region near the decision plane, statistical method is used to classify the samples instead of SVM, and in the region far away from the decision plane, SVM is used. In this way, the misclassification by SVM near the decision plane can be decreased significantly. A higher F-measure for Chinese NE recognition can be achieved.

In the following sections, we shall describe our approach in details.

2 Recognition of Chinese Named Entity Using SVM

Firstly, we segment and assign part-of-speech (POS) tags to words in the texts using a Chinese lexical analyzer. Secondly, we break segmented words into characters and assign each character its features. Lastly, a model based on SVM to identify Chinese named entities is set up by choosing a proper kernel function.

In the following, we will exemplify the person names and location names to illustrate the identification process.

2.1 Support Vector Machines

Support Vector Machines first introduced by Vapnik (1996) are learning systems that use a hypothesis space of linear functions in a high dimensional feature space, trained with a learning algorithm from optimization theory that implements a learning bias derived from statistical theory. SVMs are based on the principle of structural risk minimization. Viewing the data as points in a high-dimensional feature space, the goal is to fit a hyperplane between the positive and negative examples so as to maximize the distance between the data points and the hyperplane.

Given training examples:

$$S = \{(x_1, y_1), (x_2, y_2), ..., (x_l, y_l)\},\ x_i \in R^n, y_i \in \{-1,+1\}, \quad (1)$$

x_i is a feature vector (n dimension) of the i-th sample. y_i is the class (positive(+1) or negative(-1) class) label of the i-th sample. l is the number of the given training samples. SVMs find an "optimal" hyperplane: $(wx + b) = 0$ to separate the training data into two classes. The optimal hyperplane can be found by solving the following quadratic programming problem (we leave the details to Vapnik (1998)):

$$\max \quad \sum_{i=1}^{l} \alpha_i - \frac{1}{2}\sum_{i=1}^{l}\sum_{j=1}^{l} \alpha_i y_i \alpha_j y_j K(x_i, x_j) \quad (2)$$

$$\text{subject to} \quad \sum_{i=1}^{l} y_i \alpha_i = 0, \quad 0 \le \alpha_i \le c, i = 1,2,..., l.$$

The function $K(x_i, x_j) = \varphi(x_i) \cdot \varphi(x_j)$ is called kernel function, $\varphi(x)$ is the mapping from primary input space to feature space. Given a test example, its label y is decided by the following function:

$$f(x) = \text{sgn}[\sum_{x_i \in sv} \alpha_i y_i K(x_i, x) + b]. \quad (3)$$

Basically, SVMs are binary classifiers, and can be extended to multi-class classifiers in order to solve multi-class discrimination problems. There are two popular methods to extend a binary classification task to that of K classes: *one class vs. all others* and *pairwise*. Here, we employ the simple *pairwise* method. This idea is to build $K \times (K-1)/2$ classifiers considering all pairs of classes, and final decision is given by their voting.

2.2 Recognition of Chinese Person Names Based on SVM

We use a SVM-based chunker, YamCha (Kudo and Masumoto, 2001), to extract Chinese person names from the Chinese lexical analyzer.

1) Chinese Person Names Chunk Tags

We use the Inside/Outside representation for proper chunks:

I Current token is inside of a chunk.

O Current token is outside of any chunk.

B Current token is the beginning of a chunk.

A chunk is considered as a Chinese person name in this case. Every character in the training set is given a tag classification of B, I or O, that is, $y_i \in \{B, I, O\}$. Here, the multi-class decision method pairwise is selected.

2) Features Extraction for Chinese Person Names

Since Chinese person names are identified from the segmented texts, the mistakes of word segmentation can result in error identification of person names. So we must break words into characters and extract features for every character. Table 1 summarizes types of features and their values.

Type of feature	Value
POS tag	n-B, v-I, p-S
Whether a character is a surname	Y or N
Character	surface form of the character itself
The frequency of a character in person names table	Y or N
Previous BIO tag	B-character, I-character, O-character

Table 1. Summary of Features and Their Values

The POS tag from the output of lexical analysis is subcategorized to include the position of the character in the word. The list of POS tags is shown in Table 2.

POS tag	Description of the position of the character in a word
<POS>-S	One-character word
<POS>-B	first character in a multi-character word
<POS>-I	intermediate character in a multi-character word
<POS>-E	last character in a multi-character word

Table 2. POS Tags in A Word

If the character is a surname, the value is assigned to Y, otherwise assigned to N.

The "character" is surface form of the character in the word.

We extract all person names in January 1998 of the People's Daily to set up person names table and calculate the frequency of every character (F) of person names table in the training corpus. The frequency of F is defined as

$$P(F) = \frac{\textit{the number of F as a character of person names}}{\textit{the total number of F}}, \quad (4)$$

if $P(F)$ is greater than the given threshold, the value is assigned to Y, otherwise assigned to N.

We also use previous BIO-tags as features.

Whether a character is inside a person name or not, it depends on the context of the character. Therefore, we use contextual information of two previous and two successive characters of the current character as features.

Figure 1 shows an example of features extraction for the *i*-th character. When training, the features of the character "Min" contains all the features surrounded in the frames. If the same sentence is used as testing, the same features are used.

			i		
Position	−2	−1	0	+1	+2
Character	Jiang	Ze	Min	zhu	xi
POS tags	n-S	n-B	n-E	n-B	n-E
Whether the character is a surname	Y	N	N	N	Y
The frequency of a character in the person names table	Y	Y	Y	N	N
Previous BIO tags	B	I	I	0	0

Figure 1. An example of features extraction

3) Choosing Kernel Functions

Here, we choose polynomial kernel functions: $K(x, x_i) = [(x \cdot x_i) + 1]^d$ to build an optimal separating hyperplane.

2.3 Recognition of Chinese Location Names Based on SVM

The identification process of location names is the same as that of person names except for the features extraction. Table 3 summarizes types of features and their values of location names extraction.

Type of feature	Value
POS tag	n-B, v-I, p-S
Whether a character appears in location names characteristic table	Y or N
Character	surface form of the character itself
Previous BIO tag	B-character, I-character, O-character

Table 3. Summary of Features and Their Values

The location names characteristic table is set up in advance, and it includes the characters or words expressing the characteristics of location names such as "sheng (province)", "shi (city)", "xian (county)"etc. If the character is in the location names characteristic table, the value is assigned to Y, otherwise assigned to N.

3 Statistical Models

Many statistical models for NER have been presented (Zhang et al., 1992; Huang et al., 2003 etc). In this section, we proposed our statistical models for Chinese person names recognition and Chinese location names recognition.

3.1 Chinese Person Names

We define a function to evaluate the person name candidate *PN*. The evaluated function *Total-Probability*(*PN*) is composed of two parts: the lexical probability *LP*(*PN*) and contextual probability *CP*(*PN*) based on POS tags.

$$TotalProbability(PN) = \alpha LP(PN) + (1-\alpha)CP(PN), \quad (5)$$

where *PN* is the evaluated person name and α is the balance cofficient.

1) lexical probability *LP(PN)*

We establish the surname table (*SurName*) and the first name table (*FirstName*) from the students of year 1999 in a university (containing 9986 person names).

Suppose $PN=LF_1F_2$, where L is the surname of the evaluated person name *PN*, F_i (i=1,2) is the *i*-th first name of the evaluated person name *PN*.

The probability of the surname $P_l(L)$ is defined as

$$P_l(L) = \frac{P_{l0}(L)}{\sum_{y \in SurName} P_{l0}(y)}, \quad (6)$$

where $P_{l0}(L) = \log_2(N(L)+2)$, $N(L)$ is the number of L as the single or multiple surname of person names in the *SurName*.

The probability of the first name $P_f(F)$ is defined as

$$P_f(F) = \frac{P_{f0}(F)}{\sum_{y \in FirstName} P_{f0}(y)}, \quad (7)$$

where $P_{f0}(F) = \log_2(N(F)+2)$, $N(F)$ is the number of F in the *FirstName*.

The lexical probability of the person name *PN* is defined as

$$\begin{aligned} LP(PN) &= P_l(L) \times P_f(F_1) & \textit{if}(PN = LF_1) \\ LP(PN) &= P_l(L) \times C_b \times (P_f(F_1) + P_f(F_2)) & \textit{if}(PN = LF_1F_2), \end{aligned} \quad (8)$$

where C_b is the balance cofficient between the single name and the double name. Here, C_b=0.844 (Huang et al., 2001).

2) contextual probability based on POS tags *CP(PN)*

Chinese person names have characteristic contexual POS tags in real Chinese texts, for example, in the phrase "dui Zhangshuai shuo (say to Zhangshuai)", the POS tag before the person name "Zhangshuai" is prepnoun and verb occurs after the person name. We define the bigram contextual probability *CP(PN)* of the person name *PN* as the following equation:

$$CP(PN) = \frac{PersonPOS(<lpos, PN, rpos>)}{TotalPOS}, \quad (9)$$

where *lpos* is the POS tag of the character before *PN* (called POS forward), *rpos* is the POS tag of the character after *PN* (called POS backward), and $PersonPOS(<lpos, PN, rpos>)$ is the number of *PN* as a pereson name whose POS forward is *lpos* and POS backward is *rpos* in training corpus. *TotalPOS* is the total number of the contexual POS tags of every person name in the whole training corpus.

3.2 Chinese Location Names

We also define a function to evaluate the location name candidate *LN*. The evaluated function *TotalProbability(LN)* is composed of two parts: the lexical probability *LP (LN)* and contextual probability *CP (LN)* based on POS tags.

$$TotalProbability(LN) = \alpha LP(LN) + (1-\alpha)CP(LN), \quad (10)$$

where *LN* is the evaluated location name and α is the balance cofficient.

1) lexical probability *LP (LN)*

Suppose $LN=F_0F^+S$, $F^+=F_1 \ldots F_n$, (i=1,…,n), where F_0 is the first character of the evaluated location name *LN*, F^+ is the middle characters of the evaluated location name *LN*, *S* is the last character of the evaluated location name *LN*.

The probability of the first character of the evaluated location name $P_h(F_0)$ is defined as

$$P_h(F_0) = \frac{P_{h0}(F_0)}{P'_{h0}(F_0)}, \quad (11)$$

where $P_{h0}(F_0) = \log_2(C(F_0)+2)$, $C(F_0)$ is the number of F_0 as the first character of location names in the Chinese Location Names Record.

$P'_{h0}(F_0) = \log_2(C'(F_0)+2)$, $C'(F_0)$ is the total number of F_0 in the Chinese Location Names Record.

The probability of the middle character of the evaluated location name $P_f(F^+)$ is defined as

$$P_f(F^+) = \sum_{i=1}^{n} \frac{P_f(F_i)}{P'_f(F_i)}, \quad (12)$$

where $P_f(F_i) = \log_2(C(F_i)+2)$, $C(F_i)$ is the number of F_i as the *i*-th middle character of location names in the Chinese Location Names Record.

$P'_f(F_i) = \log_2(C'(F_i)+2)$, $C'(F_i)$ is the total number of F_i in the Chinese Location Names Record.

The probability of the last character of the evaluated location name $P_l(S)$ is defined as

$$P_l(S) = \frac{P_l(S)}{P'_l(S)}, \quad (13)$$

where $P_l(S) = \log_2(C'(S)+2)$, $C(S)$ is the number of S as the last character of location names in the Chinese Location Names Record.

$P'_l(S) = \log_2(C'(S)+2)$, $C'(S)$ is the total number of *S* in the Chinese Location Names Record.

The lexical probability of the location name *LN* is defined as

$$LN = (P_h(F_0) + P_f(F^+) + P_l(S)) / Len(LN), \quad (14)$$

where *Len(LN)* is the length of the evaluated location name *LN*.

2) contextual probability based on POS tags *CP (LN)*

Location names also have characteristic contexual POS tags in real Chinese texts, for example, in the phrase "zai Chongqing shi junxing (to be held in Chongqing)", the POS tag before the location name "Chongqing"is prepnoun and verb occurs after the location name. We define the bigram contextual probability *CP(LN)* of the location name *LN* similar to that of the person name *PN* in equation (9), where *PN* is replaced with *LN*.

4 Recognition of Chinese Named Entity Using Hybrid Model

Analyzing the classification results (obtained by sole SVMs described in section 2) between B and I, B and O, I and O respectively, we find that the error is mainly caused by the second classification. The samples which attribute to B class are misclassified to O class, which leads to B class vote's diminishing and the corresponding named entities are lost. Therefore the Recall is lower. In the meantime, the number of the misclassified samples whose function distances to the hyperplane of SVM in feature space are less than 1 can reach over 83% of the number of total misclassified samples. That means the misclassification of a classifier is occurred in the region of two overlapping classes. Considering this fact, we can expect to improve SVM using the following hybrid model.

The hybrid model includes the following procedure:

1) compute the distance from the test sample to the hyperplane of SVM in feature space.

2) compare the distance with given threshold.

The algorithm of hybrid model can be described as follows:

Suppose T is the testing set,

(1) if $T \neq \Phi$, select $x \in T$, else stop;

(2) compute $g(x) = \sum_{i=1}^{l} \alpha y_i K(x_i, x) + b$

(3) if $|g(x)| > \varepsilon$, $\varepsilon \in [0,1]$ output $f(x) = \mathrm{sgn}(g(x))$, else use the statistic models and output the returned results.

(4) $T \leftarrow T - \{x\}$, repeat(1)

5 Experiments

Our experimental results are all based on the corpus of Peking University.

5.1 Extracting Chinese Person Names

We use 180 thousand characters corpus of year 1998 from the People's Daily as the training corpus and extract other sentences (containing 1526 Chinese person names) as testing corpus to conduct an open test experiment. The results are obtained as follows based on different models.

1) Based on Sole SVM

An experiment is carried out to recognize Chinese person names based on sole SVM by the method as described in Section 2. The Recall, Precision and F-measure using different number of degree of polynomial kernel function are given in Table 4. The best result is obtained when d=2.

	Recall	Precision	F-measure
d=1	87.22%	94.26%	90.61%
d=2	87.16%	96.10%	91.41%
d=3	84.67%	95.14%	89.60%

Table 4. Results for Person Names Extraction Based on Sole SVM

2) Using Hybrid Model

As mentioned in section 4, the test samples which attribute to B class are misclassified to O class and therefore the Recall for person names extraction from sole SVM is lower. So we only deal with the test samples (B class and O class) whose function distances to the hyperplane of SVM in feature space (i.e. g(x)) is between 0 and ε. We move class-boundary learned by SVM towards the O class, that is, the O class samples are considered as B class in that area. 93.64% of the Chinese person names in testing corpus are recalled when ε=0.9 (Here, ε also represents how much the boundary is moved). However, a number of non-person names are also identified as person names wrongly and the Precision is decreased correspondingly. Table 5 shows the Recall and Precision of person names extraction with different ε.

	Recall	Precision	F-measure
ε=1	93.05%	75.17%	83.16%
ε=0.9	93.64%	81.75%	87.29%
ε=0.8	93.51%	85.91%	89.55%
ε=0.7	93.05%	88.31%	90.62%
ε=0.6	92.39%	90.21%	91.29%
ε=0.5	91.81%	91.87%	91.84%
ε=0.4	91.02%	93.28%	92.13%
ε=0.3	90.56%	95.05%	92.75%
ε=0.2	90.03%	95.48%	92.68%
ε=0.1	88.66%	95.82%	92.10%

Table 5. Results for Person Names Extraction with Different ε

We use the evaluated function *TotalProbability(PN)* as described in section 3 to filter the wrongly recalled person names using SVM. We tune α in equation (5) to obtain the best results. The results based on the hybrid model with different α are listed in Table 6 (when d=2). We can observe that the result is best when α=0.4. Table 7 shows the results based on the hybrid model with different ε when α=0.4. We can observe that the Recall rises and the Precision drops on the whole when ε increases. The synthetic index F-measures are improved when ε is between 0.1 and 0.8 compared with sole SVM. The best result is obtained when ε=0.3. The Recall and the F-measure increases 3.27% and 1.77% respectively.

	Recall	Precision	F-measure
α=0.1	90.37%	95.76%	92.99%
α=0.2	90.37%	96.03%	93.11%
α=0.3	90.43%	96.03%	93.15%
α=0.4	***90.43%***	***96.10%***	***93.18%***
α=0.5	90.63%	95.76%	93.13%
α=0.6	90.43%	95.97%	93.12%

α=0.7	90.43%	95.90%	93.09%
α=0.8	90.43%	95.90%	93.09%
α=0.9	90.37%	95.90%	93.05%

Table 6. Results for Person Names Extraction Based on The Hybrid Model with Different α

	Recall	Precision	F-measure
ε=1	92.53%	84.96%	88.58%
ε=0.9	93.05%	88.81%	90.88%
ε=0.8	92.86%	90.95%	91.89%
ε=0.7	92.46%	92.04%	92.25%
ε=0.6	91.93%	93.22%	92.58%
ε=0.5	91.48%	94.26%	92.85%
ε=0.4	90.76%	95.25%	92.95%
ε=0.3	***90.43%***	***96.10%***	***93.18%***
ε=0.2	90.04%	96.15%	92.99%
ε=0.1	88.73%	96.23%	92.32%

Table 7. Results for Person Names Extraction Based on The Hybrid Model (α=0.4)

5.2 Extracting Chinese Location Names

We use 1.5M characters corpus of year 1998 from the People's Daily as the training corpus and extract sentences of year 2000 from the People's Daily (containing 2919 Chinese location names) as testing corpus to conduct an open test experiment. The results are obtained as follows based on different models.

1) Based on Sole SVM

The Recall, Precision and F-measure using different number of degree of polynomial kernel function are given in Table 8. The best result is obtained when *d*=2.

	Recall	Precision	F-measure
d=1	84.66%	91.95%	88.16%
d=2	86.69%	93.82%	90.12%
d=3	86.27%	94.23%	90.07%

Table 8. Results for Location Names Extraction Based on Sole SVM

2) Using Hybrid Model

The results for Chinese location names extraction based on the hybrid model are listed in Table 9 (when *d*=2; α=0.2 in equation (10)). We can observe that the Recall rises and the Precision drops on the whole when ε increases. The synthetic index F-measures are improved when ε is between 0.1 and 0.7 compared with sole SVM. The best result is obtained when ε=0.3. The Recall increases 3.55%, the Precision decreases 1.05% and the F-measure increases 1.37%.

	Recall	Precision	F-measure
ε=1	90.75%	83.00%	86.71%
ε=0.9	90.85%	85.33%	88.01%
ε=0.8	91.42%	87.42%	89.37%
ε=0.7	91.65%	89.05%	90.33%
ε=0.6	91.75%	90.38%	91.06%
ε=0.5	91.32%	90.98%	91.15%
ε=0.4	90.66%	91.87%	91.26%
ε=0.3	***90.24%***	***92.77%***	***91.49%***
ε=0.2	89.10%	93.28%	91.15%
ε=0.1	87.83%	93.38%	90.52%

Table 9. Results for Location Names Extraction Based on The Hybrid Model (α=0.2)

6 Comparison with other work

The same corpus was also tested using statistics-based approach to identify Chinese person names (Huang et al, 2001) and location names (Huang and Yue, 2003). In their systems, lexical reliability and contextual reliability were used to identify person names and location names calculated from statistical information drawn from a training corpus. The results of our models and the statistics-based methods (Huang 2001; Huang 2003) are shown in Table 10 for comparison. We can see that the Recall and F-measure in our method all increase a lot.

		Recall	Precision	F-measure
Person names	Our models	90.10%	96.15%	93.03%
	Huang (2001)	88.62%	92.37%	90.46%
Location names	Our models	90.24%	92.77%	91.49%
	Huang (2003)	86.86%	91.48%	89.11%

Table 10. Results of Our Method and Huang (2001; 2003) for Comparison

7 Conclusions and Future work

We recognize Chinese named entities using a hybrid model combining support vector machines with statistical methods. The model integrates the advantages of two methods and the experimental results show that it can achieve higher F-measure than the sole SVM and individual statistical approach.

Future work includes optimizing statistical models, for example, we can add the probability information of Chinese named entities in real texts to compute lexical probability, and we can also use trigram models to compute contextual probability.

The hybrid model is expected to extend to foreign names in transliteration to obtain improved results by sole SVMs. The identification of transliterated names by SVMs has been completed (Li et al., 2004). The future work includes: set up statistical models for transliterated names and combine statistical models with SVMs to identify transliterated names.

References

William J. Black and Argyrios Vasilakopoulos. 2002. Language Independent Named Entity Classification by Modified Transformation-based Learning and by Decision Tree Induction. *The 6th Conference on Natural Language Learning*, Taipei.

Andrew Eliot Borthwick. 1999. A Maximum Entropy Approach to Named Entity Recognition. *PhD Dissertation*. New York University.

Xavier Carreras, Lluis Marquez, and Lluis Padro. 2002. Named Entity Extraction Using AdaBoost. *The 6th Conference on Natural Language Learning*, Taipei.

Michael Collins. 2002. Ranking Algorithms for Named-entity Extraction: Boosting and the Voted Perceptron. *Proceedings of the 40th Annual Meeting of the Association for Computational Linguistics* (*ACL*-2002), Philadelphia, 489-496.

Chooi-Ling Goh, Masayuki Asahara and Yuji Matsumoto. 2003. Chinese Unknown Word Identification Based on Morphological Analysis and Chunking. *The Companion Volume to the Proceedings of 41st Annual Meeting of the Association for Computational Linguistics* (*ACL-2003*), Sapporo, 197-200.

De-Gen Huang, Yuan-Sheng Yang, and Xing Wang. 2001. Identification of Chinese Names Based on Statistics. *Journal of Chinese Information Processing*, 15(2): 31-37.

De-Gen Huang and Guang-Ling Yue. 2003. Identification of Chinese Place Names Based on Statistics. *Journal of Chinese Information Processing*, 17(2): 46-52.

Thorsten Joachims. 1998. Text Categorization with Support Vector Machines: Learning with Many Relevant Features. *In Proceedings of the European Conference on Machine Learning*, 1398:137-142.

Taku Kudo and Yuji Matsumoto. 2001. Chunking with Support Vector Machines. *In Proceedings of NAACL 2001*.

Li-Shuang Li, Chun-Rong Chen, De-Gen Huang and Yuan-Sheng Yang. 2004. Identifying Pronunciation-Translated Names from Chinese Texts Based on Support Vector Machines. *Advances in Neural Networks-ISNN 2004, Lecture Notes in Computer Science*, Berlin Heidelberg, 3173: 983-988.

Scott Miller and Michael Crystal. 1998. BBN: Description of the SIFT System as Used for MUC-7. *Proceedings of 7th Message Understanding Conference*, Washington.

David D. Palmer. 1997. A Trainable Rule-Based Algorithm for Word Segmentation. *In Proc of 35th of ACL & 8th conf. of EACL*, 321-328.

Wen Qin and Chun-Fa Yuan. 2004. Identification of Chinese Unknown Word Based on Decision Tree. *Journal of Chinese Information Processing*, 18(1): 14-19.

Erik Tjong Kim Sang. 2002. Memory-based Named Entity Recognition. *The 6th Conference on Natural Language Learning*, Taipei.

Koichi Takeuchi and Nigel Collier. 2002. Use of Support Vector Machines in Extended Named Entity Recognition. *The 6th Conference on Natural Language Learning*, Taipei.

Vladimir N. Vapnik. 1995. *The Nature of Statistical Learning Theory*. Springer-Verlag, Berlin.

Vladimir N. Vapnik. 1998. *Statistical Learning Theory*. John Wiley & Sons, New York.

Ying Yu, Xiao-Long Wang, Bing-Quan Liu, and Hui Wang. 2004. Efficient SVM-based Recognition of Chinese Personal Names. *High Technology Letters*, 10(3): 15-18.

Jun-Sheng Zhang, Shun-De Chen, Ying Zheng, Xian-Zhong Liu and Shu-Jin Ke. 1992. Large-Corpus-Based Methods for Chinese Personal Name. *Journal of Chinese Information Processing*, 6(3): 7-15.

Guo-Dong Zhou and Jian Su. 2002. Named Entity Recognition Using an HMM-based Chunk Tagger. *Proceedings of the 40th Annual Meeting of the ACL*, Philadelphia, 473-480.

Realization of the Chinese BA-construction in an English-Chinese Machine Translation System

Xiaohong Wu
Centre Tesnière, Faculté des Lettres
Université de Franche-Comté
Besançon, France
wuxaiohong@voila.fr

Sylviane Cardey
Centre Tesnière, Faculté des Lettres
Université de Franche-Comté
Besançon, France
Sylviane.cardey@univ-fcomte.fr

Peter Greenfield
Centre Tesnière, Faculté des Lettres
Université de Franche-Comté
Besançon, France
Peter.greenfield@univ-fcomte.fr

Abstract

The BA-construction refers to a special grammatical structure in Mandarin Chinese. It is an extremely important syntactic structure in Chinese, which is frequently used in daily life. The study of the BA-construction has attracted the attention of almost all linguists who are interested in this language. Yet it is a quite complex and difficult linguistic phenomenon and it is hard to analyze it satisfactorily to cope with the syntactic structure(s) of another language which does not possess this kind of construction (e.g. in machine translation). This paper discusses a few methods on how some of the English imperative sentences are realized by the Chinese BA-construction which is mandatory in transferring certain source language (SL) information into target language (TL) in an experimental machine translation (MT) system. We also introduce the basic syntactic structures of the BA-construction and explain how we formalize and control these structures to satisfy our need. Some features related to the BA-construction, such as obligatoriness versus the optionality, the semantics as well as the properties of the elements preceding and following the BA are also discussed. Finally we suggest that by constraining the variations of the formalized patterns of the BA-construction, a better MT could be reached.

1 Introduction

The BA-construction ('把'字句) is a special syntactic structure in the Chinese language. It is so frequently used in everyday conversations that its usage can not be simply ignored. In fact, the BA-construction has been greatly drawing the attention of almost all linguists who are interested in the Chinese language. The reason for this concentrates not only on the fact that it is a quite special Chinese linguistic phenomenon but also that until now no consensus has been reached among linguists on whether its grammatical category belongs to that of a verb or that of a preposition. Historically speaking, much evidence shows that it was used more as a verb than as a preposition. However, recent research tends to classify the BA-construction to the category of the prepositional phrase (PP), which characterizes the pre-posed object (usually a noun phrase – NP) of a transitive verb (Zhou and PU, 1985). In the following sections we will first introduce very briefly the different points of view held by these linguists and then we will demonstrate our choice for the study of the BA-construction in our experimental English-Chinese machine translation system, which is based on the controlled language technique. We will particularly stress the problems we face when transferring certain English imperative sentences into Chinese sentences containing the BA-construction which is mandatory in some cases, while this is optional in other cases, or can be used as one of the other alternatives (between a normal syntactic structure (V + NP + X[1]) and the BA-construction (BA + NP + V + X).

2 The BA-Construction: a verb phrase or a prepositional phrase?

It is important to note that we do not pretend to give an overview of all kinds of points of view on the study of the BA-construction here, nor do we claim to justify all the different conceptions held in the literature in this short paper. Instead, we just try to verify how our practice with this construction can be better formulated for our specific purpose: to be well adapted to serve for an English-Chinese MT system.

Whether the word BA (把) in the BA-construction is a verb or a preposition is an open question in Chinese linguistics. Due to the difficulty of having sufficient and strong evidence to distinguish the BA-construction between a verb and a preposition, some linguists also call the BA and some other words which possess the same property, such as BEI (被) etc., a "coverb" (次动词或副动词, literally: a sub-verb) which share the properties of both a verb and a preposition. As a result of no consensus among linguists, the analysis of this construction is divided into two separate schools: that of a verb phrase (VP) and that of prepositional phrase (PP) or one that is more inclined to one of the schools than the other. The first school of linguists states that the BA-construction should be considered as a VP whose surface structure resembles a lot the serial-verb constructions (连动式) (Subj + V + (NP1+[2]) + V2 + (NP2) …), (see example 1 b). Like a serial verb construction, the first V can be represented by the word BA and form a BA-construction. In their opinion, the BA shows the characteristics of the other parallel verbs which are used in the serial-verb construction (refers to any surface string with more than one verb in a sentence). Furthermore, some features of the BA indicate that the elements following the BA make up a constituent in which the BA looks more like a verbal head taking a complement (Bender, 2002), (Hashimoto, 1971), (Ma, 1985), and (Her, 1990), for example:

1 a) 张三把李四打了一拳，王五踢了两脚。

(literal translation: Zhang San BA (V1) Li Si hit (V2) LE[3] (ASP) a punch, Wang Wu kick (V3) LE (ASP) two foot)

Zhang San gave Li Si a punch and Wang Wu two kicks.

b) 我开门进去取书。

(literal translation: I open (V1) door come (V2) in take (V3) book)

I opened the door and went in to take a book.

One of their supporting points is that unlike a prepositional phrase, the BA-construction can not be moved to the beginning of the sentence, for example:

c) *[4] 把李四, 张三打了一拳, 王五踢了两脚。

Compare this with the following example (with a prepositional phrase):

2 a) 他在北京买了一本书。

(literal translation: He in Beijing buy LE (ASP) a BEN (CLS[5]) book;)

He bought a book in Beijing.

b) 在北京，他买了一本书。

(literal translation: In Beijing, he buy LE(ASP) a BEN(CL) book)

In Beijing, he bought a book.

Furthermore, like the other verbs, the BA can be negated by MEIYOU (没有), for example (1 a):

张三没有把李四打一拳，王五踢两脚。

(literal translation: Zhang San, MEIYOU[6], BA Li Si hit a punch, Wang Wu kick two foot)

Zhang San did not give Li Si a punch and Wang WU two kicks.

In addition, like other monosyllable verbs, the BA as a verb can be used as the attributive of a noun by adding a structural word "DE (的)" (STR[7]) between it and the noun, for example, "念的书" (read, DE, book; the book to read); "听的歌", (listen, DE, song; a song to listen to); "把的关" (BA, DE checks; the checks to do/the pass to guard)

[1] X: a non-null variable, usually an adverb or a PP

[2] +: refers to the possibility of more than one NP.

[3] LE : Aspectual particle indicating a past action

[4] *: ungrammatical

[5] CLS: classifier

[6] MEIYOU (没有): negation = no, not or do not

[7] STR: structural word usually connects a constituent to a NP

A basic structural analysis of the first school is illustrated in Figure 1 "BA as a Verb" from the example cited from (LIN, 2004):

3) 张三把李四打了。

(literal translation: Zhang San BA Li Si hit LE)

Zhang San hit Li Si.

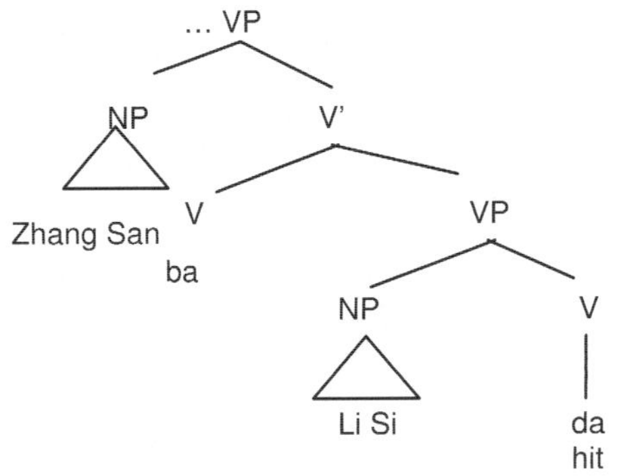

Figure 1 BA as a Verb

The second school of linguists claims that the BA-construction is actually a prepositional phrase with its head word followed by a NP complement which is moved in front of the transitive main verb in the sentence (See example 4 a) below). Furthermore, though the BA possesses the categorical features of a verb, it is hard to qualify the BA to function alone as the main verb or predicate in a sentence. In addition, in Mandarin Chinese the aspect attachments can be used as one of the conditions to test the verbhood of a word. The fact is that in most cases, if an aspect attachment, such as LE (了), GUO (过) (expressing past actions) and ZHE (着) (expressing continuous actions), is attached to the BA, the whole sentence will look strange and become ungrammatical (see below in b) and c)).

4 a) 他把刚才的话又重复了一遍。(literal translation: He, BA, just now, DE (STR), talks, again, speak, LE, one BIAN (CLS))

He repeated what he had said just now.

Compare the following with aspect attachments:

b) * 他把了刚才的话又重复了一遍。(LE)

c) * 他把过刚才的话又重复了一遍。(GUO)

d) *他把着刚才的话又重复了一遍。(ZHE)

Compare with other verb:

5 a) 他看了这本书。(LE)

(literal translation: he, look, LE, this book)

He has read the book.

b) 他看过这本书。(GUO)

(literal translation: he, look, GUO, this book)

He read the book.

c) 他看着这本书。(ZHE)

He is looking at the book.

Their point of view concerning this construction is also supported by some grammatical criteria to test the verbhood of a word. For instance, most monosyllable verbs can be duplicated as independent "AA" or "A 一 A" structures in Chinese, for example "看 (see, look)" as "看看" or "看一看"; "读 (read)" as "读读" or "读一读"; "吃 (eat)"as "吃吃" or "吃一吃"; and "走 (go or walk)" as "走走" or "走一走"; but never "把" as "*把把" or "*把一把" (some transitive verbs can be used this way without objects, but the duplicated "把把" or "把一把" as a verb must have its object following it, e.g. "把把关 (make checks; to guard a pass, etc.)" or "把一把关"). Furthermore the verb following the BA-construction is a transitive verb which in fact subcategorizes for (or still governs) the pre-posed logical object (the complement of the preposition BA) and the main verb is usually accompanied by other auxiliary constituents following or immediately preceding it. In other words, the verb can not stand alone after its object is moved in front of it (see in 6 a), 7 a) and 7 c)) in italics and in blue and the ungrammatical sentences 6 c) and 7 d)). Besides, Chinese is a thematic language, and the theme is often placed in front of the other constituents in the sentences accordingly. In many cases, we can see that the BA-construction does have an effect of emphasis on the semantic content that this structure carries (see the comparisons between 6 a) and 6 b), and between 7 a) and 7 b)). We take again the example (4), "*He repeated what he had said just now.*", and show it in (6) (HU, 1991).

Compare:

6 a)[8] 他把刚才的话又**重复**了 *一遍*。

[8] The underlined part refers to the BA-construction; the italic refers to the auxiliary constituents; and the word in bold font refers to the verb.

(Subj + BA-structure + V + auxiliary constituent)

b) 他又重复了刚才的话。(Subj + V + Obj)

c) * 他*把刚才的话*又重复。

7 a) 我把信读了*一遍*。(Subj + BA-structure V + LE + auxiliary constituent)
(literal translation: I BA letter read one BIAN (CLS)) *I read the letter once.*

b) 我读了信。(Subj + V + Obj)
I read the letter.

c) 我把信*仔细地*读*了*。(Subj + BA-structure + auxiliary constituent + V + LE)
(literal translation: I BA letter carefully read LE) *I have carefully read the letter.*

d) * 我把信读。

As shown in example (6 a, c) and (7 a, c, d), if we leave out the auxiliary constituents "*一遍*" in (6 a), and "*一遍*", "*仔细地*" and "*了*"in (7 a, c), both sentences (6 c and 7 d) become ungrammatical. Therefore, the syntactic structure of the second school can be analyzed as shown in Figure 2 "BA as a Preposition":

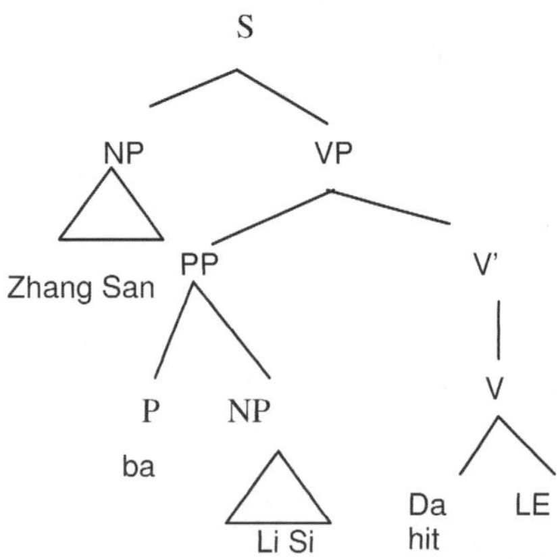

Figure 2 BA as a Preposition

Schematically, a BA-construction always has the following linear configurations:

a) NP* + BA + NP + V + X
b) NP* + BA + NP + X + V

where the sentence can have an optional (in many cases) NP* as subject, followed by BA and its NP complement, then followed by a transitive V and another constituent X (which might precede the verb as shown in (b), and usually is an adverb or a prepositional phrase).

Concerning our own view, we adopt the idea that the BA is a preposition with which the patient object is shifted to the front of the main verb and the BA structure functions as an adjunct of the verb like many other adjuncts that are often placed between the subject and the predicate verb (HU, 1991). The reason for this choice is that considering the BA-construction as a PP is easier for the syntactic analysis and formulation than taking it as a VP in a serial verb construction.

Against this background, we will demonstrate in the following section how we formalize the BA-construction to cope with its English counterpart imperative sentences in our work and how these English sentences are finally constructed into grammatical target Chinese sentences containing the BA-structure.

3 Formalization of the BA-construction

The MT system we work with is oriented to the automatic translation of medical protocols selected from two sub-domains: echinococcosis (clinical practice) and molecular cloning (laboratory practice), where the predominant sentence type is the imperative sentence. Due to the fact that the BA-construction is mandatory in transferring some of the information conveyed in these SL sentences, we have formalized some English sentences into Chinese counterpart sentences containing the BA-construction. To do this, we compare carefully each of the sentence pairs in both languages from a parallel bilingual corpus which we have constructed for our research. In this way, we obtained enough evidence to support the formalization of this special Chinese construction for our MT system. Though the BA-construction is a very productive structure from which we can derive many varieties in Mandarin Chinese, our observation of the corpus reveals that the variations are limited but nevertheless indispensable for formulation.

As we have mentioned in the above paragraph, we have constructed a parallel bilingual corpus for an experimental MT system for the purpose of automatic translation of medical protocols which are from two different sources: one is on echinococcosis, a kind of transmissible disease shared by humans and animals, and the other is on molecular cloning. Like many other scientific documents, the medical texts we collected show a high degree of homogeneity in respect of the text structure and lexical usage, but often we find very long and structurally complicated sentences which are difficult to analyze or to be formally represented. To narrow down the linguistic difficulty, we adopt the controlled language technique as a supporting method (CARDEY, et al. 2004), (WU, 2005). In other words, we first make the raw text materials simpler and easier for the computer to process, for example, to standardize the general structure of the text, the terminology, and to constrain the lexical usages and the sentence structures, which allows us to avoid many complex linguistic phenomena and which helps us to design practical controlled writing rules. Controlled language has been proved to be very feasible in machine translation by many systems, e.g. KANT (NYBERG & TERUKO, 1996). With the simpler and clearer input source sentences, the machine can generally produce better output target sentences.

We finally work with our already well-controlled final texts for linguistic analysis which is based on unification-based grammar. According to our observation, the English sentences which have to be transferred into Chinese sentences containing the BA-constructions are of two types, of which one is obligatory and the other is optional (with the BA-construction or no). The typical feature of these kinds of sentences is that the main verb in the sentence often indicates a kind of change or movement; therefore, in both the source and target sentence the goal or location of this change or movement is represented by a prepositional phrase, for example:

8) Insert a catheter in the cyst.

把导管插入到包囊中。

9) Store the tube on the ice.

把试管存放在冰上。

The syntactic structure of this kind of sentence in the SL can be represented as:

S → VP

VP → V NP PP

and we get two basic formulae by applying predicate-argument generation for example 8 and 9:

Insert (_, Compl1, in_Compl2)

Store (_, Compl1, on_Compl2)

"_" refers to the position of the verb which may vary accordingly.

From the aligned TL sentence, we can formulate the TL sentence as:

S → VP

VP → PP1 V PP2

in which the first PP is the BA-structure and the second PP corresponds to the PP in the SL. Therefore we get two corresponding formulae for example 8 and 9 in the TL respectively:

插入(BA_Compl1, _, 到_Compl2_中)

存放(BA_Compl1, _, 在_Compl2_上)

In fact, for example 8 the Chinese translation can leave out the second preposition "到... (中)", for the reason that it is more convenient if we lexicalize a Chinese equivalent for the English preposition "in" in the Chinese translation at the cost that it is a bit redundant in the TL sometimes, but completely grammatical and acceptable. Our principle here is that every word should have its status in the sentence. So whenever it is possible and, in particular acceptable in the TL, we assign a correspondence to the SL preposition (or other words like adverbs or NP as adjunct) in the TL. By doing so, the machine can have a better performance in most cases. It is particularly beneficial for bi-directional MT. The correspondence of a SL preposition is mostly composed of two Chinese characters in the structure of "X ... Y", of which "..." is the position of the complement of the preposition in question. The second element "Y" is usually considered as a noun indicating the direction or location in Chinese. However, in our case, we consider it as a disjoint part of the first preposition "X". In other words, the "X...Y" structure is considered as one language unit in our practice. The lexicalization of a prepositional phrase in the TL is also one of our criteria to test if a sentence has to be constructed with the BA-structure or not. Most importantly this practice can reduce the workload of writing too many grammatical rules for the system, for example when a preposition has to be translated into Chinese and when it needs not to, etc.

Like most of the English imperative sentences, the Chinese counterpart sentences start with verbs. However, in some cases, the BA-construction is also employed. Generally speaking, many of the sentences can be used in both ways: to start with a verb or start with the BA-construction. They do not make big differences in general. However, semantically the sentences starting with a verb tend to be more narrative while the BA-construction is more firm and authoritative in expressing the ideas, for example:

10) Store the tube on the ice.

a. 把*试管***存放**在冰上。(BA + *N* + **V** + PP)[9]

b. 在冰上**存放***试管*。(PP + V + *N*)

11) Aspirate the contrast medium from the cyst.

a. 把*造影剂*从包囊中**抽出来**。

b. 从包囊中**抽出***造影剂*。

The protocols we work with are instructions of certain step-by-step procedures of either clinical practice or laboratory practice, just like product use instructions, recipes and user's manuals. The semantic contents of these sentences should be firmly expressed as kinds of orders. Though both pairs of the Chinese sentences (10 and 11) are transferring the same idea, the BA-construction is more expressive and natural in this case (example 10 a) and 11 a).

In our corpus, we have observed that some of the English imperative sentences can be transferred into two kinds of BA-construction, that of obligatory and that of optional.

Obligatoriness:

In our work, some sentences must be constructed into Chinese BA-structure, otherwise, the whole sentence sounds either ungrammatical (see in c below) or unnatural or especially unacceptable (see in b below). The grammaticality of the sentence can be tested by moving the translated SL PP to the front of the sentence in the TL (see in c)), for example:

12 a) Inject contrast medium into the cyst.

把*造影剂***注射**进包囊中[10] 。

b) **注射***造影剂*进包囊中。

(unacceptable)

c) *进包囊中**注射***造影剂*。

As is shown in (c), if the whole sentence becomes ungrammatical after moving the PP in front of the sentence, we classify the sentence as obligatory to be transferred into to a TL sentence containing the BA-structure. We then constrain the syntactic structure to the first one as the legal structure while excluding the other two, thus the formulations are:

insert (_, Compl1, into_Compl2)

注射 (BA_Compl1, _, 进_Compl2_中)

The other two are excluded:

注射 (_, Compl1, 进_Compl2_中)

(unacceptable)

*注射 (进_Compl2_中, _, Compl1)

Notice that though the first excluded formulation in the TL shares the same structure as that of the SL, they are unacceptable in the TL. The same situation applies to the following two examples:

13 a) Leave the contrast medium in the cyst as a substitute of protoscolicide agent.

作为灭杀原头蚴剂的替代品, 把*造影剂***留**在包囊里。

b) *作为灭杀原头蚴剂的替代品, **留***造影剂*在包囊里。(ungrammatical)

c) *作为杀原头蚴剂的替代品，在包囊里**留***造影剂*。(strange and ungrammatical)

The final formulation is based on (a):

Leave (_, Compl1, in_Compl2, X)

留 (X, BA_Compl1, _, 在_Compl2_里)

The other two are excluded:

*留 (X, _, Compl1, 在_Compl2_里)

*留 (X, 在_Compl2_里, _, Compl1,)

14 a) Leave the inserted catheter in the cyst for 1-3 days.

把插入的导管**留**在包囊里 1 到 3 天。

Alternative:

把插入的导管在包囊里**留** 1 到 3 天。

b) **留***插入的导管*在包囊里 1 到 3 天。

(unacceptable)

c) *1 到 3 天在包囊里**留***插入的导管*。

(ungrammatical)

Note: for (b) a better alternative should be:

在包囊里**留** 1 到 3 天*插入的导管*。(an acceptable sentence)

The final legal formulations are:

Leave (_, Compl1, in_Compl2, T)

留(BA_Compl1, _, 在_Compl2_里, T)

The alternatives (in a) and b)) will be excluded as long as the first one (a) is a perfectly acceptable sentence. Unlike the "X" in example (13 and 14), here the "T" refers to adjuncts which refers to TIME and which usually occupies a different position in the sentence in our case.

Therefore our criterion to test the obligatoriness is to see what kind of grammatical performance a sentence will exhibit when it is used in the form shown in the above (b's and c's, especially in (c's)). If the sentence looks

---

[9] Note: the BA is underlined; the verb is in bold font; and the object (logical) is in italic.

[10] Red: refer the translated SL PP in TL.

unacceptable or is in particular ungrammatical, then it must be constructed into the TL sentence containing the BA-structure. This phenomenon is in fact closely related with the semantic contents of the verb and as well as the preposition (a goal or a location) in question (we will not discuss this aspect in this paper).

Optionality

Some sentences that we have observed can be used optionally. That is to say, we can transfer the SL sentences without employing the BA-construction, or with the BA-construction in the TL. In doing so, no significant loss of the sentence meaning will occur (except that in some cases there still exist the semantic differences where a BA-construction exhibits firmness and authority), for example:

15 a) Dissolve the nucleic acids in 50 μl of TE that contains 20 μg/ml DNase-free RNase A.

把*核酸*溶解在含有 20 μg/ 无 DNase RNase A 的 50 μl TE 中。

b) 在含有 20 μg/ml 无 DNase RNase A 的 50 μl TE 中溶解*核酸*。

Final formulations:

Dissolve (_, Compl1, in_Compl2)

溶解 (BA_Compl1, _, 在_Compl2_中)

Or:

溶解 (在_Compl2_中, _, Compl1)

16 a) Store the tube on the ice for three minutes.

把试管在冰上存放三分钟。

(linear sequence of the literal translation: BA tube, on ice, store, three minute)

b) 在冰上存放*试管*三分钟。

Alternative:

在冰上存放三分钟*试管*。

Final formulations:

Store (_, Compl1, on_Compl2, T)

存放 (BA_Compl1, _, 在_Compl2_上, T)

Or:

存放(在_Compl2_上, _, Compl1, T)

16 a) Vortex the solution gently for a few seconds.

把*溶液*轻轻振荡几秒钟。

(linear sequence: BA solution, gently, vortex, a few seconds)

b) 轻轻振荡*溶液*几秒钟。

Final formulations :

Vortex (_, Compl1, Y, T)

振荡 (BA_Compl1, Y, _, T)

Or:

振荡 (Y, _, Compl1, T)

Here "Y" refers to adverbs.

However, if the transitive verb (e.g. "vortex") is used intransitively as is often the case in our corpus, the BA-construction has to be changed to the normal sentence structure (V + (X) + PP), for example:

17) Vortex gently for a few seconds.

轻轻振荡几秒钟。

Formulation for this becomes:

Vortex (_, Y, T)

振荡 (Y, _, T)

The reason why we allow the alternative formulations in the second case is that these sentences are actually subcategorized for by the verbs and will not be confused with other similar syntactic structures (e.g. V + NP + PP) which do not employ the BA-construction in the TL while transferring the intended information. We demonstrate this with an example:

18 a) Puncture the cyst with the needle.

用针穿刺包囊。

While the machine is searching the information concerning this sentence, two major supported sources of information (lexicon and grammar rules) will help it find the correct structure for transferring the sentence into the correct TL correspondence. Therefore, the machine will not mismatch the syntactic structure for this sentence by wrongly employing the BA-construction, for example the following translation will be excluded by both the information stored in the lexicon and grammar as a legal instruction:

b) *把包囊用针穿刺。

This is an understandable but very unnatural sentence and can be regarded as ungrammatical in the target language. Though it possesses the same structure as that of the other BA-construction, the problem of this ungrammaticality is caused by the semantic content conveyed by both the verb and the preposition. Usually a BA-construction expresses the resultative or directional effect of the verb. However, what the PP "*with the needle*" expresses is the manner of the verb, that is, how the action is done. Semantically, it is not within the semantic scope of the BA-construction (though we can find few contradictory examples) and thus can not be translated into to the target language by incorrectly employing the BA-construction.

In our system prepositional phrases like, "*with the needle*" is subcategorized by the verb "*puncture*" and the syntactic rules for this verb. To demonstrate this, we simplify the lexical and syntactic information as shown in the formula below:

Puncture (_, Compl1, with_Compl2)

穿刺(用_Compl2, _, Compl1)

The above information tells us that the verb "*puncture*" of the source language, like the other verbs mentioned in the previous paragraphs, can have two complements, of which one has a preposition as the head of the second linear complement. The correspondence in the target language for this verb is "穿刺" which take two complements too. One corresponds to the first complement of the SL and is placed after the verb "穿刺", and the other complement corresponds to the second complement but is placed in front of the verb with a preposition as its head "用". The simplified syntactic structures for both sentences are:

SL: V_3[11] (_, A, P_B)
TL: V_3 (P_B, _, A)

4 Conclusion

In this paper we have discussed a special Chinese syntactic structure: the BA-construction which is quite controversial in the literature but nevertheless less problematic in our work. After comparing with other syntactic structures, we finally adopt the idea that the BA-construction shows more characteristics of a PP which is still governed by the verb which follows it, in particular in our work. We thus treat this structure as a PP rather than a VP. This is supported by the relatively simpler sentence structures found in our corpus. While constructing our grammar and formulating the BA-structure, we lay focus on the syntactic performance and semantic contents that the BA-construction exhibits. Based on the verb types and the semantic content of the preposition following the verb, we finally formulate two kinds of sentence types concerning the BA-construction in the target language which can well satisfy our purpose. Of course, like many other language-specific syntactic structures, our analysis and practice can not satisfy all situations. However, as we work on a relatively narrow domain where the sentence types by themselves do not vary greatly. We can find a better solution by controlling the syntactic types to tackle the problems concerning the BA-construction and the alike.

[11] V_3: refers to the syntactic pattern of the verb.

References

BENDER, Emily. 2002 The Syntax of Madarin Ba: Reconsidering the Verbal Analysis, Journal of East Asian Linguistics, 2002

CARDEY, Sylviane, GREENFIELD, Peter, WU Xiaohong. 2004. Desinging a Controlled Language for the Machine Translation of Medical Protocols: the Case of English to Chinese. In Proceedings of the AMTA 2004, LNAI 3265, Springer-Verlag, pp. 37-47

HASHIMOTO, Anne Yue. 1971. Descriptive adverbials and the passive construction, Unicorn, No. 7.

HER, One-Soon. 1990. Grammatical Functions and Verb Subcategorization in Madarin Chinese. PhD dissertation, University of Hawaii.

HU Yushu et al. 1991 Modern Chinese 《现代汉语》，上海教育出版社， ISBN 7- 5320-0547-X/G.456

LIN, Tzong-Hong Jonah. 2004. Grammar of Chinese, Lecture note, "The Ba construction and Bei Construction 12/21/2004, National Tsing Hua University, Taiwan, 国立清华大学语言研究所，http://www.ling.nthu.edu.tw

MA, L. 1985. The Classical Notion of Passive and the Mandarin bei. ms. Department of linguistics, Stanford University.

NYBERG, Eric H., TERUKO Mitamura. 1992. The KANT System: Fast, Accurate, High-Quality Translation in Practical Domains. Proceedings of COLING-92.

WU Xiaohong. 2005. Controlled Language – A Useful Technique to Facilitate Machine Translation of Technical Documents, In Linguisticoe Investigationes 28:1, 2005. John Benjamins Publishing Company, pp. 123-131

ZHOU Jing and PU Kan. 1985. Modern Chinese 《现代汉语》，华东师范大学出版社，ISBN 7135 104

ZHU, Dexi. 1982. 《语法讲义》 Lectures on Syntax. 北京，商务印书馆。Beijing: Commercial Press

A Hybrid Approach to Chinese Base Noun Phrase Chunking

Fang Xu **Chengqing Zong** **Jun Zhao**
National Laboratory of Pattern Recognition
Institute of Automation
Chinese Academy of Sciences, Beijing 100080,China
{fxu, cqzong, jzhao}@nlpr.ia.ac.cn

Abstract

In this paper, we propose a hybrid approach to chunking Chinese base noun phrases (base NPs), which combines SVM (Support Vector Machine) model and CRF (Conditional Random Field) model. In order to compare the result respectively from two chunkers, we use the discriminative post-processing method, whose measure criterion is the conditional probability generated from the CRF chunker. With respect to the special structures of Chinese base NP and complete analyses of the first two results, we also customize some appropriate grammar rules to avoid ambiguities and prune errors. According to our overall experiments, the method achieves a higher accuracy in the final results.

1 Introduction

Chunking means extracting the non-overlapping segments from a stream of data. These segments are called chunks (Dirk and Satoshi, 2003). The definition of base noun phrase (base NP) is simple and non-recursive noun phrase which does not contain other noun phrase descendants. Base NP chunking could be used as a precursor for many elaborate natural language processing tasks, such as information retrieval, name entity extraction and text summarization and so on. Many other problems similar to text processing can also benefit from base NP chunking, for example, finding genes in DNA and phoneme information extraction.

The initial work on base NP chunking is focused on the grammar-based method. Ramshaw and Marcus (1995) introduced a transformation-based learning method which considered chunking as a kind of tagging problem. Their work inspired many others to study the applications of learning methods to noun phrase chunking. (Cardie and Pierce, 1998, 1999) applied a scoring method to select new rules and a naive heuristic for matching rules to evaluate the results' accuracy.

CoNLL-2000 proposed a shared task (Tjong and Buchholz, 2000), which aimed at dividing a text in syntactically correlated parts of words. The eleven systems for the CoNLL-2000 shared task used a wide variety of machine learning methods. The best system in this workshop is on the basis of Support Vector Machines used by (Kudo and Matsumoto, 2000).

Recently, some new statistical techniques, such as CRF (Lafferty *et al.* 2001) and structural learning methods (Ando and Zhang, 2005) have been applied on the base NP chunking. (Fei and Fernando, 2003) considered chunking as a sequence labeling task and achieved good performance by an improved training methods of CRF. (Ando and Zhang, 2005) presented a novel semi-supervised learning method on chunking and produced performances higher than the previous best results.

The research on Chinese Base NP Chunking is, however, still at its developing stage. Researchers apply similar methods of English Base NP chunking to Chinese. Zhao and Huang (1998) made a strict definition of Chinese base NP and put forward a quasi-dependency model to analysis the structure of Chinese base NPs. There are some other methods to deal with Chinese phrase (no only base NP) chunking, such as HMM (Heng Li *et al.*, 2003), Maximum Entropy (Zhou Yaqian *et al.*, 2003), Memory-Based Learning (Zhang and Zhou, 2002) etc.

However, according to our experiments over 30,000 Chinese words, the best results of Chinese base NP chunking are about 5% less than that of English chunking (Although we should admit the chunking outcomes vary among different sizes of corpus and rely on the details of experiments). The differences between Chinese NPs and English NPs are summarized as following points: First, the flexible structure of Chinese noun phrase often results in the ambiguities during the recognition procedure. For example, many English base NPs begin with the determinative, while the margin of Chinese base NPs is more uncertain. Second, the base NPs begins with more than two noun-modifiers, such as "高(high)/JJ 新(new)/JJ 技术(technology)/NN", the noun-modifiers "高/JJ " can not be completely recognized. Third, the usage of Chinese word is flexible, as a Chinese word may serve with multi POS (Part-of-Speech) tags. For example, a noun is used as a verbal or an adjective component in the sentence. In this way the chunker is puzzled by those multi-used words. Finally, there are no standard datasets and elevation systems for Chinese base NP chunking as the CoNLL-2000 shared task, which makes it difficult to compare and evaluate different Chinese base NP chunking systems.

In this paper, we propose a hybrid approach to extract the Chinese base NPs with the help of the conditional probabilities derived from the CRF algorithm and some appropriate grammar rules. According to our preliminary experiments on SVM and CRF, our approach outperforms both of them.

The remainder of the paper is organized as follows. Section 2 gives a brief introduction of the data representations and methods. We explain our motivations of the hybrid approach in section 3. The experimental results and conclusions are introduced in section 4 and section 5 respectively.

2 Task Description

2.1 Data Representation

Ramshaw and Marcus (1995) gave mainly two kinds of base NPs representation — the open/close bracketing and IOB tagging. For example, a bracketed Chinese sentence,

[外商(foreign businessmen) 投资(investment)] 成为(become) [中国 (Chinese) 外贸(foreign trade)] [重要(important) 增长点(growth)] 。

The IOB tags are used to indicate the boundaries for each base NP where letter 'B' means the current word starts a base NP, 'I' for a word inside a base NP and 'O' for a word outside a NP chunk. In this case the tokens for the former sentence would be labeled as follows:

外商/B 投资/I 成为/V 中国/B 外贸/I 重要/B 增长点/O 。/O

Currently, most of the work on base NP identification employs the trainable, corpus-based algorithm, which makes full use of the tokens and corresponding POS tags to recognize the chunk segmentation of the test data. The SVM and CRF are two representative effective models widely used.

2.2 Chunking with SVMs

SVM is a machine learning algorithm for a linear binary classifier in order to maximize the margin of confidence of the classification on the training data set. According to the different requirements, distinctive kernel functions are employed to transfer non-linear problems into linear problems by mapping it to a higher dimension space.

By transforming the training data into the form with IOB tags, we can view the base NP chunking problem as a multi-class classification problem. As SVMs are binary classifiers, we use the pairwise method to convert the multi-class problem into a set of binary class problem, thus the I/O/B classifier is reduced into 3 kinds of binary classifier — I/O classifier, O/B classifier, B/I classifier.

In our experiments, we choose TinySVM[1] together with YamCha[2] (Kudo and Matsumoto, 2001) as the one of the baseline systems for our chunker. In order to construct the feature sets for training SVMs, all information available in the surrounding contexts, including tokens, POS tags and IOB tags. The tool YamCha makes it possible to add new features on your own. Therefore, in the training stage, we also add two new features according to the words. First, we give special tags to the noun words, especially the proper noun, as we find in the experiment the proper nouns sometimes bring on errors, such as base

[1] http://chasen.org/~taku/software/TinySVM/
[2] http://chasen.org/~taku/software/yamcha

NP "四川(Sichuan)/NR 盆地(basin)/NN", containing the proper noun "四川/NR", could be mistaken for a single base NP "盆地/NN"; Second, some punctuations such as separating marks, contribute to the wrong chunking, because many Chinese compound noun phrases are connected by separating mark, and the ingredients in the sentence are a mixture of simple nouns and noun phrases, for example,

"国家(National)/NN 统计局(Statistics Office)/NN，中国(Chinese)/NR 社会(Social Sciences)/NN 科学院(Academy)/NN 和(and)/CC 中科院(Chinese Academy of Sciences)/NN-SHORT"

The part of base NP – "中国/B 社会/I 科学院/I" can be recognized as three independent base NPs --"中国/B 社会/B 科学院/B". The kind of errors comes from the conjunction "和(and)" and the successive sequences of nouns, which contribute little to the chunker. More information and analyses will be provided in Section 4.

2.3 Conditional Random Fields

Lafferty *et al.*(2001) present the Conditional Random Fields for building probabilistic models to segment and label sequence data, which was used effectively for base NP chunking (Sha & Pereira, 2003). Lafferty *et al.* (2001) point out that each of the random variable label sequences Y conditioned on the random observation sequence X. The joint distribution over the label sequence Y given X has the form

$$p(y \mid x, \lambda) = \frac{1}{Z(x)} \exp(\sum_j \lambda_j F_j(y, x))$$

$$F(y, x) = \sum_{i=1}^{n} f(y_{i-1}, y_i, x, i)$$

where $f_j(y_{i-1}, y_i, x, i)$ is either a transition feature function $s(y_{i-1}, y_i, x, i)$ or a state feature function $t(y_{i-1}, y_i, x, i)$; y_{i-1}, y_i are labels, x is an input sequence, i is an input position, $Z(x)$ is a normalization factor; λ_k is the parameter to be estimated from training data.

Then we use the maximum likelihood training, such as the log-likelihood to train CRF given training data $T = \{(x_k, y_k)\}$,

$$L(\lambda) = \sum_k \left[\log \frac{1}{Z(x_k)} + \lambda \cdot F(y_k, x_k) \right]$$

$L(\lambda)$ is minimized by finding unique zero of the gradient

$$\nabla L(\lambda) = \sum_k [F(y_k, x_k) - E_{p(Y|x_k,\lambda)} F(Y, x_k)]$$

$E_{p(Y|x_k,\lambda)} F(Y, x_k)$ can be computed using a variant of the forward-backward algorithm. We define a transition matrix as following:

$$M_i(y', y \mid x) = \exp(\sum_j \lambda_j f_j(y', y, x, i))$$

Then,

$$p(y \mid x, \lambda) = \frac{1}{Z(x)} \prod_{i=1}^{n+1} M_i(y_{i-1}, y_i \mid x)$$

and let * denote component-wise matrix product,

$$E_{p(Y|x_k,\lambda)} F(Y, x_k) = \sum_y p(Y = y \mid x_k, \lambda) F(y, x_k)$$

$$= \sum_i \frac{\alpha_{i-1}(f_i * M_i)\beta_i^T}{Z(x)}$$

$$Z(x) = a_n \cdot 1^T$$

Where α_i, β_i as the forward and backward state-cost vectors defined by

$$\alpha_i = \begin{cases} \alpha_{i-1} M_i & 0 < i \le n \\ 1 & i = 0 \end{cases}, \beta_i^T = \begin{cases} M_{i+1}\beta_{i+1}^T & 1 \le i < n \\ 1 & i = n \end{cases}$$

Sha & Pereira (2003) provided a thorough discussion of CRF training methods including preconditioned Conjugate Gradient, limited-Memory Quasi-Newton and voted perceptron. They also present a novel approach to model construction and feature selection in shallow parsing.

We use the software CRF++[3] as our Chinese base NP chunker baseline software. The results of CRF are better than that of SVM, which is the same as the outcome of the English base NP chunking in (Sha & Pereira, 2003). However, we find CRF products some errors on identifying long-range base NP, while SVM performs well in this aspect and the errors of SVM and CRF are of different types. In this case, we develop a combination approach to improve the results.

3 Our Approach

(Tjong *et al.*, 2000) pointed out that the performance of machine learning can be improved by combining the output of different systems, so they combined the results of different classifiers

[3] http://www.chasen.org/~taku/software/CRF++/

and obtained good performance. Their combination system generated different classifiers by using different data labels and applied respective voting weights accordingly. (Kudo and Matsumoto 2001) designed a voting arrangement by applying cross validation and VC-bound and Leave-One-Out bound for the voting weights.

The voting systems improve the accuracy, the choices of weights and the balance between different weights is based on experiences, which does not concern the inside features of the classification, without the guarantee of persuasive theoretical supports. Therefore, we developed a hybrid approach to combine the results of the SVM and CRF and utilize their advantages. (Simon, 2003) pointed out that the SVM guarantees a high generalization using very rich features from the sentences, even with a large and high-dimension training data. CRF can build efficient and robust structure model of the labels, when one doesn't have prior knowledge about data. Figure 1 shows the preliminary chunking and pos-processing procedure in our experiments

First of all, we use YamCha and CRF++ respectively to treat with the testing data. We got two original results from those chunkers, which use the exactly same data format; in this case we can compare the performance between CRF and SVM. After comparisons, we can figure out the same words with different IOB tags from the two former chunkers. Afterward, there exist two problems: how to pick out the IOB tags identified improperly and how to modify those wrong IOB tags.

To solve the first question, we use the conditional probability from the CRF to help determine the wrong IOB tags. For each word of the testing data, the CRF chunker works out a conditional probability for each IOB tag and chooses the most probable tag for the output. We bring out the differences between the SVM and CRF, such as "四川 (Sichuan)" in a base noun phrase is recognized as "I" and "O" respectively, and the distance between P(I| "四川") and P(O| "四川") is tiny. According to our experiment, about 80% of the differences between SVM and CRF share the same statistical characters, which indicate the correct answers are inundated by the noisy features in the classifier.

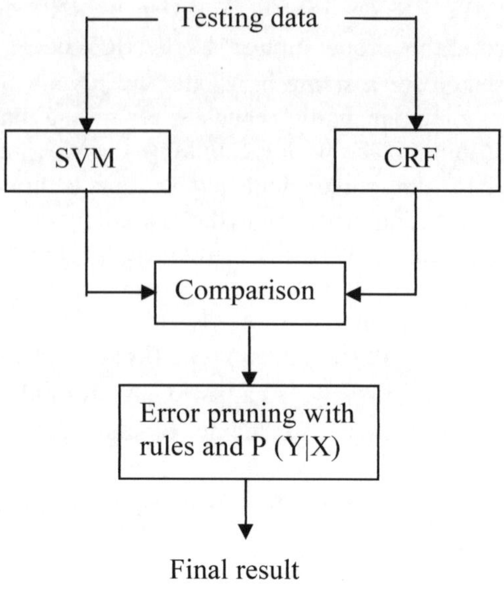

Figure 1 the Experiments' Procedure

Using the comparison between SVM and CRF we can check most of those errors. Then we could build some simple grammar rules to figure out the correct tags for the ambiguous words corresponding to the surrounding contexts. Then At the error pruning step, judging from the surrounding texts and the grammar rules, the base NP is corrected to the right form. We give 5 mainly representative grammar rules to explain how they work in the experiments.

The first simple sample of grammar rules is just like "BNP → NR NN", used to solve the proper noun problems. Take the "四川 (Sichuan)/NR/B 盆地 (basin)/NN/I" for example, the comparison finds out the base NP recognized as "四川 (Sichuan)/NR/I 盆地 (basin)/NN/B". Second, with respect to the base NP connecting with separating mark and conjunction words, two rules "BNP → BNP CC (BNP | Noun), BNP →BNP PU (BNP | Noun)" is used to figure out those errors; Third, with analyzing our experiment results, the CRF and SVM chunker recognize differently on the determinative, therefore the rule "BNP → JJ BNP", our combination methods figure out new BNP tags from the preliminary results according to this rule. Finally, the most complex situation is the determination of the Base NPs composed of series of nouns, especially the proper nouns. With figuring out the maximum length of this kind of noun phrase, we highlight the proper nouns and then separate the complex noun phrase to base noun phrases, and according to the our experiments, this method could solve close to 75% of the ambiguity in the errors from complex noun phrases. Totally, the rules could solve about 63% of the found errors.

4 Experiments

The CoNLL 2000 provided the software[4] to convert Penn English Treebank II into the IOB tags form. We use the Penn Chinese Treebank 5.0[5], which is improved and involved with more POS tags, segmentation and syntactic bracketing. As the sentences in the Treebank are longer and related to more complicated structures, we modify the software with robust heuristics to cope with those new features of the Chinese Treebank and generate the training and testing data sets from the Treebank. Afterward we also make some manual adjustments to the final data.

In our experiments, the SVM chunker uses a polynomial kernel with degree 2; the cost per unit violation of the margin, C=1; and tolerance of the termination criterion, $\varepsilon = 0.01$.

In the base NPs chunking task, the evaluation metrics for base NP chunking include precision *P*, recall *R* and the F_β. Usually we refer to the F_β as the creditable metric.

$$P = \frac{\#\ of\ correct\ proposed\ baseNP}{\#\, of\ \ proposed\ baseNP} * 100\%$$

$$R = \frac{\#\ of\ correct\ proposed\ baseNP}{\#\, of\ corect\ baseNP} * 100\%$$

$$F_\beta = \frac{(\beta^2+1)RF}{\beta^2 R + F} \qquad (\beta = 1)$$

All the experiments were performed on a Linux system with 3.2 GHz Pentium 4 and 2G memory. The total size of the Penn Chinese Treebank words is 13 MB, including about 500,000 Chinese words. The quantity of training corpus amounts to 300,000 Chinese words. Each word contains two Chinese characters in average. We mainly use five kinds of corpus, whose sizes include 30000, 40000, 50000, 60000 and 70,000 words. The corpus with an even larger size is improper according to the training corpus amount.

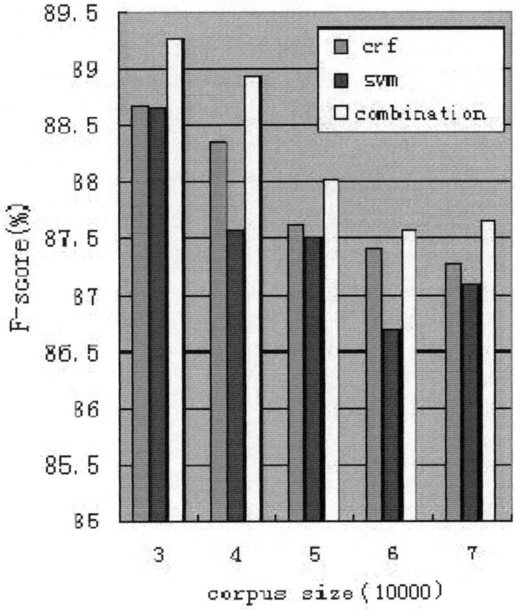

Figure 2 F-score vs. Corpus Size

From Figure 2, we can see that the results from CRF are better than that from SVM and the error-pruning performs the best. Our hybrid error-pruning method achieves an obvious improvement F-scores by combining the outcome from SVM and CRF classifiers. The test F-scores are decreasing when the sizes of corpus increase. The best performance with F-score of 89.27% is achieved by using a test corpus of 30k words. We get about 1.0% increase of F-score after using the hybrid approach. The F-score is higher than F-score 87.75% of Chinese base NP chunking systems using the Maximum Entropy method in (Zhou *et al.*, 2003),. Which used the smaller 3 MB Penn Chinese Treebank II as the corpus.

The Chinese Base NP chunkers are not superior to those for English. Zhang and Ando (2005) produce the best English base NP accuracy with F-score of 94.39+ (0.79), which is superior to our best results. The previous work mostly considered base NP chunking as the classification problem without special attention to the lexical information and syntactic dependence of words. On the other hand, we add some grammar rules to strength the syntactic dependence between the words. However, the syntactic structure derived from Chinese is much more flexible and complex than that from English. First, some Chinese words contain abundant meanings or play different syntactic roles. For example, "其中 (among which)/NN 重 庆 (Chongqing)/NR 地 区 (district)/NN" is recognized as a base NP. Actu-

[4] http://ilk.kub.nl/~sabine/chunklink/

[5] http://www.cis.upenn.edu/~chinese/

ally the Chinese word "其中/NN (among)" refers to the content in the previous sentence and "其中 (thereinto)" sometimes used as an adverb. Second, how to deal with the conjunctions is a major problem, especially the words "与 (and)" can appear in the preposition structure "与 …… 相关 (relate to)", which makes it difficult to judge those types of differences. Third, the chunkers can not handle with compact sequence data of chunks with name entities and new words (especially the transliterated words) satisfactorily, such as

"中国 (China) /NR 红十字会(Red Cross) /NR名誉 (Honorary) /NN 会长 (Chairman) /NN 江泽民(Jiang Ze-min) /NR"

As it points above, the English name entities sequences are connected with the conjunction such as "of, and, in". While in Chinese there are no such connection words for name entities sequences. Therefore when we use the statistical methods, those kinds of sequential chunks contribute slightly to the feature selection and classifier training, and are treated as the useless noise in the training data. In the testing section, it is close the separating margin and hardly determined to be in the right category. What's more, some other factors such as Idiomatic and specialized expressions also account for the errors. By highlighting those kinds of words and using some rules which emphasize on those proper words, we use our error-pruning methods and useful grammar rules to correct about 60% errors.

5 Conclusions

This paper presented a new hybrid approach for identifying the Chinese base NPs. Our hybrid approach uses the SVM and CRF algorithm to design the preliminary classifiers for chunking. Furthermore with the direct comparison between the results from the former chunkers, we figure out that those two statistical methods are myopic about the compact chunking data of sequential noun. With the intention of capturing the syntactic dependence within those sequential chunking data, we make use of the conditional probabilities of the chunking tags given the corresponding tokens derived from CRF and some simple grammar rules to modify the preliminary results.

The overall results achieve 89.27% precision on the base NP chunking. We attempt to explain some existing semantic problems and solve a certain part of problems, which have been discovered and explained in the paper. Future work will concentrate on working out some adaptive machine learning methods to make grammar rules automatically, select better features and employ suitable classifiers for Chinese base NP chunking. Finally, the particular Chinese base phrase grammars need a complete study, and the approach provides a primary solution and framework to process an analyses and comparisons between Chinese and English parallel base NP chunkers.

Acknowledgments

This work was partially supported by the Natural Science Foundation of China under Grant No. 60575043, and 60121302, the China-France PRA project under Grant No. PRA SI02-05, the Outstanding Overseas Chinese Scholars Fund of the Chinese Academy of Sciences under Grant No.2003-1-1, and Nokia (China) Co. Ltd, as well.

References

Claire Cardie and David Pierce. 1998. *Error-Driven Pruning of Treebank Grammars for Base Noun Phrase Identification.* Proceedings of the 36th ACL and COLING-98, 218-224.

Claire Cardie and David Pierce. 1999. *The role of lexicalization and pruning for base noun phrase grammars.* Proceedings of the 16th AAAI, 423-430.

Dirk Ludtke and Satoshi Sato. 2003. *Fast Base NP Chunking with Decision Trees —— Experiments on Different POS tag Settings.* CICLing 2003, 136-147. LNC S2588, Springer-Verlag Berlin Heidelberg.

Erik F. Tjong Kim Sang and Sabine Buchholz. 2000. *Introduction to the CoNLL-2000 Shared Task: Chunking*. Proceedings of CoNLL and LLL-2000, 127-132.

Erik F. Tjong Kim Sang, Walter Daelemans, Hervé Déean, Rob Koeling, Yuval Krymolowski, Vasin Punyakanok, and Dan Roth. 2000. *Applying system combination to base noun phrase identification.* Proceedings of COLING 2000, 857-863.

Fei Sha and Fernando Pereira. 2003. *Shallow Parsing with Conditional Random Fields.* Proceedings of HLT-NAACL 2003, 134-141.

Heng Li, Jonathan J. Webster, Chunyu Kit, and Tianshun Yao. 2003. *Transductive HMM based Chinese Text Chunking.* IEEE NLP-KE 2003, Beijing, 257-262.

Lance A. Ramshaw and Mitchell P. Marcus. 1995. *Text Chunking using Transformation-Based Learning.* Proceedings of the Third ACL Workshop on Very Large Corpora, 82–94.

Lafferty A. McCallum and F. Pereira. 2001. *Conditional random Fields.* Proceedings of ICML 2001, 282-289.

Rie Kubota Ando and Tong Zhang. 2004. *A framework for learning predictive structures from multiple tasks and unlabeled data.* RC23462. Technical report, IBM.

Rie Kubota Ando and Tong Zhang. 2005. *A High-Performance Semi-Supervised Learning Method for Text Chunking*. Proceedings of the 43rd Annual Meeting of ACL, 1-9.

Simon Lacoste-Julien. 2003. *Combining SVM with graphical models for supervised classification: an introduction to Max-Margin Markov Network.* CS281A Project Report, UC Berkeley.

Taku Kudo and Yuji Matsumoto. 2001. *Chunking with support vector machine.* Proceeding of the NAACL, 192-199.

Zhang Yuqi and Zhou Qiang. 2002. *Chinese Base-Phrases Chunking.* First SigHAN Workshop on Chinese Language Processing, COLING-02.

Zhao Jun and Huang Changling. 1998. *A Quasi-Dependency Model for Structural Analysis of Chinese BaseNPs.* 36th Annual Meeting of the ACL and 17th International Conference on Computational Linguistics.

Zhou Yaqian, Guo YiKun, Huang XuanLing and Wu Lide. 2003. *Chinese and English Base NP Recognition on a Maximum Entropy Model.* Vol140, No13. Journal of Computer Research and Development. (In Chinese)

A SVM-based Model for Chinese Functional Chunk Parsing

Yingze Zhao
State Key Laboratory of Intelligent Technology and Systems
Dept. of Computer Science and Technology, Tsinghua University
Beijing 100084, P. R. China
zhaoyingze@gmail.com

Qiang Zhou
State Key Laboratory of Intelligent Technology and Systems
Dept. of Computer Science and Technology, Tsinghua University
Beijing 100084, P. R. China
zq-lxd@mail.tsinghua.edu.cn

Abstract

Functional chunks are defined as a series of non-overlapping, non-nested segments of text in a sentence, representing the implicit grammatical relations between the sentence-level predicates and their arguments. Its top-down scheme and complexity of internal constitutions bring in a new challenge for automatic parser. In this paper, a new parsing model is proposed to formulate the complete chunking problem as a series of boundary detection sub tasks. Each of these sub tasks is only in charge of detecting one type of the chunk boundaries. As each sub task could be modeled as a binary classification problem, a lot of machine learning techniques could be applied.

In our experiments, we only focus on the subject-predicate (SP) and predicate-object (PO) boundary detection sub tasks. By applying SVM algorithm to these sub tasks, we have achieved the best F-Score of 76.56% and 82.26% respectively.

1 Introduction

Parsing is a basic task in natural language processing; however, it has not been successful in achieving the accuracy and efficiency required by real world applications. As an alternative, shallow parsing or partial parsing has been proposed to meet the current needs by obtaining only a limited amount of syntactic information needed by the application. In recent years, there has been an increasing interest in chunk parsing. From CoNLL-2000 to CoNLL-2005, a lot of efforts have been made in the identification of basic chunks and the methods of combining them from bottom-up to form large, complex units. In this paper, we will apply functional chunks to Chinese shallow parsing.

Functional chunks are defined as a series of non-overlapping, non-nested functional units in a sentence, such as subjects, predicates, objects, adverbs, complements and so on. These units represent the implicit grammatical relations between the sentence-level predicates and their arguments. Different from the basic chunks defined by Abney (1991), functional chunks are generated from a top-down scheme, and thus their constitutions may be very complex. In addition, the type of a functional chunk could not be simply determined by its constitution, but depends heavily on the context. Therefore, we will have new challenges in the functional chunk parsing.

Ramshaw and Marcus (1995) first introduced the machine learning techniques to chunking problem. By formulating the NP-chunking task as a tagging process, they marked each word with a tag from set {B, I, O}, and successfully applied TBL to it. Inspired by their work, we introduce SVM algorithm to our functional chunking problem. Instead of using the BIO tagging system, we propose a new model for solving this problem. In this model, we do not tag the words with BIO tags, but directly discover the chunk boundaries between every two adjacent functional chunks. Each of these chunk boundaries will be assigned a type to it, which contains the information of the functional chunk types before and after it. Then we further decompose this model into a series of sub modules, each of which is in charge of detecting only one type of the chunk boundaries. As each sub module can be modeled as a binary classifier, various machine learning techniques could be applied.

In our experiments, we focus on the subject-predicate (SP) and predicate-object (PO) boundary detection tasks, which are the most difficult but important parts in our parsing model. By applying SVM algorithm to these tasks, we achieve the best F-Score of 76.56% and 82.26% respectively.

This paper is organized as follows. In section 2, we give a brief introduction to the concept of our functional chunks. In section 3, we propose the parsing model for Chinese functional chunk parsing. In section 4, we compare SVM with several other machine learning techniques, and illustrate how competitive SVM is in our chunking task. In section 5, we build 2 sub modules based on SVM algorithm for SP and PO boundary detection tasks. In section 6, some related work on functional chunk parsing is introduced. Section 7 is the conclusion.

2 Functional Chunk Scheme

Functional chunks are defined as a series of non-overlapping, non-nested segments of text at the sentence level without leaving any words outside. Each chunk is labeled with a functional tag, such as subject, predicate, object and so on. These functional chunks in the sentence form a linear structure within which the grammatical relations between sentence-level predicates and their arguments or adjuncts are kept implicitly. Table 1 lists all the tags used in our functional chunk scheme:

Table 1. Functional Chunk Tag Set.

Chunk Tag	Basic Function Description
S	Subject
P	Predicate
O	Object
J	Raised Object
D	Adverbial adjunct
C	Complement
T	Independent constituent
Y	Modal particle

Here, we list some examples to illustrate how these functional tags are used in Chinese sentences.

1. "[D 下午/t (afternoon) ，/， [D 当/p (when) 我/rN (I) 来到/v (come to) 西柏坡村/nS (Xi Bai Po village) 东口/s (eastern entrance) 时/n ，/， [D 已/d (already) [P 有/v (there is) [J 一/m 位/qN (a) 参谋/n (brainman) [D 在/p 那里/rS (there) [P 等候/v (waiting) [Y 了/y 。/。 "

2. "[T 可以说/l (frankly speaking) ，/， [S 那/rN (that) [P 是/vC (was) [O 我/rN (I) 终生/d (lifetime) 不/dN 能/vM (can't) 忘怀/v (forget) 的/u 。/。 "

3. "[S 时间/n (time) [P 安排/v 得/u (schedule) [C 很/dD (very) 紧/a (tight) 。/。 "

Compared with the basic chunk scheme defined by Abney (1991), our functional chunk scheme has the following two main differences:

(1) Functional chunks are not constituted from bottom-up, but generated from top-down, thus some functional chunks are usually longer and more complex than the basic chunks.

We have a collection of 185 news files as our functional chunk corpus. Each file is manually annotated with functional chunks. There are about 200,000 Chinese words in the corpus. To investigate the complex constitutions of functional chunks, we list the average chunk lengths (ACL) of different types in Table 2:

Table 2. Average Chunk Lengths of Different Types.

Chunk Type	Count	Word Sum	ACL
P	21988	27618	1.26
D	19795	46919	2.37
O	14289	61401	4.30
S	11920	34479	2.89
J	855	2083	2.44
Y	594	604	1.02
T	407	909	2.23
C	244	444	1.82

From the table above, we can find that O chunk has the longest average length of 4.30 words, and S chunk has the second longest average length of 2.89 words, and D chunk has an average length of 2.37 words. Although the average length doesn't seem so long, the length of a specific chunk varies greatly.

In Table 3, we list some detailed length distributional data of three chunks.

Table 3. Length Distribution of S, O and D Chunks.

Chunk Length	# of S	# of O	# of D
1	5322	3537	12147
2	2093	2228	2499
3	1402	2117	1431
4	917	1624	1010
5	627	1108	696
>5	1559	3675	2013
Sum	11920	14289	19796

From the table above, we can find that there are totally 1559 S chunks with a length of more than 5 words which takes up 13.08% of the total number. And when we refer to the S chunks with more than 3 words, the percentage will increase to 26.03%. These long chunks are usually constituted with several complex phrases or clauses as the modifiers of a head word. Among the O chunks, 25.72% of them have a length of more than 5 words, and 44.84% of them are longer than 3 words. The reason why O chunks have a longer length may be that many of them contain the entire clauses. Although most of the D chunks are less than 5 words, some constituted with complex preposition phrases can still be very long.

The complex constitutions of S, O, D chunks are the main parsing difficulties.

(2) The type of functional chunks can't be simply determined by their constitutions, but depends heavily on their contexts.

As the constitution of a basic chunk is very simple, its type can be largely determined by its head word, but in the case of functional chunks, the relationships between the functional chunks play an important role. For example, a NP phrase before a P chunk can be identified as a subject chunk, but in other sentences, when it follows another P chunk, it will be recognized as an object chunk. Thus we can't determine the type of a functional chunk simply by its constitution.

The context dependencies of functional chunks bring a new challenge for our chunk parser.

In the next section, we will propose a top-down model for Chinese functional chunk parsing. Since the functional chunk boundaries have the information of linking two adjacent chunks, they will be very helpful in the determination of chunk types.

3 Parsing Model

The Chinese functional chunk parser takes a stream of segmented and tagged words as its input, and outputs all the functional chunk boundaries in a sentence. In this section, we will present a parsing model which formulates the functional chunk parsing problem as a boundary detection task, and then decompose this model into a series of sub modules that are easy to build.

3.1 Formulation

Functional chunks have the property of exhaustibility and no words will be left outside the chunks. Thus we don't need to find the end position for a functional chunk as it could be identified by the start of the next one. In this case, we can simply regard the chunking task as a process of cutting the input sentence into several segments of words, each of which is labeled with a functional tag. Based on this idea, we can model the functional chunk parsing problem as a boundary detection task.

Let $S=\langle W, T \rangle$ denote the input sentence to be parsed by the functional chunk parser, where $W=w_1w_2w_3 \ldots w_n$ is the sequence of words in S, and $T=t_1t_2t_3 \ldots t_n$ is sequence of the POS tags assigned to each word in W. If w_i is a punctuation mark, t_i will be equal to w_i.

A chunk boundary is defined as a pair $\langle C_1, C_2 \rangle$ where $C_1, C_2 \in \{S, P, O, J, D, C, T, Y\}$, C_1 is the chunk type before this boundary and C_2 is the chunk type following it. The output of the chunk parser is denoted as $O=\langle B, P \rangle$ where $B=b_1b_2b_3 \ldots b_m$ is the sequence of chunk boundaries generated by the parser, and $P=p_1p_2p_3 \ldots p_m$ is the corresponding positions of $b_1b_2b_3 \ldots b_m$ in the sentence.

Chinese functional chunk parser can be considered as a function h(S) which maps the input sentence S to the chunk boundary sequence O.

Take the following sentence for example:

"14 核电/n(Nuclear electricity) $_1$ 是/vC(is) $_2$ 一/m(a) $_3$ 种/qN(kind) $_4$ 安全/a(safe) $_5$ 、/、 $_6$ 清洁/a(safe) $_7$ 、/、 $_8$ 经济/a(economical) $_9$ 的/u $_{10}$ 能源/n(energy) $_{11}$ 。/。"

"Nuclear electricity is a kind of safe, clean and economical energy."

In this sentence, there are totally 12 Chinese words (punctuation marks are treated the same way as words) with 11 numbers falling between them indicating the positions where a functional chunk boundary may appear. If the input sentence is parsed correctly by the functional chunk parser, a series of boundaries will arise at position 1 and 2, which are illustrated as below:

"14 核电/n $_{\langle S, P \rangle}$ 是/vC $_{\langle P, O \rangle}$ 一/m 种/qN 安全/a 、/、 清洁/a 、/、 经济/a 的/u 能源/n 。/。"

From the information provided by these boundaries, we can easily identify the functional chunks in the sentence:

"14 [S 核电/n [P 是/vC [O 一/m 种/qN 安全/a 、/、 清洁/a 、/、 经济/a 的/u 能源/n 。/。"

3.2 Decomposition of Parsing Model

The functional chunk parser presented above could be further divided into several sub modules, each of which is only in charge of detecting one type of the chunk boundaries in a sentence. The sub module in charge of detecting boundary b could be formulated as a Boolean function $h_b(S, i)$ where S is the input sentence and i is the position between word w_i and w_{i+1}. Function $h_b(S, i)$ will take true if there is a chunk boundary of type b at position i, and it will take false if there's not. Since the Boolean function $h_b(S, i)$ can be treated as a binary classifier, many machine learning techniques could be applied.

If we combine every two chunk types in the tag set, we can make a total number of 8*8=64 boundary types in our chunking task. However, not all of them appear in the natural language text, for example, we don't have any SO boundaries in our corpus as S and O chunks can't become neighbors in a sentence without any P chunks between them. In our corpus, we could find 43 boundary types, but only a small number of them are used very frequently. In table 4, we list the 5 most frequently used boundaries in our corpus:

Table 4. The 5 Most Frequently Used Boundaries in the Corpus.

Boundary Type	Count
PO	14209
DP	11459
SD	6156
DD	5238
SP	5233

The top 5 boundaries take up 67.76% of all the 62418 boundaries in our corpus. If we further investigate the chunk types associated with these boundaries, we can find that only four types are involved: P, D, O and S. Referred to Table 2, we can find that these chunks are also the 4 most frequently used chunks in our corpus.

In most cases, S, P, and O chunks constitute the backbone of a Chinese sentence, and they usually contain the most useful information we need. Therefore, we are more concerned about S, P and O chunks. In the following sections, we will focus on the construction of sub modules for SP and PO boundary detection tasks.

4 Statistical Model Selection

After decomposing the parsing model into several sub modules, a lot of machine learning techniques could be applied to the constructions of these sub modules.

SVM [1] is a machine learning technique for solving the binary classification problems. It is well known for its good generalization performance and high efficiency. In this section, we will make a performance comparison between SVM (Vapnik, 1995) and several other machine learning techniques including Naïve Bayes, ID3 [2] (Quinlan, 1986) and C4.5[3] (Quinlan, 1993), and then illustrates how competitive SVM is in the boundary detection tasks.

4.1 Experimental Data

The corpus we use here is a collection of 185 news files which are manually corrected after automatic sentence-split, word segmentation and part-of-speech tagging. After these processes, they have been manually annotated with functional chunks. Among the 185 files, 167 of them are taken as the training data and the remaining 18 are left as the test data, which takes up approximately 10% of all the data.

In our experiments, we will use feature templates to describe which features are to be used in the generation of feature vectors. For example, if the current feature template we use is w-1t2, then the feature vector generated at position i will take the first word on the left and the second word tag on the right as its features.

Before we perform any experiments, all the data have been converted to the vectors that are acceptable by different machine learning algorithms. Thus we have a total number of 199268 feature vectors generated from the 185 files. Among them, 172465 vectors are in the training data and 26803 vectors are in the test data. Two sets of training and test data are prepared respectively for the SP and PO boundary detection tasks.

The performance of each experiment is measured with 3 rates: precision, recall and $F_{\beta=1}$, where precision is the percentage of detected boundaries that are correct, recall is the percentage of boundaries in the test data that are found by the parser, and $F_{\beta=1}$ is defined as $F_\beta=(\beta^2+1)*precision*recall/(\beta^2*precision + recall)$ with $\beta=1$.

[1] The software package we use is SVM^{light} v6.00, it is available at http://svmlight.joachims.org/. We use linear kernel function and other default parameters in our experiments.

[2] We use the weka's implementation of Naïve Bayes and ID3 algorithms. Weak 3.4 is available at http://www.cs.waikato.ac.nz/ml/weka/.

[3] We use Quinlan's C4.5 software package with its default parameters in our experiments.

4.2 Algorithm Comparison

We first use t-3t-2t-1t1t2 as the feature template, and list all the experimental results in Table 5 and Table 6. From these results, we can find that SVM has achieved the best precision, recall and F-Score in SP boundary detection task, while C4.5 has an overwhelming advantage in PO boundary detection task. In both tasks, Naïve Bayes algorithm performs the worst, which makes us very disappointed.

Table 5. Results of Different Algorithms in SP Boundary Detection Task.

Algorithm	Precision	Recall	$F_{\beta=1}$
SVM	82.21%	57.10%	67.39%
ID3	67.60%	50.70%	57.94%
C4.5	81.10%	44.60%	57.55%
Naïve Bayes	47.90%	51.00%	49.40%

Table 6. Results of Different Algorithms in PO Boundary Detection Task.

Algorithm	Precision	Recall	$F_{\beta=1}$
C4.5	72.00%	74.70%	73.33%
SVM	67.27%	64.96%	66.09%
ID3	70.70%	59.90%	64.85%
Naïve Bayes	48.10%	60.10%	53.43%

As the feature template we use here is too simple, the results we have got may not seem so persuasive. Therefore we decide to conduct another experiment using a more complex feature template.

In the following experiments, we will use w-2w-1w1w2t-2t-1t1t2 as the feature template. The experimental results are listed in Table 7 and Table 8.

After adding the word information to the feature template, the dimensions of feature vectors used by some algorithms increase dramatically. We remove Naïve Bayes algorithm from the following experiments, as it fails to deal with such high dimensional data.

Table 7. Results of Different Algorithms in SP Boundary Detection Task.

Algorithm	Precision	Recall	$F_{\beta=1}$
SVM	82.25%	61.22%	70.19%
ID3	64.70%	51.70%	57.47%
C4.5	79.70%	37.40%	50.91%

Table 8. Results of Different Algorithms in PO Boundary Detection Task.

Algorithm	Precision	Recall	$F_{\beta=1}$
SVM	74.83%	86.99%	80.45%
C4.5	67.90%	79.90%	73.41%
ID3	75.10%	57.70%	65.26%

After applying the complex feature template, SVM still keeps the first place in SP boundary detection task. In PO boundary detection task, SVM successfully takes the place of C4.5, and achieves the best recall and F-Score among all the algorithms. Although the precision of ID3 is a little better than SVM, we still prefer SVM to ID3. It seems that the word information in the feature vectors is not so beneficial to decision tree algorithms as to SVM.

We also notice that SVM can perform very efficiently even with a large number of features. In the second set experiments, it usually takes several hours to train a decision tree model, but for SVM, the time cost is no more than 20 minutes. In addition, we can expect a better result by adding more information to SVM algorithm without worrying about the dimension disaster problem in other algorithms. Therefore, we decide to base our parsing model on SVM algorithm.

5 The SVM-based Parsing Model

5.1 Baseline Models

In this section, we will build 2 baseline models based on SVM for SP and PO boundary detection tasks respectively. By comprising the results of two different feature templates, we will illustrate how useful the word information is in our SVM based models.

One feature template we use here is the simple template which only takes the POS tag information as its features. The other one is the complex template which takes both word and tag information as its features. To make sure the results are comparable, we restrict the context window to 4 words.

In the SP boundary detection sub task, we got the following results:

Table 9. SP Boundary Detection Results.

Feature template	Precision	Recall	$F_{\beta=1}$
t-2t-1t1t2	76.25%	51.99%	61.83%
w-2w-1w1w2t-2t-1t1t2	82.25%	61.22%	70.19%

In the PO boundary detection sub task, we got the following results:

Table 10. PO Boundary Detection Results.

Feature template	Precision	Recall	$F_{\beta=1}$
t-2t-1t1t2	66.42%	65.27%	65.84%
w-2w-1w1w2t-2t-1t1t2	74.83%	86.99%	80.45%

By taking the complex feature template, we have achieved the best $F_{\beta=1}$ value of 70.19% in SP boundary detection experiment and 80.45% in PO experiment, both of which are much higher than those of the simple feature templates. From these results we can conclude that word information is very helpful in our SVM based models. Thus we will only use the feature templates with word information in the succeeding experiments.

5.2 Expanding the Context Window

In the previous section, the feature templates we use are restricted to a context window of 4 words, which might not be large enough to detect the boundaries between complex chunks. For example, when parsing the sentence "[P 派出/v $_1$ [O 精干/a $_2$ 的/u $_3$ 民族/n $_4$ 政策/n $_5$ 宣传/vN $_6$ 人员/n", the algorithm fails to detect the PO boundary at position 1. If we expand the context window to the noun word "民族/n", some of these errors may disappear. In the following experiments, we will expand the context window from a size of 4 words to 10 words, and make a comparison between the different results.

The 4 feature templates used here are listed below:

T1: w-2w-1w1w2t-2t-1t1t2,

T2: w-3w-2w-1w1w2w3t-3t-2t-1t1t2t3,

T3: w-4w-3w-2w-1w1w2w3w4t-4t-3t-2t-1t1t2t3t4

T4: w-5w-4w-3w-2w-1w1w2w3w4w5t-5t-4t-3t-2t-1t1t2t3t4t5.

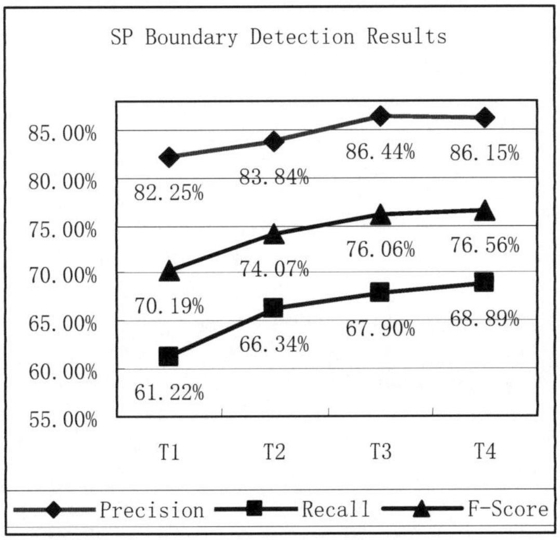

Figure 1. SP Boundary Detection Results.

As we have expected, the performance of SP boundary detection experiment has been improved as the context window expands from a size of 4 words to 8 words. However, the precision value meets its turning point at T3 after which it goes down, while F-Score and recall value still keep rising. From the curves shown in figure 1, we can find that the expansion of context window size from 4 words to 6 words has an obvious improvement for performance, and after that only F-Score and recall could be improved.

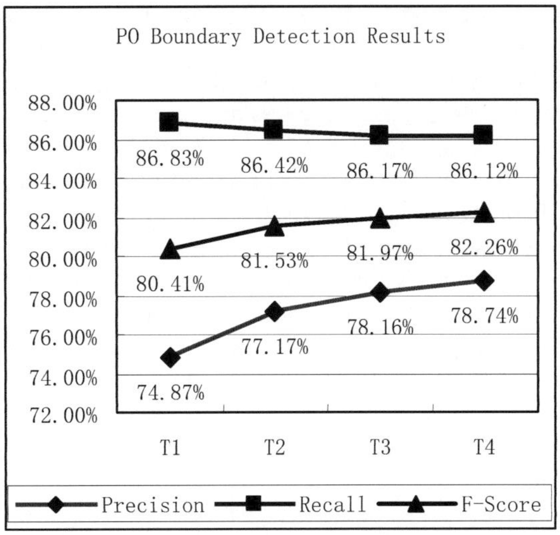

Figure 2. SP Boundary Detection Results.

In contrast to the significant improvement we have achieved in the SP experiments, the results of PO experiments are not so exciting. As the context window expands, the precision value keeps rising while the recall value keeps declining. Fortunately, we have obtained a very slight increase of F-Score from these efforts.

Although it is very difficult to improve the performance of PO boundary detection by simply expanding the context window, we've still got a better result than that of SP. If we examine the results of the two tasks carefully, we can find a very interesting difference between them: in SP boundary detection task, it's very easier to get a better precision than recall, but in PO experiment, as the O chunks have a longer length, they are more likely to be cut into small pieces, and thus it's easier to get a better recall than precision.

5.3 Error Analysis

In our experiments, the recall value can be simply raised by adding a positive bias value to the SVM classifier. However, we can't do the same thing to improve the precision value. Thus, in the following analysis, we are only focus on the errors that deter the improvement of precision value.

There are 2 kinds of errors influencing the precision value of the test results: One is the wrongly detected chunk boundaries (WDB) within chunks (these chunk boundaries are detected by the program, but they don't exist in the training data). This kind of error tends to cut a large chunk into several small pieces. The other is the misclassification of chunk boundary types (MBT) at the chunk boundaries (There exists a chunk boundary at that position, but chunk boundary type labeled by the program is wrong).

In the following analysis, by comparing the numbers of errors in the test results of T1 (w-2w-1w1w2t-2t-1t1t2) and T4 (w-5w-4w-3w-2w-1w1w2w3w4w5t-5t-4t-3t-2t-1t1t2t3t4t5), we will point out which kind of errors could be effectively eliminated by the expansion of context window and which of them couldn't. Through this analysis, we hope to get some knowledge of what efforts should be made in our further study.

In SP boundary detection task, we list the number of wrongly detected chunk boundaries (#WDB) and the corresponding chunk types (CT) where WDB arises in the following table.

Table 11. Wrongly Detected Chunk Boundaries in the Test Results of T1 and T4.

CT	#WDB of T1	#WDB of T4	T4-T1
O	17	18	1
S	17	18	1
D	7	6	-1
C	0	1	1
P	2	1	-1
T	1	1	0
Sum	44	45	1

From the above table, we find that the number of wrongly detected boundaries seems to be unchanged during the expansion of context window.

But when we refer to the second type of errors, the expansion of context window does help. We list the misclassified boundary types (MBT) and the error numbers (#MB) in the below table. In SP boundary detection task, MBT is wrongly recognized as boundary type SP.

Table 12. Misclassified Chunk Boundaries in the Test Results of T1 and T4.

MBT	#MB of T1	#MB of T4	T4-T1
OP	9	3	-6
JP	8	2	-6
DP	23	20	-3
SD	6	6	0
DS	1	1	0
Sum	47	32	-15

From the above table, we can find that the misclassifications of OP, JP and DP as SP have been largely reduced by expanding the context window, but the misclassifications of DS and SD remain the same. Therefore, we should try some other methods for D chunks in our future work.

In PO boundary detection task, the expansion of context window seems to be very effective. We list all the results in the below table:

Table 14. Wrongly Detected Chunk Boundaries in the Test Results of T1 and T4.

CT	#WDB of T1	#WDB of T4	T4-T1
O	251	196	-55
S	106	76	-30
D	92	55	-37
P	56	64	8
T	4	4	0
C	1	1	0
J	0	1	1
Sum	510	397	-113

It's very exciting to see that by expanding the window size, the number of WDB decreases dramatically from 510 to 397. But it fails to eliminate the WDB errors within P, T, C, and J chunks.

In PO boundary detection task, MBT is wrongly recognized as boundary type PO. We list the error data of T1 and T4 in the below table.

Table 13. Misclassified Chunk Boundaries in the Test Results of T1 and T4.

MBT	#MB of T1	#MB of T4	T4-T1
PJ	17	18	1
PD	9	9	0
PC	8	8	0
SP	6	6	0
PS	5	5	0
SD	5	4	-1
DP	3	2	-1
TS	3	3	0
OD	1	0	-1
PY	1	1	0
Sum	58	56	-2

In contrast to the results of SP boundary detection task, the MBT errors could not be largely reduced by simply expanding the context window. Therefore, we need to pay more attention to these problems in our future work.

6 Related works

After the work of Ramshaw and Marcus (1995) , many machine learning techniques have been applied to the basic chunking task, such as Support Vector Machines (Kudo and Matsumoto, 2001), Hidden Markov Model(Molina and Pla 2002), Memory Based Learning (Sang, 2002), Conditional Random Fields (Sha and Pereira, 2003), and so on. But only a small amount of attention has been paid to the functional chunk parsing problem.

Sandra and Erhard (2001) tried to construct the function-argument structures based on the pre-chunked input. They proposed a similarity based algorithm to assign the functional labels to complete syntactic structures, and achieved a precision of 89.73% and 90.40% for German and English respectively. Different from our top-down scheme, their function-argument structures are still constituted from bottom-up, and the pre-chunked input helps simplify the chunking process.

Elliott and Qiang Zhou (2001) used the BIO tagging system to identify the functional chunks in a sentence. In their experiments, they used C4.5 algorithm to build the parsing model, and focused their efforts on the selection of feature sets. After testing 5 sets of features, they have achieved the best f-measure of 0.741 by using feature set E which contains all the features in other feature sets. Instead of using BIO tags in our chunking task, we introduced chunk boundaries to help us identify the functional chunks, which could provide more relational information between the functional chunks.

7 Conclusions and Future Works

In this paper, we have applied functional chunks to Chinese shallow parsing. Since the functional chunks have the properties of linearity and exhaustibility, we can formulate the functional chunk parsing problem as a boundary detection task. By applying the divide-and-conquer strategy, we have further decomposed the parsing model into a series of sub modules, each of which is only in charge of one boundary type. In this way, we provide a very flexible framework within which different machine learning techniques could be applied. In our experiments, we build two sub modules based on SVM for solving the SP and PO boundary detection tasks. Thanks to the good generalization performance and high efficiency of SVM, we can successfully deal with a large number of features. By expanding the context window, we have achieved the best F-Score of 76.56% and 82.26 for SP and PO boundary detection tasks.

The 2 sub modules we have built are only parts of the Chinese functional chunk parser. Although the results we have got here seem somewhat coarse, they could already be used in some simple tasks. In the future, we will build the other sub modules for the remaining types of the chunk boundaries. After all these work, there may be some inconsistent chunk boundaries in the results, thus we need to solve the inconsistency problems and try to identify all the functional chunks in a sentence by combining these chunk boundaries.

Acknowledgements

This work was supported by the Chinese National Science Foundation (Grant No. 60573185, 60520130299).

References

Elliott Franco Drábek and Qiang Zhou. 2001. Experiments in Learning Models for Functional Chunking of Chinese Text. *IEEE International Workshop on Natural Language processing and Knowledge Engineering*, Tucson, Arizona, pages 859-864.

E.F. Tjong Kim Sang. 2002. Memory-based shallow parsing, *Journal of Machine Learning Research 2*, pages 559-594.

F. Sha and F. Pereira. 2003. Shallow parsing with conditional random fields. In *Proceedings of Human Language Technology Conference / North American Chapter of the Association for Computational Linguistics annual meeting*.

Ian H. Witten and Eibe Frank. 2005. *Data Mining: Practical machine learning tools and techniques*, 2nd Edition, Morgan Kaufmann, San Francisco.

Taku Kudo and Yuji Matsumoto. 2001. Chunking with support vector machines. *Proceedings of the Second Meeting of the North American Chapter of the Association for Computational Linguistics*. Pittsburgh, PA.

Lance Ramshaw and Mitch Marcus. 1995. Text chunking using transformation-based learning. In *Proceedings of the Third Workshop on Very Large Corpora*, pages 82—94.

Quinlan, J. Ross. 1986. Induction of decision trees. *Machine Learning*, 1(1), pages 81-106.

Quinlan, J. Ross. 1993. C4.5: *Programs for Machine Learning*. San Mateo, CA: Morgan Kaufmann.

Steven Abney. 1991. Parsing by chunks. In *Principle-Based Parsing*, Kluwer Academic Publishers, Dordrecht, pages 257—278.

Sandra Kübler and Erhard W. Hinrichs. 2001. From chunks to function-argument structure: A similarity-based approach. In *Proceedings of ACL/EACL 2001*, Toulouse, France, 2001, pages 338 - 345.

Thorsten Joachims. 1999. *Advances in Kernel Methods - Support Vector Learning*, chapter Making large-Scale SVM Learning Practical. MIT-Press.

Vladimir N. Vapnik. 1995. *The Nature of Statistical Learning Theory*. Springer, New York.

Broadcast Audio and Video Bimodal Corpus Exploitation and Application

Zou Yu, Hou Min, Chen Yudong, Hu Fengguo, Fu Li
Dept. of Applied Linguistics, Presentation Art School
Communication University of China
Beijing 100024, P. R. China
{zouiy;byhoumin;bychenyudong;bushiwoshishui;red_fuli}@cuc.edu.cn

Abstract

The main purpose of this paper is the exploitation and application of an audio and video bimodal corpus of the Chinese language in broadcasting. It deals with the designation of the size and structure of speech samples according to radio and television program features. Secondly, it discusses annotation method of broadcast speech with achievements made and suggested future improvements. Finally, it presents an attempt to describe the distribution of annotated items in our corpus.

1 Introduction

Since the year of 2002, we've been engaged in setting up the Media Language Corpus aimed to provide the language resources for the researchers who are interested in broadcasting and television media language, for teachers and for researchers of presentation art. Up till now, we have established a 50 million word text corpus involving 40 million word television program text corpora and 10 million word radio program text corpora with 10 million annotated word corpora. The work of this paper is to introduce a ten-hour segmented and prosodic labeled broadcast audio & video bimodal corpus that we built just now.

Section 2 of this paper describes a method for selection of radio and television programs to record according to program features on radio and television stations. Recording conditions are proposed to record a quality spoken language corpus. Section 3 is dedicated to annotation methods. Section 4 shows the distribution of syllables, initials, finals and tones etc. Finally, section 5 contains the conclusion and outlines of our future work in this field.

2 Corpus Information

2.1 Corpus metadata

First of all, we have to select radio and television programs to record. Since a broadcast bimodal corpus should represent the real life usages of spoken language in radio and television, the differences between radio and television, the differences between central and local televisions, and the categories of programs should all together be taken into account during the process of collecting. The followings are the framework (`.wav` files & `.mpeg` files matched with `.txt` files) of head information (metadata) of broadcast audio & video bimodal corpus that has been collected:

No.: ...
Level: central, local, Hong Kong and Taiwan
Station: CCTV, CNR, Phoenix Television...
Style: monologue, dialogue, multi-style
Register: (hypogyny of monologue) presentation,
explanation,
reading, talk
(hypogyny of dialogue) two person talk show,
three person talk show,
multi-person talk show
Content: news, literature, service
Audiences: woman, children, elder...
Program: News probe, The first time...
Sub-program: ...
Announcer: ...
Gender: Male /female
Recording condition: Pinnacle PCTV pro card...
Sample rate/Resolution: 22 KHz/16bit...
Topic: ...
Time: xxxx-xx-xx

2.2 Corpus structure

The purpose of building the broadcast spoken language corpus is to provide the service for the research of broadcast spoken language, esp. for the contrastive studies of the prosodic features of different genres of broadcast language. Hence, the selections of samples of the corpus mainly involve monologues, dialogues or both. As the performing forms of radio and television programs are getting more and more diverse, it is very difficult to decide whether a program is a monologue or dialogue, because these two genres of programs often co-occur in one program. Furthermore, these kinds of programs are increasing their share of radio and television programs. Consequently, this kind of program is most frequent in the corpus. Table 1 displays the structural framework of the broadcast audio and video bimodal corpus.

Table 1 the structure of broadcast bimodal corpus

Style		Example
Dialogue	two person talk show / interview	Face to face...etc.
	three person talk show / interview	Behind the Headlines with Wen Tao...etc.
	multi-person talk show / interview	Utterly challenge...
Mono-logue	presentation	News...etc.
	explanation	Music story... etc.
	reading	Reading and enjoying... etc.
	talk	Tonight, Weather forecast... etc.
Multi-style		News probe, The first time...etc.

2.3 Recording & management information

All the recorded data are over the programs on radio and TV, that is, it is recorded directly from radio and TV programs by Pinnacle PCTV pro card to connect cable TV with our recording computers. The recorded speech data are saved as 22 kHz and 16bit, Windows PCM waveform, the video data are saved as MPEG or WMV format file by Ulead VideoStudio in a post-processing step. Every program or segment of programs is composed of three parts: `*.wav` data, `*.txt` data, and `*.mpeg/.wmv` data.

Zhao Shixia et al (2000) pointed out that the structure of a speech corpus consists of synchronized objects (text files, wav files, and annotated prosodic files), arranged in deep hierarchies (recording environment), and labeled with speaker-attribute metadata. Therefore, the managed objects of our broadcast bimodal corpus are integrated programs or segments of programs. All data are stored separately but have complex logical inter-relations. These inter-relations can be obtained through the description of the programs. Figure 1 displays the logical structure of the broadcast bimodal corpus.

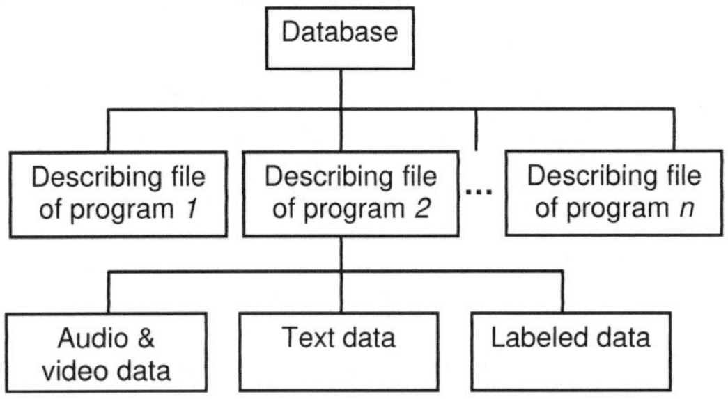

Figure 1 the logic structure of broadcast audio and video bimodal corpus

3 Annotation

Why should we annotate a corpus? An annotation is the fundamental act of associating some content to a region in a signal. The annotation quality and depth have a direct impact on the utility and possible applications of the corpus (Ding Xinshan 1998). The annotation of our corpus consists of transcription, segmental annotation, and prosodic annotation.

3.1 Transcription and segmentation

Transcription is primarily composed of *pinyin* transcription of Chinese characters. Besides, tones are annotated "1", "2", "3", and "4" after the syllable, the neutral tone is labeled "0"; final "ü" annotated as "v", and "üe" annotated as "ue", for example, "旅 (lǚ)" annotated as "lv3", "虐 (nüè)" annotated as "nue4".

In the utterance, compared with broken syllables, successive speech alters greatly, due to the influence of co-articulation, semantics and prosody. The purpose of segmental annotating is to annotate the altered phonemes in the syllables amidst the utterance. For instances, the voicing of some plosives (e.g. b, d, g); labial's influence on alveolar nasal (e.g. "-n" in "renmin" affected by the initial of "min" gradually change into "labionasal", demonstrating the similarities between alveolar nasal and labionasal initial in the frequency spectrum). In the places of unapparent pauses, the stop in the front of plosives esp. affricates often vanishes, which are called the inexistence of silence.

We transcription and segmentation we used BSCA (Broadcasting Speech Corpus Annotator) which was designed by ourselves (Hu Fengguo and Zou Yu 2005). An annotated example is shown in Figure 2:

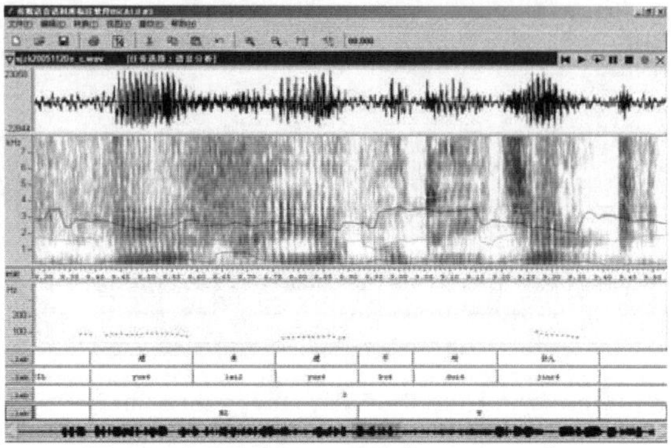
Figure 2 BSCA: a tool for annotation

3.2 Prosodic annotation tiers

Prosodic annotation increases the utility of a speech corpus. An annotated speech corpus can not only offer us a database for the research and exploration of speech information but can also enlarge our knowledge of speech and prosodic features through a visual and scientific method.

Prosodic annotation is a categorical description for the prosodic features with linguistic functions, in other words, annotation of the changes of tone, the patterns of stress, and the prosodic structure with linguistic functions. The prosodic labeling conventions are a set of machine-readable codes for transforming speech prosodies and rule conventions. Based on ToBI (Kim Silverman et al. 1992, John F. Pitrelli et al. 1994) and C-ToBI Conventions (Li Aijun 2002), according to the practical needs of broadcast speech language, the prosodic annotation mainly involves labeling the following parallel tiers: break index, stress index, and intonation construction tier (Chen Yudong 2004, Zou Yu 2004).

3.2.1 Break indices tier

Based on Cao Jianfen's (1999, 2001) categories of prosodic hierarchy structure combined with the practical needs of broadcast speech, we identified five break levels (0-4): 0 indicates the silence or the boundary of default internal syllables amidst the prosodic words. 1 stands for the boundaries of the prosodic words including the short breaks with silent pause and breaks with filled pause. The prosodic words are the fundamental prosodic units in broadcast speech. Simple prosodic words are composed of 1~3 syllables. Complex prosodic words normally contain 5~9 syllables, e.g., "Shang4hai3 he2zuo4 zu3zhi1" (i.e. the Shanghai Cooperation Organization). Break level 2 designates the boundaries of the prosodic phrases, most of which are apparent breaks with silent pause, and their patterns of pitch have also changed. Break level 3 represent the boundaries of intonational phrases, or the boundaries of sentences. Break level 4 stands for the boundaries of intonation groups, similar to the boundary of the entire piece of news in a news broadcast, or of a talker turn in dialogue. At indefinite boundaries, the code "-" is added after the numbers. The labels of the break tier occurring times are shown in table 2:

Table 2 the labels of the break tier occurring in 4 hours annotated corpora

Break index	Occurrence
1	1512
2	2998
3	1986
4	740

3.2.2 Stress indices tier

Stress is a significant prosodic feature. In training materials for broadcast announcers, emphasis is laid on labeling the stress on the basis of the purpose of the utterance, the pattern and rhythm of stresses, and the changes of emotions. Zhang Song's (1983) classification of nuclear stresses can be the guideline for broadcasting production and practice. However, there are some shortcomings in his classifications, for instances, the vague hierarchies between the sentences and discourses. This gets in the way of the formal description of the stresses by the computers. Nevertheless, his theories on the judgment of primary and minor stresses (i.e. non-stresses, minor stresses, primary stresses etc.) have some reference value for stress annotations, because distinguishing the hierarchies of stress is a crucial practical problem for annotation.

As to the problems with the hierarchies of stress, most of the experimental phonetics and speech processing researchers adopt Lin Maocan's (2001, 2002) classifications of stress hierarchies or some similar classifications. That is to say, the levels of stress include prosodic word stress, prosodic phrase stress, and sentence stress (or nuclear stress) in Chinese. According to real life broadcasting productions, this paper identifies four categories of stresses in broadcast speech: the rhythm unit, the cross rhythm unit, the clause, and the discourse. Among them, the discourse stress often occurs at the place of an accented syllable, but they are relatively more important than the other sentence stresses. The labeling methods of all the ranks are listed as follows (Chen Yudong 2004):

Table 3 the stress levels in the stress indices tier

Ranks	Labels
Rhythm unit	1
Cross rhythm unit	2
Clause	3
Discourse	4

Table 4 the stress levels' mean of duration in 4 hours annotated corpora

Stress indices	Mean of duration. (seconds)	Variance
1	.585	.09628
2	.790	.19405
3	.728	.24882
4	.821	.29456

Furthermore, Zhang Song's (1983) other criteria for stress annotation (utterance purpose and emotion change), while perceptually important, are meta-linguistic or para-linguistic in character, and will therefore not be addressed in this paper.

3.2.3 Intonation construction tier

In line with Shen Jiong's view about intonation (Shen Jiong 1994), we found that the intonation construction tier is an important component of the annotation of discourses (Chen Yudong 2004). It can display the changes of sentence intonation structures. The annotation of the intonation construction is mainly to label the relationship of other syllables to the nuclear stress apart from prehead, dissociation etc. For example:

Table 5 the labels of the intonation construction tier occurring in 4 hours annotated corpora

Labels	Description	Occurrence
P	Prehead	794
H	Head	2980
N	Nucleus	2400
T	Tail	1600
W	Weak in stress	2321
D	Dissociation	527
Top	Topic	269
Conj	Conjunction	87

A sentence can have one nuclear stress, or multiple nuclear stresses.

Single nuclear stress: representing the fore-and-aft places of the nuclear stress, the steepness of nuclear stress, and the length of nuclear stress. Examples are listed as follows:

P-H-N-T;

P-H-H-N;

… …

Among the above examples, long nuclear splitting type "H-N-T-H-N'-T", with the features of multi-nuclear "H-N1-T-H-N2-T" is greatly similar to multi-nuclear. However, "H-N-T-H-N'-T" differs from multi-nuclear in its dependent grammar unit.

Multi-nuclear stress: The two or more nuclear stresses in a multi-nuclear sentence take the patterns of like independent sentence intonation constructions, each with its own nucleus, preceded by a head and optional prehead, and followed by a tail. In other words, these relatively independent patterns already have the features of relatively independent intonation constructions, with the apparent features of "prehead, head, and nuclear ending". This kind of nuclear stress often occurs in relatively longer and more complex constructions. Intonation constructions can be labeled separately. A case in point is the contrastive sentence "zai4 wen3 ding4 de0 ji1 chu3 shang0, qu3 de2 bi3 jiao4 gao1 su4 de0 fa1 zhan3" (i.e. It got a comparative high-speed development on the stable conditions) that can be annotated as "H-N1-T, H-N2-T". For example:

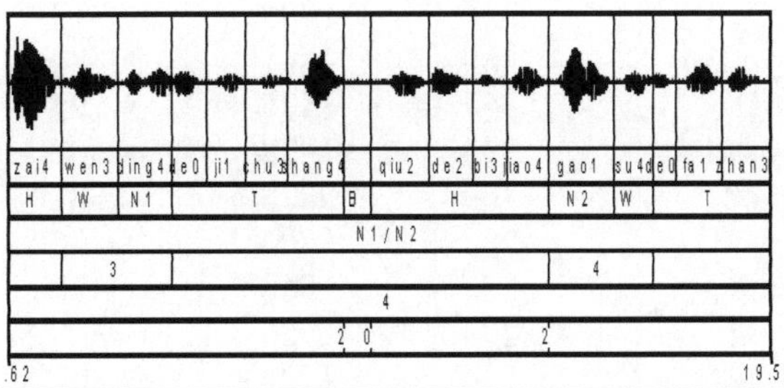

Figure 3 the contrastive sentence "zai4 wen3 ding4 de0 ji1 chu3 shang0, qu3 de2 bi3 jiao4 gao1 su4 de0 fa1 zhan3"(在稳定的基础上，取得比较高速的发展)

3.3 Other items of annotation

Some spoken language corpus can have some additional annotation information. For example, turn talking, paralinguistic and non-linguistic information (e.g. spot, background music, coughing, sobbing and sneezing) and some hosts' accents (e.g. Shanghai accent) can be annotated in talk show corpus. There are 82 times of spot and 31 times of background music in 4 hours annotated data. Furthermore, some .wav files, .mpeg files can be annotated together for discourse analysis.

4 Distribution of annotated items

We conducted a statistic analysis of some annotated items using 4 hours of annotated data in our corpus.

The syllables (initials and finals) of the 20 top frequent occurring are given in Table 6. In addition to this, the duration and variance distribution for them are calculation shown as follows.

Table 6 the mean of duration and variance of the top 20 frequent occurring syllables

Syllable	Occurrence	Mean of duration. (seconds)	Variance
de0	1993	.1167	.00232
shi4	912	.2051	.00572
shi2	626	.2054	.00625
zai4	602	.1889	.00341
le0	540	.1325	.00334
ta1	442	.1765	.00461
bu4	423	.1492	.00267
guo2	404	.1673	.00328
yi4	398	.1656	.00350
zhong1	395	.1996	.00390
ren2	394	.1959	.00625
zhe4	386	.1499	.00317
you3	380	.1841	.00480
yi1	357	.1475	.00295
dao4	335	.1778	.00367
he2	309	.2078	.00687
wo3	287	.1704	.00755
men0	287	.1568	.00426
yi2	274	.1555	.00320
jiu4	250	.1724	.00332

Table 7 Distribution of initials (4 hours data)

Initials	Times	Initials	Times
b	1076	j	3136
p	443	q	1464
m	1636	x	2146
f	972	zh	2953
d	4635	ch	1112
t	1561	sh	3406
n	1085	r	895
l	2569	z	1705
g	2162	c	512
k	879	s	700
h	2071	?	6099

Table 8 Distribution of finals (4 hours data)

Finals	Times	Finals	Times	Finals	Times
a	1653	ian	1767	ua	229
ai	1909	iang	919	uai	136
an	1425	iao	773	uan	632
ang	1192	ie	838	uang	389
ao	1205	in	1175	uei	1317
e	5074	ing	1480	uen	368
ei	807	iong	128	ueng	3
en	1515	iou	1144	uo	1760
eng	1237	o	176	v	932
er	353	ong	1658	van	432
i	6856	ou	831	ve	474
ia	586	u	2533	vn	209

Table 9 Distribution of tones (4 hours data)

Tones	1	2	3	4	0
Occurrence	8948	9194	7401	14683	6134

The occurrence distribution of initial, final, and tone are calculated. These are shown in table 7, 8 and 9 respectively.

We also measured the mean duration and F0 of each tone in three speaking styles are listed in Table 10 and 11.

Table 10 Mean duration of tones in various speaking styles (seconds)

	T1	T2	T3	T4	T0
Presentation	.189	.199	.192	.180	.129
Reading	.338	.337	.324	.335	.277
Talk	.167	.173	.163	.163	.154

Table 11 F0 of tones in various speaking styles (Hz)

	Presentation	Reading	Talk
T1	162.78	158.86	207.37
min. of T2	126.39	134.46	168.73
max. of T2	147.27	155.34	180.94
range of T2	79.12	20.88	12.21
min. of T3	101.94	119.12	151.21
max. of T4	163.96	170.07	209.86
min. of T4	113.39	120.98	175.49
range of T4	50.57	49.09	34.37

To summarize, we conclude that the mean duration of tones of reading style is longer than that of presentation style; that of talk style is the shortest among three styles. As for the F0 of each tone, the F0 and pitch range of presentation style is high and has big fluctuation; that of talk style is high and has small fluctuation. However, the F0 of tone 3 of presentation style is lower than that of reading and talk styles.

5 Further study

The broadcast audio and video bimodal corpus[1] is a presentation art-oriented corpus with radio and television news as its basis. This paper probes the development and compilation of broadcast audio and video bimodal corpus.

Firstly, on the collection of the corpus, what sort of audio and video corpus can represent the features of radio and television speech language? How can we auto-annotate the audio and video corpus? ...These are the problems that have always been bothering us.

Secondly, this corpus can be a platform for further research into non-accented or accented syllables, intonation construction, the prosodic functions of paragraphs and discourses, the emotions of speech, and genre styles.

Finally, we can statistically analyze the spectral and prosodic characteristics of various speaking styles by the corpora, such as presentation, reading and talk. All speaking styles would be synthesized based on the analysis results. This is also work for the future.

6 Acknowledgements

We would like to thank Prof. Wolfgang Teubert for his guidance and comments on this paper. I would also like to thank Mr. Daniel Zhang, Jan Van der Ven for their kind help.

References

Cao Jianfen. 1999. *Acoustic-phonetic Characteristics of the Rhythm of Standard Chinese*, In Proceedings of 4th National Conference on Modern Phonetics, Beijing, pp.155~159.

Cao Jianfen. 2001. *Phonetic and Linguistic Cues in Chinese Prosodic Segmentation and Grouping*, In Proceedings of 5th National Conference on Modern Phonetics, Beijing, pp.176~179.

Chen Yudong. 2004. *The Utterance Construction and Adjustment in Media Spoken Language*, PhD thesis, Peking University.

Ding Xinshan.1998. *Development and Research of Corpus Linguistics*, Contemporary Linguistics, 1: 4~12.

Hu Fengguo, Zou Yu. 2005. *The Design and Exploitation of Broadcasting Speech Corpus System*, In Proceedings of the Eighth Joint Seminar of Computational Linguistics (JSCL-2005), Nanjing, China, pp.521~527.

John F. Pitrelli, Mary E. Beckman, and Julia Hirschberg. 1994. *Evaluation of Prosodic Transcription Labeling reliability in the ToBI Framework*, In Proceedings of the 1994 International Conference on Spoken Language Processing(ICSLP), Yokohama, Japan, pp.123-126.

Kim Silverman, Mary Beckman, John Pitrelli, Mari Ostendorf, Colin Wightman, Patti Price, Janet Pierrehumbert, and Julia Hirschberg. 1992. *ToBI: A Standard for Labeling English Prosody*, In Proceedings of the 1992 International Conference on Spoken Language Processing(ICSLP), Banff, Alberta, Canada, vol.2, pp.867-870.

Li Aijun. 2002. *Chinese Prosody and Prosodic Labeling of Spontaneous Speech*, In Speech Prosody 2002 An International Conference, Aix-en-Provence, France.

Lin Maocan. 2001. *Prosodic Structure and F0 Declination in Sentence of Standard Chinese*, In Proceedings of 5th National Conference on Modern Phonetics, Beijing, pp.180~184.

Lin Maocan. 2002. *Prosodic Structure and Construction of F0 Top-Line and Bottom-Line in Utterances of Standard Chinese*, Contemporary Linguistics, 4: 254~265.

Shen Jiong. 1994. *Chinese Intonation structure and category*, Dialect, 4: 221~228.

Zhang Song. 1983. *Recitation*, Changsha: Hunan Education Press.

Zhao Shixia, Cai Lianhong, Chang Xiaolei. 2000. *Construction of Mandarin Corpus for Chinese Speech Synthesis*, Mini-Micro System, Vol.21 (3): 295~297.

Zou Yu. 2004. *Primary Research on Prosodic Labeling in Chinese News Broadcasting Speech*, In Proceedings of the 2nd Student Workshop on Computational Linguistics (SWCL2004), Beijing, pp.1-7.

[1] This research was supported by the National Working Committee on Language and Characters, project no. YB105-61A and Communication University of China, project no. BBU211-15.

The Third International Chinese Language Processing Bakeoff: Word Segmentation and Named Entity Recognition

Gina-Anne Levow
University of Chicago
1100 E. 58th St.
Chicago, IL 60637 USA
levow@cs.uchicago.edu

Abstract

The Third International Chinese Language Processing Bakeoff was held in Spring 2006 to assess the state of the art in two important tasks: word segmentation and named entity recognition. Twenty-nine groups submitted result sets in the two tasks across two tracks and a total of five corpora. We found strong results in both tasks as well as continuing challenges.

1 Introduction

Many important natural language processing tasks ranging from part of speech tagging to parsing to reference resolution and machine translation assume the ready availability of a tokenization into words. While such tokenization is relatively straight-forward in languages which use whitespace to delimit words, Chinese presents a significant challenge since it is typically written without such separation. Word segmentation has thus long been the focus of significant research because of its role as a necessary pre-processing phase for the tasks above. However, word segmentation remains a significant challenge both for the difficulty of the task itself and because standards for segmentation vary and human segmenters may often disagree.

SIGHAN, the Special Interest Group for Chinese Language Processing of the Association for Computational Linguistics, conducted two prior word segmentation bakeoffs, in 2003 and 2005(Emerson, 2005), which established benchmarks for word segmentation against which other systems are judged. The bakeoff presentations at SIGHAN workshops highlighted new approaches in the field as well as the crucial importance of handling out-of-vocabulary (OOV) words.

A significant class of OOV words is Named Entities, such as person, location, and organization names. These terms are frequently poorly covered in lexical resources and change over time as new individuals, institutions, or products appear. These terms also play a particularly crucial role in information retrieval, reference resolution, and question answering. As a result of this importance, and interest in expanding the scope of the bakeoff expressed at the Fourth SIGHAN Workshop, in the Winter of 2005 it was decided to hold a new bakeoff to evaluate both continued progress in Word Segmentation (WS) and the state of the art in Chinese Named Entity Recognition (NER).

2 Details of the Evaluation

2.1 Corpora

Five corpora were provided for the evaluation: three in Simplified characters and two in traditional characters. The Simplified character corpora were provided by Microsoft Research Asia (MSRA) for WS and NER, by University of Pennsylvania/University of Colorado (UPUC) for WS, and by the Linguistic Data Consortium (LDC) for NER. The Traditional character corpora were provided by City University of Hong Kong (CITYU) for WS and NER and by the Chinese Knowledge Information Processing Laboratory (CKIP) of the Academia Sinica, Taiwan for WS. Each data provider offered separate training and test corpora. General information for each corpus appears in Table 1.

All data providers were requested to supply the training and test corpora in both the standard local encoding and in Unicode (UTF-8) in a standard XML format with sentence and word tags, and named entity tags if appropriate. For

Source	Encodings	Training (Wds/Types)	Test (Wds/Types)
CITYU	BIG5HKSCS/Unicode	1.6M/76K	220K/23K
CKIP	BIG5/Unicode	5.5M/146K	91K/15K
LDC	Unicode	632K (est. wds)	61K (est. wds)
MSRA	GB18030/Unicode	1.3M/63K	100K/13K
UPUC	GB/Unicode	509K/37K	155K/17K

Table 1: Overall corpus statistics

all providers except the LDC, missing encodings were transcoded by the organizers using the appropriate Python CJK codecs.

Primary training and truth data for word segmentation were generated by the organizers via a Python script by replacing sentence end tags with newlines and word end tags with a single whitespace character, deleting all other tags and associated newlines. For test data, end of sentence tags were replaced with newlines and all other tags removed. Since the UPUC truth corpus was only provided in white-space separated form, test data was created by automatically deleting line-internal whitespace.

Primary training and truth data for named entity recognition were converted from the provided XML format to a two-column format similar to that used in the CoNLL 2002 NER task(Sang, 2002) adapted for Chinese, where the first column is the current character and the second column the corresponding tag. Format details may be found at the bakeoff website (`http://www.sighan.org/bakeoff2006/`). For consistency, we tagged only "<NAMEX>" mentions, of either (PER)SON, (LOC)ATION, (ORG)ANIZATION, or (G)EO-(P)OLITICAL (E)NTITY as annotated in the corpora.[1] Test was generated as above.

The LDC required sites to download training data from their website directly in the ACE[2] evaluation format, restricted to "NAM" mentions. The organizers provided the sites with a Python script to convert the LDC data to the CoNLL format above, and the same script was used to create the truth data. Test data was created by splitting on newlines or Chinese period characters.

Comparable XML format data was also provided for all corpora and both tasks.

The segmentation and NER annotation standard, as appropriate, for each corpus was made available on the bakeoff website. As observed in previous evaluations, these documents varied widely in length, detail, and presentation language.

Except as noted above, no additional changes were made to the data furnished by the providers.

2.2 Rules and Procedures

The Third Bakeoff followed the structure of the first two word segmentation bakeoffs. Participating groups ("sites") registered by email form; only the primary contact was required to register, identifying the corpora and tasks of interest. Training data was released for download from the websites (both SIGHAN and LDC) on April 17, 2006. Test data was released on May 15, 2006 and results were due 14:00 GMT on May 17. Scores for all submitted runs were emailed to the individual groups by May 19, and were made available to all groups on a web page a few days later.

Groups could participate in either or both of two tracks for each task and corpus:

- In the *open* track, participants could use any external data they chose in addition to the provided training data. Such data could include external lexica, name lists, gazetteers, part-of-speech taggers, etc. Groups were required to specify this information in their system descriptions.

- In the *closed* track, participants could only use information found in the provided training data. Information such as externally obtained word counts, part of speech information, or name lists was excluded.

Groups were required to submit fully automatic runs and were prohibited from testing on corpora which they had previously used.

Scoring was performed automatically using a combination of Python and Perl scripts, facilitated by stringent file naming conventions. In cases

[1] Only the LDC provided GPE tags.

[2] http://www.ldc.upenn.edu/projects/ACE

where naming errors or minor divergences from required file formats arose, a mix of manual intervention and automatic conversion was employed to enable scoring. The primary scoring scripts were made available to participants for followup experiments.

3 Participating Sites

A total of 36 sites registered, and 29 submitted results for scoring. The greatest number of participants came from the People's Republic of China (11), followed by Taiwan (7), the United States (5), Japan (2), with one team each from Singapore, Korea, Hong Kong, and Canada. A summary of participating groups with task and track information appears in Table 2. A total of 144 official runs were scored: 101 for word segmentation and 43 for named entity recognition.

4 Results & Discussion

We report results below first for word segmentation and second for named entity recognition.

4.1 Word Segmentation Results

To provide a basis for comparison, we computed baseline and possible topline scores for each of the corpora. The baseline was constructed by left-to-right maximal match implemented by Python script, using the training corpus vocabulary. The topline employed the same procedure, but instead used the test vocabulary. These results are shown in Tables 3 and 4.

For the WS task, we computed the following measures using the *score*(Sproat and Emerson, 2003) program developed for the previous bakeoffs: recall (R), precision (P), equally weighted F-measure ($F = \frac{2PR}{(P+R)}$), the rate of out-of-vocabulary words (OOV rate) in the test corpus, the recall on OOV (R_{oov}), and recall on in-vocabulary words (R_{iv}). In and out of vocabulary status are defined relative to the training corpus. Following previous bakeoffs, we employ the Central Limit Theorem for Bernoulli trials (Grinstead and Snell, 1997) to compute 95% confidence interval as $\pm 2\sqrt{(\frac{p(1-p)}{n})}$, assuming the binomial distribution is appropriate. For recall, C_r, we assume that recall represents the probability of correct word identification. Symmetrically, for precision, we compute C_p, setting p to the precision value. One can determine if two systems may then be viewed as significantly different at a 95% confidence level by computing whether their confidence intervals overlap.

Word segmentation results for all runs grouped by corpus and track appear in Tables 5-12; all tables are sorted by F-score.

4.2 Word Segmentation Discussion

Across all corpora, the best F-score was achieved in the MSRA Open Track at 0.979. Overall, as would be expected, the best results on Open track runs had higher F-scores than the best results for Closed Track runs on the same corpora. Likewise, the OOV recall rates for the best Open Track systems exceed those of the best Closed Track runs on comparable corpora by exploiting outside information. Unfortunately, few sites submitted runs in both conditions making strong direct comparisons difficult.

Many systems strongly outperformed the baseline runs, though none achieved the topline. The closest approach to the topline score was on the CITYU corpus, with the best performing runs achieving 99% of the topline F-score.

It is also informative to observe the rather wide variation in scores across the test corpora. The maximum scores were achieved on the MSRA corpus closely followed by the CITYU corpus. The best score achieved on the UPUC Open track condition, however, was lower than all scores but one on the MSRA Open track. However, a comparison of the baseline, topline, and especially the OOV rates may shed some light on this disparity. The UPUC training corpus was only about one-third the size of the MSRA corpus, and the OOV rate for UPUC was more than double that of any of the other corpora, yielding a challenging task, especially in the Closed track. This high OOV rate may also be attributed to a change in register, since the training data for UPUC had been drawn exclusively from the Chinese Treebank and the test data also included data from other newswire and broadcast news sources. In contrast, the MSRA corpus had both the highest baseline and highest topline scores, possibly indicating an easier corpus in some sense. The differences in topline also suggest a greater degree of variance in the UPUC, and in fact all other corpora, relative the MSRA corpus. These differences highlight the continuing challenges of handling out-of-vocabulary words and performing segmentation across different reg-

Site Name	Site ID	Country	CITYU WS	CKIP WS	MSRA WS	UPUC WS	CITYU NER	LDC NER	MSRA NER
Natural Language Processing Lab, Northeastern University of China	1	ZH	C	C	C	C			
Language Technologies Institute, Carnegie Mellon University	2	US	O	O	O	O			
National Institute of Information and Communications Technology, Japan	3	JP					C	C	C
Basis Technology Corp.	4	US	C	C	C	C			
Pattern Recognition and Intelligent System Laboratory,Beijing University of Posts and Telecommunications	5	ZH			C	C			
HKUST, Human Language Technology Center	6	HK					O	O	O
The University of Tokyo	7	JP			O	O		O	O
Institute of Software, Chinese Academy of Sciences	8	ZH	C	C	C	C	C	C	OC
Alias-i, Inc.	9	US	C	C	C	C	C		C
Beijing University of Posts and Telecommunications	10	ZH			O	O			O
France Telecom R&D Beijing	11	ZH	C		OC				O
NETEASE Information Technology (Beijing) Co., Ltd.	12	ZH				O			O
AI Lab., Dept of Information Management, Huafan University, Taiwan.	13	TW	OC	OC					
Nanjing University, China	14	ZH			O				OC
Intelligent Agent Systems Lab (IASL), Academia Sinica	15	TW	C	C	C				
Simon Fraser University	16	CA	C		C	C			
Tung Nan Institute of Technology	18	TW			C				
Institute of Information Science, Taiwan	19	TW					C		C
Microsoft Research Asia	20	ZH	OC	OC		OC			
Yahoo!	21	US					C		C
CKIP, Academia Sinica, Taiwan	22	TW	O						
Kookmin University	23	KO	C	C	C	C			
Shenyang Institute of Aeronautical Engineering	24	ZH			OC	OC			
Institute for Infocomm Research, Singapore	26	SG	C	C	C	C	C		C
National Taiwan University	29	TW					C		
ITNLP, Harbin Institute of Technology, China	30	ZH			OC				O
National Central University at Taiwan	31	TW				C	C		
National Laboratory on Machine Perception, Peking University, China	32	ZH	OC	OC	OC	OC			O
University of Texas at Austin	34	US	O	O	O	O			

Table 2: Participating Sites by Corpus, Task, and Track

Source	Recall	Precision	F-measure	OOV Rate	R_{oov}	R_{iv}
CITYU	0.930	0.882	0.906	0.040	0.009	0.969
CKIP	0.915	0.870	0.892	0.042	0.030	0.954
MSRA	0.949	0.900	0.924	0.034	0.022	0.981
UPUC	0.869	0.790	0.828	0.088	0.011	0.951

Table 3: Baselines: WS: Maximum match with training vocabulary

Source	Recall	Precision	F-measure	OOV Rate	R_{oov}	R_{iv}
CITYU	0.982	0.985	0.984	0.040	0.993	0.981
CKIP	0.980	0.987	0.983	0.042	0.997	0.979
MSRA	0.991	0.993	0.992	0.034	0.999	0.991
UPUC	0.961	0.976	0.968	0.088	0.989	0.958

Table 4: Toplines: WS: Maximum match with testing vocabulary

Site	RunID	R	C_r	P	C_p	F	R_{oov}	R_{iv}
15	d	0.973	±0.000691	0.972	±0.000703	0.972	0.787	0.981
15	b	0.973	±0.000691	0.972	±0.000703	0.972	0.787	0.981
20		0.972	±0.000703	0.971	±0.000715	0.971	0.792	0.979
32		0.969	±0.000739	0.970	±0.000727	0.970	0.773	0.978
1	a	0.971	±0.000715	0.965	±0.000783	0.968	0.719	0.981
15	c	0.965	±0.000783	0.967	±0.000761	0.966	0.792	0.972
15	a	0.966	±0.000772	0.967	±0.000761	0.966	0.786	0.973
26		0.968	±0.000750	0.961	±0.000825	0.965	0.633	0.983
11		0.962	±0.000815	0.962	±0.000815	0.962	0.722	0.972
16		0.963	±0.000805	0.958	±0.000855	0.961	0.689	0.974
9		0.966	±0.000772	0.957	±0.000865	0.961	0.555	0.983
1	b	0.958	±0.000855	0.963	±0.000805	0.960	0.714	0.968
8		0.952	±0.000911	0.954	±0.000893	0.953	0.747	0.960
23		0.950	±0.000929	0.949	±0.000938	0.949	0.638	0.963
4	b	0.845	±0.001543	0.844	±0.001547	0.844	0.632	0.854
4	a	0.841	±0.001559	0.844	±0.001547	0.843	0.506	0.855
13	1	0.589	±0.002097	0.589	±0.002097	0.589	0.022	0.613

Table 5: CITYU: Word Segmentation: Closed Track

Site	RunID	R	C_r	P	C_p	F	R_{oov}	R_{iv}
20		0.978	±0.000625	0.977	±0.000639	0.977	0.840	0.984
32		0.979	±0.000611	0.976	±0.000652	0.977	0.813	0.985
34		0.971	±0.000715	0.967	±0.000761	0.969	0.795	0.978
22		0.970	±0.000727	0.965	±0.000783	0.967	0.761	0.979
2		0.964	±0.000794	0.964	±0.000794	0.964	0.787	0.971
13	2	0.544	±0.002123	0.549	±0.002121	0.547	0.194	0.559
13	3	0.524	±0.002129	0.503	±0.002131	0.513	0.195	0.538
13	1	0.497	±0.002131	0.467	±0.002127	0.481	0.057	0.516

Table 6: CITYU: Word Segmentation: Open Track

Site	RunID	R	C_r	P	C_p	F	R_{oov}	R_{iv}
20		0.961	±0.001280	0.955	±0.001371	0.958	0.702	0.972
15	a	0.961	±0.001280	0.953	±0.001400	0.957	0.658	0.974
15	b	0.961	±0.001280	0.952	±0.001414	0.957	0.656	0.974
32		0.958	±0.001327	0.948	±0.001468	0.953	0.646	0.972
26		0.958	±0.001327	0.941	±0.001558	0.949	0.554	0.976
1	b	0.947	±0.001482	0.943	±0.001533	0.945	0.601	0.962
1	a	0.949	±0.001455	0.940	±0.001571	0.944	0.694	0.960
9		0.951	±0.001428	0.935	±0.001630	0.943	0.389	0.976
23		0.937	±0.001607	0.933	±0.001654	0.935	0.547	0.954
8		0.939	±0.001583	0.929	±0.001699	0.934	0.606	0.954
4	a	0.836	±0.002449	0.834	±0.002461	0.835	0.521	0.849
4	b	0.836	±0.002449	0.828	±0.002496	0.832	0.590	0.847
13	1	0.747	±0.002875	0.677	±0.003093	0.710	0.036	0.778

Table 7: CKIP: Word Segmentation: Closed Track

Site	RunID	R	C_r	P	C_p	F	R_{oov}	R_{iv}
20		0.964	±0.001232	0.955	±0.001371	0.959	0.704	0.975
34		0.959	±0.001311	0.949	±0.001455	0.954	0.672	0.972
32		0.958	±0.001327	0.948	±0.001468	0.953	0.647	0.972
2	a	0.953	±0.001400	0.946	±0.001495	0.949	0.679	0.965
2	b	0.951	±0.001428	0.944	±0.001521	0.948	0.676	0.964
13	2	0.724	±0.002956	0.668	±0.003115	0.695	0.161	0.749
13	3	0.736	±0.002915	0.653	±0.003148	0.692	0.160	0.761
13	1	0.654	±0.003146	0.573	±0.003271	0.611	0.057	0.680

Table 8: CKIP: Word Segmentation: Open Track

Site	RunID	R	C_r	P	C_p	F	R_{oov}	R_{iv}
32		0.964	±0.001176	0.961	±0.001222	0.963	0.612	0.976
26		0.961	±0.001222	0.953	±0.001336	0.957	0.499	0.977
9		0.959	±0.001252	0.955	±0.001309	0.957	0.494	0.975
1	a	0.955	±0.001309	0.956	±0.001295	0.956	0.650	0.966
15	d	0.953	±0.001336	0.956	±0.001295	0.955	0.574	0.966
11	a	0.955	±0.001309	0.953	±0.001336	0.954	0.575	0.969
15	b	0.952	±0.001350	0.956	±0.001295	0.954	0.575	0.966
15	c	0.949	±0.001389	0.957	±0.001281	0.953	0.673	0.959
15	a	0.949	±0.001389	0.958	±0.001266	0.953	0.672	0.959
16		0.952	±0.001350	0.954	±0.001323	0.953	0.604	0.964
11	b	0.950	±0.001376	0.954	±0.001323	0.952	0.602	0.962
5		0.956	±0.001295	0.947	±0.001414	0.951	0.493	0.972
1	b	0.946	±0.001427	0.952	±0.001350	0.949	0.568	0.959
18	c	0.950	±0.001376	0.930	±0.001611	0.940	0.272	0.974
30	a	0.963	±0.001192	0.918	±0.001732	0.940	0.175	0.991
18	b	0.954	±0.001323	0.921	±0.001703	0.937	0.163	0.981
8		0.933	±0.001578	0.942	±0.001476	0.937	0.640	0.943
23		0.933	±0.001578	0.939	±0.001511	0.936	0.526	0.948
24		0.923	±0.001683	0.929	±0.001621	0.926	0.554	0.936
18	a	0.949	±0.001389	0.897	±0.001919	0.922	0.022	0.982
4	a	0.830	±0.002371	0.832	±0.002360	0.831	0.473	0.842
4	b	0.817	±0.002441	0.821	±0.002420	0.819	0.491	0.829

Table 9: MSRA: Word Segmentation: Closed Track

Site	RunID	R	C_r	P	C_p	F	R_{oov}	R_{iv}
11	a	0.980	±0.000884	0.978	±0.000926	0.979	0.839	0.985
11	b	0.977	±0.000946	0.976	±0.000966	0.977	0.840	0.982
14		0.975	±0.000986	0.976	±0.000966	0.975	0.811	0.981
32		0.977	±0.000946	0.971	±0.001059	0.974	0.675	0.988
10		0.970	±0.001077	0.970	±0.001077	0.970	0.804	0.976
30	a	0.977	±0.000946	0.960	±0.001237	0.968	0.624	0.989
34		0.959	±0.001252	0.961	±0.001222	0.960	0.711	0.968
2		0.949	±0.001389	0.954	±0.001323	0.952	0.692	0.958
7		0.953	±0.001336	0.940	±0.001499	0.947	0.503	0.969
24		0.938	±0.001522	0.946	±0.001427	0.942	0.706	0.946

Table 10: MSRA: Word Segmentation: Open Track

Site	RunID	R	C_r	P	C_p	F	R_{oov}	R_{iv}
20		0.940	±0.001207	0.926	±0.001330	0.933	0.707	0.963
32		0.936	±0.001244	0.923	±0.001355	0.930	0.683	0.961
1	a	0.940	±0.001207	0.914	±0.001425	0.927	0.634	0.969
26	a	0.936	±0.001244	0.917	±0.001402	0.926	0.617	0.966
26	b	0.932	±0.001279	0.910	±0.001454	0.921	0.577	0.966
16		0.929	±0.001305	0.909	±0.001462	0.919	0.628	0.958
5		0.932	±0.001279	0.904	±0.001497	0.918	0.546	0.969
1	b	0.922	±0.001363	0.914	±0.001425	0.918	0.637	0.949
8		0.922	±0.001363	0.912	±0.001440	0.917	0.680	0.945
31	1	0.917	±0.001402	0.904	±0.001497	0.910	0.676	0.940
9		0.919	±0.001387	0.895	±0.001558	0.907	0.459	0.964
23		0.915	±0.001417	0.896	±0.001551	0.905	0.565	0.949
24		0.902	±0.001511	0.887	±0.001609	0.895	0.568	0.934
4	a	0.831	±0.001905	0.819	±0.001957	0.825	0.487	0.864
4	b	0.809	±0.001998	0.827	±0.001922	0.818	0.637	0.825

Table 11: UPUC: Word Segmentation: Closed Track

Site	RunID	R	C_r	P	C_p	F	R_{oov}	R_{iv}
34		0.949	±0.001118	0.939	±0.001216	0.944	0.768	0.966
2		0.942	±0.001188	0.928	±0.001314	0.935	0.711	0.964
20		0.940	±0.001207	0.927	±0.001322	0.933	0.741	0.959
7		0.944	±0.001169	0.922	±0.001363	0.933	0.680	0.970
12		0.933	±0.001271	0.916	±0.001410	0.924	0.656	0.959
32		0.940	±0.001207	0.907	±0.001476	0.923	0.561	0.976
24		0.928	±0.001314	0.906	±0.001483	0.917	0.660	0.954
10		0.925	±0.001339	0.897	±0.001545	0.911	0.593	0.957

Table 12: UPUC: Word Segmentation: Open Track

isters and writing styles.

4.3 Named Entity Results

We employed a slightly modified version of the CoNLL 2002 scoring script to evaluate NER task submissions. For each submission, we compute overall phrase precision (P), recall(R), and balanced F-measure (F), as well as F-measure for each entity type (PER-F,ORG-F,LOC-F,GPE-F).

For each corpus, we compute a baseline performance level as follows. Based on the training data, using a left-to-right pass over the test data, we assign a named entity tag to a span of characters if it was tagged with a single unique NE tag (PER/LOC/ORG/GPE) in the training data.[3] All In the case of overlapping spans, we tag the maximal span. These scores for all NER corpora are found in Table 13.

4.4 Named Entity Discussion

Though fewer sites participated in the NER task, performances overall were very strong, with only two runs performing below baseline. The best F-score overall on the MSRA Open Track reached 0.912, with ten other scores for MSRA and CITYU Open Track above 0.85. Only two sites submitted runs in both Open and Closed Track conditions, and few Open Track runs were submitted at all, again limiting comparability. For the only corpus with substantial numbers of both Open and Closed Track runs, MSRA, the top three runs outperformed all Closed Track runs.

System scores and baselines were much higher for the CITYU and MSRA corpora than for the LDC corpus. This disparity can, in part, also be attributed to a substantially smaller training corpus for the LDC than the other two collections. The presence of an additional category, Geo-political entity, which is potentially confused for either location or organization also enhances the difficulty of this corpus. Training requirements, variation across corpora, and most extensive tag sets will continue to raise challenges for named entity recognition.

Named entity recognition results for all runs grouped by corpus and track appear in Tables 14-19; all tables are sorted by F-score.

[3]If the span was a single character and appeared UNtagged in the corpus, we exclude it. Longer spans are retained for tagging even if they might appear both tagged and untagged in the training corpus.

[4]This result indicates a rescoring of the run below with all

Source	P	R	F	PER-F	ORG-F	LOC-F	GPE-F
CITY	0.611	0.467	0.529	0.587	0.516	0.503	N/A
LDC	0.493	0.378	0.428	0.395	0.29	0.259	0.539
MSRA	0.59	0.488	0.534	0.614	0.469	0.531	N/A

Table 13: Baselines: NER: Maximal match with unique tag in training corpus

Site	RunID	P	R	F	ORG-F	LOC-F	PER-F
3		0.9143	0.8676	0.8903	0.8046	0.9211	0.9087
19	ccrf	0.9201	0.8545	0.8861	0.8054	0.9251	0.8872
21	a	0.9266	0.8475	0.8853	0.7973	0.9232	0.8937
21	b	0.9242	0.8491	0.8850	0.7976	0.9236	0.8920
19	avdic	0.9079	0.8626	0.8847	0.7984	0.9233	0.8914
8		0.9276	0.8181	0.8694	0.7707	0.9114	0.8769
21	f	0.9188	0.8231	0.8683	0.7852	0.9105	0.8652
21	g	0.9164	0.8246	0.8681	0.7842	0.9114	0.8636
9		0.8690	0.8417	0.8551	0.7541	0.8861	0.8845
19	bme	0.8742	0.8307	0.8519	0.7667	0.9015	0.8395
26		0.8466	0.8061	0.8259	0.7467	0.8863	0.7927
31	1	0.9035	0.6973	0.7871	0.7703	0.8905	0.5974
29		0.7703	0.6447	0.7019	0.4948	0.7613	0.7531

Table 14: CITYU: Named Entity Recognition: Closed Track

Site	RunID	P	R	F	ORG-F	LOC-F	PER-F
6		0.8692	0.7498	0.8051	0.6801	0.8604	0.8098

Table 15: CITYU: Named Entity Recognition: Open Track

Site	RunID	P	R	F	ORG-F	LOC-F	PER-F	GPE-F
3		0.8026	0.7265	0.7627	0.6585	0.3046	0.7884	0.8204
8		0.8143	0.5953	0.6878	0.5855	0.1705	0.6571	0.7727

Table 16: LDC: Named Entity Recognition: Closed Track

Site	RunID	P	R	F	ORG-F	LOC-F	PER-F	GPE-F
7		0.7616	0.6621	0.7084	0.5209	0.2857	0.7422	0.7930
6	GPE-LOC[4]	0.6720	0.6554	0.6636	0.4553	0.7078	0.7420	
6		0.3058	0.2982	0.3019	0.4553	0.0370	0.7420	0.0

Table 17: LDC: Named Entity Recognition: Open Track

Site	RunID	P	R	F	ORG-F	LOC-F	PER-F
14		0.8894	0.8420	0.8651	0.8310	0.8545	0.9009
21	a	0.9122	0.8171	0.8620	0.8196	0.9053	0.8257
21	b	0.8843	0.8288	0.8556	0.7698	0.9013	0.8495
3		0.8814	0.8234	0.8514	0.8150	0.9062	0.7938
21	f	0.8845	0.7931	0.8363	0.8071	0.9003	0.7568
21	g	0.8661	0.8032	0.8335	0.7742	0.8991	0.7753
19	avdic	0.8637	0.7767	0.8179	0.8138	0.8233	0.8126
19	dcrf	0.8623	0.7740	0.8158	0.8141	0.8207	0.8093
9		0.8188	0.8097	0.8142	0.7295	0.8529	0.8196
19	cnoword	0.8670	0.7554	0.8074	0.8100	0.8257	0.7764
19	bvoting	0.8583	0.7606	0.8065	0.8145	0.8133	0.7899
26		0.8105	0.7882	0.7992	0.7491	0.8385	0.7699
21	r	0.8748	0.7168	0.7880	0.7288	0.8604	0.7107
8		0.8164	0.3124	0.4519	0.4591	0.5084	0.3521

Table 18: MSRA: Named Entity Recognition: Closed Track

Site	RunID	P	R	F	ORG-F	LOC-F	PER-F
10		0.9220	0.9018	0.9118	0.8590	0.9034	0.9604
14		0.9076	0.8922	0.8999	0.8397	0.9099	0.9261
11	b	0.8767	0.8753	0.8760	0.7611	0.8976	0.9225
11	a	0.8645	0.8399	0.8520	0.6945	0.8745	0.9199
32		0.8397	0.8184	0.8289	0.7261	0.8804	0.8207
7		0.8468	0.7822	0.8132	0.6958	0.8552	0.8280
6		0.8195	0.6926	0.7507	0.6443	0.8291	0.6955
30	a	0.8697	0.6556	0.7476	0.5841	0.7029	0.8987
8		0.8320	0.6703	0.7424	0.5651	0.8000	0.7565
12	b	0.7083	0.5464	0.6169	0.4168	0.6154	0.7171
12	a	0.7395	0.5186	0.6096	0.4168	0.6154	0.7074

Table 19: MSRA: Named Entity Recognition: Open Track

5 Conclusions & Future Directions

The Third SIGHAN Chinese Language Processing Bakeoff successfully brought together a collection of 29 strong research groups to assess the progress of research in two important tasks, word segmentation and named entity recognition, that in turn enable other important language processing technologies. The individual group presentations at the SIGHAN workshop detail the approaches that yielded strong performance for both tasks. Issues of out-of-vocabulary word handling, annotation consistency, character encoding and code mixing of Chinese and non-Chinese text all continue to challenge system designers and bakeoff organizers alike.

In future analyses, we hope to develop additional analysis tools to better assess progress in these fundamental tasks, in a more corpus independent fashion. Microsoft Research Asia has been pursuing work along these lines focusing on improvements in F-score and OOV F-score relative to more intrinsic corpus measures, such as baselines and toplines.[5] Such developments will guide the planning of future evaluations.

Finally, while word segmentation and named entity recognition are important in themselves, it is also important to assess the impact of improvements in these enabling technologies on broader downstream applications. More tightly coupled experiments that involve joint word segmentation and named entity recognition could provide insight. Integration of WS and NER with a higher level task such as parsing, reference resolution, or machine translation could allow the development of more refined, task-oriented metrics to evaluate WS and NER and focus attention on improvements to the fundamental techniques which enhance performance on higher level tasks.

GPE tags in the truth data mapped to LOC, since no GPE tags were present in the results.

[5]Personal communication, Mu Li, Microsoft Research Asia.

Acknowledgements

We gratefully acknowledge the generous assistance of the organizations and individuals listed below who provided the data for this bakeoff; without their support, it could not have taken place:

- Chinese Knowledge Information Processing Group, Academia Sinica, Taiwan: Keh-Jiann Chen, Henning Chiu
- City University of Hong Kong: Benjamin K. Tsou, Olivia Oi Yee Kwong
- Linguistic Data Consortium: Stephanie Strassel
- Microsoft Research Asia: Mu Li
- University of Pennsylvania/University of Colorado, USA: Martha Palmer, Nianwen Xue

We also thank Hwee Tou Ng and Olivia Oi Yee Kwong, the co-organizers of the fifth SIGHAN workshop, in conjunction with which this bakeoff takes place. Olivia Kwong merits special thanks both for her help in co-organizing this bakeoff and in coordinating publications. Finally, we thank all the participating sites who enabled the success of this bakeoff.

References

Thomas Emerson. 2005. The Second International Chinese Word Segmentation Bakeoff. In *Proceedings of the Fourth SIGHAN Workshop on Chinese Language Processing*, Jeju Island, Republic of Korea.

Charles M. Grinstead and J. Laurie Snell. 1997. *Introduction to Probability*. American Mathematical Society, Providence, RI.

Erik F. Tjong Kim Sang. 2002. Introduction to the CoNLL-2002 Shared Task: Language-Independent Named Entity Recognition. In *Proceedings of the 6th Conference on Natural Language Learning 2002 (CoNLL-2002)*.

Richard Sproat and Thomas Emerson. 2003. The First International Chinese Word Segmentation Bakeoff. In *Proceedings of the Second SIGHAN Workshop on Chinese Language Processing*, Sapporo, Japan.

Chinese Named Entity Recognition with Conditional Random Fields

Wenliang Chen and **Yujie Zhang** and **Hitoshi Isahara**
Computational Linguistics Group
National Institute of Information and Communications Technology
3-5 Hikari-dai, Seika-cho, Soraku-gun, Kyoto, Japan, 619-0289
{chenwl, yujie, isahara}@nict.go.jp

Abstract

We present a Chinese Named Entity Recognition (NER) system submitted to the close track of Sighan Bakeoff2006. We define some additional features via doing statistics in training corpus. Our system incorporates basic features and additional features based on Conditional Random Fields (CRFs). In order to correct inconsistently results, we perform the post-processing procedure according to n-best results given by the CRFs model. Our final system achieved a F-score of 85.14 at MSRA, 89.03 at CityU, and 76.27 at LDC.

1 Introduction

Named Entity Recognition task in the 2006 Sighan Bakeoff includes three corpora: Microsoft Research (MSRA), City University of Hong Kong (CityU), and Linguistic Data Consortium (LDC). There are four types of Named Entities in the corpora: Person Name, Organization Name, Location Name, and Geopolitical Entity (only included in LDC corpus).

We attend the close track of all three corpora. In the close track, we can not use any external resources. Thus except basic features, we define some additional features by applying statistics in training corpus to replace external resources. Firstly, we perform word segmentation using a simple left-to-right maximum matching algorithm, in which we use a word dictionary generated by doing n-gram statistics. Then we define the features based on word boundaries. Secondly, we generate several lists according to the relative position to Named Entity (NE). We define another type of features based on these lists. Using these features, we build a Conditional Random Fields(CRFs)-based Named Entity Recognition (NER) System. We use the system to generate n-best results for every sentence, and then perform a post-processing.

2 Conditional Random Fields

2.1 The model

Conditional Random Fields(CRFs), a statistical sequence modeling framework, was first introduced by Lafferty et al(Lafferty et al., 2001). The model has been used for chunking(Sha and Pereira, 2003). We only describe the model briefly since full details are presented in the paper(Lafferty et al., 2001).

In this paper, we regard Chinese NER as a sequence labeling problem. For our sequence labeling problem, we create a linear-chain CRFs based on an undirected graph $G = (V, E)$, where V is the set of random variables $Y = \{Y_i|1 \leq i \leq n\}$, for each of n tokens in an input sentence and $E = \{(Y_{i-1}, Y_i)|1 \leq i \leq n\}$ is the set of $n-1$ edges forming a linear chain. For each sentence x, we define two non-negative factors:
$exp(\sum_{k=1}^{K} \lambda_k f_k(y_{i-1}, y_i, x))$ for each edge
$exp(\sum_{k=1}^{K'} \lambda'_k f'_k(y_i, x))$ for each node
where f_k is a binary feature function, and K and K' are the number of features defined for edges and nodes respectively. Following Lafferty et al(Lafferty et al., 2001), the conditional probability of a sequence of tags y given a sequence of tokens x is:

$$P(y|x) = \frac{1}{Z(x)} exp(\sum_{i,k} \lambda_k f_k(y_{i-1}, y_i, x) + \sum_{i,k} \lambda'_k f'_k(y_i, x)) \quad (1)$$

where $Z(x)$ is the normalization constant. Given the training data D, a set of sentences (characters

Tag	Meaning
0 (zero)	Not part of a named entity
PER	A person name
ORG	An organization name
LOC	A location name
GPE	A geopolitical entity

Table 1: Named Entities in the Data

with their corresponding tags), the parameters of the model are trained to maximize the conditional log-likelihood. When testing, given a sentence x in the test data, the tagging sequence y is given by $Argmax_{y'} P(y'|x)$.

CRFs allow us to utilize a large number of observation features as well as different state sequence based features and other features we want to add.

2.2 CRFs for Chinese NER

Our CRFs-based system has a first-order Markov dependency between NER tags.

In our experiments, we do not use feature selection and all features are used in training and testing. We use the following feature functions:

$$f(y_{i-1}, y_i, x, i) = p(x, i)q(y_{i-1}, y_i) \quad (2)$$

where $p(x, i)$ is a predicate on the input sequence x and current position i and $q(y_{i-1}, y_i)$ is a predicate on pairs of labels. For instance, $p(x, i)$ might be "the char at position i is 和(and)".

In our system, we used CRF++ (V0.42)[1] to implement the CRFs model.

3 Chinese Named Entity Recognition

The training data format is similar to that of the CoNLL NER task 2002, adapted for Chinese. The data is presented in two-column format, where the first column consists of the character and the second is a tag.

Table 1 shows the types of Named Entities in the data. Every character is to be tagged with a NE type label extended with B (Beginning character of a NE) and I (Non-beginning character of a NE), or 0 (Not part of a NE).

To obtain a good-quality estimation of the conditional probability of the event tag, the observations should be based on features that represent the difference of the two events. In our system, we define three types of features for the CRFs model.

[1]CRF++ is available at http://chasen.org/ taku/software/CRF++/

3.1 Basic Features

The basic features of our system list as follows:

- . $C_n (n = -2, -1, 0, 1, 2)$
- . $C_n C_{n+1} (n = -1, 0)$

Where C refers to a Chinese character while C_0 denotes the current character and $C_n(C_{-n})$ denotes the character n positions to the right (left) of the current character.

For example, given a character sequence "张福贵先生", when considering the character C_0 denotes "贵", C_{-1} denotes "福", $C_{-1}C_0$ denotes "富贵", and so on.

3.2 Word Boundary Features

The sentences in training data are based on characters. However, there are many features related to the words. For instance, the word "先生" can be a important feature for Person Name. We perform word segmentation using the left-to-right maximum matching algorithm, in which we use a word dictionary generated by doing n-gram statistics in training corpus. Then we use the word boundary tags as the features for the model.

Firstly, we construct a word dictionary by extracting N-grams from training corpus as follows:

1. Extract arbitrary N-grams ($2 \leq n \leq 10$, $Frequency \geq 10$) from training corpus. We get a list W_1.

2. Use a tool to perform statistical substring reduction in W_1[described in (Lv et al., 2004)][2]. We get a list W_2.

3. Construct a character list (CH)[3], in which the characters are top 20 frequency in training corpus.

4. Remove the strings from W_2, which contain the characters in the list CH. We get final N-grams list W_3.

Secondly, we use W_3 as a dictionary for left-to-right maximum matching word segmentation. We assign word boundary tags to sentences. Each character can be assigned one of 4 possible boundary tags: "B" for a character that begins a word and is followed by another character, "M" for a

[2]Tools are available at http://homepages.inf.ed.ac.uk/s0450736/Software

[3]To collect some characters such as punctuation, "的", "了" and so on.

character that occurs in the middle of a word, "E" for a character that ends a word, and "S" for a character that occurs as a single-character word.

The word boundary features of our system list as follows:

- . $WT_n(n = -1, 0, 1)$

Where WT refers to the word boundary tag while WT_0 denotes the tag of current character and $WT_n(WT_{-n})$ denotes the tag n positions to the right (left) of the current character.

3.3 Char Features

If we can use external resources, we often use the lists of surname, suffix of named entity and prefix of named entity for Chinese NER. In our system, we generate these lists automatically from training corpus by the procedure as follows:

- PSur: uni-gram characters, first characters of Person Name. (surname)
- PC: uni-gram characters in Person Name.
- PPre: bi-gram characters before Person Name. (prefix of Person Name)
- PSuf: bi-gram characters after Person Name. (suffix of Person Name)
- LC: uni-gram characters in Location Name or Geopolitical entity.
- LSuf: uni-gram characters, the last characters of Location Name or Geopolitical Entity. (suffix of Location Name or Geopolitical Entity)
- OC: uni-gram characters in Organization Name.
- OSuf: uni-gram characters, the last characters of Organization Name. (suffix of Organization Name)
- OBSuf: bi-gram characters, the last two characters of Organization Name. (suffix of Organization Name)

We remove the items in uni-gram lists if their frequencies are less than 5 and in bi-gram lists if their frequencies are less than 2. Based on these lists, we assign the tags to every character. For instance, if a character is included in PSur list, then we assign a tag "PSur_1", otherwise assign a tag "PSur_0". Then we define the char features as follows:

- . $PSur_0PC_0$;
- . $PSur_nPC_nPSur_{n+1}PC_{n+1}(n = -1, 0)$;
- . $PPre_0$;
- . $PSuf_0$;
- . LC_0OC_0;
- . $LC_nOC_nLC_{n+1}OC_{n+1}(n = -1, 0)$;
- . $LSuf_0OSuf_0$;
- . $LSuf_nOSuf_nLSuf_{n+1}OSuf_{n+1}(n = -1, 0)$;

```
S is the list of sentences, S = {s1, s2, ..., sn}.
T is m-best results of S, T = {t1, t2, ..., tn}, which ti
is a set of m-best results of si.
pij is the score of tij, that is the jth result in ti.

Collect NE list:
Loop i in [1, n]
 if(pi0 ≥ 0.5){
  Exacting all NEs from ti0 to add into NEList.}

Replacing:
Loop i in [1, n]
 if(pi0 ≥ 0.5){
  FinalResult(si) = ti0.}
 else{
  TmpResult = ti0.
  Loop j in [m, 1]
   if(the NEs in tij is included in NEList){
    Replace the matching string in TmpResult with new
NE tags.}
   FinalResult(si) = TmpResult.
 }
```

Table 2: The algorithm of Post-processing

4 Post-Processing

There are inconsistently results, which are tagged by the CRFs model. Thus we perform a post-processing step to correct these errors.

The post-processing tries to assign the correct tags according to n-best results for every sentence. Our system outputs top 20 labeled sequences for each sentence with the confident scores. The post-processing algorithm is shown at Table 2. Firstly, we collect NE list from high confident results. Secondly, we re-assign the tags for low confident results using the NE list.

5 Evaluation Results

5.1 Results on Sighan bakeoff 2006

We evaluated our system in the close track, on all three corpora, namely Microsoft Research (MSRA), City University of Hong Kong (CityU), and Linguistic Data Consortium (LDC). Our official Bakeoff results are shown at Table 3, where the columns P, R, and FB1 show precision, recall and F measure($\beta = 1$). We used all three types of features in our final system.

In order to evaluate the contribution of features, we conducted the experiments of each type of features using the test sets with gold-standard dataset. Table 4 shows the experimental results,

MSRA	P	R	FB1
LOC	92.81	88.53	90.62
ORG	81.93	81.07	81.50
PER	85.41	74.15	79.38
Overall	88.14	82.34	85.14
CityU	P	R	FB1
LOC	92.21	92.00	92.11
ORG	87.83	74.23	80.46
PER	92.77	89.05	90.87
Overall	91.43	86.76	89.03
LDC	P	R	FB1
GPE	83.78	80.36	82.04
LOC	51.11	21.70	30.46
ORG	71.79	60.82	65.85
PER	82.40	75.58	78.84
Overall	80.26	72.65	76.27

Table 3: Our official Bakeoff results

	MSRA	CityU	LDC
F1	84.73	88.26	76.18
+F2		88.67	76.30
+F3		88.74	
Post	85.23	89.03	76.66

Table 4: Results of different combinations

where F1 refers to use basic features, F2 refers to use the word boundary features, F3 refers to use the char features, and Post refers to perform the post-processing.

The results indicated that word boundary features helped on LDC and CityU, char features only helped on CityU and the post-processing always helped to improve the performance.

6 Conclusion

This paper presented our Named Entity Recognition system for the close track of Bakeoff2006. Our approach was based on Conditional Random Fields model. Except basic features, we defined the additional features by doing statistics in training corpus. In addition, we performed a post-processing according to n-best results generated by the CRFs model. The evaluation results showed that our system achieved state-of-the-art performance on all three corpora in the close track.

References

John Lafferty, Andrew McCallum, and Fernando Pereira. 2001. Conditional random fields: Probabilistic models for segmenting and labeling sequence data. In *International Conference on Machine Learning (ICML01)*.

Xueqiang Lv, Le Zhang, and Junfeng Hu. 2004. Statistical substring reduction in linear time. In *Proceedings of IJCNLP-04*, HaiNan island, P.R.China.

Fei Sha and Fernando Pereira. 2003. Shallow parsing with conditional random fields. In *Proceedings of HLT-NAACL03*.

France Telecom R&D Beijing Word Segmenter for Sighan Bakeoff 2006

Wu Liu
France Telecom R&D Beijing
wu.liu@francetelecom.com

Heng Li
France Telecom R&D Beijing
heng.li@francetelecom.com

Yuan Dong
Beijing University of Posts and Telecommunications
yuandong@bupt.edu.cn

Nan He
Beijing University of Posts and Telecommunications
hn.ft.pris@gmail.com

Haitao Luo
Northeastern University of China
luoht@ics.neu.edu.cn

Haila Wang
France Telecom R&D Beijing
haila.wang@francetelecom.com

Abstract

This paper presents two word segmentation (WS) systems and a named entity recognition (NER) system in France Telecom R&D Beijing. The one system of WS is for open tracks based on n-gram language model and another one is for closed tracks based on maximum entropy approach. The NER system uses a hybrid algorithm based on Class-based language model and rule-based knowledge. These systems are all augmented with a set of post-processors.

1 Introduction

The FTRD team participated in MSRA Open, MSRA Closed and CityU Closed tracks of the WS bakeoff and MSRA Open track of the NER bakeoff, and achieved the state-of-the-art performance in these tracks. Analysis of the results shows that each component of these systems contributed to the scores.

2 System Description

2.1 MSRA Open track of WS

The system used in open track of WS is based on the system (Li 2005) participated in the second international WS bakeoff. We mainly modify the factoid detection rules and add the GKB (The Grammatical Knowledge-base of Contemporary Chinese) dictionary. The system also has a few postprocessors. The main postprocessors include named entity recognizers and TBL (Transformation-Based Learning) component.

2.1.1 Basic system

In our basic system, Chinese words can be categorized into one of the following types: lexicon words, morphological words, factoids, name entities. These types of words were processed in different ways in our system, and were incorporated into a unified statistical framework of the trigram language model. The details about the basic system are reported in (Li 2005).

2.1.2 Factoid detection

The factoid rules used in the basic system were summarized according to the MSRA training data. The Tokenization Guidelines of Chinese Text (V5.0) was provided by MSRA in this bakeoff. We used the Guidelines to rewrite the factoid rules, and the performance had the distinct improvement.

2.1.3 Named entity identification

The named entity recognizer is the one participated in the NER bakeoff, as shown in figure 1. In the section **2.3**, we will describe in detail.

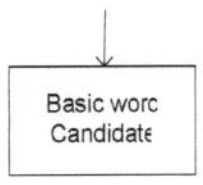

2.2 System Used in Close tracks

The system used in closed tracks of WS is based on maximum entropy approach. The system also has a few postprocessors. The main postprocessors include combining the separated words and TBL component.

2.2.1 Basic system

The basic system is similar to (Ng and Low, 2004). We used the Tsujii laboratory maximum entropy package v2.0 (http://www-tsujii.is.s.u-tokyo.ac.jp/~tsuruoka/maxent/) to train our models. For CityU closed track, the basic features are the same as (Ng and Low, 2004). For MSRA closed track, we used two sets of basic features. The one is similar to (Ng and Low, 2004) and we change the window size of another one from 2 to 3, so we trained two models for MSRA closed track and submitted two results.

2.2.2 Post processing

Firstly, we extracted one lexicon from each training data. For MSRA closed track, the postprocessor only combined the words which appeared in the lexicon but were separated in the test result. For CityU closed track, we firstly used the factoid tool provided by the open system of WS to combine the separated factoid words, and then we used the lexicon to combine the separated words, at last the TBL was applied to the test result.

2.3 MSRA Open track of NER

The system used a hybrid algorithm which can combine a class-based statistical model (Gao 2004) with various types of rule-based knowledge very well. All the words were categorized into three types: Lexicon words (LWs), Factoid words (FTs), Named Entity (NEs). Accordingly, three main components were included to identify each kind of named entities: basic word candidates, NE combination and Viterbi search, as shown in Figure 1.

Table 1 presents the results of this track. For comparison, we also include in the table (Row 1) the results of basic system. From Row 2 to Row 11, it shows the relative contribution of each component and resource to the overall word segmentation performance. The second column shows the recall, the third column the precision, and the fourth column F-score. The last two columns present the recall of the OOV words and the recall of IV words, respectively.

(%)	R	P	F	R_{oov}	R_{iv}
1.basic system	0.971	0.958	0.964	0.590	0.984
2.1+new factoid	0.966	0.958	0.962	0.642	0.978
3.1+GKB lexicon	0.975	0.966	0.971	0.716	0.984
4.3+new factoid	0.971	0.967	0.969	0.768	0.978
5. 4+NE	0.971	0.973	0.972	0.838	0.975
6. 5+TBL	0.977	0.976	0.977	0.840	0.982
7.5+new TBL	0.980	0.978	0.979	0.839	0.985
8. 4+TBL	0.977	0.970	0.974	0.769	0.984
9.4+new TBL	0.980	0.971	0.975	0.769	0.987
10. 8+NE	0.977	0.976	0.977	0.840	0.982
11. 9+NE	0.979	0.978	0.979	0.841	0.984

Table1: Our system results on Open tracks

From Table 1 we can find that, in Row 1, the basic system participated in the last bakeoff already achieves quite good recall, but the recall of OOV is not very good because it cannot correctly identify unknown words that are not in the lexicon such as factoids and name entities (especially the nested named entity) and new words (except factoids, named entities and words abstracted from training data). In Row 2, we only rewrite the factoid rules according to the MSRA Guidelines, and the recall of OOV improves significantly while the recall of IV falls slightly. It shows that the factoid detection affects the recall of IV. As shown in Table 1, the GKB lexicon has made significant and persistent progress in all performance because the GKB lexicon is refined and the words are conformed to the MSRA standard. We also find that the NE postprocessor can improve the recall of OOV but affects slightly the recall of IV in all experiments. It shows that our named entity recognition has make improvement compared with that of last year. As shown in Table 1, TBL has made slightly but persistent progress in all steps it applies to. After TBL adaptation OOV recall stays almost unchanged, for the rules are derived from training corpus, and no OOV words would meet the condition of applying them in theory, but IV recall improves, which compensates the loss of IV recall caused by NE post-process and the factoid detection. It is interesting comparing the performance of two TBL template sets, the first template set is simple and the threshold for generating rules is 3 by default (called TBL in Table 1), and the second is more complicated with a "0" threshold (called New TBL in Table 1). The number of rules generated is 1061 and 12135 respectively. Our experiments demonstrate that more precise rule template set with low threshold always leads to better performance, for they could cover more situations, although a simple rule template set with high threshold does better in OOV word recognition.

3.1.2 MSRA Open track of NER

In the track, we used People's Daily 2000 corpus (Yu, 2003) for building our lexicon and training our model.

Considering that organization names are irregular in their forms compared with person names and location names, and there are many abbreviations and anaphora, TBL adaptation may degrade the performance of organization, we submitted two results, as shown in Table 2. 1+TBL1 means that TBL only adapt person and location results of basic system, the organization performance of basic system and 1+TBL1 would be identical. 1+TBL2 means TBL adapt all three types of NE. For comparison, we list (Column 2) the results of basic system. The Row 2 to Row 13 shows the recall, the precision, and the F-score of PN, LN, ON and total.

(%)		1.basic	1+TBL1	1+TBL2
PN	R	87.28	91.43	91.74
	P	90.63	92.56	92.77
	F	88.92	91.99	92.25
LN	R	80.18	87.39	89.74
	P	81.68	87.51	89.77
	F	80.92	87.45	89.76
ON	R	65.59	65.59	76.48
	P	73.80	73.80	75.44
	F	69.45	69.45	76.11
Total	R	79.31	83.99	87.53
	P	82.98	86.45	87.67
	F	81.10	85.20	87.60

Table 2: MSRA Open track of NER

To our surprise, performance listed in Table 2 demonstrates that applying TBL causes a dramatic improvement in all three types of NE, especially organization performance. The great similarity between training corpus and test corpus of MSRA may explain this. For the inconsistency of standard between MSRA and PKU, the recall, especially of the ONs, is not very good. We did some effort in the standard adaptation, such as constraint the length and type of candidate words in combining the named entities, but the result is not very good.

3.2 Closed tracks

The Table 3 and Table 4 present the results of MSRA and CityU closed tracks respectively.

(%)	R	P	F	R_{oov}	R_{iv}
1.basic system(2)	0.924	0.877	0.900	0.575	0.936
2.1+training lexicon	0.955	0.953	0.954	0.575	0.969
3.2+TBL	0.960	0.955	0.958	0.575	0.973
4.basic system(3)	0.919	0.880	0.899	0.602	0.930
5.4+training lexicon	0.950	0.954	0.952	0.602	0.962
6.5+TBL	0.954	0.955	0.955	0.603	0.966

Table 3: Our system results on MSRA Closed

(%)	R	P	F	R_{oov}	R_{iv}
1.basic system	0.947	0.916	0.931	0.716	0.957
2.1+training lexicon	0.959	0.960	0.959	0.716	0.969
3.2+TBL	0.969	0.964	0.967	0.716	0.980
4.1+factoid tool	0.946	0.915	0.931	0.713	0.956
5.4+training lexicon	0.958	0.959	0.959	0.713	0.968
6.5+TBL	0.969	0.964	0.966	0.712	0.980
6'	0.962	0.962	0.962	0.722	0.972

Table 4: Our system results on CityU Closed

In Table 3, the basic system (2) shows the window size of the template is 2 and the basic system (3) is 3. As is shown in the table, except the precision and the recall of OOV, the performance of window size with 2 outperforms that of window size with 3.

In Table 4, the system 6' is the one we submitted in this closed CityU track, but the system 6 is better than the system 6'. In TBL training, we made a mistake that the training data weren't processed by factoid tool and lexicon combining. We also can find that the factoid tool doesn't improve the performance. The system 6 isn't the best one (system 3).

Combining the separated words according to training lexicon improved the performance of both MSRA and CITYU closed track. In the meantime, TBL worked considerably well in all closed tracks.

4 Conclusions

The evaluation results show that the performance of NER need be improved in abbreviations recognition and anaphora resolution.

Acknowledgements

The work reported here was a team effort. We thank Yonggang Xue, Duo Ji, Haitao Luo, Nan He and Xinnian Mao for their help in the experimentation and evaluation of the system. We also thank Prof. Shiwen Yu for the People's Daily 2000 corpus (Yu 2003) and GKB (Yu 2002) lexicon.

References

Heng Li, etc. 2005. Chinese Word Segmentation in FTRD Beijing. Proceedings of the Fourth SIGHAN workshop on Chinese Language Processing. Pages:150-154

Hwee Tou Ng, Jin Kiat Low. 2004. Chiense part-of-speech tagging: One-at-a-time or all-at-once? Word-based or character-based?. Proceedings of the 2004 conference on Empirical Methods in Natural Language Processing. Pages:277-284

Jianfeng Gao, Mu Li, Andi Wu and Chang-Ning Huang. 2004a. Chinese word segmentation: a pragmatic approach. Microsoft Research Technical Report, MSR-TR-2004-123.

Nianwen Xue, Libin Shen. July 2003. Chinese word segmentation as LMR tagging. Proceedings of the Second SIGHAN workshop on Chinese Language Processing. Pages:176-179.

Shiwen Yu, etc. 2003. Specification for Corpus Processing at Peking University:Word Segmentation, POS Tagging and Phonetic Notation. Journal of Chinese Language and Computing, 13(2) 121-158.

Shiwen Yu, etc. 2002. The Grammatical Knowledge-base of Contemporary Chinese --- A Complete Specification. Tsinghua University Press.

Voting between Dictionary-based and Subword Tagging Models for Chinese Word Segmentation

Dong Song and **Anoop Sarkar**
School of Computing Science, Simon Fraser University
Burnaby, BC, Canada V5A1S6
{dsong,anoop}@cs.sfu.ca

Abstract

This paper describes a Chinese word segmentation system that is based on majority voting among three models: a forward maximum matching model, a conditional random field (CRF) model using maximum subword-based tagging, and a CRF model using minimum subword-based tagging. In addition, it contains a post-processing component to deal with inconsistencies. Testing on the closed track of CityU, MSRA and UPUC corpora in the third SIGHAN Chinese Word Segmentation Bakeoff, the system achieves a F-score of 0.961, 0.953 and 0.919, respectively.

1 Introduction

Tokenizing input text into words is the first step of any text analysis task. In Chinese, a sentence is written as a string of characters, to which we shall refer by their traditional name of *hanzi*, without separations between words. As a result, before any text analysis on Chinese, word segmentation task has to be completed so that each word is "isolated" by the word-boundary information.

Participating in the third SIGHAN Chinese Word Segmentation Bakeoff in 2006, our system is tested on the closed track of CityU, MSRA and UPUC corpora. The sections below provide a detailed description of the system and our experimental results.

2 System Description

In our segmentation system, a hybrid strategy is applied (Figure 1): First, forward maximum matching (Chen and Liu, 1992), which is a dictionary-based method, is used to generate a segmentation result. Also, the CRF model using maximum subword-based tagging (Zhang et al., 2006) and the CRF model using minimum subword-based tagging, both of which are statistical methods, are used individually to solve the problem. In the next step, the solutions from these three methods are combined via the *hanzi*-level majority voting algorithm. Then, a post-processing procedure is applied in order to to get the final output. This procedure merges adjoining words to match the dictionary entries and then splits words which are inconsistent with entries in the training corpus.

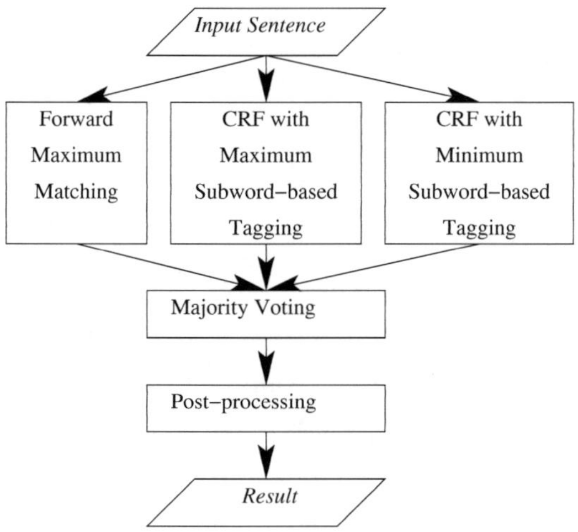

Figure 1: Outline of the segmentation process

2.1 Forward Maximum Matching

The maximum matching algorithm is a greedy segmentation approach. It proceeds through the sentence, mapping the longest word at each point with an entry in the dictionary. In our system, the well-known forward maximum matching algorithm (Chen and Liu, 1992) is implemented.

The maximum matching approach is simple and efficient, and it results in high in-vocabulary accuracy; However, the small size of the dictionary, which is obtained only from the training data, is a major bottleneck for this approach to be applied by itself.

2.2 CRF Model with Maximum Subword-based Tagging

Conditional random fields (CRF), a statistical sequence modeling approach (Lafferty et al., 2001), has been widely applied in various sequence learning tasks including Chinese word segmentation. In this approach, most existing methods use the character-based IOB tagging. For example, "都(all) 至关重要(extremely important)" is labeled as "都(all)/O 至(until)/B 关(close)/I 重(heavy)/I 要(demand)/I".

Recently (Zhang et al., 2006) proposed a maximum subword-based IOB tagger for Chinese word segmentation, and our system applies their approach which obtains a very high accuracy on the shared task data from previous SIGHAN competitions. In this method, all single-*hanzi* words and the top frequently occurring multi-*hanzi* words are extracted from the training corpus to form the lexicon subset. Then, each word in the training corpus is segmented for IOB tagging, with the forward maximum matching algorithm, using the formed lexicon subset as the dictionary. In the above example, the tagging labels become "都(all)/O 至(until)/B 关(close)/I 重要(important)/I", assuming that "重要(important)" is the longest subword in this word, and it is one of the top frequently occurring words in the training corpus.

After tagging the training corpus, we use the package CRF++[1] to train the CRF model. Suppose w_0 represents the current word, w_{-1} is the first word to the left, w_{-2} is the second word to the left, w_1 is the first word to the right, and w_2 is the second word to the right, then in our experiments, the types of unigram features used include w_0, w_{-1}, w_1, w_{-2}, w_2, w_0w_{-1}, w_0w_1, $w_{-1}w_1$, $w_{-2}w_{-1}$, and w_2w_0. In addition, only combinations of previous observation and current observation are exploited as bigram features.

2.3 CRF Model with Minimum Subword-based Tagging

In our third model, we applies a similar approach as in the previous section. However, instead of finding the maximum subwords, we explore the minimum subwords. At the beginning, we build the dictionary using the whole training corpus. Then, for each word in the training data, a forward shortest matching is used to get the sequence of minimum-length subwords, and this sequence is tagged in the same IOB format as before. Suppose "a", "ac", "de" and "acde" are the only entries in the dictionary. Then, for the word "acde", the sequence of subwords is "a", "c" and "de", and the tags assigned to "acde" are "a/B c/I de/I".

After tagging the training data set, CRF++ package is executed again to train this type of model, using the identical unigram and bigram feature sets that are used in the previous model. Meanwhile, the unsegmented test data is segmented by the forward shortest matching algorithm. After this initial segmentation process, the result is fed into the trained CRF model for re-segmentation by assigning IOB tags.

2.4 Majority Voting

Having the segmentation results from the above three models in hand, in this next step, we adopt the *hanzi*-level majority voting algorithm. First, for each *hanzi* in a segmented sentence, we tag it either as "B" if it is the first *hanzi* of a word or a single-*hanzi* word, or as "I" otherwise. Then, for a given *hanzi* in the results from those three models, if at least two of the models provide the identical tag, it will be assigned that tag. For instance, suppose "a c de" is the segmentation result via forward maximum matching, and it is also the result from CRF model with maximum subword-based tagging, and "ac d e" is the result from the third model. Then, for "a", since all of them assign "B' to it, "a" is given the "B" tag; for "c", because two of segmentations tag it as "B", "c" is given the "B" tag as well. Similarly, the tag for each remaining *hanzi* is determined by this majority voting process, and we get "a c de" as the result for this example.

To test the performance of each of the three models and that of the majority voting, we divide the MSRA corpus into training set and held-out set. Throughout all the experiments we conducted, we discover that those two CRF models perform much better than the pure *hanzi*-based CRF method, and that the voting process improves the performance further.

2.5 Post-processing

While analyzing errors with the segmentation result from the held-out set, we find two inconsistency problems: First, the inconsistency between the dictionary and the result: that is, certain words that appear in the dictionary are separated into consecutive words in the test result; Second,

[1] available from http://www/chasen.org/~taku/software

the inconsistency among words in the dictionary; For instance, both "科学研究"(scientific research) and "科学(science) 研究(research)" appear in the training corpus.

To deal with the first phenomena, for the segmented result, we try to merge adjoining words to match the dictionary entries. Suppose "a b c de" are the original voting result, and "ab", "abc" and "cd" form the dictionary. Then, we merge "a", "b" and "c" together to get the longest match with the dictionary. Therefore, the output is "abc de".

For the second problem, we introduce the *split* procedure. In our system, we only consider two consecutive words. First, all bigrams are extracted from the training corpus, and their frequencies are counted. After that, for example, if "a b" appears more often than "ab", then whenever in the test result we encounter "ab", we split it into "a b".

The post-processing steps detailed above attempt to maximize the value of known words in the training data as well as attempting to deal with the word segmentation inconsistencies in the training data.

3 Experiments and Analysis

The third International Chinese Language Processing Bakeoff includes four different corpora, Academia Sinica (CKIP), City University of Hong Kong (CityU), Microsoft Research (MSRA), and University of Pennsylvania and University of Colorado, Boulder (UPUC), for the word segmentation task.

In this bakeoff, we test our system in CityU, MSRA and UPUC corpora, and follow the closed track. That is, we only use training material from the training data for the particular corpus we are testing on. No other material or any type of external knowledge is used, including part-of-speech information, externally generated word-frequency counts, Arabic and Chinese numbers, feature characters for place names and common Chinese surnames.

3.1 Results on SIGHAN Bakeoff 2006

To observe the result of majority voting and the contribution of the post-processing step, the experiment is ran for each corpus by first producing the outcome of majority voting and then producing the output from the post-processing. In each experiment, the precision (P), recall (R), F-measure (F), Out-of-Vocabulary rate (OOV), OOV recall rate (R_{OOV}), and In-Vocabulary rate (R_{IV}) are recorded. Table 1,2,3 show the scores for the CityU corpus, for the MSRA corpus, and for the UPUC corpus, respectively.

	Majority Voting	Post-processing
P	0.956	0.958
R	0.962	0.963
F	0.959	0.961
OOV	0.04	0.04
R_{OOV}	0.689	0.689
R_{IV}	0.974	0.974

Table 1: Scores for CityU corpus

	Majority Voting	Post-processing
P	0.952	0.954
R	0.952	0.952
F	0.952	0.953
OOV	0.034	0.034
R_{OOV}	0.604	0.604
R_{IV}	0.964	0.964

Table 2: Scores for MSRA corpus

	Majority Voting	Post-processing
P	0.908	0.909
R	0.927	0.929
F	0.918	0.919
OOV	0.088	0.088
R_{OOV}	0.628	0.628
R_{IV}	0.956	0.958

Table 3: Scores for UPUC corpus

From those tables, we can see that a simple majority voting algorithm produces accuracy that is higher than each individual system and reasonably high F-scores overall. In addition, the post-processing step indeed helps to improve the performance.

3.2 Error analysis

The errors that occur in our system are mainly due to the following three factors:

First, there is inconsistency between the gold segmentation and the training corpus. Although the inconsistency problem within the training corpus is intended to be tackled in the post-processing step, we cannot conclude that the segmentation for certain words in the gold test set always follows the convention in the training data set. For example, in the MSRA training corpus, "中国政府"(Chinese government) is usually considered as a single word; while in the gold test set, it is separated as two words "中国"(Chinese) and "政府"(government). This inconsistency issue lowers the system performance. This problem, of course, affects all competing systems.

Second, we don't have specific steps to deal with words with postfixes such as "者"(person). Compared to our system, (Zhang, 2005) proposed a segmentation system that contains morphologically derived word recognition post-processing component to solve this problem. Lacking of such a step prevents us from identifying certain types of words such as "劳动者"(worker) to be a single word.

In addition, the unknown words are still troublesome because of the limited size of the training corpora. In the class of unknown words, we encounter person names, numbers, dates, organization names and words translated from languages other than Chinese. For example, in the produced CityU test result, the translated person name "米哈伊洛维奇"(Mihajlovic) is incorrectly separated as "米哈伊洛" and "维奇". Moreover, in certain cases, person names can also create ambiguity. Take the name "秋北方"(Qiu, Beifang) in UPUC test set for example, without understanding the meaning of the whole sentence, it is difficult even for human to determine whether it is a person name or it represents "秋"(autumn), "北方"(north), with the meaning of "the autumn in the north".

4 Alternative to Majority Voting

In designing the voting procedure, we also attempt to develop and use a segmentation lattice, which proceeds using a similar underlying principle as the one applied in (Xu et al., 2005).

In our approach, for an input sentence, the segmentation result using each of our three models is transformed into an individual lattice. Also, each edge in the lattice is assigned a particular weight, according to certain features such as whether or not the output word from that edge is in the dictionary. After building the three lattices, one for each model, we merge them together. Then, the shortest path, referring to the path that has the minimum weight, is extracted from the merged lattice, and therefore, the segmentation result is determined by this shortest path.

However, in the time we had to run our experiments on the test data, we were unable to optimize the edge weights to obtain high accuracy on some held-out set from the training corpora. So instead, we tried a simple method for finding edge weights by uniformly distributing the weight for each feature; Nevertheless, by testing on the shared task data from the 2005 SIGHAN bakeoff, the performance is not competitive, compared to our simple majority voting method described above. As a result, we decide to abandon this approach for this year's SIGHAN bakeoff.

5 Conclusion

Our Chinese word segmentation system is based on majority voting among the initial outputs from forward maximum matching, from a CRF model with maximum subword-based tagging, and from a CRF model with minimum subword-based tagging. In addition, we experimented with various steps in post-processing which effectively boosted the overall performance.

In future research, we shall explore more sophisticated ways of voting, including the continuing investigation on the segmentation lattice approach. Also, more powerful methods on how to accurately deal with unknown words, including person and place names, without external knowledge, will be studied as well.

References

Keh-jiann Chen, and Shing-Huan Liu. 1992. Word Identification for Mandarin Chinese Sentences. In *Fifth International Conference on Computational Linguistics*, pages 101–107.

John Lafferty, Andrew McCallum, and Fernando Pereira. 2001. Conditional Random Fields: Probabilistic Models for Segmenting and Labeling Sequence Data. In *Proc. of ICML-2001*, pages 591–598.

Jia Xu, Evgeny Matusov, Richard Zens, and Hermann Ney. 2005. Integrated Chinese Word Segmentation in Statistical Machine Translation. In *Proc. of IWSLT-2005*.

Huipeng Zhang, Ting Liu, Jinshan Ma, and Xiantao Liu. 2005. Chinese Word Segmentation with Multiple Postprocessors in HIT-IRLab. In *Proceedings of the Fourth SIGHAN Workshop on Chinese Language Processing*, pages 172–175.

Ruiqiang Zhang, Genichiro Kikui, and Eiichiro Sumita. 2006. Subword-based Tagging by Conditional Random Fields for Chinese Word Segmentation. In *Proc. of HLT-NAACL 2006*.

BMM-based Chinese Word Segmentor with Word Support Model for the SIGHAN Bakeoff 2006

Jia-Lin Tsai
Tung Nan Institute of Technology, Department of Information Management
Taipei 222, Taiwan, R.O.C.
tsaijl@mail.tnit.edu.tw

Abstract

This paper describes a Chinese word segmentor (CWS) for the third International Chinese Language Processing Bakeoff (SIGHAN Bakeoff 2006). We participate in the word segmentation task at the Microsoft Research (MSR) closed testing track. Our CWS is based on backward maximum matching with word support model (WSM) and contextual-based Chinese unknown word identification. From the scored results and our experimental results, it shows WSM can improve our previous CWS, which was reported at the SIGHAN Bakeoff 2005, about 1% of F-measure.

1 Introduction

A high-performance Chinese word segmentor (CWS) is a critical processing stage to produce an intermediate result for later processes, such as search engines, text mining, word spell checking, text-to-speech and speech recognition, etc. As per (Lin et al. 1993; Tsai et al. 2003; Tsai, 2005), the bottleneck for developing a high-performance CWS is to comprise of high performance Chinese unknown word identification (UWI). It is because Chinese is written without any separation between words and more than 50% words of the Chinese texts in web corpus are out-of-vocabulary (Tsai et al. 2003). In our report for the SIGHAN Bakeoff 2005 (Tsai, 2005), we have shown that a highly performance of 99.1% F-measure can be achieved while a BMM-based CWS using a perfect system dictionary (Tsai, 2005). A perfect system dictionary means all word types of the dictionary are extracted from training and testing gold standard corpus.

Conventionally, there are four approaches to develop a CWS: (1) **Dictionary-based approach** (Cheng et al. 1999), especial forward and backward maximum matching (Wong and Chan, 1996); (2) **Linguistic approach** based on syntax-semantic knowledge (Chen et al. 2002); (3) **Statistical approach** based on statistical language model (SLM) (Sproat and Shih, 1990; Teahan et al. 2000; Gao et al. 2003); and (4) **Hybrid approach** trying to combine the benefits of dictionary-based, linguistic and statistical approaches (Tsai et al. 2003; Ma and Chen, 2003). In practice, statistical approaches are most widely used because their effective and reasonable performance.

To develop UWI, there are three approaches: (1) **Statistical approach**, researchers use common statistical features, such as maximum entropy (Chieu *et al.* 2002), association strength, mutual information, ambiguous matching, and multi-statistical features for unknown word detection and extraction; (2) **Linguistic approach**, three major types of linguistic rules (knowledge): morphology, syntax, and semantics, are used to identify unknown words; and (3) **Hybrid approach**, recently, one important trend of UWI follows a hybrid approach so as to take advantage of both merits of statistical and linguistic approaches. Statistical approaches are simple and efficient whereas linguistic approaches are effective in identifying low frequency unknown words (Chen *et al.* 2002).

To develop WSD, there are two major types of word segmentation ambiguities while there are no unknown word problems with them: (1) **Overlap Ambiguity** (OA). Take string C1C2C3 comprised of three Chinese characters C1, C2 and C3 as an example. If its segmentation can be either C1C2/C3 or C1/C2C3 depending on context meaning, the C1C2C3 is called an overlap ambiguity string (OAS), such as "將軍(a general)/用(use)" and "將(to get)/軍用(for military use)" (the symbol "/" indicates a word boundary). (2) **Combination Ambiguity** (CA). Take string C1C2 comprised of two Chinese characters C1 and C2 as an example. If its segmentation can be either C1/C2 or C1C2 depending on context meaning, the C1C2 is called a combination ambiguity string (CAS), such as "才(just)/能(can)" and "才能(ability)." Besides the OA and CA problems, the other two types of word segmentation errors are caused by unknown word problems. They are: (1) **Lack of unknown word** (LUW), it means segmentation error occurred by lack of an unknown word in the system dictionary, and (2) **Error identified word** (EIW), it means segmentation error occurred by an error identified unknown words.

The goal of this paper is to report the approach and experiment results of our backward maximum matching-based (BMM-based) CWS with word support model (WSM) for the SIGHAN Bakeoff 2006. In (Tsai, 2006), WSM has been shown effectively to improve Chinese input system. In the third Bakeoff, our CWS is mainly addressed on improving its performance of OA/CA disambiguation by WSM. We show that WSM is able to improve our BMM-based CWS, which reported at the SIGHAN Bakeoff 2005, about 1% of F-measure.

The remainder of this paper is arranged as follows. In Section 2, we present the details of our BMM-based CWS comprised of WSM. In Section 3, we present the scored results of the CWS at the Microsoft Research closed track and give our experiment results and analysis. Finally, in Section 4, we give our conclusions and future research directions.

2 BMM-based CWS with WSM

From our work (Tsai et al. 2004), the Chinese word segmentation performance of BMM technique is about 1% greater than that of forward maximum matching (FMM) technique. Thus, we adopt BMM technique as base to develop our CWS. In this Bakeoff, we use context-based Chinese unknown word identification (CCUWI) (Tsai, 2005) to resolve unknown word problem. The CCUWI uses template matching technique to extract unknown words from sentences. The context template includes triple context template (TCT) and word context template (WCT). The details of the CCUWI can be found in (Tsai, 2005). In (Tsai, 2006), we propose a new language model named word support model (WSM) and shown it can effectively perform homophone selection and word-syllable segmentation to improve Chinese input system. For this Bakeoff, we use WSM to resolve OA/CA problems.

The two steps of our BMM-based CWS with WSM are as below:

Step 1. Generate the BMM segmentation for the given Chinese sentence by system dictionary.

Step 2. Use WSM to resolve OA/CA problems for the BMM segmentation of Step 1. Now, we give a brief description of how we use WSM to resolve OA/CA problem. Firstly, we pre-collect OA/CA pattern-pairs (such as "就/是"-"就是") by compare each training gold segmentation and its corresponding BMM segmentation. The pattern of OA/CA pattern-pairs can be a segmentation pattern, such as "就/是," or just a word, such as "就是." Secondly, for a BMM segmentation of Step 1, if one pattern matching (matching pattern) with at least one pattern of those pre-collected OA/CA pattern-pairs (matching OA/CA pattern-pairs), CWS will compute the word support degree for each pattern of the matching OA/CA pattern-pair. Finally, select out the pattern with maximum word support degree as its segmentation for the matching pattern. If the patterns of the matching OA/CA pattern-pair having the same word support degree, randomly select one to be its segmentation. The details of WSM can be found in (Tsai, 2006).

3 Scored Results and Our Experiments

In the SIGHAN Bakeoff 2006, there are four training corpus for word segmentation (WS) task: AS (Academia Sinica) and CU (City University of Hong Kong) are traditional Chinese corpus; PU (Peking University) and Microsoft Research (MSR) are simplified Chinese corpus. And, for each corpus, there are closed and open track. In the Bakeoff 2006, we attend the Microsoft Research closed (MSR_C) track.

3.1 Scored Results and our Experiments

Tables 1a and 1b show the details of MSR training and testing corpus for 2nd (2005) and 3rd (2006) bakeoff. From Table 1a and 1b, it indicates that MSR track of 3rd bakeoff seems to be a more difficult WS task than that of 2nd bakeoff, since (1) the training size of 2nd bakeoff is two times as great as that of 3rd bakeoff; (2) in training data, the word type number of 3rd bakeoff is less than that of 2nd bakeoff, and (3) in testing data, the word type number of 3rd bakeoff is greater than that of 2nd bakeoff.

	Training	Testing
Sentences	86,924	3,985
Word types	88,119	12,924
Words	2,368,391	109,002
Character types	5,167	2,839
Characters	4,050,469	184,356

Table 1a. Details of MSR_C corpus of 2nd bakeoff.

	Training	Testing
Sentences	46,364	4356
Word types	63,494	13,461
Words	1,266,169	100,361
Character types	4,767	3,103
Characters	2,169879	172,601

Table 1b. Details of MSR_C corpus of 3rd bakeoff.

Table 2 shows the scored results of our CWS at the MSR_C track of this bakeoff. In Table 2, the symbols a, b and c stand for the CWS with a, b and c system dictionary. The system dictionary "a" is the dictionary comprised of all word types found in the MSR training corpus. The system dictionary "b" is the dictionary comprised of "a" system dictionary and the word types found in the testing corpus by CCUWI with TCT knowledge. The system dictionary "c" is the dictionary comprised of "a" system dictionary and the word types found in the testing corpus by CCUWI with TCT and WCT knowledge. Table 3 is F-measure differences between the BMM-based CWS system and it with WSM and CCUWI using "a", "b" and "c" system dictionary in the MSR_C track.

From Tables 2 and 3, we conclude that our CWS of 3rd bakeoff improve the CWS of 2nd bakeoff about 1.8% of F-measure. Among the 1.8% F-measure improvement, 1% is contributed by WSM for resolving OA/CA problems and the other 0.8% is contributed by CCUWI for resolving UWI problem.

System	R	P	F	R_{OOV}	R_{IV}
a	0.949	0.897	0.922	0.022	0.982
b	0.954	0.921	0.937	0.163	0.981
c	0.950	0.930	0.940	0.272	0.974

Table 2. The scored results of our CWS in the MSR_C track (OOV is 0.034) for 3rd bakeoff.

System	R	P	F	Improve
a1.BMM	0.949	0.897	0.922	
a2.BMM+WSM	0.958	0.907	0.932	0.010
b1.BMM	0.946	0.911	0.928	
b2.BMM+WSM	0.954	0.921	0.937	0.009
c1.BMM	0.938	0.920	0.929	
c2.BMM+WSM	0.950	0.930	0.940	0.011

Table 3. The F-measure improvement between the BMM-based CWS and it with WSM in the MSR_C track (OOV is 0.034) using a, b, and c system dictionary.

3.2 Error Analysis

Table 4 shows the F-measure and R_{OOV} differences between each result of our CWS with a, b and c system dictionaries. From Table 4, it indicates that the most contribution for increasing the overall performance (F-measure) of our CWS is occurred while our CWS comprised of WSM and CCUWI with TCT knowledge.

System	F	F(d)	R_{OOV}	R_{OOV}(d)
a	0.922	-	0.022	-
b	0.937	0.015	0.163	0.141
c	0.940	0.003	0.272	0.109

Table 4. The differences of F-measure and ROOV between near-by steps of our CWS.

	OA	CA	LUW	EIW
a	667(389)	403(194)	3268(2545)	0(0)
c	160(147)	231(150)	2310(1887)	805(605)

Table 5. The number of OAS (types), CAS (types), LUW (types) and EIW (types) for our CWS.

Table 5 shows the distributions of four segmentation error types (OA, CA, LUW and EIW) for each result of our CWS with a and c system dictionaries. From Table 5, it shows CCUWI with the knowledge of TCT and WCT can be used to optimize the LUW-EIW tradeoff. Moreover, it shows that WSM can effectively to reduce the number of OA/CA segmentation errors from 1,070 to 391.

4 Conclusions and Future Directions

In this paper, we have applied a BMM-based CWS comprised of a context-based UWI and word support model to the Chinese word segmentation. While we repeat the CWS with the MSR_C track data of 2nd bakeoff, we obtained 96.3% F-measure, which is 0.8% greater than that (95.5%) of our CWS at 2nd bakeoff. To sum up the results of this study, we have following conclusions and future directions:

(1) **UWI and OA/CA problems could be independent tasks for developing a CWS**. The experiment results of this study support this observation. It is because we found 1% improvement is stable contributed by WSM and the other 0.8% improvement is stable contributed by the CCUWI while the BMM-based CWS with difference a, b and c system dictionaries and different MSR_C training and testing data of 2nd and 3rd bakeoff.

(2) About 89% of segmentation errors of our CWS caused by unknown word problem. In the 89%, we found 66% is LUW problem and 23% is EIW problem. This result indicates that the major target to improve our CWS is CCUWI. The result also supports that a high performance CWS is relied on a high performance Chinese UWI (Tsai, 2005).

(3) We will continue to expand our CWS with other unknown word identification techniques, especially applying n-gram extractor with the TCT and WCT template matching technique to improve our CCUWI for attending the fourth SIGHAN Bakeoff.

References

Chen, Keh-Jiann and Wei-Yun, Ma. 2002. Unknown Word Extraction for Chinese Documents, *Proceedings of 19th COLING 2002*, Taipei, 169-175.

Cheng, Kowk-Shing, Gilbert H. Yong and Kam-Fai Wong.. 1999. A study on word-based and integral-bit Chinese text compression algorithms. *JASIS*, 50(3): 218-228.

Chieu, H.L. and H.T. Ng. 2002. Named Entity Recognition: A Maximum Entropy Approach Using Global Information. *Proceedings of 19th COLING 2002*, Taipei, 190-196.

Gao, Jianfeng, Mu Li and Chang-Ning uang. 2003. Improved Source-Channel Models for Chinese Word Segmentation. *Proceedings of the 41st Annual Meeting of the Association for Computational Linguistics*, 272-279.

Lin, Ming-Yu, Tung-Hui Chiang and Keh-Yi Su. 1993. A preliminary study on unknown word problem in Chinese word segmentation. ROCLING 6, 119-141.

Ma, Wei-Yun and Keh-Jiann Chen, 2003, "Introduction to CKIP Chinese Word Segmentation System for the First International Chinese Word Segmentation Bakeoff", *Proceedings of ACL, Second SIGHAN Workshop on Chinese Language Processing*, pp168-171.

Sproat, R. and C., Shih. 1990. A Statistical Method for Finding Word Boundaries in Chinese Text. Computer proceeding of Chinese and Oriental Language, 4(4):336 349.

Teahan, W. J., Yingying Wen, Rodger McNad and Ian Witten. 2000. A compression-based algorithm for Chinese word segmentation. *Computational Linguistics*, 26(3): 375-393.

Tsai, Jia-Lin, C.L., Sung and W.L., Hsu. 2003. Chinese Word Auto-Confirmation Agent, *Proceedings of ROCLING XV*, Taiwan, 175-192.

Tsai, Jia-Lin, G., Hsieh and W.L., Hsu. 2004. Auto-Generation of NVEF knowledge in Chinese, *Computational Linguistics and Chinese Language Processing*, 9(1):41-64.

Tsai, Jia-Lin. 2005. A Study of Applying BTM Model on the Chinese Chunk Bracketing. *Proceedings of IJCNLP, 6th International Workshop on Linguistically Interpreted Corpora*, Jeju Island.

Tsai, Jia-Lin. 2006. Using Word Support Model to Improve Chinese Input System. *Proceedings of ACL/COLING 2006*, Sydney.

Wong, Pak-Kwong and Chorkin ChanWong. 1996. Chinese Word Segmentation. based on Maximum Matching and Word Binding Force. *Proceedings of the 16th International conference on Computational linguistic*, 1:200-203.

On Closed Task of Chinese Word Segmentation: An Improved CRF Model Coupled with Character Clustering and Automatically Generated Template Matching

Richard Tzong-Han Tsai, Hsieh-Chuan Hung, Cheng-Lung Sung, Hong-Jie Dai, and Wen-Lian Hsu
Intelligent Agent Systems Lab
Institute of Information Science, Academia Sinica
No. 128, Sec. 2, Academia Rd., 115 Nankang, Taipei, Taiwan, R.O.C.
{thtsai,yabt,clsung,hongjie,hsu}@iis.sinica.edu.tw

Abstract

This paper addresses two major problems in closed task of Chinese word segmentation (CWS): tagging sentences interspersed with non-Chinese words, and long named entity (NE) identification. To resolve the former, we apply K-means clustering to identify non-Chinese characters, and then adopt a two-tagger architecture: one for Chinese text and the other for non-Chinese text. For the latter problem, we apply postprocessing to our CWS output using automatically generated templates. The experiment results show that, when non-Chinese characters are sparse in the training corpus, our two-tagger method significantly improves the segmentation of sentences containing non-Chinese words. Identification of long NEs and long words is also enhanced by template-based postprocessing. In the closed task of SIGHAN 2006 CWS, our system achieved F-scores of 0.957, 0.972, and 0.955 on the CKIP, CTU, and MSR corpora respectively.

1 Introduction

Unlike Western languages, Chinese does not have explicit word delimiters. Therefore, word segmentation (CWS) is essential for Chinese text processing or indexing. There are two main problems in the closed CWS task. The first is to identify and segment non-Chinese word sequences in Chinese documents, especially in a closed task (described later). A good CWS system should be able to handle Chinese texts peppered with non-Chinese words or phrases. Since non-Chinese language morphologies are quite different from that of Chinese, our approach must depend on how many non-Chinese words appear, whether they are connected with each other, and whether they are interleaved with Chinese words. If we can distinguish non-Chinese characters automatically and apply different strategies, the segmentation performance can be improved. The second problem in closed CWS is to correctly identify longer NEs. Most ML-based CWS systems use a five-character context window to determine the current character's tag. In the majority of cases, given the constraints of computational resources, this compromise is acceptable. However, limited by the window size, these systems often handle long words poorly.

In this paper, our goal is to construct a general CWS system that can deal with the above problems. We adopt CRF as our ML model.

2 Chinese Word Segmentation System

2.1 Conditional Random Fields

Conditional random fields (CRFs) are undirected graphical models trained to maximize a conditional probability (Lafferty *et al.*, 2001). A linear-chain CRF with parameters $\Lambda=\{\lambda_1, \lambda_2, \ldots\}$ defines a conditional probability for a state sequence $\mathbf{y} = y_1 \ldots y_T$, given that an input sequence $\mathbf{x} = x_1 \ldots x_T$ is

$$P_\Lambda(\mathbf{y} \mid \mathbf{x}) = \frac{1}{Z_\mathbf{x}} \exp\left(\sum_{t=1}^{T} \sum_{k} \lambda_k f_k(y_{t-1}, y_t, \mathbf{x}, t) \right), \quad (1)$$

where Z_x is the normalization factor that makes the probability of all state sequences sum to one; $f_k(y_{t-1}, y_t, \mathbf{x}, t)$ is often a binary-valued feature function and λ_k is its weight. The feature functions can measure any aspect of a state transition, $y_{t-1} \rightarrow y_t$, and the entire observation sequence, x, centered at the current time step, t. For example, one feature function might have the value 1 when y_{t-1} is the state B, y_t is the state I, and x_t is the character "国".

2.2 Character Clustering

In many cases, Chinese sentences may be interspersed with non-Chinese words. In a closed task, there is no way of knowing how many languages there are in a given text. Our solution is to apply a clustering algorithm to find homogeneous characters belonging to the same character clusters. One general rule we adopted is that a language's characters tend to appear together in tokens. In addition, character clusters exhibit certain distinct properties. The first property is that the order of characters in some pairs can be interchanged. This is referred to as *exchangeability*. The second property is that some characters, such as lowercase characters, can appear in any position of a word; while others, such as uppercase characters, cannot. This is referred to as *location independence*. According to the general rule, we can calculate the pairing frequency of characters in tokens by checking all tokens in the corpus. Assuming the alphabet is Σ, we first need to represent each character as a |Σ|-dimensional vector. For each character c_i, we use v_j to represent its j-dimension value, which is calculated as follows:

$$v_j = \alpha + (1-\alpha)[\min(f_{ij}, f_{ji})]^{\gamma}, \qquad (2),$$

where f_{ij} denotes the frequency with which c_i and c_j appear in the same word when c_i's position precedes that of c_j. We take the minimum value of f_{ij} and f_{ji} because even when c_i and c_j have a high co-occurrence frequency, if either f_{ij} or f_{ji} is low, then one order does not occur often, so v_j's value will be low. We use two parameters to normalize v_j within the range 0 to 1; α is used to enlarge the gap between non-zero and zero frequencies, and γ is used to weaken the influence of very high frequencies.

Next, we apply the K-means algorithm to generate candidate cluster sets composed of K clusters (Hartigan et al., 1979). Different K's, α's, and γ's are used to generate possible character cluster sets. Our K-means algorithm uses the cosine distance.

After obtaining the K clusters, we need to select the N_1 best character clusters among them. Assuming the angle between the cluster centroid vector and (1, 1, ..., 1) is θ, the cluster with the largest cosine θ will be removed. This is because characters whose co-occurrence frequencies are nearly all zero will be transformed into vectors very close to (α, α, ..., α); thus, their centroids will also be very close to (α, α, ..., α), leading to unreasonable clustering results.

After removing these two types of clusters, for each character c in a cluster M, we calculate the inverse relative distance (IRDist) of c using (3):

$$\text{IRDist}(c) = \log\left(\frac{\sum_i \cos(c, m_i)}{\cos(c, m)}\right), \qquad (3)$$

where m_i stands for the centroid of cluster M_i, and m stands for the centroid of M.

We then calculate the average inverse distance for each cluster M. The N_1 best clusters are selected from the original K clusters.

The above K-means clustering and character cluster selection steps are executed iteratively for each cluster set generated from K-means clustering with different K's, α's, and γ's.

After selecting the N_1 best clusters for each cluster set, we pool and rank them according to their inner ratios. Each cluster's inner ratio is calculated by the following formula:

$$\text{inner}(M) = \frac{\sum_{c_i, c_j \in M} \text{co-occurence}(c_i, c_j)}{\sum_{c_i, c_j} \text{co-occurence}(c_i, c_j)}, \qquad (4)$$

where co-occurrence(c_i, c_j) denotes the frequency with which characters c_i and c_j co-occur in the same word.

To ensure that we select a balanced mix of clusters, for each character in an incoming cluster M, we use Algorithm 1 to check if the frequency of each character in $C \cup M$ is greater than a threshold τ.

Algorithm 1 Balanced Cluster Selection

Input: A set of character clusters $P=\{M_1, \ldots, M_K\}$
Number of selections N_2,
Output: A set of clusters $Q=\{M'_1, \ldots, M'_{N_2}\}$.

```
C={}
sort the clusters in P by their inner ratios;
while |C|<=N2 do
    pick the cluster M that has highest inner ratio;
    for each character c in M do
        if the frequency of c in C∪M is over threshold τ
            P←P−M;
            continue;
        else
```

```
            C←C∪M;
            P←P−M;
      end;
  end;
end
```

The above algorithm yields the best N_1 clusters in terms of exchangeability. Next, we execute the above procedures again to select the best N_2 clusters based on their location independence and exchangeability. However, for each character c_i, we use v_j to denote the value of its j-th dimension. We calculate v_j as follows:

$$v'_j = \alpha + (1-\alpha)[\min(\overline{f_{ij}}, f'_{ij}, \overline{f_{ji}}, f'_{ji})]^{\gamma}, \qquad (5)$$

where $\overline{f_{ij}}$ stands for the frequency with which c_i and c_j appear in the same word when c_i is the first character; and f'_{ij} stands for the frequency with which c_i and c_j co-occur in the same word when c_i precedes c_j but not in the first position. We choose the minimum value from $\overline{f_{ij}}$, f'_{ij}, $\overline{f_{ji}}$, and f'_{ji} because if c_i and c_j both appear in the first position of a word and their order is exchangeable, the four frequency values, including the minimum value, will all be large enough.

Type	Cluster	Inner	(K, α, γ)
EX	,.0123456789	0.94	(10, 0.60, 0.16)
	-/ABCDEFGHIKLMNOPRSTUVWabcdefghiklmnoprstuvwxy	0.93	(10, 0.70, 0.16)
EL	－／ABCDEFGHIKLMNOPRSTUVWabcdefghiklmnoprstvwxy	0.84	(10, 0.50, 0.25)
	０１２３４５６７８９	0.76	(10, 0.50, 0.26)

Table 1. Clustering Results of the CTU corpus

Our next goal is to create the best hybrid of the above two cluster sets. The set selected for exchangeability is referred to as the EX set, while the set selected for both exchangeability and location independence is referred to as the EL set. We create a development set and use the best first strategy to build the optimal cluster set from EX∪EL. The EX and EL for the CTU corpus are shown in Table 1.

2.3 Handling Non-Chinese Words

Non-Chinese characters suffer from a serious data sparseness problem, since their frequencies are much lower than those of Chinese characters. In bigrams containing at least one non-Chinese character (referred as non-Chinese bigrams), the problem is more serious. Take the phrase "約莫 20 歲" (about 20 years old) for example. "2" is usually predicted as *I*, (i.e., "約莫" is connected with "2") resulting in incorrect segmentation, because the frequency of "2" in the *I* class is much higher than that of "2" in the *B* class, even though the feature $C_{-2}C_{-1}$="約莫" has a high weight for assigning "2" to the *B* class.

Traditional approaches to CWS only use one general tagger (referred as the G tagger) for segmentation. In our system, we use two CWS taggers. One is a general tagger, similar to the traditional approaches; the other is a specialized tagger designed to deal with non-Chinese words. We refer to the composite tagger (the general tagger plus the specialized tagger) as the GS tagger.

Here, we refer to all characters in the selected clusters as non-Chinese characters. In the development stage, the best-first feature selector determines which clusters will be used. Then, we convert each sentence in the training data and test data into a normalized sentence. Each non-Chinese character c is replaced by a cluster representative symbol σ_M, where c is in the cluster M. We refer to the string composed of all σ_M as F. If the length of F is more than that of W, it will be shortened to W. The normalized sentence is then placed in one file, and the non-Chinese character sequence is placed in another. Next, we use the normalized training and test file for the general tagger, and the non-Chinese sequence training and test file for the specialized tagger. Finally, the results of these two taggers are combined.

The advantage of this approach is that it resolves the data sparseness problem in non-Chinese bigrams. Consider the previous example in which σ stands for the numeral cluster. Since there is a phrase "約莫 8 年" in the training data, $C_{-1}C_0$= "莫 8" is still an unknown bigram using the G tagger. By using the GS tagger, however, "約莫 20 歲" and "約莫 8 年" will be converted as "約莫 σσ 歲" and "約莫 σ 年", respectively. Therefore, the bigram feature $C_{-1}C_0$="莫 σ" is no longer unknown. Also, since σ in "莫 σ" is tagged as *B*, (i.e., "莫" and "σ" are separated), "莫" and "σ" will be separated in "約莫 σσ 歲".

2.4 Generating and Applying Templates

Template Generation

We first extract all possible word candidates from the training set. Given a minimum word length *L*, we extract all words whose length is greater than or equal to *L*, after which we align all word pairs. For each pair, if more than fifty percent of the characters are identical, a template will be generated to match both words in the pair.

Template Filtering

We have two criteria for filtering the extracted templates. First, we test the matching accuracy of each template t on the development set. This is calculated by the following formula:

$$A(t) = \frac{\#\text{ of matched strings with no separators}}{\#\text{ of all matched strings}}.$$

In our system, templates whose accuracy is lower than the threshold τ_1 are discarded. For the remaining templates, we apply two different strategies. According to our observations of the development set, most templates whose accuracy is less than τ_2 are ineffective. To refine such templates, we employ the character class information generated by character clustering to impose a class limitation on certain template slots. This regulates the potential input and improves the precision. Consider a template with one or more wildcard slots. If any string matched with these wildcard slots contains characters in different clusters, this template is also discarded.

Template-Based Post-Processing (TBPP)

After the generated templates have been filtered, they are used to match our CWS output and check if the matched tokens can be combined into complete words. If a template's accuracy is greater than τ_2, then all separators within the matched strings will be eliminated; otherwise, for a template t with accuracy between τ_1 and τ_2, we eliminate all separators in its matched string if no substring matched with t's wildcard slots contains characters in different clusters. Resultant words of less than three characters in length are discarded because CRF performs well with such words.

3 Experiment

3.1 Dataset

We use the three larger corpora in SIGHAN Bakeoff 2006: a Simplified Chinese corpus provided by Microsoft Research Beijing, and two Traditional Chinese corpora provided by Academia Sinica in Taiwan and the City University of Hong Kong respectively. Details of each corpus are listed in Table 2.

Corpus	Training Size		Test Size	
	Types	Words	Types	Words
CKIP	141 K	5.45 M	19 K	122 K
City University (CTU)	69 K	1.46 M	9 K	41 K
Microsoft Research (MSR)	88 K	2.37 M	13 K	107 K

Table 2. Corpora Information

3.2 Results

Table 3 lists the best combination of n-gram features used in the G tagger.

Uni-gram	Bigram
C_{-2}, C_{-1}, C_0, C_1	$C_{-2}C_{-1}$, $C_{-1}C_0$, C_0C_1, $C_{-3}C_{-1}$, $C_{-2}C_0$, $C_{-1}C_1$

Table 3. Best Combination of N-gram Features

Table 4 compares the baseline G tagger and the enhanced GST tagger. We observe that the GST tagger outperforms the G tagger on all three corpora.

Conf	R	P	F	R_{OOV}	R_{IV}
CKIP-g	0.958	0.949	0.954	0.690	0.969
CKIP-gst	0.961	0.953	0.957	0.658	0.974
CTU-g	0.966	0.967	0.966	0.786	0.973
CTU-gst	0.973	0.972	0.972	0.787	0.981
MSR-g	0.949	0.957	0.953	0.673	0.959
MSR-gst	0.953	0.956	0.955	0.574	0.966

Table 4 Performance Comparison of the G Tagger and the GST Tagger

4 Conclusion

The contribution of this paper is two fold. First, we successfully apply the K-means algorithm to character clustering and develop several cluster set selection algorithms for our GS tagger. This significantly improves the handling of sentences containing non-Chinese words as well as the overall performance. Second, we develop a post-processing method that compensates for the weakness of ML-based CWS on longer words.

References

Hartigan, J. A., & Wong, M. A. (1979). A K-means Clustering Algorithm. *Applied Statistics, 28*, 100-108.

Lafferty, J., McCallum, A., & Pereira, F. (2001). *Conditional Random Fields: Probabilistic Models for Segmenting and Labeling Sequence Data.* Paper presented at the ICML-01.

Chinese Word Segmentation with Maximum Entropy and N-gram Language Model

Wang Xinhao, Lin Xiaojun, Yu Dianhai, Tian Hao, Wu Xihong
National Laboratory on Machine Perception,
School of Electronics Engineering and Computer Science,
Peking University, China, 100871
{wangxh,linxj,yudh,tianhao,wxh}@cis.pku.edu.cn

Abstract

This paper presents the Chinese word segmentation systems developed by Speech and Hearing Research Group of National Laboratory on Machine Perception (NLMP) at Peking University, which were evaluated in the third International Chinese Word Segmentation Bakeoff held by SIGHAN. The Chinese character-based maximum entropy model, which switches the word segmentation task to a classification task, is adopted in system developing. To integrate more linguistics information, an n-gram language model as well as several post processing strategies are also employed. Both the closed and open tracks regarding to all four corpora MSRA, UPUC, CITYU, CKIP are involved in our systems' evaluation, and good performance are achieved. Especially, in the closed track on MSRA, our system ranks 1st.

1 Introduction

Chinese word segmentation is one of the core techniques in Chinese language processing and attracts lots of research interests in recent years. Several promising methods are proposed by previous researchers, in which Maximum Entropy (ME) model has turned out to be a successful way for this task (Hwee Tou Ng et al., 2004; Jin Kiat Low et al., 2005). By employing Maximum Entropy (ME) model, the Chinese word segmentation task is regarded as a classification problem, where each character will be classified to one of the four classes, i.e., the *beginning*, *middle*, *end* of a multi-character word and a single-character word.

However, in a high degree, ME model pays its emphasis on Chinese characters while debases the consideration on the relationship of the context words. Motivated by this view, several strategies used for reflecting the context words' relationship and integrating more linguistics information, are employed in our systems.

As known, an n-gram language model could express the relationship of the context words well, it therefore as a desirable choice is imported in our system to modify the scoring of the ME model. An analysis on our preliminary experiments shows the combination ambiguity is another issue that should be specially tackled, and a division and combination strategy is then adopted in our system. To handle the numeral words, we also introduce a number conjunction strategy. In addition, to deal with the long organization names problem in MSRA corpus, a post processing strategy for organization name is presented.

The remainder of this paper is organized as follows. Section 2 describes our system in detail. Section 3 presents the experiments and results. And in last section, we draw our conclusions.

2 System Description

With the ME model, n-gram language model, and several post processing strategies, our systems are established. And detailed description on these components are given in following subsections.

2.1 Maximum Entropy Model

The ME model used in our system is based on the previous works (Jin Kiat Low et al., 2005; Hwee Tou Ng et al., 2004). As mentioned above, the ME model based word segmentation is a 4-classes learning process. Here, we remarked four classes, i.e. the beginning, middle, end of a multi-character word and a single-character word, as b, m, e and s respectively.

In ME model, the following features (Jin Kiat Low et al., 2005) are selected:

a) c_n $(n = -2, -1, 0, 1, 2)$

b) $c_n c_{n+1}$ $(n = -2, -1, 0, 1)$

c) $c_{-1}c_{+1}$

where c_n indicates the character in the left or right position n relative to the current character c_0.

For the open track especially, three extended features are extracted with the help of an external dictionary as follows:

d) $Pu\ (c_0)$

e) L and t_0

f) $c_n t_0$ $(n = -1, 0, 1)$

where Pu(c_0) denotes whether the current character is a punctuation, L is the length of word W that conjoined from the character and its context which matching a word in the external dictionary as long as possible. t_0 is the boundary tag of the character in W.

With the features, a ME model is trained which could output four scores for each character with regard to four classes. Based on scores of all characters, a completely segmented semiangle matrix can be constructed. Each element w_{ji} in this matrix represents a word that starts at the ith character and ends at jth character, and its value $\texttt{ME}(j, i)$, the score for these $(j - i + 1)$ characters to form a word, is calculated as follow:

$$\begin{aligned}\texttt{ME}[j,i] &= -\log p(w = c_i...c_j) \\ &= -\log[p(b_{c_i})p(m_{c_{i+1}})... \\ &\qquad p(m_{c_{j-1}})p(e_{c_j})]\end{aligned} \quad (1)$$

As a consequence, the optimal segmentation results corresponding to the best path with the lowest overall score could be reached via a dynamic programming algorithm. For example:

那一年我十九岁(I was 19 years old that year)

Table 1 shows its corresponding matrix. In this example, the ultimate segmented result is:

那 一年 我 十九岁

2.2 Language Model

N-gram language model, a widely used method in natural language processing, can represent the context relation of words. In our systems, a bigram model is integrated with ME model in the phase of calculating the path score. In detail, the score of a path will be modified by adding the bigram of words with a weight λ at the word boundaries. The approach used for modifying path score is based on the following formula.

$$\begin{aligned}V[j,i] &= \texttt{ME}[j,i] \\ &\quad + \min_{k=1}^{i-1}\{[(V[i-1,k] \\ &\quad + \lambda\texttt{Bigram}(w_{k,i-1}, w_{i,j})\}\end{aligned} \quad (2)$$

where V[j,i] is the score of local best path which ends at the jth character and the last word on the path is $w_{i,j} = c_i...c_j$, the parameter λ is optimized by the test set used in the 2nd International Chinese Word Segmentation Bakeoff. When scoring the path, if one of the words $w_{k,i-1}$ and $w_{i,j}$ is out of the vocabulary, their bigram will backoff to the unigram. And the unigram of the OOV word will be calculated as:

$$\texttt{Unigram(OOV Word)} = p^l \quad (3)$$

where p is the minimal unigram value of words in vocabulary; l is the length of the word acting as a punishment factor to avoid overemphasizing the long OOV words.

2.3 Post Processing Strategies

The analysis on preliminary experiments, where the ME model and n-gram language model are involved, lead to several post processing strategies in developing our final systems.

2.3.1 Division and Combination Strategy

To handle the combination ambiguity issue, we introduce a division and combination strategy which take in use of unigram and bigram. For each two words A and B, if their bigrams does not exist while there exists the unigram of word AB, then they can be conjoined as one word. For example, "十月(August)" and "革命(revolution)" are two segmented words, and in training set the bigram of "十月" and "革命" is absent, while the word "十月革命(the August Revolution)" appeares, then the character string "十月革命" is conjoined as one word. On the other hand, for a word C which can be divided as AB, if its unigram does not exit in training set, while the bigram of its subwords A and B exits, then it will be resegmented. For example, Taking the word "经济体制改革(economic system reform)" for instance, if its corresponding unigram is absent in training set, while the bigram of two subwords "经济体

		那	一	年	我	十	九	岁
		1	2	3	4	5	6	7
那	1	**6.3180e-07**						
一	2	33.159	7.5801					
年	3	26.401	**0.0056708**	5.2704				
我	4	71.617	45.221	49.934	**3.1001e-07**			
十	5	83.129	56.734	61.446	33.869	7.0559		
九	6	90.021	63.625	68.337	40.760	12.525	12.534	
岁	7	77.497	51.101	55.813	28.236	**0.0012012**	10.077	10.055

Table 1: A completely segmented matrix

制(economic system)" and "改革(reform)" exists, as a consequence, it will be segmented into two words "经济体制" and "改革".

2.3.2 Numeral Word Processing Strategy

The ME model always segment a numeral word into several words. For instance, the word "4.34元(RMB Yuan 4.34)", may be segmented into two words "4." and "34元". To tackle this problem, a numeral word processing strategy is used. Under this strategy, those words that contain Arabic numerals are manually marked in the training set firstly, then a list of high frequency characters which always appear alone between the numbers in the training set can be extracted, based on which numeral word issue can be tackled as follows. When segmenting one sentence, if two conjoint words are numeral words, and the last character of the former word is in the list, then they are combined as one word.

2.3.3 Long Organization Name Processing Strategy

Since an organization name is usually an OOV, it always will be segmented as several words, especially for a long one, while in MSRA corpus, it is required to be recognized as one word. In our systems, a corresponding strategy is presented to deal with this problem. Firstly a list of organization names is manually selected from the training set and stored in the prefix-tree based on characters. Then a list of prefixes is extracted by scanning the prefix-tree, that is, for each node, if the frequencies of its child nodes are all lower than the predefined threshold *k* and half of the frequency of the current node, the string of the current node will be extracted as a prefix; otherwise, if there exists a child node whose frequency is higher than the threshold *k*, scan the corresponding subtree. In the same way, the suffixes can also be extracted. The only difference is that the order of characters is inverse in the lexical tree.

During recognizing phase, to a successive words string that may include 2-5 words, will be combined as one word, if all of the following conditions are satisfied.

a) Does not include numbers, full stop or comma.

b) Includes some OOV words.

c) Has a tail substring matching some suffix.

d) Appears more than twice in the test data.

e) Has a higher frequency than any of its substring which is an OOV word or combined by multiple words.

f) Satisfy the condition that for any two successive words w_1 w_2 in the strings, freq($w_1 w_2$)/freq(w_1)$\geq$0.1, unless w_1 contains some prefix in its right.

3 Experiments and Results

We have participated in both the closed and open tracks of all the four corpora. For MSRA corpus and other three corpora, we build System I and System II respectively. Both systems are based on the ME model and the Maximum Entropy Toolkit [1], provided by Zhang Le, is adopted.

Four systems are derived from System I with regard to whether or not the n-gram language model and three post processing strategies are used on the closed track of MSRA corpus. Table 2 shows the results of four derived systems.

System	R	P	F	R_{OOV}	R_{IV}
IA	95.0	95.7	95.3	66.0	96.0
IB	96.0	95.6	95.8	60.3	97.3
IC	96.4	96.0	96.2	60.3	97.7
ID	96.4	96.1	96.3	61.2	97.6

Table 2: The effect of ME model, n-gram language model and three post processing strategies on the closed track of MSRA corpus.

System **IA** only adopts the ME model. System **IB** integrates the ME model and the bigram language model. System **IC** integrates the division and combination strategy and the numeral words

[1] http://homepages.inf.ed.ac.uk/s0450736/maxent_toolkit.html

processing strategy. System **ID** adds the long organization name processing strategy.

For the open track of MSRA, an external dictionary is utilized to extract the *e* and *f* features. The external dictionary is built from six sources, including the Chinese Concept Dictionary from Institute of Computational Linguistics, Peking University(72,716 words), the LDC dictionary(43,120 words), the Noun Cyclopedia(111,633), the word segmentation dictionary from Institute of Computing Technology, Chinese Academy of Sciences(84,763 words), the dictionary from Institute of Acoustics, and the dictionary from Institute of Computational Linguistics, Peking University(68,200 words) and a dictionary collected by ourselves(63,470 words).

The union of the six dictionaries forms a *big dictionary*, and those words appearing in five or six dictionaries are extracted to form a *core dictionary*. If a word belongs to one of the following dictionaries or word sets, it is added into the external dictionary.

a) The core dictionary.

b) The intersection of the big dictionary and the training data.

c) The words appearing in the training data twice or more times.

Those words in the external dictionaries will be eliminated, if in most cases they are divided in the training data. Table 3 shows the effect of ME model, n-gram language model, three post processing strategies on the open track of MSRA. Here System IO only adopts the basic features, while the external dictionary based features are used in four derived systems related to open track: IA, IB, IC, ID.

System	R	P	F	R_{OOV}	R_{IV}
IO	96.0	96.5	96.3	71.1	96.9
IA	97.5	96.9	97.2	65.9	98.6
IB	97.6	96.8	97.2	64.8	98.7
IC	97.7	97.0	97.4	66.8	98.8
ID	97.7	97.1	97.4	67.5	98.8

Table 3: The effect of ME model, n-gram language model, three post processing strategies on the open track of MSRA.

System II only adopts ME model, the division and combination strategy and the numeral word processing strategy. In the open track of the corpora CKIP and CITYU, the training set and test set from the 2nd Chinese Word Segmentation Backoff are used for training. For the corpora UPUC and CITYU, the external dictionaries are used, which is constructed in the same way as that in the open track of MSRA Corpus. Table 4 shows the official results of system II on UPUC, CKIP and CITYU.

Corpus	R	P	F	R_{OOV}	R_{IV}
UPUC-C	93.6	92.3	93.0	68.3	96.1
UPUC-O	94.0	90.7	92.3	56.1	97.6
CKIP-C	95.8	94.8	95.3	64.6	97.2
CKIP-O	95.8	94.8	95.3	64.7	97.2
CITYU-C	96.9	97.0	97.0	77.3	97.8
CITYU-O	97.9	97.6	97.7	81.3	98.5

Table 4: Official results of our systems on UPUC CKIP and CITYU

On the UPUC corpus, an interesting observation is that the performance of the open track is worse than the closed track. The investigation and analysis lead to a possible explanation. That is, the segmentation standard of the dictionaries, which are used to construct the external dictionary, is different from that of the UPUC corpus.

4 Conclusion

In this paper, a detailed description on several Chinese word segmentation systems are presented, where ME model, n-gram language model as well as three post processing strategies are involved. In the closed track of MSRA, the integration of bigram language model greatly improves the recall ratio of the words in vocabulary, although it will impairs the performance of system in recognizing the words out of vocabulary. In addition, three strategies are introduced to deal with combination ambiguity, numeral word, long organization name issues. And the evaluation results reveal the validity and effectivity of our approaches.

References

Jin Kiat Low, Hwee Tou Ng and Wenyuan Guo. A maximum Entropy Approach to Chinese Word Segmentation. 2005. *Preceedings of the Fourth SIGHAN Workshop on Chinese Language Processing*, pp. 161-164.

Hwee Tou Ng and Jin Kiat Low. Chinese part-of-speech tagging: One-at-a-time or all-at-once? word-based or character-based? 2004. *Preceedings of the 2004 Conference on Empirical Methods in Natural Language Processing(EMNLP)*, pp. 277-284.

Zhang Huaping and Liu Qun. Model of Chinese Words Rough Segmentation Based on N-Shortest-Paths Method. 2002. *Journal of Chinese Information Processing*, 28(1):pp. 1-7.

On Using Ensemble Methods for Chinese Named Entity Recognition

Chia-Wei Wu **Shyh-Yi Jan** **Richard Tzong-Han Tsai** **Wen-Lian Hsu**

Institute of Information Science, Academia Sinica, Nankang, Taipei,115, Taiwan
{cwwu,shihyi,thtsai,Hsu}@iis.sinica.edu.tw

Abstract

In sequence labeling tasks, applying different machine learning models and feature sets usually leads to different results. In this paper, we exploit two ensemble methods in order to integrate multiple results generated under different conditions. One method is based on majority vote, while the other is a memory-based approach that integrates maximum entropy and conditional random field classifiers. Our results indicate that the memory-based method can outperform the individual classifiers, but the majority vote method cannot.

1 Introduction

Sequence labeling and segmentation tasks have been studied extensively in the fields of computational linguistics and information extraction. Several tasks, including, word segmentation, and semantic role labeling, provide rich information for various applications, such as segmentation in Chinese information retrieval and named entity recognition in biomedical literature mining.

Probabilistic state automata models, such as the Hidden Markov model (HMM) [6] and conditional random fields (CRF) [5] are some of best, and therefore most popular, approaches for sequence labeling tasks. Both HMM and CRF consider that the state transition and the state prediction are conditional on the observation of data. The advantage of the CRF model is that richer feature sets can be considered, because, unlike HMM, it does not make a dependence assumption. However, the obvious drawback of the CRF model is that it needs more computing resources, so we can not apply all the features of the model. One possible way to resolve this problem is to effectively combine the results of various individual classifiers trained with different feature sets. In this paper, we use two ensemble methods to combine the results of the classifiers. We also combine the results generated by two machine learning models: maximum entropy (ME) [1] and CRF. One ensemble method is based on the majority vote [3], and the other is the memory based learner [7]. Although the ensemble methods have been applied in some sequence labeling tasks [2],[3], similar work in Chinese named entity recognition is scarce.

Our Chinese named entity tagger uses a character-based model. For English named entity tasks, a character-based NER model proposed by Dan Klein [4] proves the usefulness of substrings within words. In Chinese NER, the character-based model is more straightforward, since there are no spaces between Chinese words and each Chinese character is actually meaningful. Another reason for using a character-based model is that it can avoid the errors sometimes made by a Chinese word segmentor.

The remainder of this paper is organized as follows. In the Section 2, we introduce the machine learning models, the features we apply in the machine learning models, and the ensemble methods. In Section 3, we briefly describe the experimental data and the experiment results. Then, in Section 4, we present our conclusions..

2 Method

2.1 Machine Learning Models

In this section, we introduce ME and CRF.

Maximum Entropy

ME[1] is a statistical modeling technique used for estimating the conditional probability of a target label based on given information. The technique computes the probability $p(y|x)$, where y denotes all possible outcomes of the space, and x denotes all possible features of the space. The computation of $p(y|x)$ depends on a set of fea-

tures in x; the features are helpful for making predictions about the outcomes, y.
Given a set of features and a training set, the ME estimation process produces a model, in which every feature f_i has a weight λ_i. The ME model can be represented by the following formula:

$$p(y \mid x) = \frac{1}{z(x)} \exp\left(\sum_i \lambda_i f_i(x, y) \right),$$

$$z(x) = \sum_y \exp\left(\sum_i \lambda_i f_i(x, y) \right).$$

The probability is derived by multiplying the weights of the active features (i.e., those f_i (y,x) = 1).

Conditional Random Field

A conditional random field (CRF)[5] can be seen as an undirected graph model in which the nodes corresponding to the label sequence $\boldsymbol{y}$ are conditional on the observed sequence $\boldsymbol{x}$. The goal of CRF is to find the label sequence $\boldsymbol{y}$ that has the maximized probability, given an observation sequence $\boldsymbol{x}$. The formula for the CRF model can be written as:

$$P(\mathbf{y} \mid \mathbf{x}) = \frac{1}{Z(\mathbf{x})} \exp\left(\sum_j \lambda_j F_j(\mathbf{y}, \mathbf{x}) \right),$$

where λ_j is the parameter of a corresponding feature F_j, Z(x) is an normalizing factor, and F_j can be written as:

$$F_j(\mathbf{y}, \mathbf{x}) = \sum_{i=0}^{n} f_i(y_{i-1}, y_i, \mathbf{x}, i),$$

where i means the relative position in the sequence, and y_{i-1} and y_i denote the label at position $i-1$ and i respectively. In this paper, we only consider linear chain and first-order Markov assumption CRFs. In NER applications, a feature function f_j (y_{i-1}, y_i, x, i) can be set to check whether x is a specific character, and whether y_{i-1} is a label (such as *Location*) and y_i is a label (such as *Others*).

2.2 Chinese Named Entity Recognition

In this section, we present the features applied in our CRF and ME models, namely, characters, words, and chuck information.

Character Features

The character features we apply in the CRF model and the ME model are presented in Tables 1 and 2 respectively. The numbers listed in the feature type column indicate the relative position of a character in the sliding window. For example, -1 means the previous character of the target character. Therefore, the characters in those positions are applied in the model. The numbers in parentheses mean that the feature includes a combination of the characters in those positions.
The unigrams in Tables 1 and 2 indicate that the listed features only consider to their own labels, whereas the bigram model considers the combination of the current label and the previous label. Since ME does not consider multiple states in a single feature, there are only unigrams in Table 2. In addition, as ME can handle more features than CRF, we apply extra features in the ME model

Table 1 Character features for CRF

	Feature Types
unigram	-2, -1, 0, 1, 2, (-2,-1), (-1,0), (0,1), (1,2), (-1,0,1)
bigram	-2 -1 0 +1 +2, (0,1)

Table 2 Character features for ME

	Feature Types
unigram	-2, -1, 0, 1, 2, (-2,-1), (-1,0), (0,1), (1,2), (-1,0,1) (-1,1)

Word Information

Because of the limitations of the closed task, we use the NER corpus to train the segmentors based on the CRF model. To simulate noisy word information in the test corpus, we use a ten-fold method for training segmentors to tag the training corpus. The word features we apply in our NER systems are presented in Tables 3 and 4.
In addition to the word itself, chuck information, i.e., the relative position of a character in a word, is also valuable information. Hence, we also add chuck information to our models. As the diversity of Chinese words is greater than that of Chinese characters, the number of features that can be used in CRF is much lower than the number that can be used in ME.

Table 3 Word features for CRF

	Feature Types
unigram	0
bigram	0

Table 4 Word features for ME

	Feature Types
unigram	-1, 0, 1, (-2,-1), (-1,0), (0,1), (1,2)

2.3 Ensemble Methods

Majority vote

We can not put all the features into the CRF model because of its limited resources. Therefore, we train several CRF classifiers with different feature sets so that we can use as many features as possible. Then, we use the following simple, equally weighted linear equation, called majority vote, to combine the results of the CRF classifiers.

$$S(y,x)=\sum_{i=0}^{T} C_i(y,x),$$

where S(y,x) is the score of a label y and a character x respectively; T denotes the total number of CRF models; and the value of C_i(y,x) is 1 if the decision of the result of the i_{th} CRF model is y, otherwise it is zero. The highest score of y is chosen as the label of x. The results are incorporated into the Viterbi algorithm to search for the path with the maximum scores.

In this paper, the first step in the majority vote experiment is to train three CRF classifiers with different feature sets. Then, in the second step, we use the results obtained in the first step to generate the voting scores for the Viterbi algorithm.

Memory Based learner

The memory-based learning method memorizes all examples in a training corpus. If a word is unknown, the memory-based classifier uses the k-nearest neighbors to find the most similar example as the answer. Instead of using the complete algorithm of the memory-based learner, we do not handle unseen data. In our memory- based combination method, the learner remembers all named entities from the results of the various classifiers and then tags the characters that were originally tagged as "Other". For example, if a character x is tagged by one classifier as "0" ("Others" tag) and if the memory-based classifier learns from another classifier that this character is tagged as PER, then x will be tagged as "B-PER" by the memory-based classifier.

The obvious drawback of this method is that the precision rate might decrease as the recall rate increases. Therefore, we set the following three rules to filter out samples that are likely to have a high error rate.

1. Named entities can not be tagged as different named entity tags by different classifiers.
2. We set an absolute frequency threshold to filter out examples that occur less than the threshold.
3. We set a relative frequency threshold to filter out examples that occur less than the threshold. For example, if a word x appears 10 times in the corpus, then half of the instances of x have to be tagged as named entities; otherwise, x will be filtered out of the memory classifier.

In our experiment, we used the memory-based learner to memorize the named entities from the tagging results of an ME classifier and a CRF classifier, and then tagged the tagging results of the CRF classifier.

3 Experiments

3.1 Data

We selected the corpora of City University of Hong Kong (CityU) and Microsoft Research (MSRA) corpora to evaluate our methods. CityU is a Traditional Chinese corpus, and MSRA is Simplified Chinese corpus.

3.2 Results

Table 5 shows the results of several methods applied to the MSRA corpus. The memory-based ensemble method, which combines the results of a maximum entropy model and those of a CRF classifier, achieves the best performance. The majority vote combined with the results of three CRF models based on different feature sets has the worst performance.

Table 5 msra

	Precision	Recall	FB1
Memory based	86.21	78.14	81.98
Majority Vote	85.83	76.06	80.65
Only-Character	86.70	75.54	80.74
CRF	86.23	77.40	81.58

The results obtained on Cityu, presented in Table 6, show that the single CRF classifier achieved the best performance. None of the ensemble methods can outperform the non-ensemble methods.

Table 6 cityu

	Precision	Recall	FB1
Memory based	90.79	86.26	88.47
Majority Vote	90.52	84.15	87.22
Only-Character	91.32	84.55	87.80
CRF	92.01	85.45	88.61

Tables 7 and 8 show the results of the memory-based ensemble methods under different rules. We set the frequency threshold as 2 and the relative frequency threshold as 0.5. The results show that the relative frequencies rule effectively reduces the loss of precision caused by more entities being tagged by the memory-based classifier. The memory-based ensemble method works well on the MSRA corpus, but not on the CityU corpus. In the MSRA corpus, the memory-based ensemble method outperforms the individual CRF model by approximately 0.4 % in FB1. We found that the memory-based classifier can not achieve a better performance than the CRF model because it misclassifies many organizations' names. Therefore, we chose another strategy that restricts the memory-based classifier to tagging person names only. Under this restriction, the performance of the memory-based classifier improves FB1 by approximately 0.2%.

Table 7 msra- The performances of memory based ensemble methods under different rules.

	Precision	Recall	FB1
Frequency Threshold	86.18	78.16	81.97
Relative Frequency Threshold	86.21	78.14	81.98
Only Person	86.27	77.58	81.69

Table 8 cityu- The performances of memory based ensemble methods under different rules.

	Precision	Recall	FB1
Frequency Threshold	90.69	86.55	88.57
Relative Frequency Threshold	90.87	86.29	88.52
Only Person	92.00	85.66	88.72

4 Conclusion

In this paper, we use ME and CRF models to train a Chinese named entity tagger. Like previous researchers, we found that CRF models outperform ME models. We also apply two ensemble methods, namely, majority vote and memory-based approaches, to the closed NER shared task. Our results show that integrating individual classifiers as the majority vote approach does not outperform the individual classifiers. Furthermore, a memory-based combination only seems to work when we restrict the memory-based classifier to handling person names.

Acknowledgement

We are grateful for the support of National Science Council under Grant NSC 95-2752-E-001-001-PAE.

References

1. Berger, A., Pietra, S.A.D. and Pietra, V.J.D. A Maximum Entropy Approach to Natural Language Processing. Computer Linguistic, 22. 1996 39-71.
2. Florian, R., Ittycheriah, A., Jing, H. and Zhang, T., Named Entity Recognition through Classifier Combination. in Proceedings of Conference on Computational Natural Language Learning, 2003, 168-171.
3. Halteren, H.v., Zavrel, J. and Daelemans, W. Improving accuracy in word class tagging through combination of machine learning systems. Computational Linguistics, 27 (2). 2001 199-230.
4. Klein, D., Smarr, J., Nguyen, H. and Manning, C.D., Named Entity Recognition with Character-Level Models. in Conference on Computational Natural Language Learning, 2003, 180-183.
5. Lafferty, J., McCallum, A. and Pereira, F. Conditional random fields: Probabilistic models for segmenting and labeling sequence data. International Conference on Machine Learning. 2001 282-289.
6. Rabiner, L. A tutorial on hidden Markov models and selected applications in speech recognition. Proceedings of the IEEE, 77 (2). 1989 257-286.
7. Sutton, C., Rohanimanesh, K. and McCallum, A., Dynamic Conditional Random Fields: Factorized Probabilistic Models for Labeling and Segmenting Sequence Data. in Proceedings of the Twenty-First International Conference on Machine Learning, 2004, 99-107.
8. Zavrel, J. and Daelemans, W. Memory-based learning: using similarity for smoothing. Proceedings of the eighth conference on European chapter of the Association for Computational Linguistics. 1997 436 - 443.

Chinese Word Segmentation and Named Entity Recognition by Character Tagging

Kun Yu[1] Sadao Kurohashi[2] Hao Liu[1] Toshiaki Nakazawa[1]

Graduate School of Information Science and Technology, The University of Tokyo, Tokyo, Japan, 113-8656[1]

Graduate School of Informatics, Kyoto University, Kyoto, Japan, 606-8501[2]

{kunyu, liuhao, nakazawa}@kc.t.u-tokyo.ac.jp[1]

kuro@i.kyoto-u.ac.jp[2]

Abstract

This paper describes our word segmentation system and named entity recognition (NER) system for participating in the third SIGHAN Bakeoff. Both of them are based on character tagging, but use different tag sets and different features. Evaluation results show that our word segmentation system achieved 93.3% and 94.7% F-score in UPUC and MSRA open tests, and our NER system got 70.84% and 81.32% F-score in LDC and MSRA open tests.

1 Introduction

Dealing with word segmentation as character tagging showed good results in last SIGHAN Bakeoff (J.K.Low et al.,2005). It is good at unknown word identification, but only using character-level features sometimes makes mistakes when identifying known words (T.Nakagawa, 2004). Researchers use word-level features (J.K.Low et al.,2005) to solve this problem. Based on this idea, we develop a word segmentation system based on character-tagging, which also combine character-level and word-level features. In addition, a character-based NER module and a rule-based factoid identification module are developed for post-processing.

Named entity recognition based on character-tagging has shown better accuracy than word-based methods (H.Jing et al.,2003). But the small window of text makes it difficult to recognize the named entities with many characters, such as organization names (H.Jing et al.,2003). Considering about this, we developed a NER system based on character-tagging, which combines word-level and character-level features together. In addition, in-NE probability is defined in this system to remove incorrect named entities and create new named entities as post-processing.

2 Character Tagging for Word Segmentation and NER

2.1 Basic Model

We look both word segmentation and NER as character tagging, which is to find the tag sequence T^* with the highest probability given a sequence of characters $S=c_1c_2...c_n$.

$$T^* = \arg\max_T P(T \mid S) \tag{1}$$

Then we assume that the tagging of one character is independent of each other, and modify formula 1 as

$$\begin{aligned} T^* &= \arg\max_{T=t_1t_2...t_n} P(t_1t_2...t_n \mid c_1c_2...c_n) \\ &= \arg\max_{T=t_1t_2...t_n} \prod_{i=1}^{n} P(t_i \mid c_i) \end{aligned} \tag{2}$$

Beam search (n=3) (Ratnaparkhi,1996) is applied for tag sequence searching, but we only search the valid sequences to ensure the validity of searching result. SVM is selected as the basic classification model for tagging because of its robustness to over-fitting and high performance (Sebastiani, 2002). To simplify the calculation, the output of SVM is regarded as $P(t_i|c_i)$.

2.2 Tag Definition

Four tags 'B, I, E, S' are defined for the word segmentation system, in which 'B' means the character is the beginning of one word, 'I' means the character is inside one word, 'E' means the character is at the end of one word and 'S' means the character is one word by itself.

For the NER system, different tag sets are defined for different corpuses. Table 1 shows the tag set defined for MSRA corpus. It is the product of Segment-Tag set and NE-Tag set, because not only named entities but also words are segmented in this corpus. Here NE-Tag 'O' means the character does not belong to any named entities. For LDC corpus, because there is no segmentation information, we delete NE-Tag 'O' but add tag 'NONE' to indicate the character does not belong to any named entities (Table 2).

Table 1 Tags of NER for MSRA corpus

Segment-Tag	×	NE-Tag
B, I, E, S		PER, LOC, ORG, O

Table 2 Tags of NER for LDC corpus

Segment Tag	×	NE Tag	+	NONE
B, I, E, S		PER, LOC, ORG, GPE		

2.3 Feature Definition

First, some features based on characters are defined for the two tasks, which are:

(a) C_n (n=-2,-1,0,1,2)

(b) $Pu(C_0)$

Feature C_n (n=-2,-1,0,1,2) mean the Chinese characters appearing in different positions (the current character and two characters to its left and right), and they are binary features. A character list, which contains all the characters in the lexicon introduced later, is used to identify them. Besides of that, feature $Pu(C_0)$ means whether C_0 is in a punctuation character list. It is also binary feature and all the punctuations in the punctuation character list come from Penn Chinese Treebank 5.1 (N.Xue et al.,2002).

In addition, we define some word-level features based on a lexicon to enlarge the window size of text in the two tasks, which are:

(c) W_n (n=-1,0,1)

Feature W_n (n=-1,0,1) mean the lexicon words in different positions (the word containing C_0 and one word to its left and right) and they are also binary features. We select all the possible words in the lexicon that satisfy the requirements, not like only selecting the longest one in (J.K.Low et al.,2005). To create the lexicon, we use following steps. First, a lexicon from NICT (National Institute of Information and Communications Technology, Japan) is used as the basic lexicon, which is extracted from Peking University Corpus of the second SIGHAN Bakeoff (T.Emerson, 2005), Penn Chinese Treebank 4.0 (N.Xue et al.,2002), a Chinese-to-English Wordlist[1] and part of NICT corpus (K.Uchimoto et al.,2004; Y.J.Zhang et al.,2005). Then, all the words containing digits and letters are removed from this lexicon. At last, all the punctuations in Penn Chinese Treebank 5.1 (N.Xue et al.,2002) and all the words in the training data of UPUC and MSRA corpuses are added into the lexicon.

Besides of above features, some extra features are defined only for NER task.

First, we add some character-based features to improve the accuracy of person name recognition, which are CN_n (n=-2,-1,0,1,2). They mean whether C_n (n=-2,-1,0,1,2) belong to a Chinese surname list. All of them are binary features. The Chinese surname list contains the most famous 100 Chinese surnames, such as 赵, 钱, 孙, 李 (Zhao, Qian, Sun, Li).

Then, we add some word-based features to help identify the organization name, which are $WORG_n$ (n=-1,0,1). They mean whether W_n (n=-1,0,1) belong to an organization suffix list. All of them are also binary features. The organization suffix list is created by extracting the last word from all the organization names in the training data of both MSRA and LDC corpuses.

3 Post-processing

Besides of the basic model, a NER module and a factoid identification module are developed in our word segmentation system for post-processing. In addition, we define in-NE probability to delete the incorrect named entities and identify new named entities in the post-processing phrase of our NER system.

3.1 Named Entity Recognition for Word Segmentation

In this module, if two or more segments in the outputs of basic model are recognized as one named entity, we combine them as one segment.

This module uses the same basic NER model as what we introduced in the previous section. But it only identifies person and location names, because organization names often contain more than one word. In addition, to keep the high accuracy of person name recognition, the features about organization suffixes are not used here.

3.2 Factoid Identification for Word Segmentation

Rules are used to identify the following factoids among the segments from the basic word segmentation model:

NUMBER: Integer, decimal, Chinese number

PERCENT: Percentage and fraction

DATE: Date

FOREIGN: English words

[1] http://projects.ldc.upenn.edu/Chinese/

Table 3 shows some rules defined here.

Table 3 Some Rules for Factoid Identification

Factoid	Rule
NUMBER	If previous segment ends with DIGIT and current segment starts with DIGIT, then combine them.
PERCENT	If previous segment is composed of DIGIT and current segment equals '%', then combine them.
DATE	If previous segment is composed of DIGIT and current segment is in the list of '年, 月, 日, 号 (Year, Month, Day, Day)', then combine them.
FOREIGN	Combine the consequent letters as one segment.

(DIGIT means both Arabic and Chinese numerals)

3.3 NER Deletion and Creation

In-word probability has been used in unknown word identification successfully (H.Q.Li et al., 2004). Accordingly, we define in-NE probability to help delete and create named entities (NE).

Formula 3 shows the definition of in-NE probability for character sequence $c_i c_{i+1} \ldots c_{i+n}$. Here '# of $c_i c_{i+1} \ldots c_{i+n}$ as NE' is defined as $Time_{InNE}$ and the occurrence of $c_i c_{i+1} \ldots c_{i+n}$ in different type of NE is treated differently.

$$P_{InNE}(c_i c_{i+1} .. c_{i+n}) = \frac{\#\text{ of } c_i c_{i+1} .. c_{i+n} \text{ as NE}}{\#\text{ of } c_i c_{i+1} .. c_{i+n} \text{ in testing data}} \quad (3)$$

Then, we use some criteria to delete the incorrect NE and create new possible NE, in which different thresholds are set for different tasks.

Criterion 1: If $P_{InNE}(c_i c_{i+1} \ldots c_{i+n})$ of one NE type is lower than T_{Del}, and $Time_{InNE}(c_i c_{i+1} \ldots c_{i+n})$ of the same NE type is also lower than T_{Time}, then delete this type of NE composed of $c_i c_{i+1} \ldots c_{i+n}$.

Criterion 2: If $P_{InNE}(c_i c_{i+1} \ldots c_{i+n})$ of one NE type is higher than T_{Cre}, and in other places the character sequence $c_i c_{i+1} \ldots c_{i+n}$ does not belong to any NE, then create a new NE containing $c_i c_{i+1} \ldots c_{i+n}$ with this NE type.

4 Evaluation Results and Discussion

4.1 Evaluation Setting

SVMlight (T.Joachims, 1999) was used as SVM tool. In addition, we used the MSRA training corpus of NER task in this Bakeoff to train our NER post-processing module.

4.2 Results of Word Segmentation

We attended the open track of word segmentation task for two corpuses: UPUC and MSRA. Table 4 shows the evaluation results.

Table 4 Results of Word Segmentation Task (in percentage %)

Corpus	Pre.	Rec.	F-score	Roov	Riv
UPUC	94.4	92.2	93.3	68.0	97.0
MSRA	94.0	95.3	94.7	50.3	96.9

The F-score of our word segmentation system in UPUC corpus ranked 4th (same as that of the 3rd group) among all the 8 participants. And it was only 1.1% lower than the highest one and 0.2% lower than the second one. It showed that our character-tagging approach was feasible. But the F-score of MSRA corpus was only higher than one participant in all the 10 groups (the highest one was 97.9%). Error analysis shows that there are two main reasons.

First, in MSRA corpus, they tend to segment one organization name as one word, such as 美国中国商会(China Chamber of Commerce in USA). But our basic segmentation model segmented such word into several words, e.g. 美国/中国/商会(USA/China/Chamber of Commerce), and our post-processing NER module does not consider about organization names.

Second, our factoid identification rule did not combine the consequent DATE factoids into one word, but they are combined in MSRA corpus. For example, our system segmented the word 晚上 9 时整 (9 o'clock in the evening) into three parts 晚上/9 时/整 (Evening/9 o'clock/Exact). This error can be solved by revising the rules for factoid identification.

Besides of that, we also found although our large lexicon helped identify the known word successfully, it also decreased the recall of OOV words (our Riv of UPUC corpus ranked 2nd, with only 0.6% decrease than the highest one, but Roov ranked 4th, with 8.8% decrease than the highest one). The large size of this lexicon is looked as the main reason.

Our lexicon contains 221,407 words, in which 6,400 words are single-character words. It made our system easy to segment one word into several words, for example word 经济组 (Economy Group) in UPUC corpus was segmented into 经济 (Economy) and 组(Group). Moreover, the large size of this lexicon also brought errors of combining two words into one word if the word was in the lexicon. For example, words 只 (Only) and 有 (Have) in MSRA corpus were identified as one word because there existed the word 只有 (Only) in our lexicon. We will reduce our lexicon to a reasonable size to solve these problems.

4.3 Results of NER

We also attended the open track of NER task for both LDC corpus and MSRA corpus. Table 5 and Table 6 give the evaluation results.

There were only 3 participants in the open track of LDC corpus and our group got the best F-score. In addition, among all the 11 participants for MSRA corpus, our system ranked 6th by F-score. It showed the validity of our character-tagging method for NER. But for location name (LOC) in LDC corpus, both the precision and recall of our NER system were very low. It was because there were too few location names in the training data (there were only 476 LOC in the training data, but 5648 PER, 5190 ORG and 9545 GPE in the same data set).

Table 5 Results of NER Task for LDC corpus (in percentage %)

	PER	LOC	ORG	GPE	Overall
Pre.	83.29	58.52	61.48	78.66	76.16
Rec.	66.93	18.87	45.19	79.94	66.21
F-score	74.22	28.57	52.09	79.30	70.84

Table 6 Results of NER Task for MSRA corpus (in percentage %)

	PER	LOC	ORG	Overall
Pre.	90.76	85.62	73.90	84.68
Rec.	76.13	85.41	65.74	78.22
F-score	82.80	85.52	69.58	81.32

Besides of that, error analysis shows there are four types of main errors in the NER results.

First, some organization names were very long and can be divided into several words, in which parts of them can also be looked as named entities. In such case, our system only recognized the small parts as named entities. For example, 哈佛大学费正清东亚研究中心 (Fei Zhengqing Eastern Asia Research Center of Harvard Univ.) was an organization name. But our system recognized it as 哈佛大学(Harvard Univ.)/ORG+费正清 (Fei Zheng Qing)/PER+ 东亚 (Eastern Asia)/LOC+ 研究中心(Research Center)/ORG. Adding more context features may be useful to resolve this issue.

In addition, our system was not good at recognizing foreign person names, such as 赖尔登 (Riordan), and abbreviations, such as 洛市 (Los Angeles), if they seldom or never appeared in training corpus. It is because the use of the large lexicon decreased the unknown word identification ability of our NER system simultaneously.

Third, the in-NE probability used in post-processing is helpful to identify named entities which cannot be recognized by the basic model. But it also recognized some words which can only be regarded as named entities in the local context incorrectly. For example, our system recognized 南京 (Najing) as GPE in 送到南京医治 (Send to Najing for remedy) in LDC corpus. We will consider about adding the in-NE probability as one feature into the basic model to solve this problem.

At last, in LDC corpus, they combine the attributive of one named entity (especially person and organization names) with the named entity together. But our system only recognized the named entity by itself. For example, our system only recognized 刘桂芳 (Liu Gui Fang) as PER in the reference person name 不知内情的刘桂芳 (Liu Gui Fang who does not know the inside).

5 Conclusion and Future Work

Through the participation of the third SIGHAN Bakeoff, we found that tagging characters with both character-level and word-level features was effective for both word segmentation and NER. While, this work is only our preliminary attempt and there are still many works needed to do in the future, such as the control of lexicon size, the use of extra knowledge (e.g. pos-tag), the feature definition, and so on. In addition, our word segmentation system only combined the NER module as post-processing, which resulted in that lots of information from NER module cannot be used by the basic model. We will consider about combining the NER and factoid identification modules into the basic word segmentation model by defining new tag sets in our future work.

Acknowledgement

We would like to thank Dr. Kiyotaka Uchimoto for providing the NICT lexicon.

Reference

T.Emerson. 2005. The Second International Chinese Word Segmentation Bakeoff. In *the 4th SIGHAN Workshop*. pp. 123-133.

H.Jing et al. 2003. HowtogetaChineseName(Entity): Segmentation and Combination Issues. In *EMNLP 2003*. pp. 200-207.

T.Joachims. 1999. Making large-scale SVM learning practical. *Advances in Kernel Methods - Support Vector Learning*. MIT-Press.

H.Q.Li et al. 2004. The Use of SVM for Chinese New Word Identification. In *IJCNLP 2004*. pp. 723-732.

J.K.Low et al. 2005. A Maximum Entropy Approach to Chinese Word Segmentation. In *the 4th SIGHAN Workshop*. pp. 161-164.

T.Nakagawa. 2004. Chinese and Japanese Word Segmentation Using Word-level and Character-level Information. In *COLING 2004*. pp. 466-472.

A.Ratnaparkhi. 1996. A Maximum Entropy Model for Part-of-Speech Tagging. In *EMNLP 1996*.

F.Sebastiani. 2002. Machine learning in automated text categorization. *ACM Computing Surveys*. 34(1): 1-47.

K.Uchimoto et al. 2004. Multilingual Aligned Parallel Treebank Corpus Reflecting Contextual Information and its Applications. In *Proceedings of the MLR 2004*. pp. 63-70.

N.Xue et al. 2002. Building a Large-Scale Annotated Chinese Corpus. In *COLING 2002*.

Y.J.Zhang et al. 2005. Building an Annotated Japanese-Chinese Parallel Corpus – A part of NICT Multilingual Corpora. In *Proceedings of the MT SummitX*. pp. 71-78.

Boosting for Chinese Named Entity Recognition

Xiaofeng Yu **Marine Carpuat** **Dekai Wu***
Human Language Technology Center
HKUST
Department of Computer Science and Engineering
University of Science and Technology
Clear Water Bay, Hong Kong
{xfyu,marine,dekai}@cs.ust.hk

Abstract

We report an experiment in which a high-performance boosting based NER model originally designed for multiple European languages is instead applied to the Chinese named entity recognition task of the third SIGHAN Chinese language processing bakeoff. Using a simple character-based model along with a set of features that are easily obtained from the Chinese input strings, the system described employs boosting, a promising and theoretically well-founded machine learning method to combine a set of weak classifiers together into a final system. Even though we did no other Chinese-specific tuning, and used only one-third of the MSRA and CityU corpora to train the system, reasonable results are obtained. Our evaluation results show that 75.07 and 80.51 overall F-measures were obtained on MSRA and CityU test sets respectively.

1 Introduction

Named entity recognition (NER), which includes the identification and classification of certain proper nouns, such as person names, organizations, locations, temporal, numerical and monetary phrases, plays an important part in many natural language processing applications, such as machine translation, information retrieval, information extraction and question answering. Much of the NER research was pioneered in the MUC/DUC and Multilingual Entity Task (MET) evaluations, as a result of which significant progress has been made and many NER systems of fairly high accuracy have been constructed. In addition, the shared tasks of CoNLL-2002 and CoNLL-2003 helped spur the development toward more language-independent NER systems, by evaluating four types of entities (people, locations, organizations and names of miscellaneous entities) in English, German, Dutch and Spanish.

However, these are all European languages, and Chinese NER appears to be significantly more challenging in a number of important respects. We believe some of the main reasons to be as follows: (1) Unlike European languages, Chinese lacks capitalization information which plays a very important role in identifying named entities. (2) There is no space between words in Chinese, so ambiguous segmentation interacts with NER decisions. Consequently, segmentation errors will affect the NER performance, and vice versa. (3) Unlike European languages, Chinese allows an open vocabulary for proper names of persons, eliminating another major source of explicit clues used by European language NER models.

This paper presents a system that introduces boosting to Chinese named entity identification and classification. Our primary aim was to conduct a controlled experiment to test how well the boosting based models we designed for European languages would fare on Chinese, *without* major modeling alterations to accommodate Chinese. We evaluated the system using data from the third SIGHAN Chinese language processing bakeoff, the goal of which was to perform NER on three types of named entities: PERSON, LOCATION and ORGANIZATION.[1] Three training corpora from MSRA, CityU and LDC were given. The MSRA and LDC corpora were simplified Chinese texts while the CityU corpus was traditional

*This work was supported in part by DARPA GALE contract HR0011-06-C-0023, and by the Hong Kong Research Grants Council (RGC) research grants RGC6083/99E, RGC6256/00E, and DAG03/04.EG09.

[1]Except in the LDC corpus, which contains four types of entities: PERSON, LOCATION, ORGANIZATION and GEOPOLITICAL.

Chinese. In addition, the competition also specified open and closed tests. In the open test, the participants may use any other material including material from other training corpora, proprietary dictionaries, and material from the Web besides the given training corpora. In the closed test, the participants can only use the three training corpora. No other material or knowledge is allowed, including part-of-speech (POS) information, externally generated word-frequency counts, Arabic and Chinese numbers, feature characters for place names, common Chinese surnames, and so on.

The approach we used is based on selecting a number of features, which are used to train several weak classifiers. Using boosting, which has been shown to perform well on other NLP problems and is a theoretically well-founded method, the weak classifiers are then combined to perform a strong classifier.

2 Boosting

The main idea behind the boosting algorithm is that a set of many simple and moderately accurate weak classifiers (also called **weak hypotheses**) can be effectively combined to yield a single strong classifier (also called the **final hypothesis**). The algorithm works by training weak classifiers sequentially whose classification accuracy is slightly better than random guessing and finally combining them into a highly accurate classifier. Each weak classifier searches for the hypothesis in the hypotheses space that can best classify the current set of training examples. Based on the evaluation of each iteration, the algorithm reweights the training examples, forcing the newly generated weak classifier to give higher weights to the examples that are misclassified in the previous iteration. The boosting algorithm was originally created to deal with binary classification in supervised learning. The boosting algorithm is simple to implement, does feature selection resulting in a relatively simple classifier, and has fairly good generalization.

Based on the boosting framework, our system uses the AdaBoost.MH algorithm (Schapire and Singer, 1999) as shown in Figure 1, an n-ary classification variant of the original well-known binary AdaBoost algorithm (Freund and Schapire, 1997). The original AdaBoost algorithm was designed for the binary classification problem but did not fulfill the requirements of the Chinese NER task. AdaBoost.MH has shown its usefulness on standard machine learning tasks through extensive theoretical and empirical studies, where different standard machine learning methods have been used as the weak classifier (e.g., Bauer and Kohavi (1999), Opitz and Maclin (1999), Schapire (2002)). It also performs well on a number of natural language processing problems, including text categorization (e.g., Schapire and Singer (2000), Sebastiani *et al.* (2000)) and word sense disambiguation (e.g., Escudero *et al.* (2000)). In particular, it has also been demonstrated that boosting can be used to build language-independent NER models that perform exceptionally well (Wu *et al.* (2002), Wu *et al.* (2004), Carreras *et al.* (2002)).

Input: A training set $T_r = \{< d_1, C_1 >, \ldots, < d_g, C_g >\}$ where $C_j \subseteq C = \{c_1, ..., c_m\}$ for all $j = 1, \ldots, g$.
Output: A final hypothesis $\Phi(d, c) = \sum_{s=1}^{S} \alpha_s \Phi_s(d, c)$.
Algorithm: Let$D_1(d_j, c_i) = \frac{1}{mg}$ for all $j = 1, \ldots, g$ and for all $i = 1, \ldots, m$. For $s = 1, \ldots, S$ do:

- pass distribution $D_s(d_j, c_i)$to the weak classifier;
- derive the weak hypothesis Φ_s from the weak classifier;
- choose $\alpha_s \in R$;
- set $D_{s+1}(d_j, c_i) = \frac{D_s(d_j, c_i)\exp(-\alpha_s C_j[c_i]\Phi_s(d_j, c_i))}{Z_s}$ where $Z_s = \sum_{i=1}^{m} \sum_{j=1}^{g} D_s(d_j, c_i)\exp(-\alpha_s C_j[c_i]\Phi_s(d_j, c_i))$ is a normalization factor chosen so that $\sum_{i=1}^{m} \sum_{j=1}^{g} D_{s+1}(d_j, c_i) = 1$.

Figure 1: The AdaBoost.MH algorithm.

The weak classifiers used in the boosting algorithm come from a wide range of machine learning methods. We have chosen to use a simple classifier called a **decision stump** in the algorithm. A decision stump is basically a one-level decision tree where the split at the root level is based on a specific attribute/value pair. For example, a possible attribute/value pair could be W_2 = 香港.

3 Experiment Details

In order to implement the boosting/decision stumps, we used the publicly available software AT&T BoosTexter (Schapire and Singer, 2000), which implements boosting on top of decision stumps. For preprocessing we used an off-the-shelf Chinese lexical analysis system, the open source ICTCLAS (Zhang *et al.*, 2003), to segment and POS tag the training and test corpora.

3.1 Data Preprocessing

The training corpora provided by the SIGHAN bakeoff organizers were in the CoNLL two column format, with one Chinese character per line and hand-annotated named entity chunks in the second column.

In order to provide basic features for training the decision stumps, the training corpora were segmented and POS tagged by ICTCLAS, which labels Chinese words using a set of 39 tags. This module employs a hierarchical hidden Markov model (HHMM) and provides word segmentation, POS tagging and unknown word recognition. It performs reasonably well, with segmentation precision recently evaluated at 97.58%.[2] The recall rate of unknown words using role tagging was over 90%.

We note that about 200 words in each training corpora remained untagged. For these words we simply assigned the most frequently occurring tags in each training corpora.

3.2 Feature Set

The boosting/decision stumps were able to accommodate a large number of features. The primitive features we used were:

- The current character and its POS tag.
- The characters within a window of 2 characters before and after the current character.
- The POS tags within a window of 2 characters before and after the current character.
- The chunk tags (gold standard named entity label during the training) of the previous two characters.

The chunk tag is the **BIO** representation, which was employed in the CoNLL-2002 and CoNLL-2003 evaluations. In this representation, each character is tagged as either the beginning of a named entity (**B** tag), a character inside a named entity (**I** tag), or a character outside a named entity (**O** tag).

When we used conjunction features, we found that they helped the NER performance significantly. The conjunction features used are basically conjunctions of 2 consecutive characters and 2 consecutive POS tags. We also found that a larger context window (3 characters instead of 2 before and after the current character) to be quite helpful to performance.

Apart from the training and test corpora, we considered the gazetteers from LDC which contain about 540K persons, 242K locations and 98K organization names. Named entities in the training corpora which appeared in the gazetteers were identified lexically or by using a maximum forward match algorithm. Once named entities have been identified, each character can then be annotated with an NE chunk tag. The boosting learner

[2]Results from the recent official evaluation in the national 973 project.

Table 1: Dev set results on MSRA and CityU.

	Precision	*Recall*	$F_{\beta=1}$
MSRA			
LOC	82.00%	85.93%	83.92
ORG	76.99%	61.44%	68.34
PER	89.33%	74.47%	81.22
Overall	82.62%	76.45%	79.41
CityU			
LOC	88.62%	81.69%	85.02
ORG	82.50%	66.44%	73.61
PER	84.05%	84.58%	84.31
Overall	86.46%	79.26%	82.71

Table 2: Test set results on MSRA, CityU, LDC.

	Precision	*Recall*	$F_{\beta=1}$
MSRA			
LOC	84.98%	80.94%	82.91
ORG	72.82%	57.78%	64.43
PER	82.89%	59.91%	69.55
Overall	81.95%	69.26%	75.07
CityU			
LOC	88.65%	83.58%	86.04
ORG	83.75%	57.25%	68.01
PER	86.11%	76.42%	80.98
Overall	86.92%	74.98%	80.51
LDC			
LOC	65.84%	76.51%	70.78
ORG	53.69%	39.52%	45.53
PER	80.29%	68.97%	74.20
Overall	67.20%	65.54%	66.36
LDC (w/GPE)			
GPE	0.00%	0.00%	0.00
LOC	1.94%	37.74%	3.70
ORG	53.69%	39.52%	45.53
PER	80.29%	68.97%	74.20
Overall	30.58%	29.82%	30.19

can view the NE chunk tag as an additional feature. Here we used binary gazetteer features. If the character was annotated with an NE chunk tag, its gazetteer feature was set to 1; otherwise it was set to 0. However we found that adding binary gazetteer features does not significantly help the performance when conjunction features were used. In fact, it actually hurt the performance slightly.

The features used in the final experiments were:

- The current character and its POS tag.
- The characters within a window of 3 characters before and after the current character.
- The POS tags within a window of 3 characters before and after the current character.
- A small set of conjunctions of POS tags and characters within a window of 3 characters of the current character.
- The BIO chunk tags of the previous 3 characters.

4 Results

Table 1 presents the results obtained on the MSRA and CityU development test set. Table 2 presents the results obtained on the MSRA, CityU and LDC test sets. These numbers greatly underrepresent what could be expected from the boosting model, since we only used one-third of MSRA and CityU training corpora due to limitations of the boosting software. Another problem for the LDC corpus was training/testing mismatch: we did not train any models at all with the LDC training corpus, which was the only training set annontated with geopolitical entities (GPE). Instead, for the LDC test set, we simply used the system trained on the MSRA corpus. Thus, when we consider the geopolitical entity (GPE), our low overall F-measure on the LDC test set cannot be interpreted meaningfully.[3] Even so, using only one-third of the training data, the results on the MSRA and CityU test sets are reasonable: 75.07 and 80.51 overall F-measures were obtained on the MSRA and CityU test sets, respectively.

5 Conclusion

We have described an experiment applying a boosting based NER model originally designed for multiple European languages instead to the Chinese named entity recognition task. Even though we only used one-third of the MSRA and CityU corpora to train the system, the model produced reasonable results, obtaining 75.07 and 80.51 overall F-measures on MSRA and CityU test sets respectively.

Having established this baseline for comparison against our multilingual European language boosting based NER models, our next step will be to incorporate Chinese-specific attributes into the model to compare with.

[3]Our LDC test result was scored twice by the organizer.

References

Eric Bauer and Ron Kohavi. An empirical comparison of voting classification algorithms: Bagging, boosting, and variants. *Machine Learning*, 36:105–142, 1999.

Xavier Carreras, Lluís Màrquez, and Lluís Padró. Named entity extraction using AdaBoost. In *Computational Natural Language Learning (CoNLL-2002), at COLING-2002*, pages 171–174, Taipei, Sep 2002.

Gerard Escudero, Lluís Màrquez, and German Rigau. Boosting applied to word sense disambiguation. In *11th European Conference on Machine Learning (ECML-00)*, pages 129–141, 2000.

Yoav Freund and Robert E. Schapire. A decision-theoretic generalization of on-line learning and an application to boosting. *Computer and System Sciences*, 55(1):119–139, 1997.

David Opitz and Richard Maclin. Popular ensemble methods: An empirical study. *Journal of Artificial Intelligence Research*, 11:169–198, 1999.

Robert E. Schapire and Yoram Singer. Improved boosting algorithms using confidence-rated predictions. *Machine Learning*, 37(3):297–336, 1999.

Robert E. Schapire and Yoram Singer. Boostexter: A boosting-based system for text categorization. *Machine Learning*, 39(2-3):135–168, 2000.

Robert E. Schapire. The boosting approach to machine learning: An overview. In *MSRI workshop on Nonlinear Estimation and Classification*, 2002.

Fabrizio Sebastiani, Alessandro Sperduti, and Nicola Valdambrini. An improved boosting algorithm and its application to automated text categorization. In *Proceedings of 9th ACM International Conference on Information and Knowledge Management*, pages 78–85, 2000.

Dekai Wu, Grace Ngai, Marine Carpuat, Jeppe Larsen, and Yongsheng Yang. Boosting for named entity recognition. In *Computational Natural Language Learning (CoNLL-2002), at COLING-2002*, pages 195–198, Taipei, Sep 2002.

Dekai Wu, Grace Ngai, and Marine Carpuat. Why nitpicking works: Evidence for Occam's razor in error correctors. In *20th International Conference on Computational Linguistics (COLING-2004)*, Geneva, 2004.

Hua Ping Zhang, Qun Liu, Xue-Qi Cheng, Hao Zhang, and Hong Kui Yu. Chinese lexical analysis using Hierarchical Hidden Markov Model. In *Proceedings of the second SIGHAN workshop on Chinese language processing*, volume 17, pages 63–70, 2003.

Chinese word segmentation and named entity recognition based on a context-dependent Mutual Information Independence Model

Zhang Min Zhou GuoDong Yang LingPeng Ji DongHong

Institute for Infocomm Research
21 Heng Mui Keng Terrace
Singapore, 119613
Email: (mzhang, zhougd, lpyang, dhji)@i2r.a-star.edu.sg

Abstract

This paper briefly describes our system in the third SIGHAN bakeoff on Chinese word segmentation and named entity recognition. This is done via a word chunking strategy using a context-dependent Mutual Information Independence Model. Evaluation shows that our system performs well on all the word segmentation closed tracks and achieves very good scalability across different corpora. It also shows that the use of the same strategy in named entity recognition shows promising performance given the fact that we only spend less than three days in total on extending the system in word segmentation to incorporate named entity recognition, including training and formal testing.

1 Introduction

Word segmentation and named entity recognition aim at recognizing the implicit word boundaries and proper nouns, such as names of persons, locations and organizations, respectively in plain Chinese text, and are critical in Chinese information processing. However, there exist two problems when developing a practical word segmentation or named entity recognition system for large open applications, i.e. the resolution of ambiguous segmentations and the identification of OOV words or OOV entity names.

In order to resolve above problems, we developed a purely statistical Chinese word segmentation system and a named entity recognition system using a three-stage strategy under an unified framework.

The first stage is called known word segmentation, which aims to segment an input sequence of Chinese characters into a sequence of known words (called word atoms in this paper). In this paper, all Chinese characters are regarded as known words and a word unigram model is applied to perform this task for efficiency. Also, for convenience, all the English characters are transformed into the Chinese counterparts in preprocessing, which will be recovered just before outputting results.

The second stage is the word and/or named entity identification and classification on the sequence of atomic words in the first step. Here, a word chunking strategy is applied to detect words and/or entity names by chunking one or more atomic words together according to the word formation patterns of the word atoms and optional entity name formation patterns for named entity recognition. The problem of word segmentation and/or entity name recognition are re-cast as chunking one or more word atoms together to form a new word and/or entity name, and a discriminative Markov model, named Mutual Information Independence Model (MIIM), is adopted in chunking. Besides, a SVM plus sigmoid model is applied to integrate various types of contexts and implement the discriminative modeling in MIIM.

The third step is post processing, which tries to further resolve ambiguous segmentations and unknown word segmentation. Due to time limit, this is only done in Chinese word segmentation. No post processing is done on Chinese named entity recognition.

The rest of this paper is as follows: Section 2 describes the context-dependent Mutual Information Independence Model in details while purely statistical post-processing in Chinese word segmentation is presented in Section 3. Finally, we report the results of our system in Chinese word segmentation and named entity recognition in Section 4 and conclude our work in Section 5.

2 Mutual Information Independence Model

In this paper, we use a discriminative Markov model, called Mutual Information Independence Model (MIIM) as proposed by Zhou et al (2002), for Chinese word segmentation and named entity recognition. MIIM is derived from a conditional probability model. Given an observation sequence $O_1^n = o_1 o_2 \cdots o_n$, MIIM finds a stochastic optimal state(tag) sequence $S_1^n = s_1 s_2 \cdots s_n$ that maximizes:

$$\log P(S_1^n \mid O_1^n) = \sum_{i=2}^{n} PMI(s_i, S_1^{i-1}) + \sum_{i=1}^{n} \log P(s_i \mid O_1^n)$$

We call the above model the Mutual Information Independence Model due to its Pair-wise Mutual Information (PMI) assumption (Zhou et al 2002). The above model consists of two sub-models: the state transition model $\sum_{i=2}^{n} PMI(s_i, S_1^{i-1})$, which can be computed by applying ngram modeling, and the output model $\sum_{i=1}^{n} \log P(s_i \mid O_1^n)$, which can be estimated by any probability-based classifier, such as a maximum entropy classifier or a SVM plus sigmoid classifier (Zhou et al 2006). In this competition, the SVM plus sigmoid classifier is used in Chinese word segmentation while a simple backoff approach as described in Zhou et al (2002) is used in named entity recognition.

Here, a variant of the Viterbi algorithm (Viterbi 1967) in decoding the standard Hidden Markov Model (HMM) (Rabiner 1989) is implemented to find the most likely state sequence by replacing the state transition model and the output model of the standard HMM with the state transition model and the output model of the MIIM, respectively. The above MIIM has been successfully applied in many applications, such as text chunking (Zhou 2004), Chinese word segmentation (Zhou 2005), English named entity recognition in the newswire domain (Zhou et al 2002) and the biomedical domain (Zhou et al 2004; Zhou et al 2006).

For Chinese word segmentation and named entity recognition by chunking, a word or a entity name is regarded as a chunk of one or more word atoms and we have:

- $o_i = < p_i, w_i >$; w_i is the $i-th$ word atom in the sequence of word atoms $W_1^n = w_1 w_2 \cdots w_n$; p_i is the word formation pattern of the word atom w_i. Here p_i measures the word formation power of the word atom w_i and consists of:
  - The percentage of w_i occurring as a whole word (round to 10%)
  - The percentage of w_i occurring at the beginning of other words (round to 10%)
  - The percentage of w_i occurring at the end of other words (round to 10%)
  - The length of w_i
  - Especially for named entity recognition, the percentages of a word occurring in different entity types (round to 10%).
- s_i : the states are used to bracket and differentiate various types of words and optional entity types for named entity recognition. In this way, Chinese word segmentation and named entity recognition can be regarded as a bracketing and classification process. s_i is structural and consists of two parts:
  - **Boundary category (B)**: it includes four values: {O, B, M, E}, where O means that current word atom is a whOle word or entity name and B/M/E means that current word atom is at the Beginning/in the Middle/at the End of a word or entity name.
  - **Unit category (W)**: It is used to denote the type of the word or entity name.

Because of the limited number of boundary and unit categories, the current word atom formation pattern p_i described above is added into the state transition model in MIIM. This makes the above MIIM context dependent as follows:

$$\log P(S_1^n \mid O_1^n) = \sum_{i=2}^{n} PMI(s_i, S_1^{i-1} \mid p_{i-1} p_i) + \sum_{i=1}^{n} \log P(s_i \mid O_1^n)$$

3 Post Processing in Word Segmentation

The third step is post processing, which tries to resolve ambiguous segmentations and false unknown word generation raised in the second step. Due to time limit, this is only done in Chinese word segmentation, i.e. no post processing is done on Chinese named entity recognition.

A simple pattern-based method is employed to capture context information to correct the segmentation errors generated in the second steps. The pattern is designed as follows:

<Ambiguous Entry (*AE*)> | <Left Context, Right Context> => <Proper Segmentation>

The ambiguity entry (*AE*) means ambiguous segmentations or forced-generated unknown words. We use the 1st and 2nd words before *AE* as the left context and the 1st and 2nd words after *AE* as the right context. To reduce sparseness, we also only use the 1st left and right words as context. This means that there are two patterns generated for the same context. All the patterns are automatically learned from training corpus using the following algorithm.

LearningPatterns()

// Input: training corpus

// Output: patterns

BEGIN

(1) Training a MIIM model using training corpus

(2) Using the MIIM model to segment training corpus

(3) Aligning the training corpus with the segmented training corpus

(4) Extracting error segmentations

(5) Generating disambiguation patterns using the left and right context

(6) Removing the conflicting entries if two patterns have the same left hand side but different right hand side.

END

---

4 Evaluation

We first develop our system using the PKU data released in the Second SIGHAN Bakeoff last year. Then, we train and evaluate it on the Third SIGHAN Bakeoff corpora without any fine-tuning. We only carry out our evaluation on the closed tracks. It means that we do not use any additional knowledge beyond the training corpus. Precision (**P**), Recall (**R**), F-measure (**F**), OOV Recall and IV Recall are adopted to measure the performance of word segmentation. Accuracy (**A**), Precision (**P**), Recall (**R**) and F-measure (**F**) are adopted to measure the performance of NER. Tables 1, 2 and 3 in the next page report the performance of our algorithm on different corpus in the SIGHAN Bakeoff 02 and Bakeoff 03, respectively. For the performance of other systems, please refer to http://sighan.cs.uchicago.edu/bakeoff2005/data/results.php.htm for the Chinese bakeoff 2005 and http://sighan.cs.uchicago.edu/bakeoff2006/longstats.html for the Chinese bakeoff 2006.

Comparison against other systems shows that our system achieves the state-of-the-art performance on all Chinese word segmentation closed tracks and shows good scalability across different corpora. The small performance gap should be able to overcome by replacing the word unigram model with the more powerful word bigram model. Due to very limited time of less than three days, although our NER system under the unified framework as Chinese word segmentation does not achieve the state-of-the-art, its performance in NER is quite promising and provides a good platform for further improvement. Error analysis reveals that OOV is still an open problem that is far from to resolve. In addition, different corpus defines different segmentation principles. This will stress OOV handling in the extreme. Therefore a system trained on one genre usually performances worse when faced with text from a different register.

5 Conclusion

This paper proposes a purely unified statistical three-stage strategy in Chinese word segmentation and named entity recognition, which are based on a context-dependent Mutual Information Independence Model. Evaluation shows that our system achieves the states-of-the-art segmentation performance and provides a good platform for further performance improvement of Chinese NER.

References

Rabiner L. 1989. A Tutorial on Hidden Markov Models and Selected Applications in Speech Recognition. *IEEE 77(*2), pages257-285.

Viterbi A.J. 1967. Error Bounds for Convolutional Codes and an Asymptotically Optimum Decoding Algorithm. *IEEE Transactions on Information Theory,* IT 13(2), 260-269.

Zhou GuoDong and Su Jain. 2002. Named Entity Recognition Using a HMM-based Chunk Tagger, *Proceedings of the 40th Annual Meeting of the Association for Computational Linguistics (ACL'2002).* Philadelphia. July 2002. pp473-480.

Zhou GuoDong, Zhang Jie, Su Jian, Shen Dan and Tan ChewLim. 2004. Recognizing Names in Biomedical Texts: a Machine Learning Approach. *Bioinformatics*. 20(7): 1178-1190. DOI: 10.1093/bioinformatics/bth060. 2004. ISSN: 1460-2059

Zhou GuoDong. 2004. Discriminative hidden Markov modeling with long state dependence using a kNN ensemble. *Proceedings of 20th International Conference on Computational Linguistics (COLING'2004)*. 23-27 Aug, 2004, Geneva, Switzerland.

Zhou GuoDong. 2005. A chunking strategy towards unknown word detection in Chinese word segmentation. *Proceedings of 2nd International Joint Conference on Natural Language Processing (IJCNLP'2005), Lecture Notes in Computer Science (LNCS 3651)*

Zhou GuoDong. 2006. Recognizing names in biomedical texts using Mutual Information Independence Model and SVM plus Sigmod. *International Journal of Medical Informatics* (Article in Press). ISSN 1386-5056

Tables

Task	P	R	F	OOV Recall	IV Recall
CityU	0.9 38	0.952	94.5	0.578	0.967
MSRA	0.952	0.962	95.7	0.51	0.98
CKIP	0.94	0.957	94.8	0.502	0.976
PKU	0.952	0.952	95.2	0.71	0.967

Table 1: Performance of Word Segmentation on Closed Tracks in the SIGHAN Bakeoff 02

Task	P	R	F	OOV Recall	IV Recall
CityU	0.968	0.961	96.5	0.633	0.983
MSRA	0.961	0.953	95.7	0.499	0.977
CKIP	0.958	0.941	94.9	0.554	0.976
UPUC	0.936	0.917	92.6	0.617	0.966

Table 2: Performance of Word Segmentation on Closed Tracks in the SIGHAN Bakeoff 03

Task	A	P	R	F
MSRA	0.9743	0.8150	0.7882	79.92
CityU	0.9725	0.8466	0.8061	82.59

Table 3: Performance of NER on Closed Tracks in the SIGHAN Bakeoff 03

Word Segmentation and Named Entity Recognition for SIGHAN Bakeoff3

Zhang Suxiang
CISTR,
Beijing University of Posts and Telecommunications
zsuxiang@163.com

Qin Ying
CISTR,
Beijing University of Posts and Telecommunications
qinyingmail@163.com

Wen Juan
CISTR,
Beijing University of Posts and Telecommunications
mystery999@163.com

Wang Xiaojie
CISTR,
Beijing University of Posts and Telecommunications
xjwang@bupt.edu.cn

Abstract

We have participated in three open tracks of Chinese word segmentation and named entity recognition tasks of SIGHAN Bakeoff3. We take a probabilistic feature based Maximum Entropy (ME) model as our basic frame to combine multiple sources of knowledge. Our named entity recognizer achieved the highest F measure for MSRA, and word segmenter achieved the medium F measure for MSRA. We find effective combining of the external multi-knowledge is crucial to improve performance of word segmentation and named entity recognition.

1 Introduction

Word Segmentation (WS) and Named Entity Recognition (NER) are two basic tasks for Chinese Processing. The main difficulty is ambiguities widely exist in these two tasks. Our system is thus pay special attentions on various ambiguities resolution. After preprocessing we take Maximum Entropy (ME) model as the unified frame for WS and NER. ME is a effective model which often used to combine multiple sources of knowledge into various features. For finer-grain utilization of features, we use probabilistic features instead of binary features normally used. By exploring some often used features and some new features, our system performs well in this SIGHAN contest.

In the rest sections of this paper, we give a brief introduction to our system sequentially. Section 2 describes the preprocessing in the system, including rough segmentation and factoid identification. Section 3 is on ambiguity resolution of WS. NER is introduced in Section 4. We give some experimental results in Section 5. Finally we draw some conclusions.

2 Preprocessing

The first step in preprocessing is to do a rough segmentation. By using both Forward Maximum Matching (FMM) and Backward Maximum Matching (BMM) approaches, we get an initial segmentation simultaneously detecting some of segmentation ambiguities in text. We use two different wordlists in this step. One is a basic wordlists with about 60 thousands words. We think this wordlist is relatively steady in Chinese. Another includes some words from special training corpus.

We then cope with factoid recognition by using automata. Four automata are built to identify time, date, number and other (like telephone number and model of product) respectively. For covering some exceptional structures, we use some templates to post-process some outputs from automata.

Overlapping and combination ambiguities detected in preprocessing will be treated in next round of our system. It is the topic of next section.

3 Disambiguation

3.1 Overlapping ambiguity

We only detect overlapping ambiguity with length of chain no more than 3 because these kinds of overlapping account for over 98% of all occurrences according to (Yan, 2000). The class-based bigram model trained on tagged corpus of People's Daily 2000 (about 12 million Chinese characters) is applied to resolve the ambiguities. In class-based bigram, all named entities, all punctuation and factoids is one class separately and each word is one class. For MSRA test we evaluate the performance of our overlapping disambiguation with precision of 84.1%.

3.2 Combination ambiguity

We use some templates to describe the POS properties of combination ambiguity and their segmentation words. In our system there are 155 most frequent combination words. Due to the fact that instances of combination ambiguity is deficient in given training corpus, to enlarge training examples we convert the People Daily 2000 to meet the standard of different guidelines then extract examples for training besides the given training corpora. For example, 结果 is a combination ambiguity according to the guideline of MSRA whereas it is always one unit in People Daily 2000. Noticing that when 结果 takes the sense of result, it is always tagged as a noun and a verb when it takes the meaning of fructification, we can easily enlarge the training examples of 结果.

We then use ME model to combination ambiguity resolution. There are six features used in the model as below.

(1) Contextual words;

(2) Contextual characters;

(3) Bigram collocations;

(4) If the transfer probability of adjacent words to the target word exists;

(5) If keywords indicate segmentation exists;

(6) The most frequent segmentation from prior distribution

4 Named entity recognition

4.1 Personal name recognition

We propose a probabilistic feature based maximum entropy approach to NER. Where, probabilistic feature functions are used instead of binary feature functions, it is one of the several differences between this model and the most of the previous ME based model. We also explore several new features in our model, which includes confidence functions, position of features etc. Like those in some previous works, we use sub-models to model Chinese Person Names, Foreign Names respectively, but we bring some new techniques in these sub-models.

In standard ME, feature function is a binary function, for example, if we use CPN denotes the Chinese person Name, SN denotes Surname, a typical feature is:

$$f_i(x,y)=\begin{cases}1 & y\in CPN \quad and \quad x\in SN\\ 0 & otherwise\end{cases} \qquad (1)$$

But in Chinese, firstly, most of words used as surname are also used as normal words. The probabilities are different for them to be used as surname. Furthermore, a surname is not always followed by a given name, both cases are not binary. To model these phenomena, we give probability values to features, instead of binary values.

For example, a feature function can be set value as follows:

$$f(x,y)=\begin{cases}0.985 \text{ if } y\in \text{CPN and } x\in \text{郭}\\ 0 \quad otherwise\end{cases} \qquad (2)$$

Or

$$f(x,y)=\begin{cases}0.01805 \text{ if } y\in \text{CPN } and \text{ x}\in \text{于}\\ 0 \quad otherwise\end{cases} \qquad (3)$$

Chinese characters used for translating foreign personal name are different from those in Chinese personal name. We built the foreign name model by collecting suffixes, prefixes, frequently-used characters, estimate their probabilities used in foreign personal name. These probabilities also used in model as probability features.

We also design a confidence function for a character sequence $W = C_1C_2...C_n$ to help model to estimate the probability of W as a person name. C_i may be a character or a word. Let f_{1F} is probability of the C_1, f_{iM} is the probability of the C_i, f_{nE} is the probability of the C_n. So the confidence function is

$$K(w, PERSON) = f_{1F} + \sum_{2<=i<=n-1} f_{iM} + f_{nE} \qquad (4)$$

This function is included in ME frame as a feature.

Candidate person name collection is the first step of NER. Since the ambiguity of Chinese word segmentation always exists. We propose some patterns for model different kind of segmentation ambiguity. Some labels are used to express specific roles of Chinese characters in person names.

We have seven patterns as follows; first two patterns are non-ambiguity, while the others model some possible ambiguity in Chinese person name brought by word segmenter.

(1) BCD: the Chinese personal name is composed of three Hanzi ((Chinese character).

B: Surname of a Chinese personal name.

C: Head character of 2-Hanzi given names.

D: Tail character of 2-Hanzi of given names.

(2) BD: the Chinese personal name is composed of two Hanzi (Chinese character).

(3) BCH:

H: the last given name and its next context are composed of a word.

(4) UCD:

U: the surname and its previous context are composed of a word.

(5) BE:

E: the first given name and the last given name are composed of a word.

(6) UD:

U: the surname and the first given name are composed of a word.

(7) CD：The Chinese personal name is only composed of two given names.

Based on the People's Daily corpus and maximum entropy, we achieve models of Chinese personal name and transliterated personal name respectively.

Here, How can we know whether a person name is composed of two or three Hanzi, we used another technology to limit boundary. We think out the co-appearing about the last given name and its next context, now, we have made a statistics about personal name and its next context to decide the length of the Chinese personal name. For example:

"李超为宁波拿下了一分",

In this sentence, we collect a candidate Chinese person name "李超为", but the last given name "为" is a specific character, it has different meaning, now, we make a decision whether "为" is belong to personal name or not.

$$number(NR \quad 宁波) < number(NR \quad 为) \qquad (3)$$

So, "为" is not included in the personal name, "李超" is a correct choice.

Another problem we have met is to recognize transliterated personal name, because many transliterated personal characters has included the Chinese surname, however, the condition that we can recognize the Chinese personal name is Chinese surname, therefore, a section of the transliterated personal name will often be recognized a Chinese personal name.

In our system, we design a dynamitic priority method to check ambiguous character, when we examine a ambiguous character like "谢" or "马", we will search different characters which maybe belong to Chinese personal name or transliterated personal name with forward and backward direction. According to the collection result, we will decide to use Chinese personal model or transliterated personal model to recognize personal name.

For example:

"印/方/重工业/和/国营/企业/部/部长/马/诺/哈/尔/・/乔/希/、/随/访/的/部分/议员/以及/印度/驻/华/大使/南/威/哲/等/参加/了会见/。"

The correct candidate personal name is "马诺哈尔・乔希" and not "马诺哈".

4.2 Location recognition

We collect 196 keywords such like "省,村,川,河,湖,角", when the system search these keywords in a string, it will collect some characters or words which maybe belong to a location with backward direction, and the candidate location can be inputted into location model to recognize. The approach is similar to the personal name recognition, the difference is its contextual, the contextual used for location is $w_{i-2} \quad w_{i-1} \quad w_i \quad w_{i+1} \quad w_{i+2}$, which always can be used as feature during location entity recognition.

We trained model based on the People's Daily.

We design some rules to help rectify wrong result, when a transliterated location name is lack of keyword like "省", it maybe recognized as a transliterated personal name. We collect some specific words list such as "奔赴,赴,圣地,故都" to correct the wrong personal name. If the current word is in the list, the following words are accepted as candidate location entity.

4.3 Organization recognition

Organization name recognition is very different from other kinds of entities. An organization is often composed of several characters or words, and its length is dynamitic. According to statistical result about People's Daily and MSR corpus, we decided the maximum length of an organization is 7 in a sentence.

We computed the probability of every word or character of an organization, and defined the probability threshold.

According to the different keyword, we designed sixteen classifiers; every classifier has its knowledge base, the different classifier can achieve organization recognition goal.

We computed the probability threshold (>0.02) of a candidate organization.

Combined the BIO-tagged method and the probability threshold, the organization can be recognized.

4.4 Combination of Knowledge from Various Sources

Human knowledge is very useful for NER. Knowledge from various sources can be incorporated into ME model, which are shown as follows.

1. Chinese family name list (including 925 items) and given names list (including 2453 items):

2. Transliterated character list (including 1398 items).

3. Location keyword list (including 607 items): If the word belongs to the list, 2~6 words before the salient word are accepted as candidate Location.

4. Abbreviated location like "京/Beijing", "津/Tianjin" name list. Moreover, on Microsoft corpus, the word "中" of "古今中外" is also labeled as location "中国/China".

5. Organization keyword list (including 875 items): If the current word is in organization keyword list, 2~6 words before keywords are accepted as the candidate Organization.

6. A location name dictionary. Some frequently used locations are included in the dictionary, like "美国/United States" and "新加坡/Singapore".

7. An organization name dictionary. Some frequently used organization names are included in the dictionary, like "国务院/State Council" and "联合国/United Nations".

8. Person name list: we collect some person names which come from the MSR train corpus. Moreover, the famous person name are included in the list such as "江泽民,李瑞环".

5 Evaluation result

We evaluated our word segmenter and named entity recognizer on the SIGHAN Microsoft Research Asia (MSRA) corpus in open track. The Table 1 is the official result of word segmentation by our system.

Corpus	OOV-Rate	OOV-Recall	IV Recall-rate	F measure
MSR	0.034	0.804	0.976	0.97
UPUC	0.087	0.593	0.957	0.911

Table 1 Official SIGHAN evaluation result for word segmentation in the open track

Table 2 shows the official result of entity recognition.

Type	R	P	F
Person	95.39%	96.71%	96.04%
Location	87.77%	93.06%	90.34%
Organization	87.68%	84.20%	85.90%

Table2 Official SIGHAN evaluation result for entity recognition in the open track

6 Conclusions

A probabilistic feature based ME model is used to Chinese word segmentation and named entity recognition tasks. Our word segmenter achieved the medium result in the open word segmentation track of MSRA corpus, while entity recognition achieved the top one performance.

Acknowledgement

The research work is supported by China Ministry Of Education funded project (MZ115-022): "Tools for Chinese and Minority Language Processing"

References

A L Berger. 1996. *A Maximum Entropy Approach to Natural Language Processing*. Computational Linguistic, 22 (1): 39- 71.

Yan Yintang, Zhou XiaoQiang. 2000.12 *Study of Segmentation Strategy on Ambiguous Phrases of Overlapping Type* Journal of The China Society For Scientific and Technical Information Vol. 19 , №6

Liang NanYuan. 1987 A *Written Chinese Segmentation system– CDWS*. Journal of Chinese Information Processing, Vol.2: 44-52

ZHANG Hua-ping and Liu Qun. 2004 *Automatic Recognition of Chinese Personal Name Based on Role Tagging*. CHINESE JOURNAL OF COMPUTERS Vol (27) pp 85-91.

Lv YaJuan, ZhaoTie-jun et al. 2001. *Leveled unknown Chinese Words resolution by dynamic programming*. Journal Information Processing, 15(1): 28-33.

Borthwick .A 1999. *Maximum Entropy Approach to Named Entity Recognition*. hD Dissertation.

An Improved Chinese Word Segmentation System with Conditional Random Field

Hai Zhao, Chang-Ning Huang and Mu Li
Microsoft Research Asia,
49, Zhichun Road, Haidian District,
Beijing, P. R. China, 100080
Email: {f-hzhao,cnhuang}@msrchina.research.microsoft.com,
muli@microsoft.com

Abstract

In this paper, we describe a Chinese word segmentation system that we developed for the Third SIGHAN Chinese Language Processing Bakeoff (Bakeoff-2006). We took part in six tracks, namely the closed and open track on three corpora, Academia Sinica (CKIP), City University of Hong Kong (CityU), and University of Pennsylvania/University of Colorado (UPUC). Based on a conditional random field based approach, our word segmenter achieved the highest F measures in four tracks, and the third highest in the other two tracks. We found that the use of a 6-tag set, tone feature of Chinese character and assistant segmenters trained on other corpora further improve Chinese word segmentation performance.

1 Introduction

Conditional random field (CRF) is a statistical sequence modeling framework first introduced into language processing in (Lafferty et al., 2001). Work by Peng et al. first used this framework for Chinese word segmentation by treating it as a binary decision task, such that each Chinese character is labeled either as the beginning of a word or not (Peng et al., 2004).

Since two participants, Ng and Tseng in Bakeoff-2005, gave the best results in almost all test corpora (Low et al., 2005), (Tseng et al., 2005), we continue to improve CRF-based tagging method of Chinese word segmentation on their track. Our implementation used CRF++ package Version 0.41[1] by Taku Kudo.

In our system, a Chinese character is labeled by a tag which stands for its position in the Chinese word that the character belongs to. We handle closed test and open test in the same way. The difference is that those features concerned with additional linguistic resources are added in the feature set of closed test to produce the feature set used in open test.

2 Tag Set Selection

Character based tagging method for Chinese word segmentation, either based on maximum entropy or CRF, views Chinese word segmentation as a label tagging problem, which is described in detail in (Ratnaparkhi, 1996).

The probability model and corresponding feature function is defined over the set $H \times T$, where H is the set of possible contexts (or any predefined condition) and T is the set of possible tags. Generally, a feature function can be defined as follows,

$$f(h,t) = \begin{cases} 1, & \text{if } h = h_i \text{ is satisfied and } t = t_j \\ 0, & \text{otherwise,} \end{cases} \quad (1)$$

where $h_i \in H$ and $t_j \in T$.

For convenience, features are generally organized into some groups, which used to be called feature templates. For example, a bigram feature template C_1 stands for the next character occurring in the corpus after each character.

[1] http://chasen.org/ taku/software/CRF++/

As for tag set, there are two kinds of schemes that are used to distinguish the character position in a word in the previous work, i.e., 4-tag set and 2-tag set. The details are listed in Table 1. Notice Xue and Ng use a 4-tag set in maximum entropy model. While Peng and Tseng used a 2-tag set in CRF model.

Table 1: Tag sets in Chinese word segmentation in the previous work

4-tag set Ng/(Xue)		2-tag set Peng/Tseng	
Function	Tag	Function	Tag
begin	B(LL)	start	Start
middle	M(MM)	continuation	NoStart
end	E(RR)		
single	S(LR)		

Generally speaking, activated feature functions in practice like (1) are determined by both feature template and tag set. In the existing work, tag set is specified aforehand. To effectively perform tagging for those long words, we extend the 4-tag set of Ng/Xue into a 6-tag set. Two tags, 'B2' and 'B3', are added into a 4-tag set to form a 6-tag set, each additional tag stands for the second and the third character position in a Chinese word, respectively.

3 Feature Templates for Closed Test

The feature template set we selected for closed test is shown in Table 2. We give an explanation to feature template (e) and (f).

Feature template (e) is improved from the corresponding one in (Low et al., 2005). $T_n, n = -1, 0, 1$ stands for predefined class. There are four classes defined: numbers represent class 1, those characters whose meanings are dates represent class 2, English letters represent class 3, and other characters represent class 4.

As for feature template (f), $To(C_0)$ stands for the tone of current character. There are five possible types of tones for Chinese characters in mandarin, we just assign 0, 1, 2, 3 and 4 as feature values. For example, consider some characters, '中','国','很','大' and '吗', $To(C_0)$ is 1, 2, 3, 4 and 0, respectively.

4 Feature Templates for Open Test

In open test, we use two kinds of additional feature templates to improve the performance upon closed test.

4.1 External Dictionary

This method was firstly introduced in (Low et al., 2005). We continue to use the online dictionary from Peking University downloadable from the Internet [2], consisting of about 108,000 words of length one to four characters. If there is some sequence of neighboring characters around C_0 in the sentence that matches a word in this dictionary, then we greedily choose the longest such matching word W in the dictionary. The following features derived from the dictionary are added:

(g) Lt_0

(h) $C_n t_0 (n = -1, 0, 1)$

where t_0 is the boundary tag of C_0 in W, and L is the number of characters in W.

4.2 Assistant Segmenter

We observed that although there exists different segmentation standards, most words are still segmented in the same way according to different segmentation standards. Thus, though those segmenters trained on different corpora will give some different segmentation results, they agree on most cases. In fact, we find that it is feasible to customize a pre-defined standard into any other standards with TBL method in (Gao, 2005). And it is also valuable to incorporate different segmenters into one segmenter based on the current standard. For convenience, we call the segmenter subjected to the current standard main segmenter, and the other assistant segmenters.

A feature template will be added for a assistant segmenter:

(i) $t(C_0)$

[2] http://ccl.pku.edu.cn/doubtfire/Course/Chinese %20Information%20Processing/Source Code/ Chapter 8/Lexicon full 2000.zip

Table 2: Feature templates

Code	Type	Feature	Function
a	Unigram	$C_n, n = -1, 0, 1$	The previous (current, next) character
b	Bigram	$C_n C_{n+1}, n = -1, 0$	The previous (next) character and current character
c	Jump	$C_{-1} C_1$	The previous character and next character
d	Punctuation	$Pu(C_0)$	Current character is a punctuation or not
e	Date, Digital and Letter	$T_{-1} T_0 T_1$	Types of previous, current and next character
f	Tone	$To(C_0)$	Tone of current character

where $t(C_0)$ is the output tag of the assistant segmenter for the current character C_0. For example, consider character sequence, '我们都是中国人', an assistant segmenter gives the tag sequence 'BESSBES' according to its output segmentation, then $t(C_0)$ by this assistant segmenter is 'B', 'E', 'S', 'S', 'B', 'E', and 'S' for each current character, respectively.

In our system, we integrate all other segmenters that are trained on all corpora from Bakeoff-2003, 2005 and 2006 with the feature set used in closed test. The segmenter, MSRSeg, described in (Gao, 2003) is also integrated, too.

Our assistant segmenter method is more convenient compared to the additional training corpus method in (Low et al., 2005). Firstly, the performance of additional corpus method depends on the performance of the trained segmenter that carries out the corpus extraction task. If the segmenter is not well-trained, then it cannot effectively extract the most wanted additional corpus to some extent. Secondly, additional corpus method is only able to integrate useful corpus, but it cannot integrate a well-trained segmenter while the corpus cannot be accessed. Finally, additional corpus method is very difficult to use in CRF model, the reason is that the increase of corpus can lead to a dramatic increase of memory and time consuming in this case, while assistant segmenters just lead to little increase of memory and time consuming in training.

It is more interesting that we may also regard the external dictionary method as another assistant segmenter in some degree, that is, a maximal matching segmenter with the specified external dictionary. Thus, all of our additional methods in open test can be viewed as assistant segmenter ones.

5 Evaluation Results

We took part in six segmentation tasks in Bakeoff-2006, namely the closed and open track on three corpora, Academia Sinica (CKIP), City University of Hong Kong (CityU), and University of Pennsylvania/University of Colorado (UPUC).

The comparison between our official results and best results in Bakeoff-2006 are shown in Table 3.

Our system achieved the highest F measures in four tracks, and the third highest in the other two tracks. However, a format error unfortunately occurred in the open test of UPUC corpus as we submitted our final results. Thus an abnormal result in this task is obtained, the official F measure in open test is the same as that in closed test. We get the actual F measure of 0.953 after the bug is fixed.

The results in MSRA corpus from our evaluation are listed in Table 4.

Table 4: Comparison between our results and best results of Bakeoff-2006 on MSRA corpora

Type	F Measures	
	Bakeoff-2006	Ours
Closed Test	0.963	0.970
Open Test	0.979	0.982

The sizes of training corpora (in number of characters) and difference of our results between open

Table 3: Comparison between our official results and best results of Bakeoff-2006

Type	Participant	F measures on Different Corpora		
		CKIP	CityU	UPUC
Closed	Best results of Bakeoff-2006	0.958	0.972	0.933
Test	Our results	0.958	0.971	0.933
Open	Best results of Bakeoff-2006	0.959	0.977	0.944
Test	Our results	0.959	0.977	0.933

test and closed test are shown in Table 5. This illustrates how much assistant segmenters improve the performance of segmentation in different sizes of training corpora, also, this shows how the size of training corpus affects the improvement contributed by assistant segmenters.

Table 5: The sizes of training corpora and difference of our results between open test and closed test

	F Measures			
	CKIP	CityU	MSRA	UPUC
$F_{open} - F_{closed}$	0.001	0.006	0.012	0.020
Size of training corpus	9M	2.9M	2.3M	0.88M

References

Jianfeng Gao, Mu Li, Andi Wu and Chang-Ning Huang. 2005. Chinese Word Segmentation and Named Entity Recognition: A Pragmatic Approach. *Computational Linguistics*, Vol. 31(4): 531-574.

Nianwen Xue. 2003. Chinese Word Segmentation as Character Tagging. *Computational Linguistics and Chinese Language Processing*, Vol. 8(1): 29-48.

Nianwen Xue and Libin Shen. 2003. Chinese Word Segmentation as LMR Tagging. In *Proceedings of the 2nd SIGHAN Workshop on Chinese Language Processing, in conjunction with ACL'03*, 176-179. Sapporo, Japan

Richard Sproat and Thomas Emerson. 2003. The First International Chinese Word Segmentation Bakeoff. *The Second SIGHAN Workshop on Chinese Language Processing*, 133-143. Sapporo, Japan.

Thomas Emerson. 2005. The Second International Chinese Word Segmentation Bakeoff. *Proceedings of the Fourth SIGHAN Workshop on Chinese Language Processing*, 123-133. Jeju Island, Korea.

Jin Kiat Low, Hwee Tou Ng and Wenyuan Guo 2005. A Maximum Entropy Approach to Chinese Word Segmentation. *Proceedings of the Fourth SIGHAN Workshop on Chinese Language Processing*, 161-164. Jeju Island, Korea.

Huihsin Tseng, Pichuan Chang, Galen Andrew, Daniel Jurafsky, Christopher Manning. 2005. A Conditional Random Field Word Segmenter for Sighan Bakeoff 2005. *Proceedings of the Fourth SIGHAN Workshop on Chinese Language Processing*, 168-171. Jeju Island, Korea.

Fuchun Peng, Fangfang Feng and Andrew McCallum. 2004. Chinese Segmentation and New Word Detection Using Conditional Random Fields. In *COLING 2004*, 562-568. August 23-27, 2004, Geneva, Switzerland

John Lafferty, A. McCallum and F. Pereira. 2001. Conditional Random Field: Probabilistic Models for Segmenting and Labeling Sequence Data. In *Proceedings of the Eighteenth International Conference on Machine Learning*, 282-289. June 28-July 01, 2001

Adwait Ratnaparkhi. 1996. A Maximum Entropy Part-of-speech Tagger. In *Proceedings of the Empirical Method in Natural Language Processing Conference*, 133-142. University of Pennsylvania.

Jianfeng Gao, Mu Li, and Chang-Ning Huang. 2003. Improved Source-Channel Models for Chinese Word Segmentation. In *Proceedings 41nd Annual Meeting of the Association for Computational Linguistics*, 272-279. Sapporo, Japan, July 7-12, 2003.

Chinese Word Segmentation using Various Dictionaries

Guo-Wei Bian
Department of Information Management
Huafan University, Taiwan, R.O.C.
gwbian@cc.hfu.edu.tw

Abstract

Most of the Chinese word segmentation systems utilizes monolingual dictionary and are used for monolingual processing. For the tasks of machine translation (MT) and cross-language information retrieval (CLIR), another translation dictionary may be used to transfer the words of documents from the source languages to target languages. The inconsistencies resulting from the two types of dictionaries (segmentation dictionary and transfer dictionary) may produce some problems for MT and CLIR. This paper shows the effectiveness of the external resources (bilingual dictionary and word list) for Chinese word segmentations.

1 Introduction

Most of the Chinese word segmentations are used for monolingual processing. In general, the word segmentation program utilizes the word entries, part-of-speech (POS) information (Chen and Liu, 1992) in a monolingual dictionary, segmentation rules (Palmer, 1997), and some statistical information (Sproat, *et al*., 1994). For the tasks of machine translation (MT) (Bian and Chen, 1998) and cross-language information retrieval (CLIR) (Bian and Chen, 2000), another translation dictionary may be used to transfer the words of documents from the source languages to target languages. Because of the inconsistencies resulting from the two types of dictionaries (segmentation dictionary and transfer dictionary), this approach has the problems that some segmented words cannot be found in the transfer dictionary.

In this paper, we focus on the effectiveness of the Chinese word segmentation using different dictionaries. Four different dictionaries (or word lists) and two different testing collections (testing data) are used to evaluate the results of the Chinese word segmentation.

2 Chinese Word Segmentation System

The segmentation system used only the various dictionaries in this design. In this paper, the other possible resources (POS, segmentation rules, word segmentation guide, and statistical information) are ignored to test the average performance between different testing collections specially followed the different segmented guidelines.

The longest-matching method is adopted in this Chinese segmentation system. The segmentation processing searches for a dictionary entry corresponding to the longest sequence of Chinese characters from left to right. The system provided the approximate matching to search a substring of the input with the entry in the dictionary if no total matching is found. For example, the system will segment the input "看著隨時可能結束生命的妹妹" as "看著 | 隨時 | 可能 | 結束 | 生 | 命 | 的 | 妹妹" which matched the term with the entry "看著辦" in dictionary if no entry "看著" found.

2.1 Various Dictionaries

The word segmentation are evaluated using different dictionaries (or word lists) and different testing collections (testing data). There are four dictionaries are used: the first one is converted from an English-Chinese bilingual dictionary, and the other three are extracted from the training corpora.

The original English-Chinese dictionary (Bian and Chen, 1998), which containing about 67,000 English word entries, is converted to a new Chinese-English dictionary (called CEDIC later). There are 125,719 Chinese word entries in this CEDIC.

The terms in the various training corpora (the Sinica Corpus and the City University Corpus) are extracted to build the different word lists as the segmentation dictionaries (called CKIP and CityU later). The tokens starting with the special characters or punctuation marks are ignored. The following shows some examples:

(, (0 2), (1), cm, $, %, ☆, , –, –W h y, ◢ M 4 5, 【, ○○○, ..., 「, 」 / u s r / m a n, ‖ , , , , #, .com,

Table 1 lists the number of tokens (#tokens), the number of ignored tokens (#ignored), the number of words (#words), and the unique words (#unique) for each dictionaries. There are 140,971 unique words are extracted from the training collection of Sinica Corpus, and 75,433 respected to the training set of the City University Corpus. These two dictionaries are combined to another dictionary which containing 174,398 unique words.

	#Tokens	#Ignored	#Words	#Unique
CKIP (CK)	5,468,793	894,686	4,574,107	140,971
CityU (CT)	1,643,421	257,032	1,386,389	75,433
CKIP+CityU (CK + CT)	7,112,214	1,151,718	5,960,496	174,398

Table 1. Statistical Information of the Extracted Dictionaries

3 Experimental Results

To evaluate the results of Chinese word segmentations, we implement 8 experiments (runs) using the 4 different dictionaries (CEDIC, CK, CT, and CK+CT) mentioned in previous section. Two test collections (the Sinica Corpus and the City University Corpus) are used to measure the precision, recall, and an evenly-weighted F-measure for the Chinese words segmentations.

Table 2 shows the F-measure of the experimental results, and the Figure 1 illustrates the comparisons of the segmentation performances. The symbol (*) indicates that the run is a closed test, which only uses the training material from the training data for the particular corpus. We can find that the larger dictionary (CK+CT) produces better segmentation results even the word lists are combined from the different resources (corpora) and followed the different guidelines of word segmentations.

	CEDIC	CK + CT	CK	CT
CKIP	0.710	0.695	0.692*	0.611
CityU	0.481	0.589	0.547	0.513*

Table 2. The F-measure results of segmentation performances using various dictionaries (*: closed test)

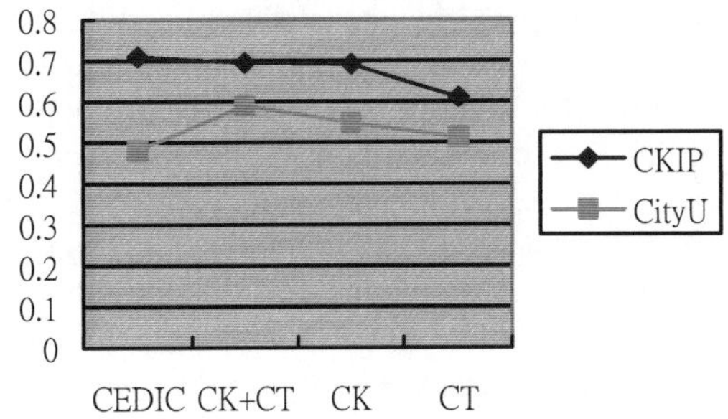

Figure 1. The comparison of segmentation performances using various dictionaries (*: close test)

3.1 Error Analysis

3.1.1 Format Error of Result File

The results file for word segmentation is required to appear with one line for each sentence/line in the test file with words and punctuation separated by whitespace. Our system makes some mistakes to produce no whitespace before English terms and Arabic numbers, and produce no whitespace after Chinese punctuation marks. This formatting problem has made many adjacent segmented words to be evaluated as errors. A sentence with such errors is listed below

(Our Answer)

與 大珠三角 相鄰 、相互 間 經貿 關係 密切 的 福建 、江西 、湖南 、廣東 、廣西 、海南 、四川 、貴 州 、雲南 9 個 省區 ，以及 香港 、澳門 特別 行政區 （簡 稱 "9+2 " ）。

(Standard)

與 大珠三角 相鄰 、 相互 間 經貿 關係 密切 的 福建 、 江西 、 湖南 、 廣東 、 廣西 、 海南 、 四川 、 貴州 、 雲南 9 個 省區 ， 以及 香港 、 澳門 特別 行政區 （ 簡稱 " 9+2 " ）。

The standard answer of the testing collection (CityU) of the City University Corpus has 7,512 sentences and 220,147 words. The total number of English terms, Arabic numbers, and Chinese punctuation marks is 37,644. Such formatting problem makes the error rate of about 30% for the City University Corpus.

3.1.2 Different Viewpoints of Segmentations

In our experiments, there are different word lists extracted from the different training corpora. Some errors are produced because of the different results of word segmentations in the training corpora according to the different guidelines. Table 3 shows some different results. The first column (CKIP) is the standard answer of the testing collection of Sinica Corpus, and the second column (HFUIM) is our answer. The third and fourth columns are the words with their frequencies appeared in the training collections of Sinica Corpus and City University Corpus. For example, our system produces the word "心中", but the standard answer of Sinica Corpus is "心" and "中". However, the word "心中" appear 61 times in the training collection of City University Corpus.

CKIP	HFUIM	CKIP-Training	CityU-Training
林婦	林婦	林婦 (0)	
整 夜	整夜	整 (1839) 夜 (366)	整夜 (2)
看 著	看著	看著辦 (4) 眼看著 (20)	
心 中	心中	心 (2551) 中 (16694)	心中 (61)
這 個	這個	這 (32409) 個 (39558)	這個 (714)
死 後	死後	死 (984) 後 (7967)	死後 (18)
所 需	所需	所 (9012) 需 (963)	所需 (35)

Table 3. The Different Segmentation Results

3.1.3 Inconsistency of Word Segmentation

Some errors of word segmentations are reported because of the inconsistency of word segmentations. The following shows such a problem. For example, the word "還有" appears 317 times in the training data, but it has been treated as two terms ("還" and "有") 19 times in the golden standard of the testing data.

(Training data)

- 歐盟 委員會 設置 等 問題 上 還有 一些 不同 聲音

(Golden Standard)

- 目前 兩 地 機場 還有 一些 商業 問題 要談
- 鍾麗緹 透露 身上 還 有 一 個 紋身 圖案
- 還 有 其他 歐國盃 的 有趣 專題 ， 萬勿錯過 已 出版 的 《 明報 歐洲 國家盃 特刊 》 。

4 Conclusion

In this paper, we discuss the effectiveness of the Chinese word segmentation using various dictionaries. In the experimental results, we can find that the larger dictionary will produce better segmentation results even the word lists are combined from the different resources (corpora) and followed the different guidelines of word segmentations. Some results show that the external resource (e.g., the bilingual dictionary) can perform the task of Chinese word segmentation better than the monolingual dictionary which extracted from the training corpus.

Reference

Bian, G.W. and Chen, H.H. (2000). "Cross Language Information Access to Multilingual Collections on the Internet." *Journal of American Society for Information Science & Technology (JASIST), Special Issue on Digital Libraries*, 51(3), 2000, 281-296.

Bian, G.W. and Chen, H.H. (1998). "Integrating Query Translation and Document Translation in a Cross-Language Information Retrieval System." *Machine Translation and the Information Soap (AMTA '98),* D. Farwell, L Gerber, and E. Hovy (Eds.), Lecture Notes in Computer Science, Vol. 1529, Springer-Verlag, pp. 250-265, 1998

Chen, K.J and Liu, S.H (1992), "word identification for Mandarin Chinese sentences" Proceedings of the 14th conference on Computational linguistics, pp. 101-107, France, 1992

Palmer, D. (1997), "A trainable rule-based algorithm for word segmentation", Proceeding of ACL'97, 321-328, 1997.

Sproat, R., *et al.* (1994) "A Stochastic Finite-State Word-Segmentation Algorithm for Chinese", *Proceeding of 32nd Annual Meeting of ACL*, New Mexico, pp. 66-73.

Character Language Models for Chinese Word Segmentation and Named Entity Recognition

Bob Carpenter
Alias-i, Inc.
carp@alias-i.com

Abstract

We describe the application of the LingPipe toolkit to Chinese word segmentation and named entity recognition for the 3rd SIGHAN bakeoff.

1 Word Segmentation

Chinese is written without spaces between words. For the word segmentation task, four training corpora were provided with one sentence per line and a single space character between words. Test data consisted of Chinese text, one sentence per line, without spaces between words. The task is to insert single space characters between the words. For this task and named entity recognition, we used the UTF8-encoded Unicode versions of the corpora converted from their native formats by the bakeoff organizers.

2 Named Entity Recognition

Named entities consist of proper noun mentions of persons (`PER`), locations (`LOC`), and organizations (`ORG`). Two training corpora were provided. Each line consists of a single character, a single space character, and then a tag. The tags were in the standard BIO (begin/in/out) encoding. `B-PER` tags the first character in a person entity, `I-PER` tags subsequent characters in a person, and `O` characters not part of entities. We segmented the data into sentences by taking Unicode character `0x3002`, which is rendered as a baseline-aligned small circle, as marking end of sentence (`EOS`). As judged by our own sentence numbers (see Figures 1 and 2), this missed around 20% of the sentence boundaries in the City U NE corpus and 5% of the boundaries in the Microsoft NE corpus. Test data is in the same format as the word segmentation task.

3 LingPipe

LingPipe is a Java-based natural language processing toolkit distributed with source code by Alias-i (2006). For this bakeoff, we used two LingPipe packages, `com.aliasi.spell` for Chinese word segmentation and `com.aliasi.chunk` for named-entity extraction. Both of these depend on the character language modeling package `com.aliasi.lm`, and the chunker also depends on the hidden Markov model package `com.alias.hmm`. The experiments reported in this paper were carried out in May 2006 using (a prerelease version of) LingPipe 2.3.0.

3.1 LingPipe's Character Language Models

LingPipe provides n-gram based character language models with a generalized form of Witten-Bell smoothing, which performed better than other approaches to smoothing in extensive English trials (Carpenter 2005). Language models provide a probability distribution $P(\sigma)$ defined for strings $\sigma \in \Sigma^*$ over a fixed alphabet of characters Σ. We begin with Markovian language models normalized as random processes. This means the sum of the probabilities for strings of a fixed length is 1.0.

The chain rule factors $P(\sigma c) = P(\sigma) \cdot P(c|\sigma)$ for a character c and string σ. The n-gram Markovian assumption restricts the context to the previous $n-1$ characters, taking $P(c_n|\sigma c_1 \cdots c_{n-1}) = P(c_n|c_1 \cdots c_{n-1})$.

The maximum likelihood estimator for n-grams is $\hat{P}_{\text{ML}}(c|\sigma) = \mathsf{count}(\sigma c)/\mathsf{extCount}(\sigma)$, where $\mathsf{count}(\sigma)$ is the number of times the sequence σ was observed in the training data and $\mathsf{extCount}(\sigma)$

is the number of single-character extensions of σ observed: $\mathsf{extCount}(\sigma) = \sum_c \mathsf{count}(\sigma c)$.

Witten-Bell smoothing uses linear interpolation to form a mixture model of all orders of maximum likelihood estimates down to the uniform estimate $P_U(c) = 1/|\Sigma|$. The interpolation ratio $\lambda(d\sigma)$ ranges between 0 and 1 depending on the context:

$$\begin{aligned} \hat{P}(c|d\sigma) &= \lambda(d\sigma)P_{\mathrm{ML}}(c|d\sigma) \\ &+ (1-\lambda(d\sigma))\hat{P}(c|\sigma) \\ \hat{P}(c) &= \lambda()P_{\mathrm{ML}}(c) \\ &+ (1-\lambda())(1/|\Sigma|) \end{aligned}$$

Generalized Witten-Bell smoothing defines the interpolation ratio with a hyperparameter θ:

$$\lambda(\sigma) = \frac{\mathsf{extCount}(\sigma)}{\mathsf{extCount}(\sigma) + \theta \cdot \mathsf{numExts}(\sigma)}$$

We take $\mathsf{numExts}(\sigma) = |\{c|\mathsf{count}(\sigma c) > 0\}|$ to be the number of different symbols observed following σ in the training data. The original Witten-Bell estimator set the hyperparameter $\theta = 1$. LingPipe's default sets θ equal to the n-gram order.

3.2 Noisy Channel Spelling Correction

LingPipe performs spelling correction with a noisy-channel model. A noisy-channel model consists of a source model $P_s(\mu)$ defining the probability of message μ, coupled with a channel model $P_c(\sigma|\mu)$ defining the likelihood of a signal σ given a message μ. In LingPipe, the source model P_s is a character language model. The channel model P_c is a (probabilistically normalized) weighted edit distance (with transposition). LingPipe's decoder finds the most likely message μ to have produced a signal σ: $\mathrm{argmax}_\mu P(\mu|\sigma) = \mathrm{argmax}_\mu P(\mu) \cdot P(\sigma|\mu)$.

For spelling correction, the channel $P_c(\sigma|\mu)$ is a model of what is likely to be typed given an intended message. Uniform models work fairly well and ones tuned to brainos and typos work even better. The source model is typically estimated from a corpus of ordinary text.

For Chinese word segmentation, the source model is trained over the corpus with spaces inserted. The noisy channel deterministically eliminates spaces so that $P_c(\sigma|\mu) = 1.0$ if σ is identical to μ with all of the spaces removed, and 0.0 otherwise. This channel is easily implemented as a weighted edit distance where deletion of a single space is 100% likely (log probability edit "cost" is zero) and matching a character is 100% likely, with any other operation being 0% likely (infinite cost). This makes any segmentation equally likely according to the channel model, reducing decoding to finding the highest likelihood hypothesis consisting of the test string with spaces inserted. This approach reduces to the cross-entropy/compression-based approach of (Teahan et al. 2000). Experiments showed that skewing these space-insertion/matching probabilities reduces decoding accuracy.

3.3 LingPipe's Named Entity Recognition

LingPipe 2.1 introduced a hidden Markov model interface with several decoders: first-best (Viterbi), n-best (Viterbi forward, A* backward with exact Viterbi estimates), and confidence-based (forward-backward).

LingPipe 2.2 introduced a chunking implementation that codes a chunking problem as an HMM tagging problem using a refinement of the standard BIO coding. The refinement both introduces context and greatly simplifies confidence estimation over the approach using standard BIO coding in (Culotta and McCallum 2004). The tags are `B-`*T* for the first character in a multi-character entity of type *T*, `M-`*T* for a middle character in a multi-character entity, `E-`*T* for the end character in a multi-character entity, and `W-`*T* for a single character entity. The out tags are similarly contextualized, with additional information on the start/end tags to model their context. Specifically, the tags used are `B-O-`*T* for a character not in an entity following an entity of type T, `I-O` for any middle character not in an entity, and `E-O-`*T* for a character not in an entity but preceding a character in an entity of type *T*, and finally, `W-O-`*T* for a character that is a single character between two entities, the following entity being of type *T*. Finally, the first tag is conditioned on the begin-of-sentence tag (*BOS*) and after the last tag, the end-of-sentence tag (*EOS*) is generated. Thus the probabilities normalize to model string/tag joint probabilities.

In the HMM implementation considered here, transitions between states (tags) in the HMM are modeled by a maximum likelihood estimate over the training data. Tag emissions are generated by bounded character language models. Rather than the process estimate $P(X)$, we use $P(X\#|\#)$, where $\#$ is a distinguished boundary character

Corpus	*Encod*	*Sents*	*Chars*	*Uniq*	*Words*	*Uniq*	*Test S*	*Test Ch*	*Unseen*
City U HK	HKSCS (trad)	57K	4.3M	5113	1.6M	76K	7.5K	364K	0.046%
Microsoft	gb18030 (simp)	46K	3.4M	4768	1.3M	63K	4.4K	173K	0.046%
Ac Sinica	Big5 (trad)	709K	13.2M	6123	5.5M	146K	11.0K	146K	0.560%
Penn/Colo	CP936 (simp)	19K	1.3M	4294	0.5M	37K	5.1K	256K	0.160%

Figure 1: Word Segmentation Corpora

Corpus	*Sents*	*Chars*	*Uniq*	*LOC*	*PER*	*ORG*	*Test S*	*Test Ch*	*Unseen*
City U HK	48K	2.7M	5113	48.2K	36.4K	27.8K	7.5K	364K	0.046%
Microsoft	44K	2.2M	4791	36.9K	17.6K	20.6K	4.4K	173K	0.046%

Figure 2: Named Entity Recognition Corpora

not in the training or test character sets. We also train with boundaries. For Chinese at the character level, this bounding is irrelevant as all tokens are length 1, so probabilities are already normalized and there is no contextual position to take account of within a token. In the more usual word-tokenized case, it normalizes probabilities over all strings and accounts for the special status of prefixes and suffixes (e.g. capitalization, inflection).

Consider the chunking consisting of the string *John J. Smith lives in Seattle.* with *John J. Smith* a person mention and *Seattle* a location mention. In the coded HMM model, the joint estimate is:

$$\hat{P}_{\text{ML}}(\texttt{B-PER}|\texttt{BOS}) \cdot \hat{P}_{\texttt{B-PER}}(John\#|\#)$$
$$\cdot \hat{P}_{\text{ML}}(\texttt{I-PER}|\texttt{B-PER}) \cdot \hat{P}_{\texttt{I-PER}}(J\#|\#)$$
$$\cdot \hat{P}_{\text{ML}}(\texttt{I-PER}|\texttt{I-PER}) \cdot \hat{P}_{\texttt{I-PER}}(.\#|\#)$$
$$\cdot \hat{P}_{\text{ML}}(\texttt{E-PER}|\texttt{I-PER}) \cdot \hat{P}_{\texttt{E-PER}}(Smith\#|\#)$$
$$\cdot \hat{P}_{\text{ML}}(\texttt{B-O-PER}|\texttt{E-PER}) \cdot \hat{P}_{\texttt{B-O-PER}}(lives\#|\#)$$
$$\cdot \hat{P}_{\text{ML}}(\texttt{E-O-LOC}|\texttt{B-O-PER}) \cdot \hat{P}_{\texttt{E-O-LOC}}(in\#|\#)$$
$$\cdot \hat{P}_{\text{ML}}(\texttt{W-LOC}|\texttt{E-O-LOC}) \cdot \hat{P}_{\texttt{W-LOC}}(Seattle\#|\#)$$
$$\cdot \hat{P}_{\text{ML}}(\texttt{W-O-EOS}|\texttt{W-LOC}) \cdot \hat{P}_{\texttt{W-O-EOS}}(.\#|\#)$$
$$\cdot \hat{P}_{\text{ML}}(\texttt{EOS}|\texttt{W-O-EOS})$$

LingPipe 2.3 introduced an n-best chunking implementation that adapts an underlying n-best chunker via rescoring. In rescoring, each of these outputs is scored on its own and the new best output is returned. The rescoring model is a longer-distance generative model that produces alternating out/entity tags for all characters. The joint probability of the specified chunking is:

$$\hat{P}_{\texttt{OUT}}(c_{\texttt{PER}}|c_{\texttt{BOS}})$$
$$\cdot \hat{P}_{\texttt{PER}}(John\ J.\ Smith c_{\texttt{OUT}}|c_{\texttt{OUT}})$$
$$\cdot \hat{P}_{\texttt{OUT}}(\ lives\ in\ c_{\texttt{LOC}}|c_{\texttt{PER}})$$
$$\cdot \hat{P}_{\texttt{LOC}}(Seattle c_{\texttt{OUT}}|c_{\texttt{OUT}})$$
$$\cdot \hat{P}_{\texttt{OUT}}(.c_{\texttt{EOS}}|c_{\texttt{LOC}})$$

where each estimator is a character language model, and where the c_T are distinct characters not in the training/test sets that encode begin-of-sentence (BOS), end-of-sentence (EOS), and type (e.g. PER, LOC, ORG). In words, we generate an alternating sequence of OUT and type estimates, starting and ending with an OUT estimate. We begin by conditioning on the begin-of-sentence tag. Because the first character is in an entity, we do not generate any text, but rather generate a character indicating that we are done generating the OUT characters and ready to switch to generating person characters. We then generate the phrase *John J. Smith* in the person model; note that type estimates always begin and end with the $c_{\texttt{OUT}}$ character, essentially making them bounded models. After generating the name and the character to end the entity, we revert to generating more out characters, starting from a person and ending with a location. Note that we are generating the phrase *lives in* including the preceding and following space. All such spaces are generated in the OUT models for English; there are no spaces in the Chinese input. Next, we generate the location phrase the same way as the person phrase. Next, we generate the final period in the OUT model and then the end-of-sentence symbol. Note that the OUT category's language model shoulders the brunt of the burden of estimating contextual effects. It conditions on the preceding type, so that the likelihood of *lives in* is conditioned on following a person entity. Furthermore, the choice to begin an entity of type location is based on the fact that it follows *lives in*. This includes begin-of-sentence and end-of-sentence effects, so the model is sensitive to initial capitalization in the out model as a distribution of character sequences likely to follow BOS. Similarly, the

Corpus	R	P	F_1	*Best* F_1	*OOV*	R_{OOV}
City Uni Hong Kong	.966	.957	.961	.972	4.0%	.555
Microsoft Research	.959	.955	.957	.963	3.4%	.494
Academia Sinica	.951	.935	.943	.958	4.2%	.389
U Penn and U Colorado	.919	.895	.907	.933	8.8%	.459

Figure 3: Word Segmentation Results (Closed Category)

Corpus	R	P	F_1	*Best* F_1	P_{LOC}	R_{LOC}	P_{PER}	R_{PER}	P_{ORG}	R_{ORG}
City Uni HK	.8417	.8690	.8551	.8903	.8961	.8762	.8749	.8943	.6997	.8176
MS Research	.8097	.8188	.8142	.8651	.8351	.8716	.7968	.8438	.7739	.6899

Figure 4: Named Entity Recognition Results (Closed Category)

end-of-sentence is conditioned on the preceding text, in this case a single period. The resulting model defines a (properly normalized) joint probability distribution over chunkings.

4 Held-out Parameter Tuning

We ran preliminary tests on MUC 6 English and City University of Hong Kong data for Chinese and found baseline performance around 72% and rescored performance around 82%. The underlying model was designed to have good recall in generating hypotheses. Over 99% of the MUC test sentences had their correct analysis in a 1024-best list generated by the underlying model. Nevertheless, setting the number of hypotheses beyond 64 did not improve results in either English or Chinese, so we reported runs with n-best set to 64. We believe this is because the two language-model based approaches make highly correlated ranking decisions based on character n-grams.

Held-out scores peaked with 5-grams for Chinese; 3-grams and 4-grams were not much worse and longer n-grams performed nearly identically. We used 7500 as the number of distinct characters, though this parameter is not at all sensitive to within an order of magnitude. We used LingPipe's default of setting the interpolation parameter equal to the n-gram length; for the final evaluation $\theta = 5.0$. Higher interpolation ratios favor precision over recall, lower ratios favor recall. Values within an order of magnitude performed with 1% F-measure and 2% precision/recall.

5 Bakeoff Time and Effort

The total time spent on this SIGHAN bakeoff was about 2 hours for the word segmentation task and 10 hours for the named-entity task (not including writing this paper). We started from a working word segmentation system for the last SIGHAN. Most of the time was spent munging entity data, with the rest devoted to held out analysis. The final code was roughly one page per task, with only a dozen or so LingPipe-specific lines. The final run, including unpacking, training and testing, took 45 minutes on a 512MB home PC; most of the time was named-entity decoding.

6 Results

Official bakeoff results for the four word segmentation corpora are shown in Figure 3, and for the two named entity corpora in Figure 4. Column labels are R for recall, P for precision, F_1 for balanced F-measure, *Best* F_1 for the best closed system's F_1 score, *OOV* for the out-of-vocabulary rate in the test corpus, and R_{OOV} for recall on the out-of-vocabulary items. For the named-entity results, precision and recall are also broken down by category.

7 Distribution

LingPipe may be downloaded from its homepage, `http://www.alias-i.com/lingpipe`. The code for the bakeoff is available via anonymous CVS from the sandbox. An Apache Ant makefile is provided to generate our bakeoff submission from the official data distribution format.

References

Carpenter, B. 2005. Scaling high-order character language models to gigabytes. *ACL Software Workshop*. Ann Arbor.

Culotta, A. and A. McCallum. 2004. Confidence estimation for information extraction. *HLT/NAACL 2004*. Boston.

Teahan, W. J., Y. Wen, R. McNab, and I. H. Witten. 2000. A compression-based algorithm for Chinese word segmentation. *Computational Linguistics*, **26**(3):375–393.

Chinese Named Entity Recognition with Conditional Probabilistic Models

Aitao Chen
Yahoo
701 First Avenue
Sunnyvale, CA 94089
aitao@yahoo-inc.com

Fuchun Peng
Yahoo
701 First Avenue
Sunnyvale, CA 94089
fuchun@yahoo-inc.com

Roy Shan
Yahoo
701 First Avenue
Sunnyvale, CA 94089
rshan@yahoo-inc.com

Gordon Sun
Yahoo
701 First Avenue
Sunnyvale, CA 94089
gzsun@yahoo-inc.com

Abstract

This paper describes the work on Chinese named entity recognition performed by Yahoo team at the third International Chinese Language Processing Bakeoff. We used two conditional probabilistic models for this task, including conditional random fields (CRFs) and maximum entropy models. In particular, we trained two conditional random field recognizers and one maximum entropy recognizer for identifying names of people, places, and organizations in un-segmented Chinese texts. Our best performance is 86.2% F-score on MSRA dataset, and 88.53% on CITYU dataset.

1 Introduction

At the third International Chinese Language Processing Bakeoff, we participated in the closed test in the Named Entity Recognition (NER) task using the MSRA corpus and the CITYU corpus. The named entity types include person, place, and organization. The training data consist of texts that are segmented into words with names of people, places, and organizations labeled. And the testing data consist of un-segmented Chinese texts, one sentence per line.

There are many well known models for English named recognition, among which Conditional Random Fields (Lafferty et al. 2001) and maximum entropy models (Berger et al. 2001) have achieved good performance in English in CoNLL NER tasks. To understand the performance of these two models on Chinese, we both models to Chinese NER task on MSRA data and CITYU data.

2 Named Entity Recognizer

2.1 Models

We trained two named entity recognizers based on conditional random field and one based on maximum entropy model. Both conditional random field and maximum entropy models are capable of modeling arbitrary features of the input, thus are well suit for many language processing tasks. However, there exist significant differences between these two models. To apply a maximum entropy model to NER task, we have to first train a maximum entropy classifier to classify each individual word and then build a dynamic programming for sequence decoding. While in CRFs, these two steps are integrated together. Thus, in theory, CRFs are superior to maximum entropy models in sequence modeling problem and this will also confirmed in our Chinese NER experiments. The superiority of CRFs on Chinese information processing was also demonstrated in word segmentation (Peng et al. 2004). However, the training speed of CRFs is much slower than that of maximum entropy models since training CRFs requires expensive forward-backward algorithm to compute the partition function.

We used Taku's CRF package[1] to train the first CRF recognizer, and the MALLET[2] package with BFGS optimization to train the second CRF recognizer. We used a C++ implementation[3] of maximum entropy modeling and wrote our own second order dynamic programming for decoding.

2.2 Features

The first CRF recognizer used the features C_{-2}, C_{-1}, C_0, C_{-1}, C_2, $C_{-2}C_{-1}$, $C_{-1}C_0$, C_0C_{-1}, C_1C_2, and $C_{-1}C_1$, where C_0 is the current character, C_1 the next character, C_2 the second character after C_0, C_{-1} the character preceding C_0, and C_{-2} the second character before C_0.

The second CRF recognizer used the same set of basic features but the feature C_2. In addition, the first CRF recognizer used the tag bigram feature, and the second CRF recognizer used word and character cluster features, obtained automatically from the training data only with distributional word clustering (Tishby and Lee, 1993).

The maximum entropy recognizer used the following unigram, bigram features, and type features: C_{-2}, C_{-1}, C_0, C_1, C_2, $C_{-4}C_{-3}$, $C_{-3}C_{-2}$, $C_{-2}C_{-1}$, $C_{-1}C_0$, C_0C_1, C_1C_2, C_2C_3, C_3C_4, and $T_{-2}T_{-1}$.

When using the first CRF package, we found the labeling scheme OBIE performs better than the OBIE scheme. In the OBI scheme, the first character of a named entity is labeled as "B", the remaining characters, including the last character, are all labeled as "I". And any character that is not part of a named entity is labeled as "O". In the OBIE scheme, the last character of a named entity is labeled as "E". The other characters are labeled in the same way as in OBIE scheme. The first CRF recognizer used the OBIE labeling scheme, and the second CRF recognizer used the OBI scheme.

We tried a window size of seven characters (three characters preceding the current character and three characters following the current character) with almost no difference in performance from using the window size of five characters.

When a named entity occurs frequently in the training data, there is a very good chance that it will be recognized when appearing in the testing data. However, for entity names of rare occurrence, they are much harder to recognize in the testing data. Thus it may be beneficial to examine the testing data to identify the named entities that occur in the training data, and assign them the same label as in the training data. From the training data, we extracted the person names of at least three characters, the place names of at least four characters, and the organization names of at least four characters. We removed from the dictionary the named entities that are also common words. We did not include the short names in the dictionary because they may be part of long names. We produced a run first using one of the NER recognizers, and then replaced the labels of a named entity assigned by a recognizer with the labels of the same named entity in the training data without considering the contexts.

3 Results

Run ID	Precision	Recall	F-Score
msra_a	91.22%	81.71%	86.20
msra_b	88.43%	82.88%	85.56
msra_f	88.45%	79.31%	83.63
msra_g	86.61%	80.32%	83.35
msra_r	87.48%	71.68%	78.80

Table 1: Official results in the closed test of the NER task on MSRA corpus.

Table 1 presents the official results of five runs in the closed test of the NER task on MSRA corpus. The first two runs, msra_a and msra_b, are produced using the first CRF recognizer; the next two runs, msra_f and msra_g, are produced using the second CRF recognizer which used randomly selected 90% of the MSRA training data. When we retrained the second CRF recognizer with the whole set of the MSRA training data, the overall F-Score is 85.00, precision 90.28%, and recall 80.31%. The last run, msra_r, is produced using the MaxEnt recognizer.

The msra_a run used the set of basic features with a window size of five characters. Slightly over eight millions features are generated from the MSRA training data, excluding features occurred only once. The training took 321 iterations to complete. The msra_b run is produced from the msra_a run by substituting the labels assigned by the recognizer to a named entity with the labels of the named entity in the training data if it occurs in the training data. For example, in the MSRA training data, the text 毕加索故居 in the sentence 我 还 到 毕 加 索 故 居 去 瞻 仰 is tagged as a place name. The same entity also appeared in MSRA testing data set. The first CRF recognizer failed to mark the text 毕加索故居 as

[1] Available from http://chasen.org/~taku/software/CRF++

[2] Available at http://mallet.cs.umass.edu

[3] Available at http://homepages.inf.ed.ac.uk/s0450736/maxent_toolkit.htm

a place name instead it tagged 毕加索 as a person name. In post-processing, the text 毕加索故居 in the testing data is re-tagged as a place name. As another example, the person name 章念生 appears both in the training data and in the testing data. The first CRF recognizer failed to recognize it as a person name. In post-processing the text 章念生 is tagged as a person name because it appears in the training data as a person name. The text "全国人大香港特别行政区筹备委员会" was correctly tagged as an organization name. It is not in the training data, but the texts "全国人大", "香港特别行政区", and "筹备委员会" are present in the training data and are all labeled as organization names. In our post-processing, the correctly tagged organization name is re-tagged incorrectly as three organization names. This is the main reason why the performance of the organization name got much worse than that without post-processing.

	Precision	Recall	F-score
LOC	94.19%	87.14%	90.53
ORG	83.59%	80.39%	81.96
PER	92.35%	74.66%	82.57

Table 2: The performance of the msra_a run broken down by entity type.

	Precision	Recall	F-score
LOC	93.09%	87.35%	90.13
ORG	75.51%	78.51	76.98
PER	91.52	79.27	84.95

Table 3: The performance of the msra_b run broken down by entity type.

Table 2 presents the performance of the msra_a run by entity type. Table 3 shows the performance of the msra_b run by entity type. While the post-processing improved the performance of person name recognition, but it degraded the performance of organization name recognition. Overall the performance was worse than that without post-processing. In our development testing, we saw large improvement in organization name recognition with post-processing.

Run ID	Precision	Recall	F-Score
cityu_a	92.66%	84.75%	88.53
cityu_b	92.42%	84.91%	88.50
cityu_f	91.88%	82.31%	86.83
cityu_g	91.64%	82.46%	86.81

Table 4: Official results in the closed test of the NER task on CITYU corpus.

Table 4 presents the official results of four runs in the closed test of the NER task on CITYU corpus. The first two runs, msra_a and msra_b, are produced using the first CRF recognizer; the next two runs, msra_f and msra_g, are produced using the second CRF recognizer. The system configurations are the same as used on the MSRA corpus. The cityu_b run is produced from cityu_a run with post-processing, and the cityu_g run produced from cityu_f run with post-processing. We used the whole set of CITYU to train the first CRF model, and 80% of the CITYU training data to train the second CRF model. No results on full training data are available at the time of submission.

All the runs we submitted are based characters. We tried word-based approach but found it was not as effective as character-based approach.

4 Discussions

Table 4 is shows the confusion matrix of the labels. The rows are the true labels and the columns are the predicated labels. An entry at row *x* and column *y* in the table is the number of characters that are predicated as *y* while the true label is *x*. Ideally, all entries except the diagonal should be zero.

The table was obtained from the result of our development dataset for MSRA data, which are the last 9,364 sentences of the MSRA training data (we used the first 37,000 sentences for training in the model developing phase). As we can see, most of the errors lie in the first column, indicating many of the entities labels are predicated as O. This resulted low recall for entities. Another major error is on detecting the beginning of ORG (B-O). Many of them are mislabeled as O and beginning of location (B-L), resulting low recall and low precision for ORG.

	O	B-L	I-L	B-O	I-O	B-P	I-P
O	406798	86	196	213	973	46	111
B-L	463	5185	54	73	29	19	7
I-L	852	25	6836	0	197	1	44
B-O	464	141	3	2693	62	17	0
I-O	1861	28	276	55	12626	2	39
B-P	472	16	2	22	3	2998	8
I-P	618	0	14	1	49	10	5502

Table 4: Confusion matrix of on the MSRA development dataset

A second interesting thing to notice is the numbers presented in Table 2. They may suggest that person name recognition is more difficult than location name recognition, which is contrary to what we believe, since Chinese person names are short and have strict structure and they should be easier to recognize than both location and organization names. We examined the MSRA testing data and found out that 617 out 1,973 person names occur in a single sentence as a list of person names. In this case, simple rule may be more effective. When we excluded the sentence with 617 person names, for person name recognition of our msra_a run, the F-score is 90.74, precision 93.44%, and recall 88.20%. Out of the 500 person names that were not recognized in our msra_a run, 340 occurred on the same line of 617 person names.

5 Conclusions

We applied Conditional Random Fields and maximum entropy models to Chinese NER tasks and achieved satisfying performance. Three systems with different implementations and different features are reported. Overall, CRFs are superior to maximum entropy models in Chinese NER tasks. Useful features include using BIOE tags instead of BIO tags and word and character clustering features.

References

Adam Berger, Stephen Della Pietra, and Vincent Della Pietra, A Maximum Entropy Approach to Natural Language Processing, *Computational Linguistics,* 22 (1)

John Lafferty, Andrew McCallum, and Fernando Pereira, Conditional random fields: Probabilistic models for segmenting and labeling sequence data. In: *Proc. 18th International Conf. on Machine Learning*, Morgan Kaufmann, San Francisco, CA (2001) 282–289

Fuchun Peng, Fangfang Feng, and Andrew McCallum, Chinese Segmentation and New Word Detection using Conditional Random Fields, In *Proceedings of The 20th International Conference on Computational Linguistics (COLING 2004)* , pages 562-568, August 23-27, 2004, Geneva, Switzerland

Naftali Tishby and Lillian Lee, Distributional Clustering of English Words, In *Proceedings of the 31st Annual Conference of Association for Computational Linguistics*, pp 183--190, 1993.

POC-NLW Template for Chinese Word Segmentation

Bo Chen
chb615@gmail.com

Weiran Xu
xuweiran@263.net

Tao Peng
ppttbupt@gmail.com

Jun Guo
guojun@bupt.edu.cn

Pattern Recognition and Intelligent System Lab
Beijing University of Posts and Telecommunications
Beijing 100876, P. R. China

Abstract

In this paper, a language tagging template named POC-NLW (position of a character within an n-length word) is presented. Based on this template, a two-stage statistical model for Chinese word segmentation is constructed. In this method, the basic word segmentation is based on n-gram language model, and a Hidden Markov tagger based on the POC-NLW template is used to implement the out-of-vocabulary (OOV) word identification. The system participated in the MSRA_Close and UPUC_Close word segmentation tracks at SIGHAN Bakeoff 2006. Results returned by this bakeoff are reported here.

1 Introduction

In Chinese word segmentation, there are two problems still remain, one is the resolution of ambiguity, and the other is the identification of so-called out-of-vocabulary (OOV) or unknown words. In order to resolve these two problems, a two-stage statistical word segmentation strategy is adopted in our system. The first stage is optional, and the whole segmentation can be accomplished in the second stage. In the first stage, the n-gram language model is employed to implement basic word segmentation including disambiguation. In the second stage, a language tagging template named POC-NLW (position of a character within an n-length word) is introduced to accomplish unknown word identification as template-based character tagging.

The remainder of this paper is organized as follows. In section 2 and section 3, a briefly description of the main methods adopted in our system is given. Results of our system at this bakeoff are reported in section 4. At last, conclusions are derived in section 5.

2 The Basic Word Segmentation Stage

In the first stage, the basic word segmentation is accomplished. The key issue in this stage is the ambiguity problem, which is mainly caused by the fact that a Chinese character can occur in different word internal positions in different words (Xue, 2003). A lot of machine learning techniques have been applied to resolve this problem, the n-gram language model is one of the most popular ones among them (Fu and Luke, 2003; Li et al., 2005). As such, we also employed n-gram model in this stage.

When a sentence is inputted, it is first segmented into a sequence of individual characters (e.g. ASCII strings, basic Chinese characters, punitions, numerals and so on), marked as $C_{1,n}$. According to the system's dictionary, several word sequences $W_{1,m}$ will be constructed as candidates. The function of the n-gram model is to find out the best word sequence W^* corresponds to $C_{1,n}$, which has the maximum integrated probability, i.e.,

$$W^* = \arg\max_{W_{1,m}} P(W_{1,m} \mid C_{1,n})$$

$$\cong \arg\max_{W_{1,m}} \prod_{i=1}^{m} P(W_i \mid W_{i-1}) \qquad \textit{for bigram}$$

$$\cong \arg\max_{W_{1,m}} \prod_{i=1}^{m} P(W_i \mid W_{i-1}, W_{i-2}) \; \textit{for trigram}$$

The Maximum Likelihood method was used to estimate the word n-gram probabilities used in our model, and the linear interpolation method (Jelinek and Mercer, 1980) was applied to smooth these estimated probabilities.

3 The OOV Word Identification Stage

The n-gram method is based on the exiting grams in the model, so it is good at judging the connecting relationship among known words, but does not have the ability to deal with unknown words in substance. Therefore, another OOV word identification model is required.

OOV words are regarded as words that do not exist in a system's machine-readable dictionary, and a more detailed definition can be found in (Wu and Jiang, 2000). In general, Chinese word can be created through compounding or abbreviating of most of existing characters and words. Thus, the key to solve the OOV word identification lies on whether the new word creation mechanisms in Chinese language can be extracted. Therefore, a POC-NLW language tagging template is introduced to explore such information on the character-level within words.

3.1 The POC-NLW Template

Many character-level based works have been done for the Chinese word segmentation, including the LMR tagging methods (Xue, 2003; Nakagawa. 2004), the IWP mechanism (Wu and Jiang, 2000). Based on these previous works, this POC-NLW template was derived. Assume that the length of a word is the number of component characters in it, the template is consist of two component: L_{max} and a *Wl-Pn* tag set. L_{max} to denote the maximum length of a word expressed by the template; a *Wl-Pn* tag denotes that this tag is assigned to a character at the *n-th* position within a *l*-length word, $n = 1,2,\cdots,l$. Apparently, the size of this tag set is $(L_{\max} + 1) \times L_{\max} / 2$

For example, the Chinese word "人民" is tagged as:

人 W2P1, 民 W2P2

and "中国人" is tagged as:

中 W3P1, 国 W3P2, 人 W3P3

In the example, two words are tagged by the template respectively, and the Chinese character "人" has been assigned two different tags.

In a sense, the Chinese word creation mechanisms could be extracted through statistics of the tags for each character on a certain large corpus.

On the other hand, while a character sequence in a sentence is tagged by this template, the word boundaries are obvious. Meanwhile, the word segmentation is implemented.

In addition, in this template, known words and unknown words are both regarded as sequences of individual characters. Thus, the basic word segmentation process, the disambiguation process and the OOV word identification process can be accomplished in a unified process. Thereby, this model can also be used alone to implement the word segmentation task. This characteristic will make the word segmentation system much more efficient.

3.2 The HMM Tagger

Form the description of POC-NLW template, it can be found that the word segmentation could be implemented as POC-NLW tagging, which is similar to the so-called part-of-speech (POS) tagging problem. In POS tagging, Hidden Markov Model (HMM) was applied as one of the most significant methods, as described in detail in (Brants, 2000). The HMM method can achieve high accuracy in tagging with low processing costs, so it was adopted in our model.

According to the definition of POC-NLW template, the state set of HMM corresponds to the *Wl-Pn* tag set, and the symbol set is composed of all characters. However, the initial state probability matrix and the state transition probability matrix are not composed of all of the tags in the state set. To express more clearly, we define two subset of the state set:

- Begin Tag Set (BTS): this set is consisted of tag which can occur in the begging position in a word. Apparently, these tags must have the *Wl-P1* form.
- *End Tag Set (ETS):* correspond to BTS, tags in this set should occur in the end position, and their form should be like *Wl-Pl*.

Apparently, the size of BTS is L_{max} as well as of ETS. Thus, the initial state probability matrix corresponds to BTS instead of the whole state set. On the other hand, because of the word internal continuity, if the current tag *Wl-Pn* is not in ETS, than the next tag must be *Wl-P(n+1)*. In other words, the case in which the transition probability is need is that when the current tag is in ETS and the next tag belongs to BTS. So, the state transition matrix in our model corresponds to $ETS \times BTS$.

The probabilities used in HMM were defined similarly to those in POS tagging, and were estimated using the Maximum Likelihood method from the training corpus.

In the two-stage strategy, the output word sequence of the first stage is transferred into the second stage. The items in the sequence, including individual characters and words, which do not have a bigram or trigram relationship with the surrounding items, are picked out with its surrounding items to compose several sequences of items. These item sequences are processed by the HMM tagger to form new item sequences. At last, these processed items sequences are combined into the whole word sequence as the final output.

4 Results and Analysis

4.1 System

The system submitted at this bakeoff was a two-stage one, as describe at beginning of this paper. The model used in the first stage was trigram, and the L_{max} of the template used in the second stage was set to 7.

In addition to the tags defined in the template before, a special tag is introduced into our *Wl-Pn* tag set to indicate all those characters that occur after the L_{max}-*th* position in an extremely long (longer than L_{max}) word., formulized as WL_{max}-$P(L_{max}+1)$. And then, there are 28 basic tags (from *W1-P1* to *W7-P7*) and the special one *W7-P8*.

For instance, using the special tag, the word "中国共产党中央委员会" (form the MSRA Corpus) is tagged as:

中 *W7-P1* 国 *W7-P2* 共 *W7-P3* 产 *W7-P4* 党 *W7-P5* 中 *W7-P6* 央 *W7-P7* 委 *W7-P8* 员 *W7-P8* 会 *W7-P8*

4.2 Results at SIGHAN Bakeoff 2006

Our system participated in the MSRA_Close and UPUC_Close track at the SIGHAN Bakeoff 2006. The test results are as showed in Table 1.

Corpus	MSRA	UPUC
F-measure	0.951	0.918
Recall	0.956	0.932
Precision	0.947	0.904
IV Recall	0.972	0.969
OOV Recall	0.493	0.546
OOV Precision	0.569	0.757

Table 1. Results at SIGHAN Bakeoff 2006

The performances of our system on the two corpuses can rank in the half-top group among the participated systems.

We notice that the accuracies on known word segmentation are relatively better than on OOV words segmentation. This appears somewhat unexpected. In the close experiments we had done on the PKU and MSR corpuses of SIGHAN Bakeoff 2005, the relative performance of OOV Recall was much more outstanding than of the F-measure.

We think this is due to the inappropriate parameters used in n-gram model, which over-guarantees the performance of basic word segmentation. It can be seen on the IV Recall (highest in UPUC_Close track). For only the best output sequence of the n-gram model is transferred to the HMM tagger, some potential unknown words may be miss-split in the early stage. Thus, the OOV Recall is not very good, and this also affects the overall performance.

On the other hand, the performances of OOV identification on UPUC are much better than on MSRA, while the performances of overall segmentation accuracy on UPUC are worse than on MSRA. This phenomenon also happened in our experiments on the Bakeoff 2005 corpuses of PKU and MSR. In the PKU test data, the rate of OOV words according is 0.058 while in MSR is 0.026. Thus, it can be conclude that the more unknown words occur, the more significant ability of OOV words identification appears.

In addition, the relative performance of OOV Precision are much better. This demonstrates that the OOV identification ability of our system is appreciable. In other words, the POC-NLW tagging method introduced is effective to some extent.

5 CONCLUSION AND FURTHER WORK

In this paper, a POC-NLW template is presented for word segmentation, which aims at exploring the word creation mechanisms in Chinese language by utilizing the character-level information to. A two-stage strategy was applied in our system to combine the n-gram model based word segmentation and OOV word identification implemented by a HMM tagger. Test results show that the method achieved high performance on word segmentation, especially on unknown words identification. Therefore, the method is a practical one that can be implemented as an integral component in actual Chinese NLP applications.

From the results, it can safely conclude that method introduced here does find some character-level information, and the information could effectively conduct the word segmentation and unknown words identification. For this is the first time we participate in this bakeoff, and the work has been done as a integral part of another system during the past two months, the implementation of the segmentation system we submitted is coarse. A lot of improvements, on either theoretical methods or implementation techniques, are required in our future work, including the smoothing techniques in the n-gram model and the HMM model, the refine of the features extraction method and the POC-NLW template itself, the more harmonious integration strategy and so on.

Acknowledgements

This work is partially supported by NSFC (National Natural Science Foundation of China) under Grant No.60475007, Key Project of Chinese Ministry of Education under Grant No.02029 and the Foundation of Chinese Ministry of Education for Century Spanning Talent.

References

Andi Wu, and Zixin Jiang. 2000. Statistically-enhanced new word identification in a rule-based Chinese system. *Proceedings of the 2nd Chinese Language Processing Workshop*, 46-51.

Frederick Jelinek, and Robert L. Mercer. 1980. Interpolated Estimation of Markov Source Parameters from Sparse Data. *Proceedings of Workshop on Pattern Recognition in Practice*, Amsterdam, 381-397.

Guohong Fu, and Kang-Kwong Luke. 2003. A Two-stage Statistical Word Segmentation System for Chinese. *Proceedings of the Second SIGHAN Workshop on Chinese Language Processing*, 156-159.

Heng Li, Yuan Dong, Xinnian Mao, Haila Wang, and Wu Liu. 2005. Chinese Word Segmentation in FTRD Beijing. *Proceedings of the Fourth SIGHAN Workshop on Chinese Language Processing*, 150-153.

Nianwen Xue. 2003. Chinese Word Segmentation as Character Tagging. *International Journal of Computational Linguistics and Chinese Language Procession*, 8(1):29–48.

Tetsuji Nakagawa. 2004. Chinese and Japanese Word Segmentation Using Word-Level and Character-Level Information. *Proceedings of the 20th International Conference on Computational Linguistics*, 466–472.

Thorsten Brants. 2000. TnT — A Statistical Part-of-Speech Tagger. *Proceedings of the Sixth Conference on Applied Natural Language Processing ANLP-2000*, 224–231.

Chinese Word Segmentation and Named Entity Recognition Based on Conditional Random Fields Models

Yuanyong Feng **Le Sun** **Yuanhua Lv**
Institute of Software, Chinese Academy of Sciences, Beijing, 100080, China
{yuanyong02, sunle, yuanhua04}@ios.cn

Abstract

This paper mainly describes a Chinese named entity recognition (NER) system NER@ISCAS, which integrates text, part-of-speech and a small-vocabulary-character-lists feature for MSRA NER open track under the framework of Conditional Random Fields (CRFs) model. The techniques used for the close NER and word segmentation tracks are also presented.

1 Introduction

The system NER@ISCAS is designed under the Conditional Random Fields (CRFs. Lafferty et al., 2001) framework. It integrates multiple features based on single Chinese character or space separated ASCII words. The early designed system (Feng et al., 2005) is used for the MSRA NER open track this year. The output of an external part-of-speech tagging tool and some carefully collected small-scale-character-lists are used as outer knowledge.

The close word segmentation and named entity recognition tracks are also based on this system by some adjustments.

The remaining of this paper is organized as follows. Section 2 introduces Conditional Random Fields model. Section 3 presents the details of our system on Chinese NER integrating multiple features. Section 4 describes the features extraction for close track. Section 5 gives the evaluation results. We end our paper with some conclusions and future works.

2 Conditional Random Fields Model

Conditional random fields are undirected graphical models for calculating the conditional probability for output vertices based on input ones. While sharing the same exponential form with maximum entropy models, they have more efficient procedures for complete, non-greedy finite-state inference and training.

Given an observation sequence $o=<o_1, o_2, ..., o_T>$, linear-chain CRFs model based on the assumption of first order Markov chains defines the corresponding state sequence s' probability as follows (Lafferty et al., 2001):

$$p_\Lambda(\mathbf{s}\,|\,\mathbf{o}) = \frac{1}{Z_\mathbf{o}}\exp(\sum_{t=1}^{T}\sum_{k}\lambda_k f_k(s_{t-1}, s_t, \mathbf{o}, t)) \qquad (1)$$

Where Λ is the model parameter set, Z_o is the normalization factor over all state sequences, f_k is an arbitrary feature function, and λ_k is the learned feature weight. A feature function defines its value to be 0 in most cases, and to be 1 in some designated cases. For example, the value of a feature named "MAYBE-SURNAME" is 1 if and only if s_{t-1} is OTHER, s_t is PER, and the t-th character in $\boldsymbol{o}$ is a common-surname.

The inference and training procedures of CRFs can be derived directly from those equivalences in HMM. For instance, the forward variable $\alpha_t(s_i)$ defines the probability that state at time t being s_i at time t given the observation sequence $\boldsymbol{o}$. Assumed that we know the probabilities of each possible value s_i for the beginning state $\alpha_0(s_i)$, then we have

$$\alpha_{t+1}(s_i) = \sum_{s'}\alpha_t(s')\exp(\sum_{k}\lambda_k f_k(s', s_i, \mathbf{o}, t) \qquad (2)$$

In similar ways, we can obtain the backward variables and Baum-Welch algorithm.

3 Chinese NER Using CRFs Model Integrating Multiple Features for Open Track

In our system the text feature, part-of-speech (POS) feature, and small-vocabulary-character-lists (SVCL) feature are combined under a unified CRFs framework.

The text feature includes single Chinese character, some continuous digits or letters.

POS feature is an important feature which carries some syntactic information. Our POS tag set follows the criterion of modern Chinese corpora construction (Yu, 1999), which contains 39 tags.

The last feature is based on lists. We first list all digits and English letters in Chinese. Then most frequently used character feature in Chinese NER are collected, including 100 single character surnames, 100 location tail characters, and 40 organization tail characters. The total number of these items in our lists is less than 600. The lists altogether make up a list feature (SVCL). Some examples of this list are given in Table 1.

Value	Description	Examples
digit	Arabic digit(s)	1,2,3
letter	Letter(s)	A,B,C,...,a, b, c
Continuous digits and/or letters (The sequence is regarded as a single token)		
chseq	Chinese order 1	(一), (1), ①, Ⅰ
chdigit	Chinese digit	１, 壹, 一
tianseq	Chinese order 2	甲, 乙, 丙, 丁
chsurn	Surname	李, 吴, 郑, 王
notname	Not name	将, 对, 那, 的, 是, 说
loctch	LOC tail character	区, 国, 岛, 海, 台, 庄, 冲
orgtch	ORG tail character	府, 团, 校, 协, 局, 办, 军
other	Other case	情, 规, 息, ！，。

Table 1. Some Examples of SVCL Feature

Each token is presented by its feature vector, which is combined by these features we just discussed. Once all token feature (Maybe including context features) values are determined, an observation sequence is feed into the model.

Each token state is a combination of the type of the named entity it belongs to and the boundary type it locates within. The entity types are person name (PER), location name (LOC), organization name (ORG), date expression (DAT), time expression (TIM), numeric expression (NUM), and not named entity (OTH). The boundary types are simply Beginning, Inside, and Outside (BIO).

4 Feature Extraction for Close Tracks

In close tracks, only character and word list features which are extracted from training data are applied for word segmentation. In NER track we also include a named entity list extracted from the training data.

To extract the list feature, we simply search each text string among the list items in maximum length forward way.

Taking the word segmentation task for instance, when a text string $c_1c_2...c_n$ is given, we tag each character into a BIO-WL style. If $c_ic_{i+1}...c_j$ matches an item I of length j-i+1 and no other item I' of length k (k>j-i+1) in the list matches $c_ic_{i+1}...c_j...c_{k+i-1}$, then the characters are tagged as follows:

c_i	c_{i+1}	...	c_j
B-WL	I-WL	...	I-WL

If no item in the list matches head subpart of the string, then c_i is tagged as 0.

The tagging operation iterates on the remaining part until all characters are tagged.

5 Evaluation

5.1 Results

The system for our MSRA NER open track submission has some bugs and was trained on a much smaller training data set than the full set the organizer provided. The results are very low, see Table 2:

Accuracy	96.28%
Precision	83.20%
Recall	67.03%
FB1	74.24%

Table 2. MSRA NER Open

When we fixed the bug and retrained on the full training corpus, the result comes out to be as follows:

Accuracy	98.24%
Precision	89.38%
Recall	83.07%
FB1	86.11%

Table 3. MSRA NER Open (retrained)

All the submissions on close tracks are trained on 80% of the training corpora, the remaining 20% parts are used for development. The results are shown in Table 4 and Table 5:

Measure	Corpus			
	UPUC	CityU	CKIP	MSRA
Recall	0.922	0.952	0.939	0.933
Precision	0.912	0.954	0.929	0.942
FB1	0.917	0.953	0.934	0.937
OOV Recall	0.680	0.747	0.606	0.640
IV Recall	0.945	0.960	0.954	0.943

Table 4. WS Close

Measure	MSRA	CityU	LDC
Accuracy	92.44	97.80	93.82
Precision	81.64	92.76	81.43
Recall	31.24	81.81	59.53
FB1	45.19	86.94	68.78

Table 5. NER Close

The reason for low measure on MSRA NER track exists in that we chose a much smaller training data file encoded in CP936 (about 7% of the full data set). This file may be an incomplete output when the organizer transfers from another encoding scheme.

5.2 Errors from NER Track

The NER errors in our system are mainly as follows:

- Abbreviations

Abbreviations are very common among the errors. Among them, a significant part of abbreviations are mentioned before their corresponding full names. Some common abbreviations has no corresponding full names appeared in document. Here are some examples:

R[1]:针对大陆人民申请进入 金 妈 地区，[内政部警政署入出境管理局 ORG][金门 GPE]、[妈祖 GPE]服务站定于明天……

K:针对大陆人民申请进入 [金 GPE][妈 GPE]地区，[内政部警政署入出境管理局 ORG][金门 GPE]、[妈祖 GPE]服务站定于明天……

R: 总后[嫩江基地 LOC]的先进事迹

K: [总后嫩江基地 LOC]的先进事迹

R: [中 丹 LOC]兩國

K: [中 LOC][丹 LOC]兩國

In current system, the recognition is fully depended on the linear-chain CRFs model, which is heavily based on local window observation features; no abbreviation list or special abbreviation recognition involved. Because lack of constraint checking on distant entity mentions, the system fails to catch the interaction among similar text fragments cross sentences.

- Concatenated Names

For many reasons, Chinese names in titles and some sentences, especially in news, are not separated. The system often fails to judge the right boundaries and the reasonable type classification. For example:

R:身边还有[张龙 赵虎 PER]王朝[马汉 PER] 四个卫士

K:身边还有[张龙 PER][赵虎 PER][王朝 PER][马汉 PER] 四个卫士

R:将[瓦西里斯 LOC]与[奥纳西斯 PER]比较

K:将[瓦西里斯 PER]与[奥纳西斯 PER]比较

- Hints

Though it helps to recognize an entity at most cases, the small-vocabulary-list hint feature may recommend a wrong decision sometimes. For instance, common surname character “王” in the following sentence is wrongly labeled when no word segmentation information given:

R:[希腊 LOC]船[王 康斯坦塔科普洛斯 PER]

K:[希腊 LOC]船 王[康斯坦塔科普洛斯 PER]

Other errors of this type may result from failing to identify verbs and prepositions, such as:

R:[中共中央 致 中国致公党十一大 ORG]的贺词……向[致公党 ORG]的同志们……

K:[中共中央 ORG]致[中国致公党十一大 ORG]的贺词……向[致公党 ORG]的同志们……

R:全国保护明天行动组委会 举行表彰会

K:[全国保护明天行动组委会 ORG]举行表彰会

R:包公 赶驴

K:[包公 PER] 赶驴

- Other Types:

R:特别助理 由喜贵 等也同机抵达。

K:特别助理[由喜贵 PER]等也同机抵达。

R:脸谱上还有 日 月 的图案

[1] R stands for system response, K for key.

K:脸谱上还有[日 LOC][月 LOC]的图案

6 Conclusions and Future Work

We mainly described a Chinese named entity recognition system NER@ISCAS, which integrates text, part-of-speech and a small-vocabulary-character-lists feature for MSRA NER open track under the framework of Conditional Random Fields (CRFs) model. Although it provides a unified framework to integrate multiple flexible features, and to achieve global optimization on input text sequence, the popular linear chained Conditional Random Fields model often fails to catch semantic relations among reoccurred mentions and adjoining entities in a catenation structure.

The situations containing exact reoccurrence and shortened occurrence enlighten us to take more effort on feature engineering or post processing on abbreviations / recurrence recognition.

Another effort may be poured on the common patterns, such as paraphrase, counting, and constraints on Chinese person name lengths.

From current point of view, enriching the hint lists is also desirable.

Acknowledgment

This work is supported by the National Science Fund of China under contract 60203007.

References

Chinese 863 program. 2005. Results on Named Entity Recognition. *The 2004HTRDP Chinese Information Processing and Intelligent Human-Machine Interface Technology Evaluation.*

Yuanyong Feng, Le Sun and Junlin Zhang. 2005. Early Results for Chinese Named Entity Recognition Using Conditional Random Fields Model, HMM and Maximum Entropy. *IEEE Natural Language Processing & Knowledge Engineering*. Beijing: Publishing House, BUPT. pp. 549~552.

John Lafferty, Andrew McCallum, and Fernando Pereira. 2001. Conditional Random Fields: Probabilistic Models for Segmenting and Labeling Sequence Data. *ICML*.

Shiwen Yu. 1999. Manual on Modern Chinese Corpora Construction. Institute of Computational Language, Peking Unversity. Beijing.

Maximum Entropy Word Segmentation of Chinese Text

Aaron J. Jacobs
Department of Linguistics
University of Texas at Austin
1 University Station B5100
Austin, TX 78712-0198 USA
aaronjacobs@mail.utexas.edu

Yuk Wah Wong
Department of Computer Sciences
University of Texas at Austin
1 University Station C0500
Austin, TX 78712-0233 USA
ywwong@cs.utexas.edu

Abstract

We extended the work of Low, Ng, and Guo (2005) to create a Chinese word segmentation system based upon a maximum entropy statistical model. This system was entered into the Third International Chinese Language Processing Bakeoff and evaluated on all four corpora in their respective open tracks. Our system achieved the highest F-score for the UPUC corpus, and the second, third, and seventh highest for CKIP, CITYU, and MSRA respectively. Later testing with the gold-standard data revealed that while the additions we made to Low et al.'s system helped our results for the 2005 data with which we experimented during development, a number of them actually hurt our scores for this year's corpora.

1 Segmenter

Our Chinese word segmenter is a modification of the system described by Low et al. (2005), which they entered in the 2005 Second International Chinese Word Segmentation Bakeoff. It uses a maximum entropy (Ratnaparkhi, 1998) model which is trained on the training corpora provided for this year's bakeoff. The maximum entropy framework used is the Python interface of Zhang Le's maximum entropy modeling toolkit (Zhang, 2004).

1.1 Properties in common with Low et al.

As with the system of Low et al., our system treats the word segmentation problem as a tagging problem. When segmenting a string of Chinese text, each character can be assigned one of four boundary tags: *S* for a character that stands alone as a word, *B* for a character that begins a multi-character word, *M* for a character in a multi-character word which neither starts nor ends the word, and *E* for a character that ends a multi-character word. The optimal tag for a given character is chosen based on features derived from the character's surrounding context in accordance with the decoding algorithm (see Section 1.2).

All of the feature templates of Low et al.'s system are utilized in our own (with a few slight modifications):

1. C_n $(n = -2, -1, 0, 1, 2)$
2. C_nC_{n+1} $(n = -2, -1, 0, 1)$
3. $C_{-1}C_1$
4. $Pu(C_0)$
5. $T(C_{-2})T(C_{-1})T(C_0)T(C_1)T(C_2)$
6. Lt_0
7. C_nt_0 $(n = -1, 0, 1)$

In the above feature templates, C_i refers to the character i positions away from the character under consideration, where negative values indicate characters to the left of the present position. The punctuation feature $Pu(C_0)$ is added only if the current character is a punctuation mark, and the function T maps characters to various numbers representing classes of characters. In addition to the numeral, date word, and English letter classes of Low et al.'s system, we added classes for punctuation and likely decimal points (which are defined by a period or the character 点 occurring between two numerals). L is defined to be the length of the longest word W in the dictionary that matches some sequence of characters around C_0

in the current context and t_0 is the boundary tag of C_0 in W. The dictionary features are derived from the use of the same online dictionary from Peking University that was used by Low et al.

In order to improve out-of-vocabulary (OOV) recall rates, we followed the same procedure as Low et al.'s system in using the other three training corpora as additional training material when training a model for a particular corpus:

1. Train a model normally using the given corpus.
2. Use the resulting model to segment the other training corpora from this year's bakeoff, ignoring the pre-existing segmentation.
3. Let C be a character in one of the other corpora D. If C is assigned a tag t by the model with probability p, t is equivalent to the tag assigned by the actual training corpus D, and p is less than 0.8, then add C (along with its associated features) as additional training material.
4. Train a new model using all of the original training data along with the new data derived from the other corpora as described in the previous step.

This procedure was carried out when training models for all of the corpora except CKIP. The model for that corpus was trained solely with its own training data due to time and memory concerns as well as the fact that our scores during development for the corresponding corpus (AS) in 2005 did not seem to benefit from the addition of data from the other corpora.

We adopt the same post-processing step as Low et al.'s system: after segmenting a body of text, any sequence of 2 to 6 words whose total length is at least 3 characters and whose concatenation is found as a single word elsewhere in the segmenter's output is joined together into that single word. Empirical testing showed that this process was actually detrimental to results in the 2005 CITYU data, so it was performed only for the UPUC, MSRA, and CKIP corpora.

1.2 Decoding algorithm

When segmenting text, to efficiently compute the most likely tag sequence our system uses the Viterbi algorithm (Viterbi, 1967). Only legal tag sequences are considered. This is accomplished by ignoring illegal state transitions (e.g. from a *B* tag to an *S* tag) during decoding. At each stage the likelihood of the current path is estimated by multiplying the likelihood of the path which it extends with the probability given by the model of the assumed tag occurring given the surrounding context and the current path. To keep the problem tractable, only the 30 most likely paths are kept at each stage.

The advantage of such an algorithm comes in its ability to 'look ahead' compared to a simpler algorithm which just chooses the most likely tag at each step and goes on. Such an algorithm is likely to run into situations where choosing the most likely tag for one character forces the choice of a very sub-optimal tag for a later character by making impossible the choice of the best tag (e.g. if *S* is the best choice but the tag assigned for the previous character was *B*). In contrast, the Viterbi algorithm entertains multiple possibilities for the tagging of each character, allowing it to choose a less likely tag now as a trade-off for a much more likely tag later.

1.3 Other outcome-independent features

To the feature templates of Low et al.'s system described in Section 1.1, we added the following three features which do not depend on previous tagging decisions but only on the current character's context within the sentence:

1. The `surname` feature is set if the current character is in our list of common surname characters, as derived from the Peking University dictionary.
2. The `redup-next` feature is set if C_1 is equal to C_0. This is to handle reduplication within words, such as in the case of 清清楚楚 'particularly clear'.
3. The `redup-prev` feature is set if C_{-1} is equal to C_0.

These features were designed to give the system hints in cases where we saw it make frequent errors in the 2005 data.

1.4 Outcome-dependent features

In addition to the features previously discussed, we added a number of features to our system that are *outcome-dependent* in the sense that their realization for a given character depends upon how the previous characters were segmented. These work in conjunction with the Viterbi algorithm discussed in Section 1.2 to make it so that a given character in a sentence can be assigned a different set of features each time it is considered, depending on the path currently being extended.

1. If the current character is one of the place characters such as 村 or 镇 which commonly occur at the end of a three-character word and the length of the current word (as determined by previous tagging decisions on the current path) including the current character is equal to three, then the feature `place-char-and-len-3` is set.

2. If the situation is as described above except the *next* character in the current context is the place character, then the feature `next-place-char-and-len-2` is set.

3. If the current character is 等 and the word before the previous word is an enumerating comma (、), then the feature `deng-list` is set. This is intended to capture situations where a list of single-word items is presented, followed by 等 to mean 'and so on'.

4. If the current character is 等 and the third word back is an enumerating comma, then the feature `double-word-deng-list` is set.

5. If the length of the previous word is at least 2 and is equal to the length of the current word, then the feature `symmetry` is set.

6. If the length of the previous word is at least 2 and is one more than the length of the current word, then the feature `almost-symmetry` is set.

7. Similar features are added if the length of the current word is equal to (or one less than) the length of the word before the last and the last word is a comma.

These features were largely designed to help alleviate problems the model had with situations in which it would otherwise be difficult to discern the correct segmentation. For example, in one development data set the model incorrectly grouped 等 at the end of a list (which should be a word on its own) with the following character to form 等同, a word found in the dictionary.

1.5 Simplified normalization

To derive the most benefit from the additional training data obtained as described in Section 1.1, before generating any sort of features from characters in training and test data, all characters are normalized by the system to their simplified variants (if any) using data from version 4.1.0 of the Unicode Standard. This is intended to improve the utility of additional data from the traditional Chinese corpora when training models for the simplified corpora, and vice versa. Due to the results of some empirical testing, this normalization was only performed when training models for the UPUC and MSRA corpora; in our testing it did not actually help with the scores for the traditional Chinese corpora.

2 Results

Table 1 lists our official results for the bakeoff. The columns show F scores, recall rates, precision rates, and recall rates on out-of-vocabulary and in-vocabulary words. Out of the participants in the bakeoff whose scores were reported, our system achieved the highest F score for UPUC, the second-highest for CKIP, the seventh-highest for MSRA, and the third-highest for CITYU.

Corpus	F	R	P	R_{OOV}	R_{IV}
UPUC	0.944	0.949	0.939	0.768	0.966
CKIP	0.954	0.959	0.949	0.672	0.972
MSRA	0.960	0.959	0.961	0.711	0.968
CITYU	0.969	0.971	0.967	0.795	0.978

Table 1: Our 2006 SIGHAN bakeoff results.

The system's F score for MSRA was higher than for UPUC or CKIP, but it did particularly poorly compared to the rest of the contestants when one considers how well it performed for the other corpora. An analysis of the gold-standard files for the MSRA test data show that out of all of the corpora, MSRA had the highest percentage of single-character words and the smallest percentage of two-character and three-character words. Moreover, its proportion of words over 5 characters in length was five times that of the other corpora. Most of the errors our system made on the MSRA test set involved incorrect groupings of true single-character words. Another comparatively high proportion involved very long words, especially names with internal syntactic structure (e.g. 中国国民党革命委员会第九次全国代表大会).

Our out of vocabulary scores were fairly high for all of the corpora, coming in first, fourth, fifth, and third places in UPUC, CKIP, MSRA, and CITYU respectively. Much of this can be attributed to the value of using an external dictionary and additional training data, as illustrated by the experiments run by Low et al. (2005) with their model.

3 Further testing

In order to get some idea of how each of our additions to Low et al.'s system contributed to our results, we ran a number of experiments with the gold-standard segmentations distributed after the completion of the bakeoff. We stripped out all of the additions and then added them back in one by one, segmenting and scoring the test data each time. What we found is that our system actually performed best with the implementation of the Viterbi algorithm (which raised F scores by an average of about 0.09 compared to simply choosing the most likely tag at each stage) but without any of the extra outcome-dependent or independent features. There were only two exceptions to this:

- The system achieved slightly higher OOV recall rates for the MSRA and CITYU corpora with the `place-char` and `deng-list` features than without.
- The system achieved a very small increase in F score for the UPUC corpus with the `place-char` feature than without.

Besides these small differences, the model was best off without any of the features enumerated in Sections 1.3 and 1.4, obtaining the scores listed in Table 2. This is a surprising result, as in our testing the added features helped to improve the F scores and OOV recall rates of the system when dealing with the 2005 bakeoff data, even if only by a small amount in some cases.

It should be noted that in our testing during development, even when we strove to create a system which matched as closely as possible the one described by Low et al. (2005), we were unable to achieve scores for the 2005 bakeoff data as high as their system did. Why this was the case remains a mystery to us. It is possible that at least some of the gap is due to implementation differences. In particular, the maximum entropy toolkit utilized along with the training algorithms chosen seem likely candidates for sources of the disparity.

Corpus	F	R	P	R_{OOV}	R_{IV}
UPUC	0.948	0.954	0.943	0.781	0.970
CKIP	0.957	0.962	0.952	0.698	0.973
MSRA	0.964	0.963	0.964	0.731	0.971
CITYU	0.974	0.976	0.972	0.816	0.983

Table 2: Our results without the extra features.

4 Conclusions

Using a maximum entropy approach based on a modification of the system described by Low, Ng, and Guo (2005), our system was able to achieve a respectable level of accuracy when evaluated on the corpora of the word segmentation task of the Third International Chinese Language Processing Bakeoff. Implementing the Viterbi decoding algorithm was very beneficial for F scores and OOV recall rates. However, it should be investigated whether the rest of the added features, especially the outcome-dependent ones, are useful in general or if they were only beneficial for the 2005 test data due to some pattern in that data, after which they were modeled.

References

Jin Kiat Low, Hwee Tou Ng, and Wenyuan Guo. 2005. A maximum entropy approach to Chinese word segmentation. In *Fourth SIGHAN Workshop on Chinese Language Processing*, pages 161–164. URL `http://www.aclweb.org/anthology/I05-3025`.

Adwait Ratnaparkhi. 1998. *Maximum Entropy Models for Natural Language Ambiguity Resolution*. Ph.D. thesis, University of Pennsylvania.

Andrew J. Viterbi. 1967. Error bounds for convolutional codes and an asymptotically optimum decoding algorithm. *IEEE Transactions on Information Theory*, 13(2):260–269.

Le Zhang, 2004. *Maximum Entropy Modeling Toolkit for Python and C++*. URL `http://homepages.inf.ed.ac.uk/s0450736/`.

A Pragmatic Chinese Word Segmentation System

Wei Jiang, Yi Guan, Xiao-Long Wang
School of Computer Science and Technology, Harbin Institute of Technology,
Heilongjiang Province, 150001, P.R.China
jiangwei@insun.hit.edu.cn

Abstract

This paper presents our work for participation in the Third International Chinese Word Segmentation Bakeoff. We apply several processing approaches according to the corresponding sub-tasks, which are exhibited in real natural language. In our system, Trigram model with smoothing algorithm is the core module in word segmentation, and Maximum Entropy model is the basic model in Named Entity Recognition task. The experiment indicates that this system achieves F-measure 96.8% in MSRA open test in the third SIGHAN-2006 bakeoff.

1 Introduction

Word is a logical semantic and syntactic unit in natural language. Unlike English, there is no delimiter to mark word boundaries in Chinese language, so in most Chinese NLP tasks, word segmentation is a foundation task, which transforms Chinese character string into word sequence. It is prerequisite to POS tagger, parser or further applications, such as Information Extraction, Question Answer system.

Our system participated in the Third International Chinese Word Segmentation Bakeoff, which held in 2006. Compared with our system in the last bakeoff (Jiang 2005A), the system in the third bakeoff is adjusted intending to have a better pragmatic performance. This paper mainly focuses on describing two sub-tasks: (1) The basic Word Segmentation; (2) Named entities recognition. We apply different approaches to solve above two tasks, and all the modules are integrated into a pragmatic system (**ELUS**).

2 System Description

All the words in our system are categorized into five types: Lexicon words (LW), Factoid words (FT), Morphologically derived words (MDW), Named entities (NE), and New words (NW). Figure 1 demonstrates our system structure.

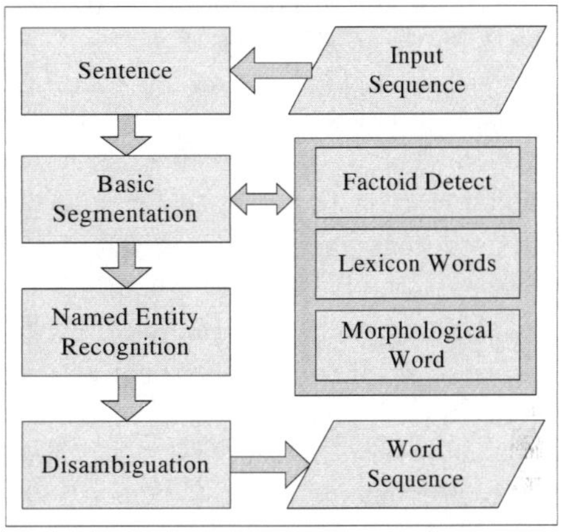

Figure 1 ELUS Segmenter and NER

The input character sequence is converted into one or several sentences, which is the basic dealing unit. The "Basic Segmentation" is used to identify the LW, FT, MDW words, and "Named Entity Recognition" is used to detect NW words. We don't adopt the New Word detection algorithm in our system in this bakeoff. The "Disambiguation" module performs to classify complicated ambiguous words, and all the above results are connected into the final result, which is denoted by XML format.

2.1 Trigram and Smoothing Algorithm

We apply the trigram model to the word segmentation task (Jiang 2005A), and make use of Absolute Smoothing algorithm to overcome the sparse data problem.

Trigram model is used to convert the sentence into a word sequence. Let $\mathbf{w} = w_1 w_2 \ldots w_n$ be a word sequence, then the most likely word sequence w* in trigram is:

$$\mathbf{w}^* = \arg\max_{w_1 w_2 \cdots w_n} \prod_{i=1}^{n} P(w_i \mid w_{i-2} w_{i-1}) \quad (1)$$

where let $P(w_0|w_{-2}\ w_{-1})$ be $P(w_0)$ and let $P(w_1|w_{-1}\ w_0)$ be $P(w_1|w_0)$, and w_i represents LW or a type of FT or MDW. In order to search the best segmentation way, all the word candidates are filled in the word lattice (Zhao 2005). And the Viterbi algorithm is used to search the best word segmentation path.

FT and MDW need to be detected when constructing word lattice (detailed in section 2.2). The data structure of lexicon can affect the efficiency of word segmentation, so we represent lexicon words as a set of TRIEs, which is a tree-like structure. Words starting with the same character are represented as a TRIE, where the root represents the first Chinese character, and the children of the root represent the second characters, and so on (Gao 2004).

When searching a word lattice, there is the zero-probability phenomenon, due to the sparse data problem. For instance, if there is no cooccurence pair "我们/吃/香蕉"(we eat bananas) in the training corpus, then P(香蕉|我们，吃) = 0. According to formula (1), the probability of the whole candidate path, which includes "我们/吃/香蕉" is zero, as a result of the local zero probability. In order to overcome the sparse data problem, our system has applied Absolute Discounting Smoothing algorithm (Chen, 1999).

$$N_{1+}(w_{i-n+1}^{i-1}\bullet) = |\{w_i : c(w_{i-n+1}^{i-1}w_i) > 0\}| \qquad (2)$$

The notation N_{1+} is meant to evoke the number of words that have one or more counts, and the • is meant to evoke a free variable that is summed over. The function $c()$ represents the count of one word or the cooccurence count of multi-words. In this case, the smoothing probability

$$p(w_i \mid w_{i-n+1}^{i-1}) = \frac{\max\{c(w_{i-n+1}^{i}) - D, 0\}}{\sum_{w_i} c(w_{i-n+1}^{i})} + (1-\lambda)p(w_i \mid w_{i-n+2}^{i-1}) \qquad (3)$$

$$\text{where, } 1-\lambda = \left(\frac{D}{\sum_{w_i} c(w_{i-n+1}^{i})} N_{1+}(w_{i-n+1}^{i-1}\bullet)\right) \qquad (4)$$

Because we use trigram model, so the maximum n may be 3. A fixed discount D ($0 \le D \le 1$) can be set through the deleted estimation on the training data. They arrive at the estimate

$$D = \frac{n_1}{n_1 + 2n_2} \qquad (5)$$

where n_1 and n_2 are the total number of n-grams with exactly one and two counts, respectively.

After the basic segmentation, some complicated ambiguous segmentation can be further disambiguated. In trigram model, only the previous two words are considered as context features, while in disambiguation processing, we can use the Maximum Entropy model fused more features (Jiang 2005B) or rule based method.

2.2 Factoid and Morphological words

All the Factoid words can be represented as regular expressions. So the detection of factoid words can be achieved by Finite State Automaton(FSA). In our system, the following categories of factoid words can be detected, as shown in table 1.

Table 1 Factoid word categories

FT type	Factoid word	Example
Number	Integer, real, percent etc.	2910, 46.12%, 二十九, 三千七百二十
Date	Date	2005年5月12日
Time	Time	8:00, 十点二十分
English	English word,	How, are, you
www	Website, IP address	http://www.hit.edu.cn 192.168.140.133
email	Email	elus@google.com
phone	Phone, fax	0451-86413322

Deterministic FSA (DFA) is efficient because a unique "next state" is determined, when given an input symbol and the current state. While it is common for a linguist to write rule, which can be represented directly as a non-deterministic FSA (NFA), i.e. which allows several "next states" to follow a given input and state.

Since every NFA has an equivalent DFA, we build a FT rule compiler to convert all the FT generative rules into a DFA. e.g.

- "< digit > -> [0..9];
- < year > ::= < digit >{< digit >+}年";
- < integer > ::= {< digit >+};

where "->" is a temporary generative rule, and "::=" is a real generative rule.

As for the morphological words, we erase the dealing module, because the word segmentation definition of our system adopts the PKU standard.

3 Named Entity Recognition

We adopt Maximum Entropy model to perform the Named Entity Recognition. The extensive evaluation on NER systems in recent years (such as CoNLL-2002 and CoNLL-2003) indicates the best statistical systems are typically achieved by using a linear (or log-linear) classification algorithm, such as Maximum Entropy model, together with a vast amount of carefully designed linguistic features. And this seems still true at present in terms of statistics based methods.

Maximum Entropy model (ME) is defined over $H \times T$ in segmentation disambiguation, where H is the set of possible contexts around target word that will be tagged, and T is the set of allowable tags, such as B-PER, I-PER, B-LOC, I-LOC etc. in our NER task. Then the model's conditional probability is defined as

$$p(t \mid h) = \frac{p(h,t)}{\sum_{t' \in T} p(h,t')} \quad (6)$$

where $p(h,t) = \pi\mu \prod_{j=1}^{k} \alpha_j^{f_j(h,t)}$ (7)

where h is the current context and t is one of the possible tags.

The several typical kinds of features can be used in the NER system. They usually include the context feature, the entity feature, and the total resource or some additional resources.

Table 2 shows the context feature templates.

Table2 NER feature template[1]

Type	Feature Template
One order feature	w_{i-2}, w_{i-1}, w_i, w_{i+1}, w_{i+2}
Two order feature	$w_{i-1:i}$, $w_{i:i+1}$
NER tag feature	t_{i-1}

While, we only point out the local feature template, some other feature templates, such as long distance dependency templates, are also helpful to NER performance. These trigger features can be collected by Average Mutual Information or Information Gain algorithm etc.

Besides context features, entity features is another important factor, such as the suffix of Location or Organization. The following 8 kinds of dictionaries are usually useful (Zhao 2006):

Table 3 NER resource dictionary[2]

List Type	Lexicon	Example
Word list	Place lexicon	北京, 纽约, 马家沟
	Chinese surname	张, 王, 赵, 欧阳
String list	Prefix of PER	老, 阿, 小
	Suffix of PLA	山, 湖, 寺, 台, 海
	Suffix of ORG	会, 联盟, 组织, 局
Character list	Character for CPER	军, 刚, 莲, 茵, 倩
	Character for FPER	科, 曼, 斯, 娃, 贝
	Rare character	滗, 胨, 薅

In addition, some external resources may improve the NER performance too, e.g. we collect a lot of entities for Chinese Daily Newspaper in 2000, and total some entity features.

However, our system is based on Peking University (PKU) word segmentation definition and PKU NER definition, so we only used the basic features in table 2 in this bakeoff. Another effect is the corpus: our system is training by the Chinese Peoples' Daily Newspaper corpora in 1998, which conforms to PKU NER definition. In the section 4, we will give our system performance with the basic features in Chinese Peoples' Daily Newspaper corpora.

[1] w_i – current word, w_{i-1} – previous word, t_i – current tag.

[2] Partial translation: 北京 BeiJing,纽约 New york;张 Zhang, 王 Wang; 老 Old;山 mountain,湖 lake;局 bureau.

4 Performance and analysis

4.1 The Evaluation in Word Segmentation

The performance of our system in the third bakeoff is presented in table 4 in terms of recall(R), precision(P) and F score in percentages. The score software is standard and open by SIGHAN.

Table 4 MSRA test in SIGHAN2006 (%)

MSRA	R	P	F	OOV	R_{oov}	R_{iv}
Close	96.3	91.8	94.0	3.4	17.5	99.1
Open	97.7	96.0	96.8	3.4	62.4	98.9

Our system has good performance in terms of R_{iv} measure. The R_{iv} measure in close test and in open test are 99.1% and 98.9% respectively. This good performance owes to class-based trigram with the absolute smoothing and word disambiguation algorithm.

In our system, it is the following reasons that the open test has a better performance than the close test:

(1) Named Entity Recognition module is added into the open test system. And Named Entities, including PER, LOC, ORG, occupy the most of the out-of-vocabulary words.

(2) The system of close test can only use the dictionary that is collected from the given training corpus, while the system of open test can use a better dictionary, which includes the words that exist in MSRA training corpus in SIGHAN2005. And we know, the dictionary is the one of important factors that affects the performance, because the LW candidates in the word lattice are generated from the dictionary.

As for the dictionary, we compare the two collections in SIGHAN2005 and SIGHAN2006, and evaluating in SIGHAN2005 MSRA close test. There are less training sentence in SIGHAN2006, as a result, there is at least 1.2% performance decrease. So this result indicates that the dictionary can bring an important impact in our system.

Table 5 gives our system performance in the second bakeoff. We'll make brief comparison.

Table 5 MSRA test in SIGHAN 2005 (%)

MSRA	R	P	F	OOV	R_{oov}	R_{iv}
Close	97.3	94.5	95.9	2.6	32.3	99.1
Open	98.0	96.5	97.2	2.6	59.0	99.0

Comparing table 4 with table 5, we find that the OOV is 3.4 in third bakeoff, which is higher than the value in the last bakeoff. Obviously, it is one of reasons that affect our performance.

In addition, based on pragmatic consideration, our system has been made some simplifier, for instance, we erase the new word detection algorithm and the is no morphological word detection.

4.2 Named Entity Recognition

In MSRA NER open test, our NER system is training in prior six-month corpora of Chinese Peoples' Daily Newspaper in 1998, which were annotated by Peking University. Table 6 shows the NER performance in the MSRA open test.

Table 6 The NER performance in MSRA Open test

MSRA NER	Precision	Recall	F Score
PER	93.68%	86.37%	89.87
LOC	85.50%	59.67%	70.29
ORG	75.87%	47.48%	58.41
Overall	86.97%	65.56%	74.76

As a result of insufficiency in preparing bake-off, our system is only trained in Chinese Peoples' Daily Newspaper, in which the NER is defined according to PKU standard. However, the NER definition of MSRA is different from that of PKU, e.g, "中华/LOC 民族", "马/PER 列/PER 主义" in MSRA, are not entities in PKU. So the training corpus becomes a main handicap to decrease the performance of our system, and it also explains that there is much difference between the recall rate and the precision in table 6.

Table 7 gives the evaluation of our NER system in Chinese Peoples' Daily Newspaper, training in prior five-month corpora and testing in the sixth month corpus. We also use the feature templates in table 2, in order to make comparison with table 6.

Table 7 The NER test in Chinese Peoples' Daily

MSRA NER	Precision	Recall	F Score
CPN	93.56	90.96	92.24
FPN	90.42	86.47	88.40
LOC	91.94	90.52	91.22
ORG	88.38	84.52	86.40
Overall	91.35	88.85	90.08

This experiment indicates that our system can have a good performance, if the test corpus and the training corpora conform to the condition of independent identically distributed attribution.

4.3 Analysis and Discussion

Some points need to be further considered:

(1) The dictionary can bring a big impact to the performance, as the LW candidates come from the dictionary. However a big dictionary can be easily acquired in the real application.

(2) Due to our technical and insufficiently preparing problem, we use the PKU NER definition, however they seem not unified with the MSRA definition.

(3) Our NER system is a word-based model, and we have find out that the word segmentation with two different dictionaries can bring a big impact to the NER performance.

(4) We erase the new word recognition algorithm in our system. While, we should explore the real annotated corpora, and add new word detection algorithm, if it has positive effect. e.g. "荷花 奖"(lotus prize) can be recognized as one word by the conditional random fields model.

5 Conclusion

We have briefly described our word segmentation system and NER system. We use word-based features in the whole processing. Our system has a good performance in terms of R_{iv} measure, so this means that the trigram model with the smoothing algorithm can deal with the basic segmentation task well. However, the result in the bakeoff indicates that detecting out-of-vocabulary word seems to be a harder task than dealing with the segmentation-ambiguity task.

The work in the future will concentrate on two sides: improving the NER performance and adding New Word Detection Algorithm.

References

HuaPing Zhang, Qun Liu etc. 2003. Chinese Lexical Analysis Using Hierarchical Hidden Markov Model, Second SIGHAN workshop affiliated with 4th ACL, Sapporo Japan, pp.63-70.

Jianfeng Gao, Mu Li et al. 2004. Chinese Word Segmentation: A Pragmatic Approach. MSR-TR-2004-123, November 2004.

Peng Fuchun, Fangfang Feng and Andrew McCallum. Chinese segmentation and new word detection using conditional random fields. In:COLING 2004.

Stanley F.Chen and J. Goodman. 1999. An empirical study of smoothing techniques for language modeling. Computer Speech and Language. 13:369-394.

Wei Jiang, Jian Zhao et al. 2005A.Chinese Word Segmentation based on Mixing Model. 4th SIGHAN Workshop. pp. 180-182.

Wei Jiang, Xiao-Long Wang, Yi Guan et al. 2005B. applying rough sets in word segmentation disambiguation based on maximum entropy model. Journal of Harbin Institute of Technology (New Series). 13(1): 94-98.

Zhao Jian. 2006. Research on Conditional Probabilistic Model and Its Application in Chinese Named Entity Recognition. Ph.D. Thesis. Harbin Institute of Technology, China.

Zhao Yan. 2005. Research on Chinese Morpheme Analysis Based on Statistic Language Model. Ph.D. Thesis. Harbin Institute of Technology, China.

NetEase Automatic Chinese Word Segmentation

Li xin **Dai shuaixiang**
NETEASE INFORMATION TECHNOLOGY (BEIJING) CO., LTD.
SP Tower D, 26th Floor, Tsinghua Science Park Building 8, No.1 Zhongguancun East Road,
Haidian District Beijing, 100084, PRC.
`lxin@corp.netease.com` `ddai@corp.netease.com`

Abstract

This document analyses the bakeoff results from *NetEase Co.* in the SIGHAN5 Word Segmentation Task and Named Entity Recognition Task. The *NetEase* WS system is designed to facilitate research in natural language processing and information retrieval. It supports Chinese and English word segmentation, Chinese named entity recognition, Chinese part of speech tagging and phrase conglutination. Evaluation result shows our WS system has a passable precision in word segmentation except for the unknown words recognition.

1 Introduction

Automatic Chinese Word Segmentation (WS) is the fundamental task of Chinese information processing [Liu, 2000].Since there are lots of works depending on the automatic segmentation of Chinese words, different Chinese NLP-enabled applications may have different requirements that call for different granularities of word segmentation. The key to accurate automatic word identification in Chinese lies in the successful resolution of those ambiguities and a proper way to handle out-of-vocabulary (OOV) words (such as person names, place names and organization name etc.).

We have applied corpus-based method to extracting various language phenomena from real texts; and have combined statistical model with rules in Chinese word segmentation, which has increased the precision of segmentation by improving ambiguous phrase segmentation and out-of-vocabulary word recognition.

In the second section of this paper, we describe a Chinese word segmentation system developed by ***NetEase***. And we present our strategies on solving the problems of ambiguous phrase segmentation and identification of Chinese people names and place names. The third section is analysis of evaluation result.

2 Modern Chinese Automatic Segmentation System

2.1 System Structure

The WS system of NETEASE CO. supports Chinese and English word segmentation, Chinese named entity recognition, Chinese part of speech tagging and phrase conglutination. In ordering to processing mass data, it is designed as an efficient system. The whole system includes some processing steps: pre-processing, number/date/time recognition, unknown words recognition, segmenting, POS tagging and post-processing, as Fig 1 shows.

The *Prehandler* module performs the pre-processing, splits the text into sentences according to the punctuations.

Number/Data/Time recognition processes the number, date, time string and English words.

Unknown word recognition includes personal name recognition and place name recognition.

Segmenter component performs word-segmenting task, matches all the candidate words and processes ambiguous lexical.

POSTagger module performs part of speech tagging task and decides the optimal word segmentation using hierarchical hidden Markov model (HHMM) [Zhang, 2003].

Posthandler retrieves phrases with multi-granularities from segmentation result and detects new words automatically etc.

2.2 Ambiguous phrase segmentation

Assume that "AJB" are character strings and that W is a word list. In the field "AJB", if "AJ" $\in$ W, and "JB" ∈ W, then "AJB" is called ambiguous phrase of overlap type. For example, in the string "*当代表*", both "*当代*" and "*代表*" are words , so "*当代表*" is an ambiguous phrase of overlap type; and there is one ambiguous string.

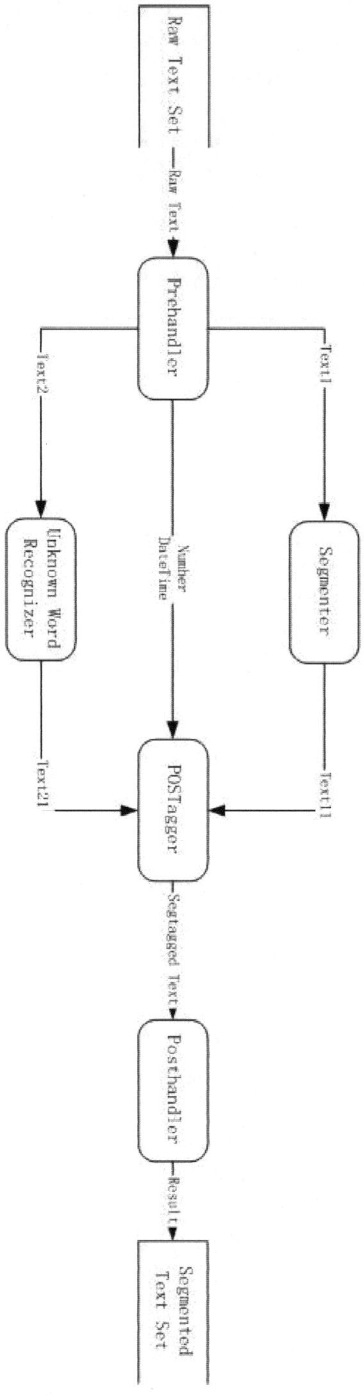

Fig 1 Structure and Components of WS

In the string "AB", if "AB" ∈ W(word), "A" ∈ W, and "B" ∈ W, then the string "AB" is called ambiguous phrase of combination type. For example, in the string "*个人*", since "*个人*", "*个*" and "*人*"are all words, so the string "*个人*" is an ambiguous phrase of combination type.

We have built an ambiguous phrase lib of overlap and combination type from tagged corpus, which contains 200,000 phrases from 1-gram to 4-gram. For example: "*才/d 能/v 创造/v, 创造/vn 作/v 准备 vn*" If one ambiguous phrase found in raw text, the potential segmentation result will be found in the lib and submit to next module. If not found, *POS tagger* module will disambiguate it.

2.3 Chinese Personal Name Recognition

At present we only consider the recognition of normal people name with both a family name and a first name. We got the statistical Character Set of Family Name and First Name data from corpus. And also consider the ability of character of constructing word. Some characters itself cannot be regarded as a word or composes a word with other characters, such as "*邓,聂,鑫*"; Some name characters which can compose word with other characters only, e.g. "*刘，张，英*" can construct words "*刘海儿，一张纸，英雄*";Some name characters are also a common words themselves, e.g. "*汤，马*" .

The recognition procedure is as follows:

1) Find the potential Chinese personal names: Family name is the trigger. Whenever a family name is found in a text, its following word is taken as a first name word, or its following two characters as the head character and the tail character of a first name. Then the family name and its following make a potential people name, the probable largest length of which is 4 when it is composed of a double-character family name and a double-character first name.

2) Based on the constructing word rules and the protective rules, sift the potential people names for the first time. For example, when raw text is "*三张…,五周…*", then the "*张,周*" were not family name. Because the "*三,五*" is number.

3) Compute the probabilities of the potential name and the threshold values of corresponding family names, then sift the people names again based on the personal name probability function and description rules.

4) According to the left-boundary rules and the right-boundary rules which base on title, for

example, "*总统, 学员*", and name frequent of context, determine the boundaries of people names.

5) Negate conflicting potential people names.

6) Output the result: The output contains every sentence in the processed text and the start and the end positions and the reliability values of all people names in it.

2.4 Chinese Place Name Recognition

By collecting a large scale of place names, For example, (1) The names of administrative regions superior to county; (2) The names of inhabitation areas; (3) The names of geographic entities, such as mountain, river, lake, sea, island etc.; (4) Other place names, e.g. monument, ruins, bridge and power station etc. building the place name dictionary.

Collecting words that can symbolize a place, e.g. "*地区*" , "*城市*" , "*乡*" etc.

Base on these knowledge we applied positive deduction mechanism. Its essence is that with reference to certain control strategies, a rule is selected; then examining whether the fact matches the condition of the rule, if it does, the rule will be triggered.

In addition, Those words that often concurrent with a place name are collected , including: "*在*" , "*位于*" etc. And which often concurrent with a people name, such as "*同志*" , "*说*" and so on, are also considered in NER.

WS system identifies all potential place names in texts by using place name base and gathers their context information; and through deduction, it utilizes rule set and knowledge base to confirm or negate a potential place name; hereupon, the remainders are recognized place name.

2.5 Multi-granularities of word segmentation

Whenever we deploy the *segmenter* for any application, we need to customize the output of the *segmenter* according to an application specific standard, which is not always explicitly defined. However, it is often implicitly defined in a given amount of application data (for example, Search engines log, Tagged corpus) from which the specific standard can be partially learned.

Most variability in word segmentation across different standards comes from those words that are not typically stored in the basic dictionary. To meet the applications of different levels, in our system, the standard adaptation is conducted by a post-processor which performs an ordered list of transformations on the output. For example: When input is "*国务院安全生产专家组*", the output will be:

1. "*国务院/安全/ 生产/ 专家组*"
2. "*国务院/安全生产/ 专家组*"
3. "*国务院/安全生产专家组*"

Result 1 is normal segmentation, also is minimum granularity of word. Result 2 and 3 is bigger granularity. Every application can select appropriate segmentation result according to its purpose.

3 Test results

The speed of *NetEase* WS system is about 1500KB/s--300KB/s in different algorithm and p4-2.8/512M computer. In SigHan5, the F-MEASURE of our word segmentation is 0.924, the IN Recall is 0.959, but OOV Recall Rate is only 0.656. This indicates that our unknown words recognition is poor; it makes a bad impact on the segmented result. It also shows our system should be improved largely in unknown words recognition. For example:

1. Name Entity Recognize: "*贝尔格勒, 中村植秀, 秋丽玲*" were falsely segment to "*贝/尔格/勒), 中村/植/秀, 秋/丽/玲*".

2. Name Entity Ambiguous: "*向/ 瑞典/LOC*" are falsely recognized "*向瑞典/PER*".

3. Abbreviations of phrase: "*所国 (所罗门)*" was segment to "*所/国*".

4. New Word: "*原著民, 宿求, 休职*"

5. Standard of Word: we think "*文化大革命*" and "*圣诞老人*" is one word, but criterion is "*文化/大/革命*", "*圣诞/老人*" etc.

In evaluation, our system's TOTAL INSERTIONS is 5292 and TOTAL DELETIONS is 2460. The result show: our WS usually segment out "shorter word", for example, "*工商企业界*", and "*血液循环*" is segmented to "*工商/企业/界*", "*血液/循环*" . But not every string is one word.

Much work needs to be done to evaluate this WS system more thoroughly. Refined pre-processing or post-processing steps could also help improve segmentation accuracy.

For example, pre-processing will split ASCII string and Chinese character, so "*DD6112H6 型, ic 卡, b p 机*" will falsely segment "*DD6112H6/ 型, ic/卡, b p/机*"; In post-processing, by using consecutive single characters "*狭/持, 败/击*" to detect the valid out-of-vocabulary words "*狭持, 败击*' also is good idea.

References

Kaiying Liu. *Automatic Chinese Word Segmentation and POS Tagging*. Business Publishing House. Beijing. 2000.

Hua-Ping Zhang etc. *Chinese Lexical Analysis Using Hierarchical Hidden Markov Model.* Second SIGHAN workshop affiliated with 41th ACL, Sapporo Japan, July, 2003, pp. 63-70

N-gram Based Two-Step Algorithm for Word Segmentation

Dong-Hee Lim
Dept. of Computer Science
Kookmin University
Seoul 136-702, Korea
nlp@cs.kookmin.ac.kr

Kyu-Baek, Hwang
School of Computing
Soongsil University
Seoul 156-743, Korea
kbhwang@ssu.ac.kr

Seung-Shik Kang
Dept. of Computer Science
Kookmin University
Seoul 136-702, Korea
sskang@kookmin.ac.kr

Abstract

This paper describes an n-gram based reinforcement approach to the closed track of word segmentation in the third Chinese word segmentation bakeoff. Character n-gram features of unigram, bigram, and trigram are extracted from the training corpus and its frequencies are counted. We investigated a step-by-step methodology by using the n-gram statistics. In the first step, relatively definite segmentations are fixed by the tight threshold value. The remaining tags are decided by considering the left or right space tags that are already fixed in the first step. Definite and loose segmentation are performed simply based on the bigram and trigram statistics. In order to overcome the data sparseness problem of bigram data, unigram is used for the smoothing.

1 Introduction

Word segmentation has been one of the very important problems in the Chinese language processing. It is a necessary in the information retrieval system for the Korean language (Kang and Woo, 2001; Lee et al, 2002). Though Korean words are separated by white spaces, many web users often do not set a space in a sentence when they write a query at the search engine. Another necessity of automatic word segmentation is the index term extraction from a sentence that includes word spacing errors.

The motivation of this research is to investigate a practical word segmentation system for the Korean language. While we develop the system, we found that ngram-based algorithm was exactly applicable to the Chinese word segmentation and we have participated the bakeoff (Kang and Lim, 2005). The bakeoff result is not satisfiable, but it is acceptable because our method is language independent that does not consider the characteristics of the Chinese language. We do not use any language dependent features except the average length of Chinese words.

Another advantage of our approach is that it can express the ambiguous word boundaries that are error-prone. So, there are a good possibility of improving the performance if language dependent functionalities are added such as proper name, numeric expression recognizer, and the postprocessing of single character words.[1]

2 N-gram Features

The n-gram features in this work are similar to the previous one in the second bakeoff. The basic segmentation in (Kang and Lim, 2005) has performed by bigram features together with space tags, and the trigram features has been used as a postprocessing of correcting the segmentation errors. Trigrams for postprocessing are the ones that are highly biased to one type of the four tag features of "A_iB_jC".[2] In addition, unigram features are used for smoothing the bigram, where bigram is not found in the training corpora. In this current work, we extended the n-gram features to a trigram.

(a) trigram: A_iB_jC
(b) bigram: $_iA_jB_k$
(c) unigram: $_iA_j$

In the above features, AB and ABC are a Chinese character sequence of bigram and trigram, respectively. The subscripts i, j, and k

[1] Single character words in Korean are not so common, compared to the Chinese language. We can control the occurrence of them through an additional processing.

[2] We applied the trigrams for error correction in which one of the trigram feature occupies 95% or more.

denote word space tags, where the tags are marked as 1(space tag) and 0(non-space tag). For the unigram ${}_iA_j$, four types of tag features are calculated in the training corpora and their frequencies are stored. In the same way, eight types of bigram features and four types of trigram features are constructed. If we take all the inside and outside space-tags of ABC, there are sixteen types of trigram features ${}_hA_iB_jC_k$ for $h,i,j,k = 0$ *or* 1. It will cause a data sparseness problem, especially for small-sized training corpora. In order to avoid the data sparseness problem, we ignored the outside-space tags h and k and constructed four types of trigram features of A_iB_jC.

Table 1 shows the number of n-gram features for each corpora. The total number of unique trigrams for CITYU corpus is 1,341,612 in which 104,852 trigrams occurred more than three times. It is less than one tenth of the total number of trigrams. N-gram feature is a compound feature of <character, space-tag> combination. Trigram classes are distinguished by the space-tag context, trigram class ${}_hA_iB_jC_k$ is named as t4-trigram or C3T4.[3] It is simplified into four classes of C3T2 trigrams of A_iB_jC, in consideration of the memory space savings and the data sparseness problem.

Table 1. The number of n-gram features

	Trigram				Bigram	Unigram
	freq≥1	freq≥2	freq≥3	freq≥4	freq≥1	freq≥1
cityu	1341612	329764	165360	104852	404411	5112
ckip	2951274	832836	444012	296372	717432	6121
msra	986338	252656	132456	86391	303443	4767
upuc	463253	96860	45775	28210	177140	4293

3 Word Segmentation Algorithm

Word segmentation is defined as to choose the best tag-sequence for a sentence.

$$\hat{T} = \arg\max_{T \in \tau} P(T \mid S)$$

where

$$T = t_1, t_2, \ldots, t_n \text{ and } S = c_1, c_2, \ldots, c_n$$

More specifically at each character position, the algorithm determines a space-tag '0' or '1' by using the word spacing features.

3.1 The Features

We investigated a two step algorithm of determining space tags in each character position of a sentence using by context dependent n-gram features. It is based on the assumption that space tags depend on the left and right context of characters together with the space tags that it accompanies. Let t_ic_i be a current <space tag, character> pair in a sentence.[4]

$$\ldots\ t_{i-2}c_{i-2}\ t_{i-1}c_{i-1}\ \mathbf{t_i}c_i\ t_{i+1}c_{i+1}\ t_{i+2}c_{i+2}\ \ldots$$

In our previous work of (Lim and Kang, 2005), n-gram features (a) and (b) are used. These features are used to determine the space tag t_i. In this work, core n-gram feature is a C3T2 classes of trigram features $c_{i-2}t_{i-1}c_{i-1}\mathbf{t_i}c_i$, $c_{i-1}\mathbf{t_i}c_it_{i+1}c_{i+1}$. In addition, a simple character trigram with no space tag "$\mathbf{t_i}c_ic_{i+1}c_{i+2}$" is added.

(a) unigram:

$t_{i-1}c_{i-1}\mathbf{t_i}$, $\mathbf{t_i}c_it_{i+1}$

(b) bigram:

$t_{i-2}c_{i-2}t_{i-1}c_{i-1}\mathbf{t_i}$, $t_{i-1}c_{i-1}\mathbf{t_i}c_it_{i+1}$, $\mathbf{t_i}c_it_{i+1}c_{i+1}t_{i+2}$

(c) trigram:

$c_{i-2}t_{i-1}c_{i-1}\mathbf{t_i}c_i$, $c_{i-1}\mathbf{t_i}c_it_{i+1}c_{i+1}$, $\mathbf{t_i}c_ic_{i+1}c_{i+2}$

Extended n-gram features with space tags are effective when left or right tags are fixed. Suppose that t_{i-1} and t_{i+1} are definitely set to 0 in a bigram context "$t_{i-1}c_{i-1}\mathbf{t_i}c_it_{i+1}$", then a feature "$0c_{i-1}\mathbf{t_i}c_i0$"($t_i$ = 0 or 1) is applied, instead of a simple feature "$c_{i-1}\mathbf{t_i}c_i$". However, none of the space tags are fixed in the beginning that simple character n-gram features with no space tag are used.[5]

3.2 Two-step Algorithm

The basic idea of our method is a cross checking the n-gram features in the space position by using three trigram features. For a character sequence "$c_{i-2}c_{i-1}\mathbf{t_i}c_ic_{i+1}c_{i+2}$", we can set a space mark '1' to t_i, if $P(t_i=1)$ is greater than $P(t_i=0)$ in all the three trigram features $c_{i-2}c_{i-1}\mathbf{t_i}c_i$, $c_{i-1}\mathbf{t_i}c_ic_{i+1}$, and $\mathbf{t_i}c_i c_{i+1}c_{i+2}$. Because no space tags are determined in

[3] 'Cn' refers to the number of characters and 'Tn' refers to the number of spae-tag. According to this notation, ${}_iA_jB_k$ and ${}_iA_j$ are expressed as C2T3 and C1T2, respectively.

[4] Tag t_i is located before the character, not after the character that is common in other tagging problem like POS-tagging.

[5] Simple n-grams with no space tags are calculated from the extended n-grams.

the beginning, word segmentation is performed in two steps. In the first step, simple n-gram features are applied with strong threshold values (t_{low1} and t_{high1} in Table 2). The space tags with high confidence are determined and the remaining space tags will be set in the next step.

Table 2. Strong and weak threshold values[6]

	t_{low1}	t_{high1}	t_{low2}	t_{high2}	t_{final}
cityu	0.36	0.69	0.46	0.51	0.48
ckip	0.37	0.69	0.49	0.51	0.49
msra	0.33	0.68	0.46	0.47	0.46
upuc	0.38	0.69	0.45	0.47	0.47

In the second step, extended bigram features are applied if any one of the left or right space tags is fixed in the first step. Otherwise, simple bigram probability will be applied, too. In this step, extended bigram features are applied with weak threshold values t_{low2} and t_{high2}. The space tags are determined by the final threshold t_{final}, if it was not determined by weak threshold values. Considering the fact that average length of Chinese words is about 1.6, the threshold values are lowered or highered.[7]

In the final step, error correction is performed by 4-gram error correction dictionary. It is constructed by running the training corpus and comparing the result to the answer. Error correction data format is 4-gram. If a 4-gram $c_{i-2}c_{i-1}c_ic_{i+1}$ is found in a sentence, then tag t_i is modified unconditionally as is specified in the 4-gram dictionary.

4 Experimental Results

We evaluated our system in the closed task on all four corpora. Table 3 shows the final results in bakeoff 2006. We expect that R_{oov} will be improved if any unknown word processing is performed. R_{iv} can also be improved if lexicon is applied to correct the segmentation errors.

Table 3. Final results in bakeoff 2006

	R	P	F	R_{oov}	R_{iv}
cityu	0.950	0.949	0.949	0.638	0.963
ckip	0.937	0.933	0.935	0.547	0.954
msra	0.933	0.939	0.936	0.526	0.948
upuc	0.915	0.896	0.905	0.565	0.949

4.1 Step-by-step Analysis

In order to analyze the effectiveness of each step, we counted the number of space positions for sentence by sentence. If the number of characters in a sentence is n, then the number of words positions is $(n-1)$ because we ignored the first tag t_0 for c_0. Table 4 shows the number of space positions in four test corpora.

Table 4. The number of space positions

	# of space positions	# of spaces	# of non-spaces
cityu	356,791	212,662	144,129
ckip	135,123	80,387	54,736
msra	168,236	95,995	72,241
upuc	251,418	149,747	101,671

As we expressed in section 3, we assumed that trigram with space tag information will determine most of the space tags. Table 5 shows the application rate with strong threshold values. As we expected, around 93.8%~95.9% of total space tags are set in step-1 with the error rate 1.5%~2.8%.

Table 5. N-gram results with strong threshold

	# of applied (%)	# of errors (%)
cityu	342,035 (95.9%)	5,024 (1.5%)
ckip	128,081 (94.8%)	2,818 (2.2%)
msra	160,437 (95.4%)	3,155 (2.0%)
upuc	235,710 (93.8%)	6,601 (2.8%)

Table 6 shows the application rate of n-gram with weak threshold values in step-2. The space tags that are not determined in step-1 are set in the second step. The error rate in step-2 is 24.3%~30.1%.

Table 6. N-gram results with weak threshold

	# of applied (%)	# of errors (%)
cityu	14,756 (4.1%)	3,672 (24.9%)
ckip	7,042 (5.2%)	1,710 (24.3%)
msra	7,799 (4.6%)	2,349 (30.1%)
upuc	15,708 (6.3%)	4,565 (29.1%)

[6] Threshold values are optimized for each training corpus.
[7] The average length of Korean words is 3.2 characters.

4.2 4-gram Error Correction

We examined the effectiveness of 4-gram error correction. The number of 4-grams that is extracted from training corpora is about 10,000 to 15,000. We counted the number of space tags that are modified by 4-gram error correction dictionary. Table 7 shows the number of modified space tags and the negative effects of 4-gram error correction. Table 8 shows the results before error correction. When compared with the final results in Table 3, F-measure is slightly lower than the final results.

Table 7. Modified space tags by error correction

	# of modified space tags (%)	Modification errors (%)
cityu	418 (0.1%)	47 (11.2%)
ckip	320 (0.2%)	94 (29.4%)
msra	778 (0.5%)	153 (19.7%)
upuc	178 (0.1%)	61 (34.3%)

Table 8. Results before error correction

	R	P	F
cityu	0.948	0.947	0.948
ckip	0.935	0.931	0.933
msra	0.930	0.930	0.930
upuc	0.915	0.895	0.905

5 Conclusion

We described a two-step word segmentation algorithm as a result of the closed track in bakeoff 2006. The algorithm is based on the cross validation of the word spacing probability by using n-gram features of <character, space-tag>. One of the advantages of our system is that it can show the self-confidence score for ambiguous or feature-conflict cases. We have not applied any language dependent resources or functionalities such as lexicons, numeric expressions, and proper name recognition. We expect that our approach will be helpful for the detection of error-prone tags and the construction of error correction dictionaries when we develop a practical system. Furthermore, the proposed algorithm has been applied to the Korean language and we achieved a good improvement on proper names, though overall performance is similar to the previous method.

Acknowledgements

This work was supported by the Korea Science and Engineering Foundation(KOSEF) through Advaned Information Technology Research Center(AITrc).

References

Asahara, M., C. L. Go, X. Wang, and Y. Matsumoto, Combining Segmenter and Chunker for Chinese Word Segmentation, Proceedings of the 2nd SIGHAN Workshop on Chinese Language Processing, pp.144-147, 2003.

Chen, A., Chinese Word Segmentation Using Minimal Linguistic Knowledge, SIGHAN 2003, pp.148-151, 2003.

Gao, J., M. Li, and C.N. Huang, Improved Source-Channel Models for Chinese Word Segmentation, ACL 2003, pp.272-279, 2003.

Kang, S. S. and C. W. Woo, Automatic Segmentation of Words using Syllable Bigram Statistics, Proceedings of NLPRS'2001, pp.729-732, 2001.

Kang, S. S. and D. H. Lim, Data-driven Language Independent Word Segmentation Using Character-Level Information, Proceedings of the 4th SIGHAN Workshop on Chinese Language Processing, pp.158-160, 2005.

Lee D. G, S. Z. Lee, and H. C. Rim, H. S. Lim, Automatic Word Spacing Using Hidden Markov Model for Refining Korean Text Corpora, Proc. of the 3rd Workshop on Asian Language Resources and International Standardization, pp.51-57, 2002.

Maosong, S., S. Dayang, and B. K. Tsou, Chinese Word Segmentation without Using Lexicon and Hand-crafted Training Data, Proceedings of the 17th International Conference on Computational Linguistics (Coling'98), pp.1265-1271, 1998.

Nakagawa, T., Chinese and Japanese Word Segmentation Using Word-Level and Character-Level Information, COLING'04., pp.466-472, 2004.

Ng, H.T. and J.K. Low, Chinese Part-of-Speech Tagging: One-at-a-Time or All-at-Once? Word-Based or Character-Based, EMNLP'04, pp.277-284, 2004.

Shim, K. S., Automated Word-Segmentation for Korean using Mutual Information of Syllables, Journal of KISS: Software and Applications, pp.991-1000, 1996.

Sproat, R. and T. Emerson, The First International Chinese Word Segmentation Bakeoff, SIGHAN 2003.

Chinese Word Segmentation based on an Approach of Maximum Entropy Modeling

Yan Song[1] **Jiaqing Guo**[1] **Dongfeng Cai**[2]
Natural Language Processing Lab
Shenyang Institute of Aeronautical Engineering
Shenyang, 110034, China
1.{mattsure,guojiaqing}@gmail.com
2.cdf@ge-soft.com

Abstract

In this paper, we described our Chinese word segmentation system for the 3rd SIGHAN Chinese Language Processing Bakeoff Word Segmentation Task. Our system deal with the Chinese character sequence by using the Maximum Entropy model, which is fully automatically generated from the training data by analyzing the character sequences from the training corpus. We analyze its performance on both closed and open tracks on Microsoft Research (MSRA) and University of Pennsylvania and University of Colorado (UPUC) corpus. It is shown that we can get the results just acceptable without using dictionary. The conclusion is also presented.

1 Introduction

In the 3rd SIGHAN Chinese Language Processing Bakeoff Word Segmentation Task, we participated in both closed and open tracks on Microsoft Research corpus (MSRA for short) and University of Pennsylvania and University of Colorado corpus (UPUC for short). The following sections described how our system works and presented the results and analysis. Finally, the conclusion is presented with discussions of the system.

2 System Overview

Using Maximum Entropy approach for Chinese Word Segmentation is not a fresh idea, some previous works (Xue and Shen, 2003; Low, Ng and Guo, 2005) have got good performance in this field. But what we consider in the process of Segmentation is another way. We treat the input text which need to be segmented as a sequence of the Chinese characters, The segment process is, in fact, to find where we should split the character sequence. The point is to get the segment probability between 2 Chinese characters, which is different from dealing with the character itself.

In this section, training and segmentation process of the system is described to show how our system works.

2.1 Pre-Process of Training

For the first step we find the Minimal Segment Unit (MSU for short) of a text fragment in the training corpus. A MSU is a character or a string which is the minimal unit in a text fragment that cannot be segmented any more. According to the corpus, all of the MSUs can be divided into 5 type classes: "C" - Chinese Character (such as "你" and "好"), "AB" - alphabetic string (such as "SIGHAN"), "EN" - digit string (such as "1234567"), "CN" - Chinese number string (such as "一百二十") and "P" - punctuation ("，", "。", "；", etc). Besides the classes above, we define a tag "NL" as a special MSU, which refers to the beginning or ending of a text fragment. So, any MSU u can be described as: $u \in C \cup AB \cup EN \cup CN \cup P \cup \{NL\}$. In order to check the capability of the pure Maximum Entropy model, in closed tracks, we didn't have any type of classes, the MSU here is every character of the text fragment, $u \in C' \cup \{NL\}$. For instance, "我们参加了SIGHAN2006分词大赛。" is segmented into these MSUs: "我/们/参/加/了/S/I/G/H/A/N/2/0/0/6/分/词/大/赛/。".

Once we get all the MSUs of a text fragment, we can get the value of the Nexus Coefficient (NC for short) of any 2 adjacent MSUs according to the training corpus. The set of NC value can be described as: $NC \in \{0, 1\}$, where 0 means those 2 MSUs are segmented and 1 means they are not segmented (Roughly, we appoint $r = 0$ if either one of the 2 adjacent MSUs is NL). For example, the NC value of these 2 MSUs "你" and "好" in the text fragment "你好" is 0 since these 2 characters is segmented according to the training corpus.

2.2 Training

Since the segmentation is to obtain NC value of any 2 adjacent MSUs (here we call the interspace of the 2 adjacent MSUs a check point, illustrated below),

$$\ldots \mathrm{U}_{-3}\,\mathrm{U}_{-2}\;\mathrm{U}_{-1}\;\mathrm{U}_{+1}\,\mathrm{U}_{+2}\,\mathrm{U}_{+3}\ldots$$

↑
Check Point of U_{-1} and U_{+1}

we built a tool to extract the feature as follows:

(α) $U_{-3}, U_{-2}, U_{-1}, U_{+1}, U_{+2}, U_{+3}$
(β) $U_{-1}U_{+1}$
(γ) $r_{-2}r_{-1}$
(δ) $U_{-3}r_{-2}, U_{-2}r_{-1}$
(ϵ) $r_{-2}U_{-2}, r_{-1}U_{-1}$

In these features above, U_{+n} (U_{-n}) refers to the following (previous) n MSU of the check point with the information of relative position (Intuitively, We consider the same MSU has different effect on the NC value of the check point when its relative position is different to check point). And $U_{-1}U_{+1}$ is the 2 adjacent MSUs of the check point. $r_{-2}r_{-1}$ is the NC value of the previous 2 check points. Similarly, the (δ) and (ϵ) features represent the MSUs with their adjacent r. For instance, in the sentence 我是一个中国人, we can extract these features for the check point between the MSU 我 and 是:

(α) *NL*$_{-3}$,*NL*$_{-2}$,我$_{-1}$,是$_{+1}$,一$_{+2}$,个$_{+3}$,
(β) 我$_{-1}$是$_{+1}$
(γ) *00* (because 我 is the boundary of the sentence)
(δ) NL_{-3}*0*,NL_{-2}*0*
(ϵ) *0*NL_{-2},*0*我$_{-1}$

and also these features for the check point between the MSU 个 and 中:

(α) 是$_{-3}$,一$_{-2}$,个$_{-1}$,中$_{+1}$,国$_{+2}$,人$_{+3}$
(β) 个$_{-1}$中$_{+1}$

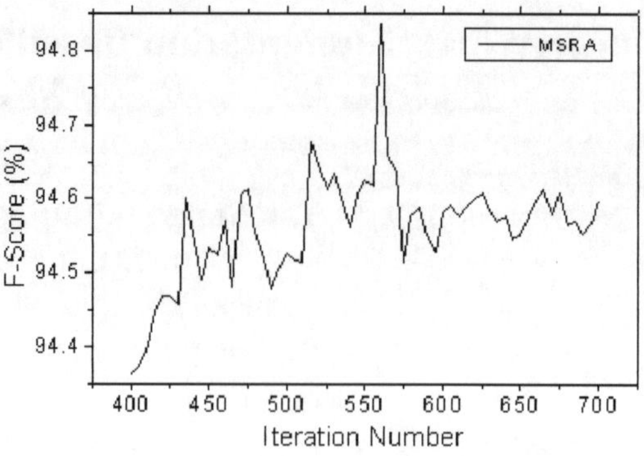

Figure 1: MSRA training curve

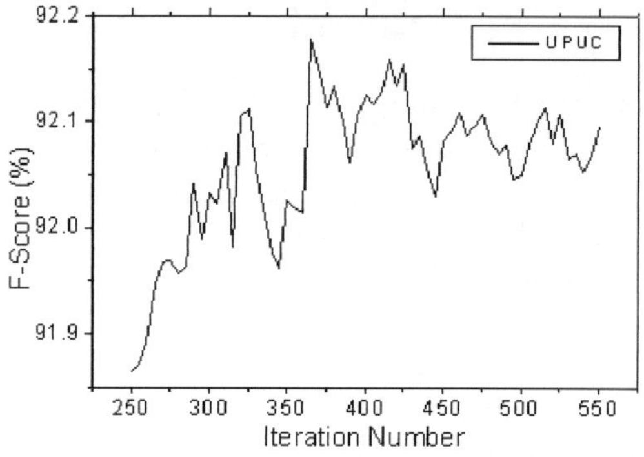

Figure 2: UPUC training curve

(γ) *01* (for UPUC corpus, here the value is 00 since 一个 is segmented into 2 characters, but in MSRA corpus, 一个 is treated as a word)
(δ) 是$_{-3}$*0*,一$_{-2}$*1*
(ϵ) *0*一$_{-2}$,*1*个$_{-1}$

After the extraction of the features, we use the ZhangLe's Maximum Entropy Toolkit[1] to train the model with a feature cutoff of 1. In order to get the best number of iteration, 9/10 of the training data is used to train the model, and the other 1/10 portion of the training data is used to evaluate the model. Figure 1 and 2 show the results of the evaluation on MSRA and UPUC corpus.

From the figures we can see the best iteration number range from 555 to 575 for MSRA corpus, and 360 to 375 for UPUC corpus. So we decide the iteration for 560 rounds for MSRA tracks and 365 rounds for UPUC tracks, respectively.

2.3 Segmentation

As we mentioned in the beginning of this section, the segmentation is the process to obtain the value

[1]Download from http://maxent.sourceforge.net

of every NC in a text fragment. This process is similar to the training process. Firstly, We scan the text fragment from start to end to get all of the MSUs. Then we can extract all of the features from the text fragment and decide which check point we should tag as $r = 0$ by this equation:

$$p(r|c) = \frac{1}{Z} \prod_{j=1}^{K} \alpha_j^{f_j(r|c)} \quad (1)$$

where K is the number of features, Z is the normalization constant used to ensure that a probability distribution results, and c represents the context of the check point. α_j is the weight for feature f_j, here $\{\alpha_1\alpha_2 \ldots \alpha_K\}$ is generated by the training data. We then compute $P(r = 0|c)$ and $P(r = 1|c)$ by the equation (1).

After one check point is treated with value of r, the system shifts backward to the next check point until all of the check point in the whole text fragment are treated. And by calculating:

$$P = \prod_{i=1}^{n-1} p(r_i|c_i) = \prod_{i=1}^{n-1} \frac{1}{Z} \prod_{j=1}^{K} \alpha_j^{f_k(r_i|c_i)} \quad (2)$$

to get an r sequence which can maximize P. From this process we can see that the sequence is, in fact, a second-order Markov Model. Thus it is easily to think about more tags prior to the check point (as an nth-order Markov Model) to get more accuracy, but in this paper we only use the previous 2 tags from the check point.

2.4 Identification of New words

We perform the new word(s) identification as a post-process by check the word formation power (WFP) of characters. The WFP of a character is defined as: $WFP(c) = N_{wc}/N_c$, where N_{wc} is the number of times that the character c appears in a word of at least 2 characters in the training corpus, N_c is the number of times the character c occurs in the training corpus. After a text fragment is segmented by our system, we extract all consecutive single characters. If at least 2 consecutive characters have the WFP larger than our threshold of 0.88, we polymerize them together as a word. For example, “州务卿” is a new word which is segmented as “州/务/卿” by our system, WFP of these 3 characters is 0.9517,0.9818 and 1.0 respectively, then they are polymerized as one word.

Besides the WFP, during the experiments, we find that the Maximum Entropy model can polymerize some MSUs as a new word (We call it polymerization characteristic of the model), such as 闻风而动 in the training corpus, we can extract 闻风而 as the previous context feature of the check point after 而, in another string 嘎然而止, we can extract the backward context 止 of the check point after 而 with $r = 1$. Then in the test, a new word 闻风而止 is recognized by the model since 闻风而 and 止 are polymerized if 而止 appears together a large number of times in the training corpus.

3 Performance analysis

Here Table 1 illustrates the results of all 4 tracks we participate. The first column is the track name, and the 2nd column presents the Recall (R), the 3rd column the Precision (P), the 4th column is F-measure (F). The R_{oov} refers to the recall of the out-of-vocabulary words and the R_{iv} refers to the recall of the words in training corpus.

Track	R	P	F	R_{oov}	R_{iv}
MSRA Closed	0.923	0.929	0.926	0.554	0.936
MSRA Open	0.938	0.946	0.942	0.706	0.946
UPUC Closed	0.902	0.887	0.895	0.568	0.934
UPUC Open	0.926	0.906	0.917	0.660	0.954

Table 1: Results of our system in 4 tracks.

3.1 Closed tracks

For all of the closed tracks, we perform the segmentation as we mentioned in the section above, without any class defined. Every MSU we extract from the training data is a character, which may be a Chinese character, an English letter or a single digit. We extract the features based on this kind of MSUs to generate the models. The results show these models are not precise.

For the UPUC closed track, the official released training data is rather small. Then the capability of the model is limited, this is the most reasonable negative effect on our F-measure 0.895.

3.2 Open tracks

The primary change between open tracks and closed tracks is that we have classified 5 classes (“C”,“AB”,“EN”,“CN” and “P”) to MSUs in order to improve the accuracy of the model. The classification really works and affects the performance of the system in a great deal. As this text fragment 1998年 can be recognized as (EN)(C), which can also presents 1644年, thus 1644年 can be easily recognized though there is no 1664年 in the training data.

The training corpus we used in UPUC open track is the same as in UPUC closed track. With those 5 classes, it is easily seen that the F-measure increased by 2.2% in the open tracks.

For the MSRA open track, we adjust the class "P" by removing the punctuation "、" from the class, because in the MSRA corpus, "、" can be a part of a organization name, such as "、" in "中俄友好、和平与发展委员会". Besides, we add the Microsoft Research training data of SIGHAN bakeoff 2005 as extended training corpus. The larger training data cooperate with the classification method, the F-measure of the open track increased to 0.942 as comparison with 0.926 of closed track.

3.3 Discussion of the tracks

Through the tracks, we tested the performance by using the pure Maximum Entropy model in closed tracks and run with the improved model with classified MSUs in open tracks. It is shown that the pure model without any additional methods can hardly make us satisfied, for the open tracks, the model with classes are just acceptable in segmentation.

In both closed and open tracks, we use the same new word identification process, and with the polymerization characteristic of the model, we find the R_{oov} is better than we expected.

On the other hand, in our system, there is no dictionary used as we described in the sections above, the R_{iv} of each track shows that affects the system performance.

Another factor affects our system in the UPUC tracks is the wrongly written characters. Consider that our system is based on the sequence of characters, this kind of mistake is fatal. For example, in the sentence 他们无愧于最可爱的人的美喻, where 美誉 is written as 美喻. The model cannot recognize it since 美喻 didn't occur in the training corpus. In the step of new word identification, the WFPs of the 2 characters 美，喻 are 0.8917 and 0.8310, thus they are wrongly segmented into 2 single characters while they are treated as a word in the gold standard corpus. Therefore, we believe the results can increase if there are no such mistakes in the test data.

4 Conclusion

We propose an approach to Chinese word segmentation by using Maximum Entropy model, which focuses on the nexus relationship of any 2 adjacent MSUs in a text fragment. We tested our system with pure Maximum Entropy models and models with simplex classification method. Compare with the pure models, the models with classified MSUs show us better performances. However, the Maximum Entropy models of our system still need improvement if we want to achieve higher performance. In future works, we will consider using more training data and add some hybrid methods with pre- and post-processes to improve the system.

Acknowledgements

We would like to thank all the colleagues of our Lab. Without their encouragement and help, this work cannot be accomplished in time.

This is our first time to participate such an international bakeoff. There are a lot of things we haven't experienced ever before, but with the enthusiastic help from the organizers, we can come through the task. Especially, We wish to thank Gina-Anne Levow for her patience and immediate reply for any of our questions, and we also thank Olivia Kwong for the advice of paper submission.

References

Nianwen Xue and Libin Shen. 2003. *Chinese Word Segmentation as LMR tagging*. In Proceedings of the Second SIGHAN Workshop on Chinese Language Processing, p176-179.

Maosong Sun, Ming Xiao, B K Tsou. 2004. *Chinese Word Segmentation without Using Dictionary Based on Unsupervised Learning Strategy*. Chinese Journal of Computers, Vol.27, #6, p736-742.

Jin Kiat Low, Hwee Tou Ng and Wenyuan Guo. 2005. *A Maximum Entropy Approach to Chinese Word Segmentation*. In Proceedings of the Fourth SIGHAN Workshop on Chinese Language Processing, p161-164.

Using Part-of-Speech Reranking to Improve Chinese Word Segmentation

Mengqiu Wang **Yanxin Shi**
Language Technologies Institute
School of Computer Science
Carnegie Mellon University
Pittsburgh, PA 15213, USA
{mengqiu,yanxins}@cs.cmu.edu

Abstract

Chinese word segmentation and Part-of-Speech (POS) tagging have been commonly considered as two separated tasks. In this paper, we present a system that performs Chinese word segmentation and POS tagging simultaneously. We train a segmenter and a tagger model separately based on linear-chain Conditional Random Fields (CRF), using lexical, morphological and semantic features. We propose an approximated joint decoding method by reranking the N-best segmenter output, based POS tagging information. Experimental results on SIGHAN Bakeoff dataset and Penn Chinese Treebank show that our reranking method significantly improve both segmentation and POS tagging accuracies.

1 Introduction

Word segmentation and Part-of-speeching (POS) tagging are the most fundamental tasks in Chinese natural language processing (NLP). Traditionally, these two tasks were treated as separate and independent processing steps chained together in a pipeline. In such pipeline systems, errors introduced at the early stage cannot be easily recovered in later steps, causing a cascade of errors and eventually harm overall performance. Intuitively, a correct segmentation of the input sentence is more likely to give rise to a correct POS tagging sequence than an incorrect segmentation. Hinging on this idea, one way to avoid error propagation in chaining subtasks such as segmentation and POS tagging is to exploit the *learning transfer* (Sutton and McCallum, 2005) among subtasks, typically through joint inference. Sutton et al. (2004) presented dynamic conditional random fields (DCRF), a generalization of the traditional linear-chain CRF that allow representation of interaction among labels. They used loopy belief propagation for inference approximation. Their empirical results on the joint task of POS tagging and NP-chunking suggested that DCRF gave superior performance over cascaded linear-chain CRF. Ng and Low (2004) and Luo (2003) also trained single joint models over the Chinese segmentation and POS tagging subtasks. In their work, they brought the two subtasks together by treating it as a single tagging problem, for which they trained a maximum entropy classifier to assign a combined word boundary and POS tag to each character.

A major challenge, however, exists in doing joint inference for complex and large-scale NLP application. Sutton and McCallum (Sutton and McCallum, 2005) suggested that in many cases exact inference can be too expensive and thus formidable. They presented an alternative approach in which a linear-chain CRF is trained separately for each subtask at training time, but at decoding time they combined the learned weights from the CRF cascade into a single grid-shaped factorial CRF to perform joint decoding and make predictions for all subtasks. Similar to (Sutton and McCallum, 2005), in our system we also train a cascade of linear-chain CRF for the subtasks. But at decoding time, we experiment with an alternative approximation method to joint decoding, by taking the n-best hypotheses from the segmentation model and use the POS tagging model for reranking. We evaluated our system on the open tracks of SIGHAN Bakeoff 2006 dataset. Furthermore, to evaluate our reranking method's impact on the POS tagging task, we also performed 10-fold cross-validation tests on the 250k Penn

Chinese Treebank (CTB) (Xue et al., 2002). Results from both evaluations suggest that our simple reranking method is very effective. We achieved a consistent performance gain on both segmentation and POS tagging tasks over linearly-cascaded CRF. Our official F-scores on the 2006 Bakeoff open tracks are 0.935 (UPUC), 0.964 (CityU), 0.952 (MSRA) and 0.949 (CKIP).

2 Algorithm

Given an observed Chinese character sequence $\mathbf{X} = \{C_1, C_2, ..., C_n\}$, let **S** and **T** denote a segmentation sequence and a POS tagging sequence over **X**. Our goal is to find a segmentation sequence $\hat{\mathbf{S}}$ and a POS tagging sequence $\hat{\mathbf{T}}$ that maximize the posterior probability :

$$P(\mathbf{S}, \mathbf{T} | \mathbf{X} = \{C_1, C_2, ..., C_n\}) \quad (1)$$

Applying chain rule, we can further derive from Equation 1 the following:

$$\begin{aligned} & < \hat{\mathbf{S}}, \hat{\mathbf{T}} > \\ = \; & \arg\max_{\mathbf{S},\mathbf{T}} P(\mathbf{T} | \mathbf{S}, \mathbf{X} = \{C_1, C_2, ..., C_n\}) \\ & \times P(\mathbf{S} | \mathbf{X} = \{C_1, C_2, ..., C_n\}) \quad (2) \end{aligned}$$

Since we have factorized the joint probability in Equation 1 into two terms, we can now model these two components using conditional random fields (Lafferty et al., 2001). Linear-chain CRF models define conditional probability, $P(\mathbf{Z}|\mathbf{X})$, by linear-chain Markov random fields. In our case, **X** is the sequence of characters or words, and **Z** is the segmentation labels for characters (START or NON-START, used to indicate word boundaries) or the POS tagging for words (NN, VV, JJ, etc.). The conditional probability is defined as:

$$P(\mathbf{Z}|\mathbf{X}) = \frac{1}{N(X)} \exp\left(\sum_{t=1}^{T} \sum_{k=1}^{K} \lambda_k f_k(\mathbf{Z}, \mathbf{X}, t)\right) \quad (3)$$

where $N(X)$ is a normalization term to guarantee that the summation of the probability of all label sequences is one. $f_k(\mathbf{Z}, \mathbf{X}, t)$ is the kth $local feature function$ at sequence position t. It maps a pair of **X** and **Z** and an index t to $\{0,1\}$. $(\lambda_1, ..., \lambda_K)$ is a weight vector to be learned from training set. A large positive value of λ_i means that the ith feature function's value is frequent to be 1, whereas a negative value of λ_i means the ith feature function's value is unlikely to be 1.

At decoding time, we are interested in finding the segmentation sequence $\hat{\mathbf{S}}$ and POS tagging sequence $\hat{\mathbf{T}}$ that maximizes the probability defined in Equation 2. Instead of exhaustively searching the whole space of all possible segmentations, we restrict our searching to $\mathcal{S} = \{\mathbf{S_1}, \mathbf{S_2}, ..., \mathbf{S_N}\}$, where $\mathcal{S}$ is the restricted search space consisting of N-best decoded segmentation sequences. This N-best list of segmentation sequences, $\mathcal{S}$, can be obtained using modified Viterbi algorithm and A* search (Schwartz and Chow, 1990).

3 Features

3.1 Features for Segmentation

We adopted the basic segmentation features used in (Ng and Low, 2004). These features are summarized in Table 1 ((1.1)-(1.7)). In these templates, C_0 refers to the current character, and C_{-n}, C_n refer to the characters *n* positions to the left and right of the current character, respectively. $Pu(C_0)$ indicates whether C_0 is a punctuation. $T(C_n)$ classifies the character C_n into four classes: numbers, dates (year, month, date), English letters and all other characters. $L_{Begin}(C_0)$, $L_{End}(C_0)$ and $L_{Mid}(C_0)$ represent the maximum length of words found in a lexicon[1] that contain the current character as either the first, last or middle character, respectively. $Single(C_0)$ indicates whether the current character can be found as a single word in the lexicon.

Besides the adopted basic features mentioned above, we also experimented with additional semantic features (Table 1 (1.8)). For (1.8), Sem_0 refers to the semantic class of current character, and Sem_{-1}, Sem_1 represent the semantic class of characters one position to the left and right of the current character, respectively. We obtained a character's semantic class from HowNet (Dong and Dong, 2006). Since many characters have multiple semantic classes defined by HowNet, it is a non-trivial task to choose among the different semantic classes. We performed contextual disambiguation of characters' semantic classes by calculating semantic class similarities. For example, let us assume the current character is 看*(look,read)* in a word context of 看报*(read*

[1]We compiled our lexicon from three external resources. HowNet: www.keenage.com; On-Line Chinese Tools: www.mandarintools.com; Online Dictionary from Peking University: http://ccl.pku.edu.cn/doubtfire/Course/Chinese%20Information%20Processing/Source_Code/Chapter_8/Lexicon_full_2000.zip

newspaper). The character 看(*look*) has two semantic classes in HowNet, i.e. 读(*read*) and 医治(*doctor*). To determine which class is more appropriate, we check the example words illustrating the meanings of the two semantic classes, given by HowNet. For 读(*read*), the example word is 看书(*read book*); for 医治(*doctor*), the example word is 看病(*see a doctor*). We then calculated the semantic class similarity scores between 报(*newspaper*) and 书(*book*), and 报(*newspaper*) and 病(*illness*), using HowNet's built-in similarity measure function. Since 报(*newspaper*) and 书(*book*) both have semantic class 文书(*document*), their maximum similarity score is 0.95, where the maximum similarity score between 报(*newspaper*) and 病(*illness*) is 0.03478. Therefore, $Sem_0 Sem_1$ =读(*read*),文书(*document*). Similarly, we can figure out $Sem_{-1} Sem_0$. For Sem_0, we simply picked the top four semantic classes ranked by HowNet, and used "'NONE'" for absent values.

Segmentation features
(1.1) $C_n, n \in [-2, 2]$
(1.2) $C_n C_{n+1}, n \in [-2, 1]$
(1.3) $C_{-1} C_1$
(1.4) $Pu(C_0)$
(1.5) $T(C_{-2})T(C_{-1})T(C_0)T(C_1)T(C_2)$
(1.6) $L_{Begin}(C_0)$, $L_{End}(C_0)$
(1.7) $Single(C_0)$
(1.8) $Sem_0, Sem_n Sem_{n+1}, n \in -1, 0$
POS tagging features
(2.1) $W_n, n \in [-2, 2]$
(2.2) $W_n W_{n+1}, n \in [-2, 1]$
(2.3) $W_{-1} W_1$
(2.4) $W_{n-1} W_n W_{n+1}, n \in [-1, 1]$
(2.5) $C_n(W_0), n \in [-2, 2]$
(2.6) $Len(W_0)$
(2.7) Other morphological features

Table 1: Feature templates list

3.2 Features for POS Tagging

The bottom half of Table 1 summarizes the feature templates we employed for POS tagging. W_0 denotes the current word. W_{-n} and W_n refer to the words *n* positions to the left and right of the current word, respectively. $C_n(W_0)$ is the nth character in current word. If the number of characters in the word is less than 5, we use "NONE" for absent characters. $Len(W_0)$ is the number of characters in the current word. We also used a group of binary features for each word, which are used to represent the morphological properties of current word, e.g. whether the current word is punctuation, number, foreign name, etc.

4 Experimental Results

We evaluated our system's segmentation results on the SIGHAN Bakeoff 2006 dataset. To evaluate our reranking method's impact on the POS tagging part, we also performed 10-fold cross-validation tests on the 250k Penn Chinese Treebank (CTB 250k). The CRF model for POS tagging is trained on CTB 250k in all the experiments. We report recall (R), precision (P), and F1-score (F) for both word segmentation and POS tagging tasks. N value is chosen to be 20 for the N-best list reranking, based on cross validation. For CRF learning and decoding, we use the CRF++ toolkit[2].

4.1 Results on Bakeoff 2006 Dataset

	R	***P***	***F***	R_{oov}	R_{iv}
UPUC	0.942	0.928	0.935	0.711	0.964
CityU	0.964	0.964	0.964	0.787	0.971
MSRA	0.949	0.954	0.952	0.692	0.958
CKIP	0.953	0.946	0.949	0.679	0.965

Table 2: Performance of our system on open tracks of SIGHAN Bakeoff 2006.

We participated in the open tracks of the SIGHAN Bakeoff 2006, and we achieved F-scores of 0.935 (UPUC), 0.964 (CityU), 0.952 (MSRA) and 0.949 (CKIP). More detailed performances statistics including in-vocabulary recall (R_{iv}) and out-of-vocabulary recall (R_{oov}) are shown in Table 2.

More interesting to us is how much the N-best list reranking method using POS tagging helped to increase segmentation performance. For comparison, we ran a linear-cascade of segmentation and POS tagging CRFs without reranking as the baseline system, and the results are shown in Table 3. We can see that our reranking method consistently improved segmentation scores. In particular, there is a greater improvement gained in recall than precision across all four tracks. We observed the greatest improvement from the UPUC track. We think it is because our POS tagging model is trained on CTB 250k, which could be drawn from the same corpus as the UPUC training data, and therefore there is a closer mapping between segmentation standard of the POS tagging training data and the segmentation training data (at this

[2]http://chasen.org/ taku/software/CRF++/

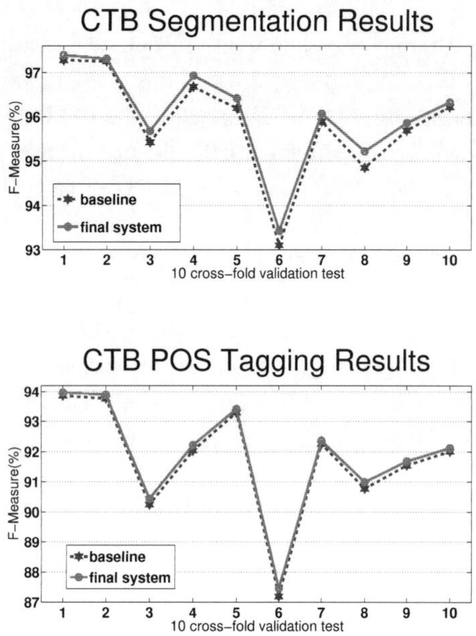

Figure 1: Segmentation and POS tagging results on CTB corpus.

point we are not sure if there exists any overlap between the UPUC test data and CTB 250k).

	Baseline system			Final system		
	R	***P***	***F***	***R***	***P***	***F***
UPUC	0.910	0.924	0.917	0.942	0.928	0.935
CityU	0.954	0.963	0.958	0.964	0.964	0.964
MSRA	0.935	0.953	0.944	0.949	0.954	0.952
CKIP	0.932	0.942	0.937	0.953	0.946	0.949

Table 3: Comparison of the baseline system (without POS reranking) and our final system.

4.2 Results on CTB Corpus

To evaluate our reranking method's impact on the POS tagging task, we also tested our systems on CTB 250k corpus using 10-fold cross-validation. Figure 1 summarizes the results of segmentation and POS tagging tasks on CTB 250k corpus. From figure 1 we can see that our reranking method improved both the segmentation and tagging accuracies across all 10 tests. We conducted pairwise t-tests and our reranking model was found to be statistically significantly better than the baseline model under significance level of 5.0^{-4} (p-value for segmentation) and 3.3^{-5} (p-value for POS tagging).

5 Conclusion

Our system uses conditional random fields for performing Chinese word segmentation and POS tagging tasks simultaneously. In particular, we proposed an approximated joint decoding method by reranking the N-best segmenter output, based POS tagging information. Our experimental results on both SIGHAN Bakeoff 2006 datasets and Chinese Penn Treebank showed that our reranking method consistently increased both segmentation and POS tagging accuracies. It is worth noting that our reranking method can be applied not only to Chinese segmentation and POS tagging tasks, but also to many other sequential tasks that can benefit from learning transfer, such as POS tagging and NP-chunking.

Acknowledgment

This work was supported in part by ARDA's AQUAINT Program.

References

Zhengdong Dong and Qiang Dong. 2006. *HowNet And The Computation Of Meaning*. World Scientific.

John Lafferty, Andrew McCallum, and Fernando Pereira. 2001. Conditional random fields: Probabilistic models for segmenting and labeling sequence data. In *Proceedings of ICML '01*.

Xiaoqiang Luo. 2003. A maximum entropy Chinese character-based parser. In *Proceedings of EMNLP '03*.

Hwee Tou Ng and Jin Kiat Low. 2004. Chinese part-of-speech tagging: One-at-a-time or all-at-once? word-based or character-based? In *Proceedings of EMNLP '04*.

Richard Schwartz and Yen-Lu Chow. 1990. The n-best algorithm: An efficient and exact procedure for finding the n most likely sentence hypotheses. In *Proceedings of ICASSP '90*.

Charles Sutton and Andrew McCallum. 2005. Composition of conditional random fields for transfer learning. In *Proceedings of HLT/EMNLP '05*.

Charles Sutton, Khashayar Rohanimanesh, and Andrew McCallum. 2004. Dynamic conditional random fields: Factorized probabilistic models for labeling and segmenting sequence data. In *Proceedings of ICML '04*.

Nianwen Xue, Fu-Dong Chiou, and Martha Stone Palmer. 2002. Building a large-scale annotated Chinese corpus. In *Proceedings of COLING '02*.

Description of the NCU Chinese Word Segmentation and Named Entity Recognition System for SIGHAN Bakeoff 2006

Yu-Chieh Wu
Dept. of Computer Science and Information Engineering
National Central University
Taoyuan, Taiwan
bcbb@db.csie.ncu.edu.tw

Jie-Chi Yang
Graduate Institute of Network Learning Technology
National Central University
Taoyuan, Taiwan
yang@cl.ncu.edu.tw

Qian-Xiang Lin
Dept. of Computer Science and Information Engineering
National Central University
Taoyuan, Taiwan
93522083@cc.ncu.edu.tw

Abstract

Asian languages are far from most western-style in their non-separate word sequence especially Chinese. The preliminary step of Asian-like language processing is to find the word boundaries between words. In this paper, we present a general purpose model for both Chinese word segmentation and named entity recognition. This model was built on the word sequence classification with probability model, i.e., conditional random fields (CRF). We used a simple feature set for CRF which achieves satisfactory classification result on the two tasks. Our model achieved 91.00 in F rate in UPUC-Treebank data, and 78.71 for NER task.

1 Introduction

With the rapid expansion of text media sources such as news articles, technical reports, there is an increasing demand for text mining and processing. Among different cultures and countries, the Asian languages are far from the other languages, there is not an explicit boundary between words, for example Chinese. Similar to English, the preliminary step of most natural language processing is to "tokenize" each word. In Chinese, the word tokenization is also known as word segmentation or Chinese word tokenization.

To support the above targets, it is necessary to detect the boundaries between words in a given sentence. In tradition, the Chinese word segmentation technologies can be categorized into three types, (heuristic) rule-based, machine learning, and hybrid. Among them, the machine learning-based techniques showed excellent performance in many research studies (Peng et al., 2004; Zhou et al., 2005; Gao et al., 2004). This method treats the word segmentation problem as a sequence of word classification. The classifier online assigns either "boundary" or "non-boundary" label to each word by learning from the large annotated corpora. Machine learning-based word segmentation method is quite similar to the word sequence inference techniques, such as part-of-speech (POS) tagging, phrase chunking (Wu et al., 2006a) and named entity recognition (Wu et al., 2006b).

In this paper, we present a prototype for Chinese word segmentation and named entity recognition based on the word sequence inference model. Unlike previous researches (Zhou et al., 2005; Shi, 2005), we argue that without using the word segmentation information, Chinese named entity recognition task can also be viewed as a variant word segmentation technique. Therefore, the two tasks can be accomplished without adapting the word sequence inference model. The preliminary experimental result show that in the word segmentation task, our method can achieve 91.00 in F rate for the UPUC Chinese Treebank data, while it at-

	帶	領	中	國	愛	樂	樂	團
WS	B-CP	I-CP	B-CP	I-CP	B-CP	I-CP	B-CP	I-CP
NER	O	O	B-LOC	I-LOC	B-ORG	I-ORG	O	O

CP: Chinese word phrase LOC: Location ORG: Organization O: Non-named entity word

Figure 1: Sequence of word classification model

tends 78.76 F rate for the Microsoft Chinese named entity recognition task.

The rest of this paper is organized as follows. Section 2 describes the word sequence inference model and the used learner. Experimental result and evaluations are reported in section 3. Finally, in section 4, we draw conclusion and future remarks.

2 System Description

In this section, we firstly describe the overall system architecture for the word segmentation and named entity recognition tasks. In section 2.2, the employed classification model- conditional random fields (CRF) is then presented.

2.1 Word Sequence Classification

Similar to English text chunking (Ramshaw and Marcus, 1995; Wu et al., 2006a), the word sequence classification model aims to classify each word via encoding its context features. An example can be shown in Figure 1. In Figure1, the model is classifying the Chinese character "國" (country). The second row in Figure 1 means the corresponding category of each in the word-segmentation (WS) task, while the third row indicates the class in the named entity recognition (NER) task. For the WS task, there are only two word types, B-CP (Begin of Chinese phrase) and I-CP (Interior of Chinese phrase). In contrast, the word types in the NER task depend on the pre-defined named class. For example, both in MSR and CityU datasets, person, location, and organization should be identified. In this paper, we used the similar IOB2 representation style (Wu et al., 2006a) to express the Chinese word structures.

By encoding with IOB style, both WS and NER problems can be viewed as a sequence of word classification. During testing, we seek to find the optimal word type for each Chinese character. These types strongly reflect the actual word boundaries for Chinese words or named entity phrases.

To effect classify each character, in this paper, we employ 13 feature templates to capture the context information of it. Table 1 lists the adopted feature templates.

Table 1: Feature template used for both Chinese word segmentation and named entity recognition tasks

Feature Type	Examples	Feature Type	Examples
W_{-2}	領	$W_0 + W_{+1}$	國+愛
W_{-1}	中	$W_{+1} + W_{+2}$	愛+樂
W_0	國	$W_{+1} + W_{+2}$	愛+樂
W_{+1}	愛	$W_{-2}+W_{-1}+W_0$	領+中+國
W_{+2}	樂	$W_{-1}+W_0+W_{+1}$	中+國+愛
$W_{-2} + W_{-1}$	領+中	$W_0+W_{+1}+W_{+2}$	國+愛+樂
$W_{-1} + W_0$	中+國		

2.2 Conditional Random Fields

Conditional random field (CRF) was an extension of both Maximum Entropy Model (MEMs) and Hidden Markov Models (HMMs) that was firstly introduced by (Lafferty et al., 2001). CRF defined conditional probability distribution $P(Y|X)$ of given sequence given input sentence where Y is the "class label" sequence and X denotes as the observation word sequence.

A CRF on (X,Y) is specified by a feature vector F of local context and the corresponding feature weight λ. The F can be treated as the combination of state transition and observation value in conventional HMM. To determine the optimal label sequence, the CRF uses the following equation to estimate the most probability.

$$y = \arg\max_y P(y \mid x, \lambda) = \arg\max_y \lambda F(y, x)$$

The most probable label sequence y can be efficiently extracted via the Viterbi algorithm. However, training a CRF is equivalent to estimate the parameter set λ for the feature set. In this paper, we directly use the quasi-Newton L-BFGS[1] method (Nocedal and Wright, 1999) to iterative update the parameters.

3 Evaluations and Experimental Result

3.1 Dataset and Evaluations

We evaluated our model in the close track on UPUC Chinese Treebank for Chinese word segmentation task, and CityU corpus for Chinese NER task. Both settings are the same for the two tasks. The evaluations of the two tasks were mainly measured by the three metrics, namely recall, precision, and f1-measurement. However, the evaluation style for the NER and WS is quite different. In WS, participant should reformulate the testing data into sentence level whereas the NER was evaluated in the token-level. Table 2 lists the results of the two tasks with our preliminary model.

Table 2: Official results on the word segmentation and named entity recognition tasks

	Dataset	F1-measure
Word segmentation	UPUC	91.00
Named entity recognition	CityU	78.71

Table 3: Experimental results for the three Chinese word segmentation datasets

Closed Task	CityU	MSR	UPUC
Recall	0.958	0.940	0.917
Precision	0.926	0.906	0.904
F-measure	0.942	0.923	0.910

3.2 Experimental Result on Word Segmentation Task

To explore the effectiveness of our method, we go on extend our model to the other three tasks for the WS track, namely CityU, MSR. Table3 shows the experimental results of our model in the all close WS track except for CKIP corpus. These results do not officially provided by the SIGHAN due to the time limitation.

[1] http://www-unix.mcs.anl.gov/tao/

3.3 Experimental Result on Named Entity Recognition Task

In the second experiment, we focus on directly adapting our method for the NER track. Table 4 lists the experimental result of our method in the CityU and MSR datasets. It is worth to note that due to the different evaluation style in NER tracks, our tokenization rules did not consistent with the SIGHAN provided testing tokens. Our preliminary tokenization rules produced 371814 characters for the testing data, while there are 364356 tokens in the official provided testing set. Such a big trouble deeply earns the actual performance of our model. To propose a reliable and actual result, we directly evaluate our method in the official provided testing set again. As shown in Table 4, the our method achieved 0.787 in F rate with non-correct version. In contrast, after correcting the Chinese tokenization rules as well as SIGHAN official provided tokens, our method significantly improved from 0.787 to 0.868. Similarly, our method performed very on the MSR track which reached 0.818 in F rate.

Table 4: Experimental results for MSR and City closed NER tasks

Closed Task	City (official result)	City (correct)	MSR
Recall	0.697	0.931	0.752
Precision	0.935	0.814	0.896
F-measure	0.787	**0.868**	**0.818**

4 Conclusions and Future Work

Chinese word segmentation is the most important foundations for many Chinese linguistic technologies such as text categorization and information retrieval. In this paper, we present simple Chinese word segmentation and named entity recognition models based on the conventional sequence classification technique. The main focus of our work is to provide a light-weight and simple model that could be easily ported to different domains and languages. Without any prior knowledge and rules, such a simple technique shows satisfactory results on both word segmentation and named entity recognition tasks. To reach state-of-the-art this model still needs to employed more detail feature engines and analysis. In the future, one of the main directions is to extend this model toward full unsupervised learning from large un-annotated text. Mining from large unlabeled data have been showed benefits to improve the original accuracy. Thus, not only the more stochastic feature analysis, but also adjust the learner from unlabeled data are important future remarks.

References

Lafferty, J., McCallum, A., and Pereira, F. 2001. Conditional Random Field: Probabilistic models for segmenting and labeling sequence data. In Proceedings of the International Conference on Machine Learning.

Gao, J., Wu, A., Li, M., Huang, C. N., Li, H., Xia, X., and Qin, H. 2004. Adaptive Chinese word segmentation. In Proceedings the 41st Annual Meeting of the Association for Computational Linguistics, pp. 21-26.

Lance A. Ramshaw and Mitchell P. Marcus. 1995. Text chunking using transformation-based learning. In Proceedings of the 3rd Workshop on Very Large Corpora, pages 82-94.

Nocedal, J., and Wright, S. 1999. Numerical optimization. Springer.

Peng, F., Feng, F., and McCallum, A. 2004. Chinese segmentation and new word detection using conditional random fields. In Porceedings of the Computational Linguistics, pp. 562-568.

Shi, W. 2005. Chinese Word Segmentation Based On Direct Maximum Entropy Model. In Proceedings of the Fourth SIGHAN Workshop on Chinese Language Processing.

Wu, Y. C., Chang, C. H. and Lee, Y. S. 2006a. A general and multi-lingual phrase chunking model based on masking method. Lecture Notes in Computer Science (LNCS): Computational Linguistics and Intelligent Text Processing, 3878: 144-155.

Wu, Y. C., Fan, T. K., Lee Y. S. and Yen, S. J. 2006b. Extracting named entities using support vector machines," Lecture Notes in Bioinformatics (LNBI): Knowledge Discovery in Life Science Literature, (3886): 91-103.

Wu, Y. C., Lee, Y. S., and Yang, J. C. 2006c. The Exploration of Deterministic and Efficient Dependency Parsing. In Proceedings of the 10th Conference on Natural Language Learning (CoNLL).

Zhou, J., Dai, X., Ni, R., Chen, J. 2005. .A Hybrid Approach to Chinese Word Segmentation around CRFs. In Proceedings of the Fourth SIGHAN Workshop on Chinese Language Processing.

Chinese Named Entity Recognition with a Multi-Phase Model

Zhou Junsheng
State Key Laboratory for Novel Software Technology, Nanjing University, China
Deptartment of Computer Science, Nanjing Normal University, China
zhoujs@nlp.nju.edu.cn

He Liang
State Key Laboratory for Novel Software Technology, Nanjing University, China
hel@nlp.nju.edu.cn

Dai Xinyu
State Key Laboratory for Novel Software Technology, Nanjing University, China
dxy@nlp.nju.edu.cn

Chen Jiajun
State Key Laboratory for Novel Software Technology, Nanjing University, China
chenjj@nlp.nju.edu.cn

Abstract

Chinese named entity recognition is one of the difficult and challenging tasks of NLP. In this paper, we present a Chinese named entity recognition system using a multi-phase model. First, we segment the text with a character-level CRF model. Then we apply three word-level CRF models to the labeling person names, location names and organization names in the segmentation results, respectively. Our systems participated in the NER tests on open and closed tracks of Microsoft Research (MSRA). The actual evaluation results show that our system performs well on both the open tracks and closed tracks.

1 Introduction

Named entity recognition (NER) is a fundamental component for many NLP applications, such as Information extraction, text Summarization, machine translation and so forth. In recent years, much attention has been focused on the problem of recognition of Chinese named entities. The problem of Chinese named entity recognition is difficult and challenging, In addition to the challenging difficulties existing in the counterpart problem in English, this problem also exhibits the following more difficulties: (1) In a Chinese document, the names do not have "boundary tokens" such as the capitalized initial letters for a person name in an English document. (2) There is no space between words in Chinese text, so we have to segment the text before NER is performed.

In this paper, we report a Chinese named entity recognition system using a multi-phase model which includes a basic segmentation phase and three named entity recognition phases. In our system, the implementations of basic segmentation components and named entity recognition component are both based on conditional random fields (CRFs) (Lafferty et al., 2001). At last, we apply the rule method to recognize some simple and short location names and organization names in the text. We will describe each of these phases in more details below.

2 Chinese NER with multi-level models

2.1 Recognition Process

The input to the recognition algorithm is Chinese character sequence that is not segmented and the output is recognized entity names. The process of recognition of Chinese NER is illustrated in figure 1. First, we segment the text with a character-level CRF model. After basic segmentation, a small number of named entities in the text, such as "山西队", "新华社", "福建省" and so on, which are segmented as a single word. These simple single-word entities will be labeled with some rules in the last phase. However, a great number of named entities in the text, such as "中国绿色照明工程办公室", "西柏坡纪念馆", are not yet segmented as a single word. Then, different from (Andrew et al. 2003), we apply three trained CRFs models with carefully designed and selected features to label person names, location names and organization names in the segmentation results, respectively. At last phase, we apply some rules to tag some names not recognized by CRFs models, and adjust part of the organization names recognized by CRFs models.

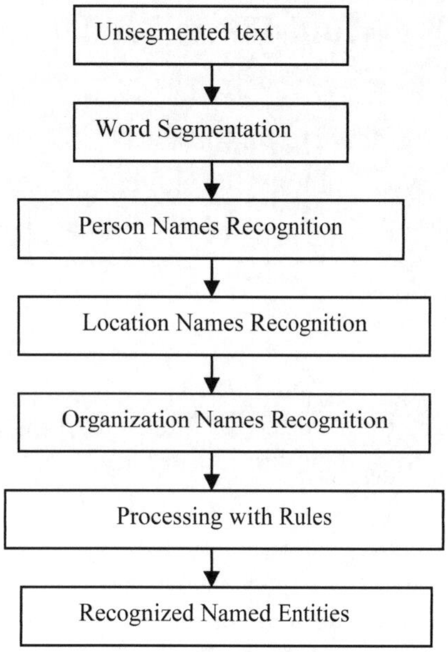

Fig1. Chinese NER process

2.2 Word segmentation

We implemented the basic segmentation component with linear chain structure CRFs. CRFs are undirected graphical models that encode a conditional probability distribution using a given set of features. In the special case in which the designated output nodes of the graphical model are linked by edges in a linear chain, CRFs make a first-order Markov independence assumption among output nodes, and thus correspond to finite state machines (FSMs). CRFs define the conditional probability of a state sequence given an input sequence as

$$P_{\mathrm{A}}(s \mid o) = \frac{1}{Z_o} \exp\left(\sum_{t=1}^{T} \sum_{k=1}^{K} \lambda_k f_k(s_{t-1}, s_t, o, t) \right)$$

Where $f_k(s_{t-1}, s_t, o, t)$ is an arbitrary feature function over its arguments, and λ_k is a learned weight for each feature function.

Based on CRFs model, we cast the segmentation problem as a sequence tagging problem. Different from (Peng et al., 2004), we represent the positions of a *hanzi* (Chinese character) with four different tags: B for a *hanzi* that starts a word, I for a *hanzi* that continues the word, F for a *hanzi* that ends the word, S for a *hanzi* that occurs as a single-character word. The basic segmentation is a process of labeling each *hanzi* with a tag given the features derived from its surrounding context. The features used in our experiment can be broken into two categories: character features and word features. The character features are instantiations of the following templates, similar to those described in (Ng and Jin, 2004), *C* refers to a Chinese *hanzi*.

(a) *Cn (n = −2,−1,0,1,2)*
(b) *CnCn+1(n = −2,−1,0,1)*
(c) *C−1C1*
(d) *Pu(C0)*

In addition to the character features, we came up with another type word context feature which was found very useful in our experiments. The feature captures the relationship between the *hanzi* and the word which contains the *hanzi*. For a two-*hanzi* word, for example, the first *hanzi* “连” within the word “连续” will have the feature WC0=TWO_F set to 1, the second *hanzi* “续” within the same word “连续” will have the feature WC0=TWO_L set to 1. For the three-*hanzi* word, for example, the first *hanzi* “梳” within a word “梳妆镜” will have the feature WC0=TRI_F set to 1, the second *hanzi* “妆” within the same word “梳妆镜” will have the feature WC0=TRI_M set to 1, and the last *hanzi* “镜” within the same word “梳妆镜” will have the feature WC0=TRI_L set to 1. Similarly, the feature can be extended to a four-*hanzi* word.

2.3 Named entity tagging with CRFs

After basic segmentation, we use three word-level CRFs models to label person names, location names and organization names, respectively. The important factor in applying CRFs model to name entity recognition is how to select the proper features set. Most of entity names do not have any common structural characteristics except for containing some feature words, such as “公司”, “学校”, “乡” , “镇” and so on. In addition, for person names, most names include a common surname, e.g. “张”, “王”. But as a proper noun, the occurrence of an entity name has the specific context. In this section, we only present our approach to organization name recognition. For example, the context information of organization name mainly includes the boundary words and some title words (e.g. 局长、董事长). By analyzing a large amount of entity name corpora, we find that the indicative intensity of different boundary words vary greatly. So we divide the left and right boundary words into two classes according to the indicative intensity. Accordingly we construct the four boundary words lexicons. To solve the problem of the selection and classification of boundary words, we make use of mutual Information *I(x, y).* If there is a genuine association between x and y, then I(x, y) >>0. If there is no interesting relationship between x and y, then I(x, y)≈0. If x and y are in complementary distribution, then I(x, y) << 0. By using mutual information, we compute the association between boundary word and the type of organization name, then select and classify the boundary words. Some example boundary words for organization names are listed in table 1.

Table 1. The classified boundary words for ORG names

Type	Class	Examples
Left boundary word	First-class	历任（6.0006）
	Second-class	接管（3.1161）
Right boundary word	First -class	管辖（5.4531）
	Second-class	规定（2.0135）

Based on the consideration given in preceding section, we constructed a set of atomic feature patterns, listed in table 2. Additionally, we defined a set of conjunctive feature patterns, which could form effective feature conjunctions to express complicated contextual information.

Table 2. Atomic feature patterns for ORG names

Atomic pattern	Meaning of pattern
CurWord	Current word
LocationName	Check if current word is a location name
PersonName	Check if current word is a person name
KnownORG	Check if current word is a known organization name
ORGFeature	Check if current word is a feature word of ORG name
ScanFeatureWord_8	Check if there exist a feature word among eight words behind the current word
LeftBoundary1_-2 LeftBoundary2_-2	Check if there exist a first-class or second-class left boundary word among two words before the current word
RightBoundary1_+2 RightBoundary2_+2	Check if there exist a first-class or second-class right boundary word among two words behind the current word

2.4 Processing with rules

There exists some single-word named entities that aren't tagged by CRFs models. We recognize these single-word named entities with some rules. We first construct two known location names and organization names dictionaries and two feature words lists for location names and organization names. In closed track, we collect known location names and organization names only from training corpus. The recognition process is described below. For each word in the text, we first check whether it is a known location or organization names according to the known location names and organization names dictionaries. If it isn't a known name, then we further check whether it is a known word. If it is not a known word also, we next check whether the word ends with a feature word of location or organization names. If it is, we label it as a location or organization name.

In addition, we introduce some rules to adjust organization names recognized by CRF model based on the labeling specification of MRSA corpus. For example, the string "阳城县李圪塔乡卫生院" is recognized as an organization name, but the string should be divided into two names: a location name ("阳城县") and a organization name ("李圪塔乡卫生院"), according to label specification, so we add some rules to adjust it.

3 Experimental results

We participated in the three GB tracks in the third international Chinese language processing bakeoff: NER msra-closed, NER msra-open and WS msra-open. In the closed track, we constructed all dictionaries only with the words appearing in the training corpus. In the closed track, we didn't use the same feature characters lists for location names and organization names as in the open tracks and we collected the feature characters from the training data in the closed track. We constructed feature characters lists for location names and organization names by the following approach. First, we extract all suffix string for all location names and organization names in the training data and count the occurrence of these suffix strings in all location names and organization names. Second, we check every suffix string to judge whether it is a known word. If a suffix string is not a known word, we discard it. Finally, in the remaining suffix words, we select the frequently used suffix words as the feature characters whose counts are greater than the threshold. We set different thresholds for single-character feature words and multi-character feature words. Similar approaches were taken to the collection of common Chinese surnames in the closed track.

While making training data for segmentation model, we adopted different tagging methods for organization names in the closed track and in the open track. In the closed track, we regard every organization name, such as "内蒙古人民出版社", as a single word. But, in the open track, we segment a long organization name into several words. For example, the organization name "内

蒙古人民出版社" would be divided into three words: "内蒙古", "人民" and "出版社". The different tagging methods at segmentation phase would bring different effect to organization names recognition. The size of training data used in the open tracks is same as the closed tracks. We have not employed any additional training data in the open tracks. Table 3 shows the performance of our systems for NER in the bakeoff.

Table 3: Named entity recognition outcome

Track	P	R	F	Per-F	Loc-F	Org-F
NER msra closed	88.94	84.20	86.51	90.09	85.45	83.10
NER msra open	90.76	89.22	89.99	92.61	90.99	83.97

For the separate word segmentation task(WS), the above NER task is performed first. Then we added several additional processing steps on the result of named entity recognition. As we all know, disambiguation problem is one of the key issue in Chinese words segmentation. In this task, some ambiguities were resolved through a rule-set which was automatically constructed based on error driven learning theory. The pre-constructed rule-set stored many pseudo-ambiguity strings and gave their correct segmentations. After analyzing the result of our NER based on CRFs model, we noticed that it presents a high recall on out-of-vocabulary. But at the same time, some characters and words were wrongly combined as new words which caused the losing of the precision of OOV and the recall of IV. To this phenomenon, we adopted an unconditional rule, that if a word, except recognized name entity, was detected as a new word and its length was more than 6 (Chinese Characters), and it should be segmented as several in-vocabulary words based on the combination of FMM and BMM methods. Table 4 shows the result of our systems for word segmentation in the bakeoff.

Table 4: Word segmentation outcome

Track	P	R	F	OOV-R	IV-R
WS msra open	0.975	0.976	0.975	0.811	0.981

4 Conclusion

We have presented our Chinese named entity recognition system with a multi-phase model and its result for Msra_open and mrsa_closed tracks. Our open and closed GB track experiments show that its performance is competitive. We will try to select more useful feature functions into the existing segmentation model and named entity recognition model in future work.

Reference

Aitao Chen. 2003. Chinese Word Segmentation Using Minimal Linguistic Knowledge. In Proceedings of the Second SIGHAN Workshop on Chinese Language Processing.

Andrew McCallum, Wei Li. 2003. Early Results for Named Entity Recognition with Conditional Random Fields, Feature Induction and Web-Enhanced Lexicons. Proceedings of the Seventh CoNLL conference, Edmonton,

J. Lafferty, A. McCallum, and F. Pereira. 2001. Conditional random fields: Probabilistic models for segmenting and labeling sequence data. In Proc. ICML 01.

Ng, Hwee Tou and Jin Kiat Low. 2004. Chinese Part-of-Speech Taging: One-at-a-Time or All at Once? Word-based or Character based? In Proceedings of the Conference on Empirical Methods in Natural Language Processing, Spain.

Peng, Fuchun, Fangfang Feng, and Andrew McCallum. 2004. Chinese Segmentation and New Word Detection using Conditional Random Fields . In Proceedings of the Twentith International Conference on Computaional Linguistics.

Designing Special Post-processing Rules for SVM-based Chinese Word Segmentation

Muhua Zhu, Yilin Wang, Zhenxing Wang, Huizhen Wang, Jingbo Zhu
Natural Language Processing Lab
Northeastern University
No.3-11, Wenhua Road, Shenyang, Liaoning, China, 110004
{zhumh, wangyl, wangzx, wanghz}@ics.neu.edu.cn
zhujingbo@mail.neu.edu.cn

Abstract

We participated in the Third International Chinese Word Segmentation Bakeoff. Specifically, we evaluated our Chinese word segmenter `NEUCipSeg` in the close track, on all four corpora, namely Academis Sinica (AS), City University of Hong Kong (CITYU), Microsoft Research (MSRA), and University of Pennsylvania/University of Colorado (UPENN). Based on Support Vector Machines (SVMs), a basic segmenter is designed regarding Chinese word segmentation as a problem of character-based tagging. Moreover, we proposed post-processing rules specially taking into account the properties of results brought out by the basic segmenter. Our system achieved good ranks in all four corpora.

1 SVM-based Chinese Word Segmenter

We built out segmentation system following (Xue and Shen, 2003), regarding Chinese word segmentation as a problem of character-based tagging. Instead of Maximum Entropy, we utilized Support Vector Machines as an alternate. SVMs are a state-of-the-art learning algorithm, owing their success mainly to the ability in control of generalization error upper-bound, and the smooth integration with kernel methods. See details in (Vapnik, 1995). We adopted `svm-light`[1] as the specific implementation of the model.

1.1 Problem Formalization

By formalizing Chinese word segmentation into the problem of character-based tagging, we assigned each character to one and only one of the four classes: `word-prefix`, `word-suffix`, `word-stem` and `single-character`. For example, given a two-word sequence "东南亚人", the Chinese words for "Southeast Asia(东南亚) people(人) ", the character "东" is assigned to the category `word-prefix`, indicating the beginning of a word; "南" is assigned to the category `word-stem`, indicating the middle position of a word; "亚" belongs to the category `word-suffix`, meaning the ending of a Chinese word; and last, "人" is assigned to the category `single-character`, indicating that the single character itself is a word.

1.2 Feature Templates

We utilized four of the five basic feature templates suggested in (Low et al. , 2005), described as follows:

- $C_n(n = -2, -1, 0, 1, 2)$
- $C_nCn + 1(n = -2, -1, 0, 1)$
- $P_u(C_0)$
- $T(C_{-2})T(C_{-1})T(C_0)T(C_1)T(C_2)$

where C refers to a Chinese character. The first two templates specify a context window with the size of five characters, where C_0 stands for the current character: the former describes individual characters and the latter presents bigrams within the context window. The third template checks if current character is a punctuation or not, and the last one encodes characters' type, including four types: numbers, dates, English letters and the type representing other characters. See detail description and the example in (Low et al. , 2005). We dropped template $C_{-1}C_1$, since,

[1] http://svmlight.joachims.org/

in experiments, it seemed not to perform well when incorporated by SVMs. Slightly different from (Low et al. , 2005), character set representing dates are expanded to include "日", "月", "年", "时", "分", "秒", the Chinese characters for "day", "month", "year", "hour","minute","second", respectively.

2 Post-processing Rules

Segmentation results of SVM-based segmenter have their particular properties. In respect to the properties of segmentation results produced by the SVM-based segmenter, we extracted solely from training data comprehensive and effective post-processing rules, which are grouped into two categories: The rules, termed `IV rules`, make efforts to fix segmentation errors of character sequences, which appear both in training and testing data; Rules seek to recall some OOV(Out Of Vocabulary) words, termed `OOV rules`. In practice, we sampled out a subset from training dataset as a development set for the analysis of segmentation results produced by SVM-based segmenter. Note that, in the following, we defined `Vocabulary` to be the collection of words appearing in training dataset and `Segmentation Unit` to be any isolated character sequence assumed to be a valid word by a segmenter. `A segmentation unit` can be a correctly segmented word or an incorrectly segmented character sequence.

2.1 IV Rules

The following rules are named `IV rules`, pursuing the consistence between segmentation results and training data. The intuition underlying the rules is that since training data give somewhat specific descriptions for most of the words in it, a character sequence in testing data should be segmented in accordance with training data as much as possible.

Ahead of post-processing, all words in the training data are grouped into two distinct sets: the `uniquity set`, which consists of words with unique segmentation in training data and the `ambiguity set`, which includes words having more than one distinct segmentations in training data. For example, the character sequence "新世纪" has two kinds of segmentations, as "新 世纪" (new century) and "新世纪" (as a component of some Named-Entity, such as the name of a restaurant).

- For each word in the uniquity set, check whether it is wrongly segmented into more than one segmentation units by the SVM-based segmenter. If true, the continuous segmentation units corresponding to the word are grouped into the united one. The intuition underlying this post-processing rule is that SVM-based segmenter prefers two-character words or single-character words when confronting the case that the segmenter has low self-confidence in some character-sequence segmentation. For example, "复制品" (duplicate) was segmented as "复 制品" and "统一" (unify) was split into "统 一". This phenomenon is caused by the imbalanced data distribution. Specifically, characters belonging to category `word-stem` are much less than other three categories.

- For each segmentation unit in the result produced by SVM-based segmenter, check whether the unit can be segmented into more than one IV words and, meanwhile, the words exist in a successive form for at least once in training data . If true, replace the segmentation unit with corresponding continuously existing words. The intuition underlying this rule is that SVM-based segmenter tends to combine a word with some suffix, such as "者"、"人", two Chinese characters representing "person". For example, "报名 者" (Person in registration) tends to be grouped as a single unit.

- For any sequence in the ambiguity set, such as "新世纪", check if the correct segmentation can be determined by the context surrounding the sequence. Without losing the generality, in the following explanation, we assume each sequence in the ambiguity set has two distinct segmentations. we collected from training data the word preceding a sequence where each existence of the sequence has one of its segmentations, into a collection, named `preceding word set`, and, correspondingly, the following word into another set, which is termed `following word set`. Analogically, we can produce `preceding word` set and following word set for another case of segmentation. When an ambiguous sequence appears in testing data, the surrounding context (in fact, just one preceding word and a following word) is extracted. If the context has overlapping with either of the pre-extracted contexts of the same sequence which are from training data, the segmentation corresponding to one of the contexts is retained.

- More over, we took a look into the annotation errors existing in training data. We assume there unavoidably exist some annotation mistakes. For example, in UPENN, the sequence "中美" (abbreviation for China and America) exists, for eighty-seven times, as a whole word and only one time, exists as "中 美". We regarded the segmentation "中 美" as an annotation error. Generally, when the ratio of two kinds of segmentations is greater than a pre-determined threshold (the value is set seven in our system), the sequence is removed from the ambiguity set and added as a word of unique segmentation into the uniquity set.

2.2 OOV Rules

The following rules are termed OOV rules, since they are utilized to recall some of the wrongly segmented OOV words. A OOV word is frequently segmented into two continuous OOV segmentation units. For example, the OOV word "梵蒂冈" (Vatican) was frequently segmented as "梵蒂 冈", where both "梵蒂" and "冈" are OOV character sequences. Continuous OOVs present a strong clue of potential segmentation errors. A rule is designed to merge some of continuous OOVs into a correct segmentation unit. The designed rule is applicable to all four corpora. Moreover, since distinction between different segmentation standards frequently leads to very different segmentation of a same OOV words in different corpora, we designed rules particularly for MSRA and UPENN respectively, to recall more OOVs.

- For two continuous OOVs, check whether at least one of them is a single-character word. If true, group the continuous OOVs into a segmentation unit. The reason for the constraint of at least one of continuous OOVs being single-character word is that not all continuous OOVs should be combined, for example, "德商 拜耳", both "德商" (Germany merchant) and "拜耳" (the company name) are OOVs, but this sequence is a valid segmentation unit. On the other hand, we assume appropriately that most of the cases for character being single-character word have been covered by training data. That is, once a single character is a OOV segmentation unit, there exists a segmentation error with high possibility.

- MSRA has very different segmentation standard from other three corpora, mainly because it requires to group several continuous words together into a Name Entity. For example, the word "中国外交部" (the Ministry of Foreign Affairs of China) appearing in MSRA is generally annotated into two words in other corpora, as "中国" (China) and "外交部" (the Ministry of Foreign Affairs). In our system, we first gathered all the words from the training data whose length are greater than six Chinese characters, filtering out dates and numbers, which was covered by Finite State Automation as a pre-processing stage. For each words collected, regard the first two and three characters as NE prefix, which indicates the beginning of a Name Entity. The collection of prefixes is termed $S_{p(refix)}$. Analogously, the collection $S_{s(uffix)}$ of suffixes is brought up in the same way. Obviously not all the prefixes (suffixes) are good indicators for Name Entities. Partly inheriting from (Brill, 1995), we applied error-driven learning to filter prefixes in S_p and suffixes in S_s. Specifically, if a prefix and a suffix are both matched in a sequence, all the characters between them, together with the prefix and the suffix, are merged into a single segmentation unit. The resulted unit is compared with corresponding sequence in training data. If they were not exactly matched, the prefix and suffix were removed from collections respectively. Finally resulted S_p and S_s are utilized to recognize Name Entities in the initial segmentation results.

- UPENN has different segmentation standard from other three corpora in that, for some

Corpus	R	P	F	R_{OOV}	R_{IV}
AS	0.949	0.940	0.944	0.694	0.960
MSRA	0.955	0.956	0.956	0.650	0.966
UPENN	0.940	0.914	0.927	0.634	0.969
CITYU	0.965	0.971	0.968	0.719	0.981

Table 1: Our official SIGHAN bakeoff results

Locations, such as "北京市" (Beijing) and Organizations, such as "外交部" (the Ministry of Foreign Affairs), the last Chinese character presents a clue that the character with high possibility is a suffix of some words. In fact, SVM-based segmenter sometimes mistakenly split an OOV word into a segmentation unit followed by a suffix. Thus, when some suffixes exist as a single-character segmentation unit, it should be grouped with the preceding segmentation unit. Undoubtedly not all suffixes are appropriate to this rule. To gather a clean collection of suffixes, we first clustered together the words with the same suffix, filtering according to the number of instances in each cluster. Second, the same as above, error-driven method is utilized to retain effective suffixes.

3 Evaluation Results

We evaluated the Chinese word segmentation system in the close track, on all four corpora, namely Academis Sinica (AS), City University of Hong Kong (CITYU), Microsoft Research (MSRA), and University of Pennsylvania/University of Colorado (UPENN). The results are depicted in Table 1, where columns R,P and F refer to Recall, Precision, F measure respectively, and R_{OOV}, R_{IV} for the recall of out-of-vocabulary words and in-vocabulary words.

In addition to final results reported in Bakeoff, we also conducted a series of experiments to evaluate the contributions of IV rules and OOV rules. The experimental results are showed in Table 2, where V1, V2, V3 represent versions of our segmenters, which compose differently of components. In detail, V1 represents the basic SVM-based segmenter; V2 represents the segmenter which applied IV rules following SVM-based segmentation; V3 represents the segmenter composing of all the components, that is, including SVM-based segmenter, IV rules and OOV rules. Since the OOV ratio is much lower than IV correspondence, the improvement made by OOV rules is not so dramatic as IV rules.

Corpus	V1	v2	v3
AS	0.932	0.94	0.944
MSRA	0.939	0.954	0.956
UPENN	0.914	0.923	0.927
CITYU	0.955	0.966	0.968

Table 2: Word segmentation accuracy(F Measure) resulted from post-processing rules

4 Conclusions and future work

We added post-processing rules to SVM-based segmenter. By doing so, we our segmentation system achieved comparable results in the close track, on all four corpora. But on the other hand, post-processing rules have the problems of confliction, which limits the number of rules. We expect to transform rules into features of SVM-based segmenter, thus incorporating information carried by rules in a more elaborate manner.

Acknowledgements

This research was supported in part by the National Natural Science Foundation of China(No. 60473140) and by Program for New Century Excellent Talents in University(No. NCET-05-0287).

References

Nianwen Xue and Libin Shen. 2003. Chinese Word segmentation as LMR tagging. *In Proceedings of the Second SIGHAN Workshop on Chinese Language Processing*,pages 176-179.

Vladimir N. Vapnik. 1995. The Nature of Statistical Learning Theory. Berlin: Springer-Verlag.

Jin Kiat Low, Hwee Tou Ng and Wenyuan Guo. 2005. A Maximum Entropy Approach to Chinese Word Segmentation. *In Proceeding of the Fifth SIGHAN Workshop on Chinese Language Processing*, pages 161-164.

Eric.Brill. 1995. Transformation-based error-driven learning and natural language processing:A case study in part-of-speech tagging. *Computational Linguistics, 21(4)*:543-565.

Author Index